Adventures *in the* Spirit

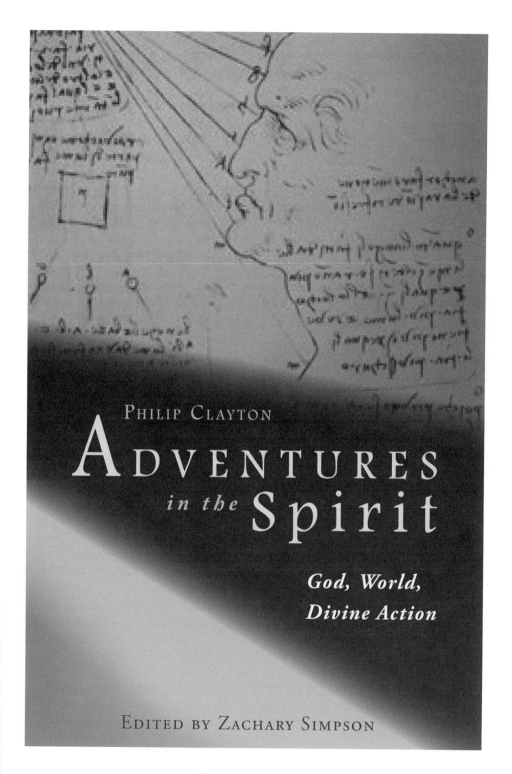

Philip Clayton

Adventures *in the* Spirit

God, World, Divine Action

Edited by Zachary Simpson

Fortress Press

MINNEAPOLIS

ADVENTURES IN THE SPIRIT
God, World, Divine Action

Cover image: Leonardo da Vinci (1452-1519), Study of the effects of light upon the human face. Photo © Scala / Art Resource, N.Y.
Cover design: Danielle Carnito
Book design: Michelle L. N. Cook

Library of Congress Cataloging-in-Publication Data
Clayton, Philip, 1956-
    Adventures in the spirit : God, world, divine action / Philip Clayton ; edited by Zachary Simpson.
        p. cm.
    Includes bibliographical references and index.
    ISBN 978-0-8006-6318-6 (alk. paper)
    1. Philosophical theology. 2. Emergence (Philosophy) 3. Pantheism. I. Simpson, Zachary R. II. Title.
    BT55.C523 2008
    230--dc22
                                    2008029738

The paper used in this publication meets the minimum requirements of American National Standard for Information Sciences—Permanence of Paper for Printed Library Materials, ANSI Z329.48-1984.

Manufactured in the U.S.A.

12   11   10   09   08   1   2   3   4   5   6   7   8   9   10

Contents

Prologue

IT IS A STRANGE PARADOX. MUCH EVIDENCE SUGGESTS THAT A GENUINELY integrative theology does not and perhaps cannot exist in our day and age. Yet the need for an open-ended dialogue between contemporary philosophy and science and the Christian tradition is greater than ever.

In the United States, by far the largest group is committed to retaining the Christian tradition intact, more or less in the form in which it has been handed down through the centuries, including miracles and the physical resurrection of Jesus from the dead. This group is sharply opposed by theologians, philosophers, and scientists who reject many of the assertions of that old tradition, treating them at best as evocative metaphors and (occasionally) helpful ethical examples. In this confrontation of worlds, one can be an evangelical theologian, or one can be a liberal theologian. One can affirm "the faith of our fathers (and mothers)," or one can affirm the modern world. One can defend "intelligent design," or one can endorse "the new atheism." One can do everything possible to preserve the tradition and to defend it from the attacks of modernity, or one can engage in the project of destroying that tradition and replacing it with something different. But, as the Latins once said, *tertium non datur*—there is no third option.

Or so we are told. The paradox is that many, many people, both in churches and outside of them, seem to be doing exactly what the common wisdom of the either/or says is impossible. As I travel around the country speaking to groups on topics in religion-science and theology, I find an active, vibrant community of persons that is deeply engaged in the very integrative project that the list of dichotomies seems to exclude. Individually and as groups, these folks acknowledge the difficulties faced by many of the traditional Christian beliefs. They worry about scientific naturalism, are hesitant about miracle claims, cannot affirm biblical literalism, and take seriously the challenges posed by other religions and by the problem of evil. At the same time, they find much of value in the Christian tradition, and they are not convinced that it should be abandoned altogether. The dichotomy "conservative evangelical or gleeful liberal" strikes them as woefully inadequate. Why can't there be a space in between? Is one really compelled, they ask, to choose the one side or the other? Is there no *via media*?

Even more disturbing is the realization that the institutions that once contributed to and lived this *via media* are rapidly disappearing. The decline in the membership and influence of the mainline churches is well known. But the crisis in institutions of theological education is even more extreme. At a number of one-time bastions of theology, such as Harvard Divinity School, little support remains for doing integrative theological work, and it is quickly being replaced by religious studies, cultural criticism, and studies of the history of religious thought. Other schools such as Pittsburgh Theological Seminary have shifted in a more conservative direction, partly because evangelical students and more conservative funders seem to offer them the only reliable source of support. The theological schools that still occupy the middle space that Harvard and others have abandoned are struggling financially, and some are now fighting for their very survival. Given decreasing church support, seminaries such as Claremont School of Theology are looking to broaden out beyond their traditional service role to their denominations to become small universities, hoping thereby to find new sources of financial support that will fill in for decreasing contributions from the mainline churches.

This book makes the case that our theologians and our media are foisting on us a false dilemma. Many more significant positions exist than the extremes of conservative evangelicalism and a liberalism that retains only ethics, politics, and a few of the old stories. Important contributions are being made to this project by thinkers and activists from a wide variety of sources. New coalitions are being formed that reject the old dichotomies. Groups and networks are putting the pieces together in new (and sometimes paradoxical-sounding) ways. Today one encounters progressive evangelicals and evangelical liberals and all around them the emerging church. Ordinary people are making common cause in new ways, with or without the leadership of their theologians. I think above all of the new networks rising up in response to the urgency of the world environmental crisis: the Network of Spiritual Progressives, for example, or the involvement of evangelical leaders in high-profile responses to global warming and the rapid loss of biodiversity worldwide. These are viable, valuable, and productive coalitions. It is high time for the theologians to catch up with them.

The theologies of integration are not merely the product of negating opposing poles. *They are the natural next step in a long succession of theologies of mediation.* Different forms of mediation and integration can be found in the biblical texts, the Patristic theologians, the medieval and Scholastic systems, the struggles of late medieval and early modern thought, and the ongoing dialogues of theologians with science and philosophy throughout the modern period. Mediating theologies today continue the same project of integrating inherited tradition with contemporary context that has animated the work of many of the great theologians over the last several centuries, from Schleiermacher to Troeltsch, from Whitehead to Tillich. Indeed, a little historical perspective shows that this integrative work actually lies at the very heart of the Christian theological project. The outliers are those who have given it up in favor of the dichotomy: preservation versus destruction.

After an opening section that presents the manifesto and unique methodological commitments of this integrative theology, I turn in parts II and III to two of its major modern supports. The concept of emergence has become the battle cry for a new way of pursuing natural science, one that no longer appeals to the philosophies of reduction as its organizing principle. Emergent thinking in the sciences was not created for the benefit of theology. It will ultimately stand (or fall) based on its adequacy to scientific research and methodology. Yet it turns out to be of immense significance for those who wonder how to affirm religious beliefs and engage in theological reflection in an age of science.

Likewise, panentheism was not invented as a cute means for splitting the difference between classical theism (with its roots in the philosophies of substance) and pantheism (with its roots in Spinoza and the Eastern traditions). Panentheism is instead a byproduct of the new concepts of personhood and subjectivity that were the major achievements of modern philosophy between Descartes and Hegel. Again, the shift from the paradigm of substance to the paradigm of subjectivity was not pursued by or for theologians. And yet, modernity's distinctively new paradigm turns out to have revolutionary—and, as I'll try to show, extremely positive—implications for constructive Christian reflection.

The problem of divine action has been called the central problem for theology in the modern age. I thus turn to this problem in part IV as the best test case for evaluating the conclusions in parts II and III. Indeed, to be concerned with the problem of divine action is already the hallmark of an integrative theology. Conservative evangelicals assert that there is no problem because they already presuppose the reality of God's miraculous action in the world, including the resurrection. And for most theologians known as "liberal" today, divine action is no longer even a topic of inquiry, because they have already decided that no such claims can be taken with intellectual seriousness in the contemporary context and hence that the question is no longer important. The volume then closes in part V with a series of applications of integrative theology to contemporary issues: theological education, deconstruction, theology and the social sciences, and the human quest for meaning.

One or another chapter in this volume may be heavy going for non-specialists, and such readers are encouraged to skim forward to greener pastures. Still, it is my sincere hope that, overall, the reflections and arguments offered here will contribute to a renewed sense of the viability of a critical religious faith—and to the life of reflection and action that it both presupposes and produces.

Adventures *in* Dialogue

Editor's Introduction

IT IS POSSIBLY OUT OF PLACE TO BEGIN THE INTRODUCTION TO SUCH A volume with a personal anecdote, but I believe that a brief tale of an interaction with Philip Clayton may help to set the tone for the essays that are to follow.

I met Philip Clayton in the fall of 2003, after enrolling in his Paul Tillich seminar. Only in my second year of graduate school, I was both awed and fearful of Clayton, who regularly read from original German texts in class, and was, on the whole, at an intellectual level that I considered wholly out of my range. Needless to say, my naïveté often showed in class. I was thus surprised when, after chatting with some of my classmates and discovering I used to play tennis, Clayton amiably asked me to play with him.

Many graduate students know this feeling all too well. Being asked to do anything of a competitive nature with a professor, much less one's future advisor, is fraught with perils. Should one simply play to his ability? Should one lose intentionally? Or should one keep things close? I opted for the latter, hoping that Clayton would meet me halfway in my venture.

Philip Clayton is a very good tennis player, and a good athlete, qualities likely owing to his competitive nature. This made my plan to "play things close" rather easy, though I did have to restrain myself at times from hitting a big shot or taking advantage of a particular weakness. My plan fell apart, however, when I apparently made it clear that I was not playing up to the best of my abilities. After hitting three consecutive balls into the net, Clayton, with hands on hips and looking rather frustrated, looked at me and said, "Either play your best, or we might as well go home." I proceeded to play the next three points as I would with any other player. After this, Clayton looked back with a smile, and said, "That's more like it."

Such an attitude, I would argue, is the prevailing tone of this volume, one which lays out many of the philosophical, theological, and scientific developments of Clayton's thought since the publication of *God and Contemporary Science* in 1997. Here the challenges are sundry, and Clayton attempts to meet them head-on. The first part, on a new method for theological reflection, lays out the ways in which one can undertake the task of religious reflection amidst pluralism, the epistemic primacy of the sciences, and existential doubt. In this volume, the attitude of having one's opponent (or interlocutor) "play their best" is written directly into a philosophical and theological method which is dialogical, which *asks* for those from the sciences, other fields of knowledge, and other religious traditions to challenge situated religious reflection. Only through a persistent give-and-take between multiple fields of inquiry does one begin to hone a theology that can be *both* relevant and internally coherent.

This adventuresome spirit sets the tone for the four parts which follow, each of which lays out themes in his previous work, but in very different form. The themes of emergence and theology, panentheism, and divine action are given fuller treatment here than in any previous publication by Clayton, though, as Clayton will argue in part I, that need not imply that any position presented here is final. Rather, each part should be seen as a progression towards a deeper understanding of a particular topic, one which has persistent, though not conclusive, resonances with the other topics explored in this book. The series of chapters presented in part II progressively refine the constraints and logic behind a theology of emergence, which is then reinforced through the metaphysical framework of part III (on panentheism) and further fortified through Clayton's work in part IV (on divine action). Conversely, Clayton's work on emergence, as he shows in chapter 8, deepens his connection to panentheism as a metaphysical doctrine and sheds light on his theory of divine action. As Clayton makes clear in Part I, the imperative here is one of coherence, or, to be altogether *passé*, of systematicity, where each doctrine is seen to be mutually reinforcing with respect to the next, and vice versa.

The final part is intended to indicate the anthropological, ethical, and political consequences of the position laid out, but, true to form, Clayton does not intend here to give final answers or normative statements. Such positions can only be hinted at, lines being drawn in directions that inevitably tail off. Instead, the book is constructed to present an iterative and intensifying understanding of a theology honed with, and against, the findings of the sciences and other fields of inquiry.

It is not my intention here to present a full introduction to this volume; Clayton's writing more than adequately speaks for itself. I do wish, however, to give a short overview of some of the parts which follow, and to provide some context for their development, as well as some critical points of emphasis. Of particular interest here will be the first and fourth parts of the present volume (on method and divine action, respectively), as they lend considerable clarity to a theological enterprise that is characterized by both its boldness and the multiple discussion partners it calls into play.

The Dialogical Challenge

Adventures in the Spirit should be seen as one attempt (among many) by Philip Clayton to continue the formulation of a compelling theological response in the present era. This statement, of course, includes within it a desideratum: one should at minimum be able to define the present era in order to qualify how one does theology against, within, or alongside it. And, if we are to take Clayton's previously published work as a clue to "what" the present era entails, we would have to include, at minimum, that the present era is one in which scientific, pluralistic, postmodern, and existential thinking has called into question our ability to make apodictic, or even true, statements about God. In *God and Contemporary Science* he gives us the following:

> The lofty aspirations of metaphysical reason are now *passé*. The claims of reason to universal validity and its claim to be able to derive important truths in an *a priori* fashion, "from reason alone," are now under severe challenge. . . . Diversity is now the name of the game; multiple perspectives are the bottom line.[1]

As Clayton makes clear in chapter 1, this still is the present context for doing theology. In the present, "postfoundationalist"[2] epoch, we often have good reason to believe that science provides more convincing answers than traditional theological dogma for explaining natural phenomena, the origins of the cosmos, and so forth.[3]

One can, of course, argue with a theological position that lends so much weight to the sciences. Yet this is not the tack of Clayton, and, given his work in *Explanation from Physics to Theology*,[4] he has strong reasons to doubt that a theological project that does not take the sciences and fallibilism seriously would have any possibility of reaching genuine accord with what we know about the world and how we seek to explain it. Rather, theology should acknowledge, if not internalize, the challenge of the sciences and other religious traditions to its own truth claims. Thus, in chapter 1, he suggests, *"perhaps we must build the problematic nature of theology into theology itself as a fundamental feature of how theological reflection is carried out in the academic context today."* What "problematic" means is clearly in need of definition, and, arguably, Clayton's *The Problem of God in Modern Thought*[5] goes some considerable distance in defining the philosophical problems posed to contemporary theology. The sciences, and specifically reductionism, as Clayton argues elsewhere,[6] pose an equally pernicious threat to theological reflection, insofar as they potentially undercut a place for divine causation or explanation.

The options for theology appear bleak. One can either fall into a form of nihilism, where all theological options are taken off the table and one simply admits that the game is over, or one can take a more reactionary tack, anxiously defending religious belief from the advance of human knowledge. Clayton does not take either path, instead opting to engage in debate, possibly at great loss, with experts from the sciences, other religious traditions, and other fields of inquiry.

The key question is whether theology will respond to contemporary skepticism and naturalism by "privatizing" Christian truth claims, relying on subjective religious experiences and appeals to the authority of scripture, or whether it will enter boldly into the debates about what constitutes knowledge, making the best case that it can for the indispensability of theological knowledge.[7]

Clayton's work, from the publication of *Explanation from Physics to Theology* to the present, clearly grapples with the theme of what it means to be both religiously and scientifically sophisticated. It is a task he describes with great passion. Here, as he states in the preface to a recent volume edited by Jean Staune, the theologian

seeks to walk the religious way with a sort of devout uncertainty, a holy agnosticism, a mystical unknowing. The "scientifically religious" acknowledge that lines of implication move outward from what the sciences know . . . in the direction of the divine. However, according to such persons, these speculative lines eventually disappear into the clouds that obscure the ontological heights.[8]

If one is to do theology *qua* science, then one must adopt, as Clayton argues, an attitude of "devout uncertainty," in which one is willing to *listen* to the sciences just as much as—if not more than—one professes one's own theology.

Unfortunately, this only describes the disposition that one must adopt when one does theology amidst the sciences, and nothing more. While this posture is critical, it continues to leave open considerable questions that are both procedural and epistemic: How does one begin such a theology? What is the goal? How does one incorporate and weed out multiple discordant voices? How does one assess truth in such a situation, or must we abandon such claims altogether?

An initial opening to this question is given by Wolfhart Pannenberg, who announces in volume 1 of his *Systematic Theology* that, "In this regard we should not think it strange if epistemologically the statements of dogmatics and the theses of the Christian doctrine which it presents are given the status of hypotheses."[9] Taking this cue, along with his work in twentieth-century philosophy of science and Imre Lakatos's concept of heuristics,[10] Clayton agrees that the "hypothetical method" shows promise for a theology that internalizes its own problematic nature. Here, "theological claims are viewed as hypotheses through which we aim to gather more information about the true nature of the world. Like hypotheses, they remain dependent on final verification from the universe itself and its history."[11] In experimental fashion, theological suppositions have the epistemic status of heuristics, which are used to further cultivate knowledge and test the fecundity of a theological program. Of course, some parts of one's theological project (to use Lakatos's term, its "core") are more necessary than others, and Clayton's hypothetical method carries with it the imperative that one be willing, in advance of theological reflection, to designate that which is essential,[12] and that which one is willing to submit to experimentation and verification.

What constitutes verification is one of the primary motifs of part I. There, in conversation with the work of Charles Sanders Peirce and Jürgen Habermas, Clayton develops a dialogical method for theological programs that allows them to be brought into conversation with science and other domains of interest. The imperative in such discourse is to make public those elements of one's theological program that are in need of testing, and, in a best-case scenario, to see how they fit with the opinions of others in relevant domains of knowledge. This is what Clayton calls "stage-three" discourse:

> This most demanding type of science-religion discourse embraces the full intent of the Peircian-Habermasian procedural account of rationality. Here one not only expresses the commitment to withdraw those claims that are counter-indicated by the evidence as a whole, but one actually *seeks out* those discursive contexts in which maximum traction between science and religion can be obtained.[13]

Clayton's use of "traction" remains an elusive term at times, and such a question will occupy this introduction in the coming pages. However, what is essential here is the *intentionality* behind Clayton's discursive method: one must be willing to submit one's theological effort, even its core if need be, to the opinion of experts in order to determine its fit with other domains of knowledge.

As one might suspect, there are both procedural and teleological questions to be answered here. Teleologically, the goal of such discourse should always be truth. As Clayton states, dialogical "inquiry presupposes *truth* as its regulating goal: all thinking is right or wrong, good or bad, depending on whether or not it leads toward that outcome."[14] However, given the epistemological uncertainty of theology itself, as well as the considerable uncertainty built into the sciences and other contemporary approaches, truth may not be entirely attainable. Similar to Kant's notion of regulative concepts in the Third Critique, truth remains the "as if" which guides a theological discourse in conversation with the sciences:

> Stage-three debate is not about short-term rational resolution, but about long-term efforts to reach intersubjective agreement and reflective equilibrium. Both Peirce and Habermas acknowledge that the final convergence lies in an indeterminate future, one that may be indefinitely deferred. . . . The link between truth and the ultimate consensus of experts thus represents a wager for all the participants.[15]

Theology-as-discourse thus remains an open-ended method of inquiry, in which one holds out the specter of truth as a guide to an indeterminate, and perhaps unforeseen, end. One works toward truth, never fully knowing when it might be reached or what it might look like.

Procedurally, theology-as-dialogue demands *prima facie* that one's presuppositions, as well as one's goals, remain public. As Clayton states, "To the extent that one declares his religious beliefs 'off limits' from this analysis, he in effect refuses to participate."[16] In contemporary discourse theory, this amounts to procedural and programmatic transparency where one does not attempt to surreptitiously steer debate towards a preconceived end. For theists, this entails a commitment to methodological agnosticism,[17] where the perceived truth of certain theological claims must be tabled in order to enter fully into debate with naturalists, social scientists, philosophers, and the like (who also must enter such inquiry with the same posture).

It is at this juncture that Clayton will invoke a procedural condition, which he calls the "Principle of Epistemic Competence." In a highly controversial move, this principle demands that, "when the question concerns phenomena that are covered by scientific laws—say, the motion of a falling rock—the presumption falls on the side of explanations given in terms of laws rather than explanations given in terms of trans-personal consciousness, gods, miracles, etc."[18] For Clayton, this represents the essence of rational discourse theory: one should grant epistemic privilege to certain fields when a particular question falls into a certain domain. In many instances, this entails the epistemic primacy of the sciences with respect to many questions that theists have traditionally held dear.

One should not see this as a "bowing out" on the part of theology. For, in rational discourse theory, the Principle of Epistemic Competence is simply a necessary procedural maneuver that allows equal access to rational debate. If anything, Clayton's discourse theory is unerringly democratic, even at the cost of precious theological claims. Only by acknowledging the success of the sciences, while holding an attitude of epistemological (and, to be sure, theological) humility, can one actually begin the process of "seeking out" ideal conversation partners.

Who these conversation partners are, and their general disposition in such discourse, remains in some question. Clayton gives some hint of these discussion partners in an unpublished lecture:

> Rational discourse is best construed . . . in terms of a series of relevant communities of inquiry or disciplines. Let's define a discipline as an organized area of inquiry aimed at explaining some specifiable domain of data. . . . Define experts as those who have achieved some level of mastery in a discipline.[19]

Here there are two non-competing notions of discourse partners: "relevant communities of inquiry" and "experts." Experts, in a favorable light, can be seen as representatives of particular discourse communities. In this way, Clayton's notion of rational discourse theory comes to represent a form of republicanism. Seen negatively, however, Clayton's concept of the expert can be (and has been) seen as a form of epistemological elitism: only those who have achieved a level of mastery, however ambiguously defined, are allowed to sit at the table of rational discourse.

Setting aside questions of the "who" of such discourse, there still remain significant procedural questions as to the aim and tenor of such debate. It is here that Clayton is apt to introduce the notion of John Rawls's "reflective equilibrium,"[20] where participants enter into an ideal discourse situation with the aim of achieving broad coherence between multiple theories, or of reaching an "ideal" rational solution to a problem set. Given the persistent deferral of truth referred to earlier, the maxim of an absolute coherence of theories remains a regulative ideal at best, but it does allow for an accommodation between multiple theories, and falsification based on internal coherence:

Since any lack of fit undercuts the rationality of the agent's overall position—she finds herself holding epistemically incompatible propositions—she will be motivated to alter her beliefs in one or both fields in order to reestablish a coherence between the two.[21]

The concept of reflective equilibrium allows for judicious falsification of theory without rendering one's entire position obsolete. At best, it provides a theory— or set of theories—which have coherence with one another and are suited to solve a number of problems that are either scientific or metaphysical in nature. At the very least, it provides the ideal format for the counter-indication[22] of scientific and metaphysical theories, and, through the process of discourse, allows for an exchange of concepts, frameworks, and presuppositions.

Yet, I would suggest, Clayton's use of Rawls's notion of reflective equilibrium is limiting, and, if extended, perhaps inadequate to the task of theological discourse. For, in Rawls's *A Theory of Justice*, reflective equilibrium is only given as the ideal outcome of a moral or political discourse that has certain preconditions. Those preconditions are telling. Rawls notes that one should be willing to: 1) generalize principles within one's particular moral domain; 2) make them public; 3) make them universal in application; and 4) agree on the finality of a solution (which, in this case, can only be a hypothetical or self-consciously deferred framework for coherence).[23] Rawls's concept of moral discourse, roughly construed, ensures transparency, universality, and unanimity. Yet, for theological discourse, such "universality," if properly pursued, undercuts Clayton's notion of the Principle of Epistemic Competence (which, if anything, endorses epistemic particularity), and potentially limits the plurality of inter-religious dialogue. Needless to say, one would have to loosen the Kantian strictures on Rawlsian discourse in order for it to be applicable to the theological domain.

This is not the most troubling problem with Rawls's concept of ideal discourse and its application to theological dialogue. What is perhaps most dangerous to theological reflection is the limitation Rawls places on the self-conscious status of the ideal discourse participant. Here, ideal discourse participants are asked to assume a "veil of ignorance" with respect to particular beliefs: "First of all, no one knows his place in society, his class position or social status; nor does he know his fortune in the distribution of natural assets and abilities, his intelligence and strength, and the like."[24] Furthermore, everyone is assumed to be "equally rational and similarly situated . . . convinced by the same arguments."[25] Only by obviating particularity in Rawls's discourse situation are discussants allowed to reach universality of opinion or of moral reasoning.[26]

Unfortunately, Rawls' injunction against particularity in *moral* discourse perhaps obscures what is precisely at issue in *theological* discourse. In theological discourse, what is at stake is one's belief, one's means of explaining the world in existential and rational terms. Not only do such beliefs constitute a significant component of theological discourse, but they are in fact the content of the discourse itself.

It is with this in mind that I would suggest amending Clayton's turn to Rawls with the work of Seyla Benhabib, who, following Habermas, suggests a more open-ended ideal discourse theory which allows for discussion with the "concrete other," not an ideally rational Kantian or Rawlsian subject. As Benhabib makes clear at multiple points, the turn to an idealized other, and the consequent elimination of their alterity[27] at the expense of universality, poses significant moral and epistemological hurdles for any ideal discourse theory such as Rawls's. "Ignoring the standpoint of the concrete other leads to epistemic incoherence or universalistic moral theories."[28] For Clayton, and for theological discourse in general, the outcome portended by Benhabib would be disastrous: theological reflection would either be sidelined by reductivist moves in science, or it would have to assume a reactionary posture.

In its stead, Benhabib recommends making one's presuppositions the very core of ideal (theological) discourse. "By allowing that the presuppositions of the moral conversation can be questioned from within the conversation itself, they are placed within the purview of argumentation."[29] Here, with respect to theological discourse with the sciences and other fields, one's metaphysical, moral, and epistemological framework is subject to debate. Not only does this broaden the scope of ideal discourse, but, I would argue, it is a sufficient condition for theological discourse in general.[30] If privatized, or if the scope of debate is limited, theological reflection stands to be in continual retreat with respect to the sciences.

However, as noted before, even if one is willing to submit to the constraints of democratic discourse, then one must accept as a precondition the possibility that truth is in some way regulative or deferred. Clayton appears willing to accept such a cost:

> Peirce thus replaces the classic correspondence definition (*adequatio rei et intellectus*) with a definition given in terms of the ultimate end of inquiry: truth is that viewpoint on which the relevant communities of inquiry would converge at "the end of inquiry"—a point which may lie finitely or infinitely in the future.[31]

"Truth" is thus replaced with such terms as "convergence" of an ideal discourse community, an infinitely deferred "consensus" and "consonance"[32] between fields of inquiry. As Benhabib notes, "our conceptions of the good life just like our conceptions of justice are matters about which intersubjective debate and reflection is possible, even if consensus on these matters, let alone legislation, is not a goal."[33]

As suggested earlier, the notion of discourse only constitutes half of Clayton's theological method. As Rawls notes, "Of course, the fact that a situation is one of equilibrium, even a stable one, does not entail that it right or just."[34] And, one would add, equilibrium, however tenuous or firm, does not entail truth, either. Questions regarding ideal discourse theory thus turn to questions of truth.

In Pannenberg's *Systematic Theology*, he outlines the dual conditions for truth in systematic theology: "The issue of truth criteria arises here, i.e, of criteria by which to decide which of the conflicting viewpoints correspond or do not correspond to the object, to reality. *Consensus* in the formation of judgment and *coherence* in interpretation have been put forward as criteria of this kind."[35] Arguably, this is precisely the orientation of Clayton's theological method: "consensus" is the goal of theological discourse, while "coherence" is the measure of any particular explanatory theory. Both are necessary for "truth" in theological discourse.

To this preceding indication Clayton would add to Pannenberg, as he does in part I, the guiding recognition that, from a phenomenological perspective, both science and religion mark out explanatory spaces in which scientific and theological truth claims have a place. Both are "situated" and situational forms of knowing. In a critique that could be similarly applied to theology, Clayton states the following: "Science does not stand completely apart from the researcher's need to construct a meaningful context for living; it is one of the projects that arises out of his life-world. . . . 'Science' is simply what persons called scientists do."[36] Interestingly, Clayton's turn to a theory of truth in theology is motivated by his examination of phenomenology. I would argue that this move is necessary for two reasons: 1) it underscores the perspectival nature of all inquiry, even science, and allows for genuine coherence to occur in which one field is debarred from claiming epistemological triumphalism; 2) it further levels the playing field for Clayton's discourse theory. Only when both theology and science are seen as "research programs" (in the Lakatosian sense) to which one adds "puzzle pieces" and reshapes an explanatory core, can one hope for consonance between the two fields.

With this addendum, Clayton can present a theory of coherence in part I that aims at internal integrity and explanatory breadth. Recalling again his work in the philosophy of science and phenomenology, he states the following:

> More likely, we can judge the relative adequacy of a given higher-order theory only on internal, coherential grounds, since all criteria of evaluation are "theory-laden." We need only recall that our experiments are suggested by our presently accepted theoretical structure, data molded by it, conclusions interpreted by it, anomalies explained away by it.[37]

Given the situated nature of human knowledge claims, one can only aim at coherence, as absolute correspondence is no longer available.

A "coherent" theology of the sort that Clayton envisions, then, must be able to reach accord between what we know about the world and how we ultimately explain it. He states such a motivation succinctly in *God and Contemporary Science*. "Any theory of God must be consistent, . . . coherent and adequately comprehensive; it must also have some explanatory power, for instance in explaining human nature and the cosmos in which we find ourselves."[38] To be sure, such words as "comprehensive," "consistent," and "coherent" indicate a more systematic direction for such a theology: coherence and broad-based accord can only be achieved if particular phenomena are linked together in an overarching framework which conforms to our experience of the world as seen through the multiple horizons of science, theology, lived experience, and so on. As Pannenberg states clearly, the truth status of theology therefore stands or falls on the systematic project: "As Christian doctrine is systematically presented by the relating of all individual themes to the reality of God, i.e., as systematic theology, the truth of Christian doctrine also becomes a theme."[39]

The task for Clayton, then, is one which he began in *God and Contemporary Science* and *The Problem of God in Modern Thought*, and which continues in this volume; namely, that of creating a clearly defined set of concepts, parameters, and constraints which, when taken as a whole, form a systematic (hypothetical) understanding of the world from a particular Christian perspective. Coherence, as a necessary element of postfoundationalist truth, demands such an effort. Clayton makes the point brilliantly clear:

> In contexts where epistemic limitations play a major role, such as theology, it's particularly important to develop a unified account. . . . The need, then, is not only to make claims about what reality is, but also to make claims about how a reality of this sort could be known in the ways we think we know it and with the degrees of certainty (or limitation) that we believe obtain in practice.[40]

The "unified account" of which Clayton speaks is nothing short of a systematic theology which attempts to make interconnections between traditional doctrines and contemporary knowledge regarding what we know—and do not know—about the world. A systematic theology of this sort, in order to be coherent, must expound not only theological dogma, but must give at least a plausible account of what the sciences, social sciences, and so forth, tell us about the world. Moreover, it must link metaphysical concepts to physical concepts in a way that responds to contemporary critiques of knowledge. Arguably, this tall order can only be fulfilled in a hypothetical theology of the sort that Clayton envisions.

If the systematic nature of Clayton's theology is not risky enough, one must keep in mind that merely being systematic is not a sufficient condition for dialogical consensus. Coherence is only a necessary condition, and it must be met at least halfway by the consensus of other interlocutors. Clayton's wager is therefore manifold. His theological methodology hopes for 1) an improbable consensus between experts, 2) a precarious balance between science and theology, 3) a coherentist explanatory account of the world, and 4) a potential linkage between items one and three in this list. These are, at minimum, the challenges inherent to Clayton's theology, which, like a tightrope walker, attempts to steer a middle course through each of these wagers without succumbing to the perils that await on either side.

Such an adventurous undertaking is what Gilles Deleuze simply calls "philosophy." Philosophy not only constructs concepts and attempts explanations, but aims for a unitary understanding of the world by interlocking concepts and joining them together on a "plane of immanence" which is spread out across phenomena:

> What defines thought in its three great forms—art, science, and philosophy—is always confronting chaos, laying out a plane [of immanence], throwing a plane over chaos. But philosophy wants to save the infinite by giving it consistency: it lays out a plane of immanence that . . . takes events or consistent concepts to infinity.[41]

For Deleuze, where "system" and "philosophy" are tantamount, philosophy proper liberates events and shows their infinite range and connectivity. Philosophy not only shows connections, it calls particular phenomena into awareness, summoning them forth. Theology in the key of philosophy is therefore a "calling" between theologians and event alike:

> The philosophical concept . . . consists, through its own creation, in setting up an event that surveys the whole of the lived no less than every state of affairs. Every concept shapes and reshapes the event in its own way. The greatness of a philosophy is measured by the nature of the events to which its concepts summon us or that it enables us to release in concepts.[42]

Thus, rather than seeing the systematic project as one which loses sight of concepts, one can alternatively see such a project as freeing particular events for awareness, drawing them into connectivity with other concepts.

I would argue that, by reading Deleuze back onto Clayton, the imperative questions for Clayton's project thus become: To which events does this system draw awareness? What is being called forth?

As Deleuze notes, such a task is always provisional, "thinking" is properly seen as "experimentation."[43] Of course, for Clayton and Deleuze alike, there are logical and epistemological constraints to such experimentation, not the least of which is coherence. But both, I would argue, add the additional demand that philosophical and theological thinking must be honest to the nature of becoming, and must be, in some sense, thought experiments in which we "live and move and have our being," as Clayton is fond of saying.

> In a great work of philosophy . . . there are two ways of considering the event. One consists in going over the event, in recording its effectuation in history, its conditioning and deterioration in history. But the other consists in it as in a becoming, becoming young again and aging in it, both at the same time, going through all its components or singularities.[44]

➤ The Problem of Divine Action

If we are to take seriously the Deleuzian command that philosophy is at once an experiment in coherence and in livability, then what follows in this volume can be seen as a partial fulfillment of Clayton's attempt to both construct, and live within the theology he is in the process of creating. If such a provisionally coherent theology is experimental in the truest sense, then it will have weaknesses, points in which the demand for coherence strains the geometries of the system itself.

One such point in the present volume, I would argue, might be Clayton's account of divine action, which can be interpreted as a working-out of the emergent theology developed in part II and the panentheistic metaphysical framework in part III. On this reading, Clayton's argument for a notion of divine action is a test case for the plausibility of both accounts and their applicability to a theistic framework.

Clayton admits the centrality of divine action in much of his work, given its interdependence with themes such as the problem of evil. As he writes in *God and Contemporary Science*, "The suffering of innocents should constantly accompany the theologian as she writes, and it is far better to be silent than to be glib in one's responses to it."[45] Thus, when considering divine action alongside the problem of evil, Clayton admits that "appeals to divine intervention in the physical world bear a special onus."[46] The challenge with respect to divine action is to establish a notion which meets head-on the irrationality and brutality of the Holocaust, while still maintaining a concept of the Divine that is sufficient for religious belief. Given Clayton's naturalistic and monistic turn in part II, as well as his panentheistic metaphysics in part III, this challenge is redoubled in intensity. How does one give an account of divine action that is responsive to evil and does not abrogate natural law, but also reflects God's ontological closeness with the universe?

For reasons that will soon become clear, Clayton's account of divine action turns on his emergentist conception of human consciousness. In his earlier work, namely *God and Contemporary Science*, Clayton discussed the possibility of divine action at the loci of quantum indeterminacy as well as human mentality.[47] In *Adventures*, however, and in the intervening years between both books, Clayton's focus has almost solely been on human mentality as a plausible site for divine agency. He does not note in this volume the reason for the change in emphasis on, if not a total move away from, quantum indeterminacy. However, I would argue that his account of human mental agency, enriched by his recent work in emergence and an emergentist philosophy of mind, potentially obviates the need for divine agency at the level of quantum effects.

What is it about human mentality, then, that provides a theoretical hinge upon which one may locate a theory of divine action? Following on his notion of emergence as the ontological irreducibility of self-organizing systems that display causal efficacy, human mentality is seen as ontologically emergent with respect to the body. Thus, one can see the "human person as [a] *psychosomatic unity*. Humans are both *body and mind,* and both in an interconnected manner."[48] Human mind, while remaining dependent upon the body (an idea that Clayton explores in his *God and Contemporary Science*),[49] exerts a form of causal efficacy that controls body, brain, and external functioning. This constitutes the "psychosomatic" unity of which Clayton speaks, indicating a causal dependence upon the body, while also marking out a distinction between "mind" and "body."

Because this concept is subject to considerable confusion, Clayton is often quick to point out that human mentality is biologically and evolutionarily contiguous with other features of the natural world. Thus, contra dualism, "emergence suggests that, if such freedom exists, it must be understood in terms of a developmental story that includes the role of physical laws, biological drives, and the increasing latitude of behavior in more complex organisms—features both shared with other animals and distinguishing us from them."[50] Yet, such statements of spatial contiguity and temporal continuity are almost always followed by a conditional "both/and." As Clayton continues,

> Organisms have a latitude of "choice" that increasingly differentiates them from non-living systems as they grow more complex, to the degree that one must, perhaps, finally acknowledge a qualitative difference. In human decision making, this range and quality of choice is manifested in a manner both continuous *and* discontinuous with the stages of development out of which it evolved.[51]

As Clayton argues in chapters 6 and 7, the human capacity for "first-person" consciousness, symbol manipulation, and culture are other distinguishing factors that constitute a "qualitative" difference between humans and our primate forebears.[52] For an emergentist like Clayton, culture, first-person introspective accounting, language, and so on synergistically combine to constitute a qualitative difference between human mental states and those of antecedent primates (much less other chordates or even cephalopods). Human mentality, while not dualistic, exhibits a form of causal efficacy and complexity hitherto unseen in the evolutionary landscape.

This view is buoyed in part by Clayton's understanding of the human brain and its neurophysiological complexity. At present, neurologists have been able to map 10^{11} neurons in the brain, and 10^{14} possible neural connections, a level of intricacy which is even further confounded by the possibility of complex neural patterning, such as that explored in recent "global workspace theory" modeling.[53] Such complexity—something hitherto unseen, at least on an individual basis—may imply that human neural machinery cannot be reduced to mere dependence relations between neurons and consciousness, much less deterministic modeling. Clayton makes this point nicely:

> One reason for the difference is that we do not now possess, and may never possess, laws of human behavior. In contrast to natural scientists, social scientists can at most ascertain broad patterns of human response, and even these evidence a virtually unlimited number of personal and cultural exceptions.[54]

Clayton refers to Donald Davidson's famous notion of "anomalous monism" in a separate chapter: "Human thought (but presumably not *only* human thought) is not reducible to algorithms. What regularities are manifested in conscious agency are the result (*inter alia*) of character, language, culture, intellectual training, the attempt to be rational, the quest to be moral, and so forth."[55] What is crucial to note here is the contention that the human mind, along with culture, language, and values, make a reductive account of human mental states, or even of laws pertaining to human mentality, *in principle* indefensible.

To many, this constitutes a potential impasse for Clayton's anthropology as well as his forthcoming account of divine action. The argument clearly hangs on the following logic: given a certain specified complexity, entities (in this case, the mind) can achieve a level of causal indeterminacy though their constituent members are causally determined (as much as cells tethered to the structure of a brain can be, at least). One should not read "causally indeterminate" as standing completely free of any inferable pattern, however:

> To accept the holism of Davidson's account of mind is to maintain that, despite the dependence of the mental on the physical, human actions are not determined by the operation of natural laws or regularities. Yet, it is not to deny that such actions manifest significant regularities.[56]

Clayton therefore makes the dual epistemological and ontological claim that one cannot know the precise functioning of the mind, and, in a stronger and more positive sense, that the specified complexity of the brain gives rise to mental states which are causally robust in their own right.

It is precisely at this juncture, one at which Clayton has established the possible causal indeterminacy or "openness" of human consciousness, that his account of focal[57] divine action can be properly argued for. Just as one cannot specify the precise causal mechanisms or constraints of human consciousness, one therefore cannot parse "divine" agency from "normal" agency in humans. "Just as no natural laws are broken when one explains the behavior of human beings in terms of their thoughts, will, and intentions, so also no laws are broken when one explains their behavior in terms that include the causal influence or 'lure' of certain higher spiritual values on their thinking and consequent actions."[58] And, as Clayton adds in an article in *Zygon*, "No physical laws are broken if there is an exchange of information between a divine source and conscious human agents. The type of influence is at least formally analogous to the chemical effects produced when an agent shifts her attention from one object to another, which are everyday occurrences."[59] The ontological openness of the human mind allows for multiple loci of causation, one of which might be the input of divine information to an agent, something similar to a lure.

Clayton's argument thus proceeds smoothly from establishing the complexity of human mental states to arguing for the plausible ontological openness of human mentality to establishing the possibility of divine influence at the level of informational input to finite agents. Though Clayton does not attempt in this volume (or elsewhere) to establish the what, when, and how of such divine influence,[60] in chapter 12 he is willing to assert that, by a lure, "God could guide the process of emergence through the introduction of new information . . . and by holding out an ideal or image that could influence development without altering the mechanisms and structures that constrain evolution from the bottom up."[61] This form of causation—one which is an amalgam of formal and final causation—Clayton and Steven Knapp term "axiological"[62] communication between God and human agents. Axiological communication, understood in this context, is the offering up of propositional content to finite agents, conforming to their place and time (otherwise it would not be special in any theological sense), and expressing the will of God. As Clayton makes clear in chapter 12 "the framework of guided emergence will not amount to the sort of control of the evolutionary process traditionally defended by theists."[63] That is, axiological communication between God and humans represents a significant step back from traditionally defended "direct" divine influence on events.

Yet it does represent, using the language and logic of emergence, a form of "downward causation" in which the analogical relationship between whole and part is used to describe God's influence on the world. God's influence can be seen as emergent upon the human consciousness, "just as our mental states can exercise downward causation on the brain as a whole and, through it, on our bodies and the world."[64] In the language of both this volume and *God and Contemporary Science*, this implies that "God's role becomes that of one who prepares and persuades, rather than one who 'brings about' human actions. . . . At the same time, it does continue to ascribe a crucial role to God in 'luring' humanity and encouraging certain types of actions. Under this model, there must be genuine openness in history."[65] Of course, the "openness in history" of which Clayton speaks is precisely the ontological openness he finds in the complexity of neurological functioning and patterning.[66] Moreover, a God that would influence human consciousness through propositional content cannot be understood as one that is coercive, much less directly influential. Rather, the onus is now borne equally by humans in Clayton's account of divine action. There is a reciprocal relationship between luring and responding, such that divine action in the more focal sense is directly contingent upon the free response of conscious agents.[67] Again, this may weaken a traditionally held concept of divine action. Yet one cannot both hold an interventionist account and remain loyal to a scientific disposition toward the natural world. As a theologian in conversation with the sciences, Clayton's goal is to see God's agency in the regularity of the world and in the indeterminacy provided through human consciousness.

This feature of Clayton's account of divine action—the persuasive influence of God on human consciousness—has direct consequences for the doctrine of God which he explores in Part II of this volume. There, owing to the "hypothetical" turn discussed earlier, Clayton advocates an analogical understanding of God in which God is seen as "not less than personal, a ground of existence to which agency may also be ascribed."[68] Or, to quote Clayton's frequent interlocutor, Arthur Peacocke, God should be deemed as "*at least personal*, or *supra-personal*."[69] The rationale for such a move is simple: once the evolutionary process has shown beings of a certain complexity (in this case, humans), then God should not be understood as *less complex* than certain structures in the universe. And, because human mental states are the most complex circuits in the universe, then God should be envisioned in no-less-than-personal terms.

In its most ostensible form, the use of human mental predicates as a condition for an analogy between humans and the divine constitutes Clayton's well-known metaphor for the relationship between God and world, that of the panentheistic analogy.

> The highest level known to us is the emergence of mind or mental properties from the most complicated biological structure known to us, the human body and brain. So the relationship suggests itself: the body is to mind as the body/mind combination —that is, human persons—are to the divine.[70]

What the panentheistic analogy evokes is not only a sense of ontological closeness between God and world, but also a direct analogical relationship between God and human mental states. In this volume, the analogy is furthered, not only making the formal analogy, God:world::mind:body, but making the additional claim that God is in some sense analogically related to mind. That is, the primary metaphors for God should be gleaned from our most up-to-date knowledge of human mental states.

As one might suspect, though, this argument is strengthened, if not transcended, through Clayton's use of human mental states as the "hinge" upon which divine action rests. In the panentheistic analogy and in the latter chapters of part II of this volume, God is envisioned as somewhat analogous to human mental states. But, as has just been argued, Clayton's account of divine action *requires* an ontological relationship between human consciousness and God, if there is to be any divine influence whatsoever upon the world. Or, in other words: Clayton's notion of divine agency extends what was cautiously extolled as an analogical relationship into an ontological relationship. Clayton, of course, would be quick to point out that his account of divine action need only be *plausible* to be theologically and existentially satisfying, but, to his credit, his notion of divine action actually reinforces his doctrine of God and forms a powerful point of overlap.

Further consonances and points of reinforcement can be found in Clayton's doctrine of God. Now, with the plausible contention that God acts at the level of sufficiently complex intentional agents, Clayton has a dual notion of divine agency:

> Every event in the world is understood as a divine act. Those events that occur with strong regularity, such as the lawlike events that physicists study, are a form of autonomic divine action, like the breathing and blood circulation that our bodies carry out without conscious direction. But in other cases God chooses to exercise a conscious influence on events, similar to the intentional actions that we can engage in.[71]

That is, God acts as both "Ground" of the universe, supporting and sustaining the processes that make collective self-organization, selection, and agency possible, as well as a "focal" agent, luring and persuading agents through God's will. If this has resonances with Whitehead's notion of God, especially that espoused in *Process and Reality*, the allusion is intentional. There, the notion of "Ground" is seen as the "Primordial" nature of God, while the focally intensive aspect examined by Clayton in his account of divine agency is the "Consequent" nature of God explored in the latter pages of *Process and Reality*. Clayton makes these connections clear in chapter 7:

> An emergentist theology of this type implicitly posits two "poles" within the divine: an antecedent nature, pre-existing the cosmos, which is responsible for its creation, and a consequent nature, which arises in relation and response to the creative activity of humans and other living things within the world.[72]

Again, Clayton's account of divine action can be seen as reinforcing the emergentist account of agency and God, as well as a more panentheistic and process-oriented metaphysical framework, thereby reinforcing Clayton's theological project as a whole.

This is not to say that there are not problems within Clayton's notion of divine action, for, just as it performs a buttressing function within his theology, it also provides additional points of weakness and places further strains on the system itself. One point of torsion is ethical. Due to Clayton's deep reliance on human mental states as the potential loci for divine action, one could claim that his account is inherently anthropocentric, a charge which would not only strike to the ethical core of Clayton's system, but would potentially push his work in the direction of dualism. He appears to admit this possibility in chapter 12. "On the one hand, this result [that of divine action on humans] makes it much more difficult to conceive a divine influence on rocks or other purely physical systems apart from the laws and initial conditions established by God at creation."[73] As some other commentators have noted,[74] this more anthropocentric notion, coupled with Clayton's constructive use of "hierarchies" in biology,[75] could lead to a form of human triumphalism, or, at the very least, a feeling of distinctiveness, and perhaps exclusivity, amongst humans.

This charge is not without its merits, and Clayton does not deal explicitly with the claim of anthropocentrism. But it should be tempered in recognition of Clayton's other work on intentionality and agency, which may suggest a more pluralistic orientation toward divine influence that can be gleaned from his work. In chapter 5 of this volume Clayton adopts the notion of "purposiveness without purpose" as it relates to intentional agents, of which he includes organs, cells, and, most obviously, organisms themselves. At other points Clayton refers to the "proto-mentality" of primates, where primate agency is akin to human agency in many respects. While these moves do not fully point to a place for sufficiently robust intentionality (and therefore a possible site for divine influence), they do at least point to a more nuanced approach to intentionality.

This contention is furthered by Clayton's recent work with the systems biologist Stuart Kauffman, in which they craft a notion of intentional agency that may allow for divine influence of the sort Clayton envisions at levels other than the human. In a recent paper in *Biology and Philosophy*, Clayton and Kauffman give five "minimal conditions" for biological agency: "autocatalytic reproduction, work cycles, boundaries for reproducing individuals, self-propagating work and constraint construction, and choice and action that have evolved to respond to (e.g.) food or poison."[76] These conditions are met minimally, they argue, in cells that display intensive behavior, such as moving across a glucose gradient, reproducing, and providing a constrained environment for cellular metabolism. Agency—the *sine qua non* of Clayton's account of divine action—is thus ascribable to cells, organ systems, and the like. Agency is also a matter of degree, and not of type: "some minimum conditions must be met for one to ascribe [agency] to it at all, and then it increases . . . until one encounters full, robust, conscious agency."[77] This appears to come close to answering a parenthetical comment Clayton makes in chapter 14 of this volume: "More generally, wherever study of the biological world reveals sufficient spontaneity, room remains for a divine influence on behavior. (Exactly what level of spontaneity is sufficient is a matter for further reflection and study.)"[78] It is unclear whether the type of agency that Clayton and Kauffman describe is "sufficient" for the sort of divine influence that Clayton articulates in part IV. Yet there is space for a more pluralistic dimension to Clayton's concept of divine action, and, I would argue, Clayton's system as a whole would benefit from an approach that married his work in philosophy of biology more explicitly with his work in divine action. Clayton's admission that "there is no obstacle to a divine influence"[79] on organisms which display a sufficient analogy to human agents should be taken as a cue to further extend his notion of focal divine influence in the direction of intentional agents in the more minimal sense.

A second criticism of Clayton's account of divine action can be registered with regard to its reliance on causal underdetermination as a possible source for divine influence on the world. As Clayton writes in *God and Contemporary Science*, "Yet, as they say, the devil lies in the details. If different outcomes are possible due to God's influence, then we *must* say that they are causally underdetermined, since the same antecedents admit of alternative results in principle."[80] What provides the ontological openness for God's influence, on Clayton's account, is precisely the indeterminate (or underdetermined) nature of mental phenomena.

There is a Janus face to this argument, however. Just as Clayton can argue that the host of causes which give rise to consciousness constitute underdeterminism, it could also easily be argued that the picture of hierarchical causation he describes in this volume, as well as in *Mind and Emergence*, points to a robust causal nexus surrounding the mental that need not include the divine. In chapter 4, Clayton notes the necessity of "pruning rules"[81] in order to model complex biological systems: systems are complex enough so as to require methods for eliminating variables that would make modeling untenable.[82] Similar to Clayton's account of biological systems, his promulgation of the human as a "psychosomatic unity" hangs on a related contention:

> Studies of the human person must be multi-dimensional because persons are the result of causal influences that operate at the physical, biological, psychological and perhaps spiritual levels—levels that, although interdependent, are not mutually reducible.[83]

Human mental states display a fundamental causal richness: physical, chemical, biological, evolutionary, historical, cultural, first-person, and possibly spiritual constraints collude to forge, in folk psychological terms, personhood.

For Clayton, the robust causal picture of the mental that he aptly describes is a fundamental precondition for divine persuasion. Yet his own picture of the mental may obviate the need for divine influence altogether. If indeed human mental states are a product of multiple nodes—if not an infinite series—of causation, then referring to a metaphysical or theistic source of additional causation may be seen as causal overdetermination. For many philosophers of mind,[84] simply admitting some form of downward causation is a hard pill to swallow. Clayton's account of divine action adds the additional problem of possible divine influence or another locus of final causation—an account that may prove decisive even for those committed to a non-reductivist picture of nature and the mental. Moreover, increasing complexity need not imply ontological openness. The increasing complexity seen from cells to organisms to human consciousness may indeed signal a "relaxation" of certain physical constraints and the emergence of different forms of causation, but it does not necessarily imply the evolution of the type of ontological openness which Clayton's account of divine action requires.

As has been stated before, however, Clayton's task in his account of divine action is not to provide a decisive theory to which all must agree. The imperative here is plausibility, and, for a liberal Christian such as Clayton, any theory must always be partial, provisional, and located. Thus, the claim of causal overdetermination, though a sticky one, is not likely to be decisive. More likely, it reveals a possible point of weakness in *any* theory which links an emergentist theory of mind, a panentheistic understanding of the God-world relationship, and a process understanding of divine activity.

➤ Conclusion

The project which unfolds in the coming pages is an ambitious one. The aim is for systematicity, in which points of overlap are staked out, reinforced, and extended. Clayton's concept of divine action is simply one example among many of such a procedure, one which reveals the striking interdependence of the doctrines he explores here. The call of coherence, however, is not an entirely unproblematic one, and, as Clayton proffers, "resistance and hostility from certain sides may serve as evidence that the theology of believing doubt is on the right track."[85]

Just as the imperative of coherence catalyzes certain dynamics within Clayton's theology, the call to communication between "concrete others" constrains the language of theology itself and influences the shape and regularity of theology from the outside. Theology in such a mode can only be hypothetical, humble, bold, and, most importantly, an adventure.

PART ONE

The Methods of Philosophy
and Theology

Critical Faith

1

Theology *in the* Midst *of the* Sciences

THE GOAL OF THESE EXPLORATIONS IS TO DEVELOP AND DEFEND A FORM of contemporary theology that shares in the adventure of human inquiry across the sciences and philosophy, across the humanities and the world religions, while maintaining contact with the broad tradition of Christian belief and practice. In earlier works I have presented the philosophical background for this project and delved into its connections with the sciences.[1] Now is the time to systematically lay out its methodological assumptions and its key results.

Six major theses serve as themes for this chapter and will accompany us in a variety of different forms through the book, to wit:

- Contemporary culture sets a radically new and increasingly urgent context for theological reflection today.
- Theologians cannot simply presuppose the truth of the Christian tradition but must be concerned in an ongoing way with the question of the truth of their central assertions.
- The work of C. S. Peirce offers an ideal model for a constructive theology that works in this new context of change and uncertainty and that remains open to the ongoing evolution of its own conclusions.
- In particular, theological inquiry cannot be pursued without ongoing feedback from other communities of discourse.
- Whether or not theologians acknowledge it, science helps to set the context within which contemporary theology is written and read.
- Although a deep and genuine engagement with the sciences and philosophy brings with it certain risks, theologians have no choice but to make themselves (and their conclusions) vulnerable in this way.

Let us examine each of these themes in turn.

The New Context for Theology

The eminent sociologist of religion Peter Berger has noted that religious believers seem to be torn between adapting to the belief systems of the surrounding world, so that no distinctiveness remains, and defining themselves in opposition to the ruling beliefs of our day.[2] With this dichotomizing of religious responses, many have begun to wonder whether Christian faith can still find a distinctive voice at all, unless it's one that is stridently raised against the dominant tenets of our age. The chapters that follow aspire to a mode of doing theology—of believing, critical reflection—that does not yet exist, or at least has not yet been formulated in a rigorous enough fashion that it can be consciously pursued and emulated.

What, then, is this new context for theology? In today's context multiple reasons are given to doubt whether the core assertions of the Christian tradition are still viable—reasons that are regarded by many as decisive objections to Christian belief and practice. (To show that they are not in fact decisive constitutes one of the central goals of our inquiry.) These reasons include:

- the ascent and unprecedented success of the sciences;
- a consequent naturalism, which broadens the scientific way of thinking into a metaphysical stance, a worldview-level assumption;
- the argument that the existence of the Christian God is incompatible with the amount of evil and suffering that we actually encounter in the world;
- the context of religious pluralism, that is, multiple religions and multiple live options for religious belief. When contrasted with the culture-transcending nature of science, this plurality leads many to conclude that the competing beliefs of the various religions cancel one another out;
- the predominance of secular worldviews and lifestyles;
- widespread secularism within the academy in most countries, with the result that religious belief and practice tends to be identified with uneducated persons and atheism with the educated elite;
- the classic liberal distinction between the "public" and "private" spheres, with all matters of religious belief falling into the "private" realm;
- the tendency to equate public-sphere matters with "objective" facts and private-sphere matters with "subjective" opinions, leading to a pervasive relativism regarding all religious matters.

In today's context it is necessary for religious persons to acknowledge that these are serious reasons for questioning many traditional religious assertions—and indeed for wondering whether religious truth claims are still viable at all in today's context.

Note that most of these factors do not apply to the various disciplines that fall under the rubric of "religious studies," disciplines that enjoy far more credibility than theology in universities today. The phenomenal growth of religious studies, though not directly related to theology, tends to lend weight to the (today widely accepted) argument that theology no longer belongs within the academy as a viable discipline. Many academics today take this conclusion to be obvious; indeed, many of them now question whether intellectuals should engage theology at all, at least with anything more than archeological interest. Perhaps, they suggest, Christian beliefs should be studied only in the way in which we now study the Greek gods: as an interesting part of the legacy of Western civilization, but not as a viable object of reasonable belief.

These and other challenges to the existence of theology within the university require us first to specify more precisely what we mean by "theology." Some years ago I defined Christian theology as "level-two discourse concerning level-one beliefs, attitudes, and practices of the Christian community."[3] More generally, then,

> as critical inquiry, [theology] is concerned with redescribing the level-one data in a systematic and self-critical manner; it is therefore methodologically related to critical inquiry in other disciplines. Because theology results in clarification of beliefs and practice, it is of vital concern and assistance to the church, and may in this sense be said to work in the service of the church. Yet because this clarification of Christian belief necessarily involves dependence on categories not drawn from the Christian tradition, as well as the use of general notions such as truth, meaning, and reference, Christian theology will also find itself in vital discourse concerning material issues with science, philosophy, and other theologies.[4]

A theology of this type continues to presuppose the life of faith; it is thus, in some sense, *believing reflection*.

But in what sense? The life of faith that provides the "level one" for this new type of theology may look very different from the life of faith of our forerunners. (I do not find this difference threatening, but many do—even heretical.) For it is now a life of faith that does not exclude but *includes* doubt and radical questioning, and sometimes even despair, within the normative, everyday experience of faith. The phenomenology of this sort of faith has been worked out in the various publications of the Yale University philosopher of religion Louis Dupré.[5] It's a faith not defined by a pre-existing realm of the sacred, radically set off from the "profane" (hence corrupt, "fallen," morally suspect) world. Rather, faith of this sort exists in, with, and through the world's ambiguities and uncertainties. It is troubled by the problem of evil, though not completely destroyed by it; it is humbled before other religious traditions, though not ready therefore to proclaim the equivalence of all faiths; it is respectful of the power of scientific predictions and explanations, though not prepared to reduce the spiritual dimension to what science can grasp of it.

In *Explanation from Physics to Theology* I described this new sort of believer as the *secular believer*:

> The secular believer may address skepticism using the formulations of his religious tradition. But, because doubts are no longer external to his religious belief, the effort to answer them in a generally acceptable manner becomes an intrinsic part of the life of faith. . . . The point here is that this effort does not need to be external or

reductionistic to religious belief, but *it can instead be internal to the dynamic of belief.* Secular believers might take the well-known quote from Diderot as their motto: "Doubts in the matter of religion, far from being acts of impiety, ought to be seen as good works, when they belong to a man who humbly recognizes his ignorance and is motivated by the fear of displeasing God by the abuse of reason."[6]

Recall the reciprocal relationship that exists between the life of faith and the manner in which one pursues and understands theology. A religious practice that depends upon the possession of absolute truths correlates with a theology that sees itself as the repository of unchanging dogmas and completed revelations. By contrast, a religious life that embraces doubt and ambiguity correlates with a theology that exists with humility in the midst of the sciences, one laborer among many.

More conservative theologians criticize this view for dispensing with the certainty of faith, for encouraging what are to them unacceptable revisions to the content of theology, and for baptizing doubt (as it were) rather than exhorting believers to avoid it.[7] The more radically liberal theologians castigate the same view for its suggestion that believing reflection might still be possible within the academy and that anything of value might still be found in the Christian theological tradition. Actually, though, it may be a good sign when one is shot at from both sides: resistance and hostility from certain quarters (say, the so-called New Atheists) may serve as evidence that contemporary constructive theology is on the right track. Theologians *should* respond to their more absolutistic brethren by reminding them that, whatever level of certainty they may experience on the inside, the public face of a theology appropriate to today's academy and society must dispense with *a priori* certainty and the accompanying dogmatism.

At the same time, theologians should respond to their critics on the other side that a certain openness—to science, to other religions, and even to the possibility of final skepticism and nihilism—is not the antithesis of believing and does not make the life of faith and practice impossible. The first step is actually to construct, and to live, a viable model of critical faith. The second step, and the major emphasis in these opening chapters, is to advance a credible methodology for the sort of theological reflection that corresponds to this critical faith. If we are successful in both steps, we will have shown that the throw-up-your-hands-in-despair hopelessness of our post-religious colleagues is neither norm nor necessity. Many have ceased to believe, and many more will; it behooves us to take seriously the reasons that have compelled them to their unbelief. But, as I hope to show in these pages, the outspoken skeptics of our day, the Dawkinses and the Harrises, are mistaken to conclude that abandoning belief altogether is the only recourse for educated men and women today.

What is the most honest response to these concerns and worries? It is, I suggest, *to acknowledge the possibility of the impossibility of religious belief.* What many believers fear but are hesitant to acknowledge publicly, and what many nonbelievers presuppose as a *fait accompli*—it is this possibility with which theologians today must grapple. Rather than considering the existence of God as an obvious truth, perhaps we need to approach it from the standpoint of its problematic status, beginning with the reasons for unbelief. To do this is to make a radical move, for one now *builds the controversial nature of religious belief into theology itself, as a fundamental feature of how reflection about God must be carried out today.*

➤ Theology Concerned with the Question of Its Own Truth

A key step in this direction was taken by Wolfhart Pannenberg some years ago in reaction to Karl Barth. Pannenberg begins his *Systematic Theology* with the claim that theology must thematize the question of its own truth:

> If the dogmas of Christians are true, they are no longer the opinions of a human school. They are divine revelation. Nevertheless, they are still formulated and proclaimed by humans, by the church and its ministers. Hence the question can and must be raised whether they are more than human opinions, whether they are not merely human inventions and traditions but an expression of divine revelation. Thus there arises once again, this time with respect to the concept of dogma, the truth question that is linked more generally to the concept of theology . . .[8]

From the start of this work Pannenberg insists that Christian theology include its own prolegomenon within itself, insofar as the authority—and truth!—of scripture cannot be presupposed at the outset but must be attested in the process of doing theology. For the collapse of the scripture principle in modern thought "simply invalidated the attempt to use the idea of verbal inspiration to establish the divine truth of scripture in all its parts as a presupposition. This thesis . . . could no longer be maintained in the face of new scientific, historical, and geographical evidence" (*ST* 1:46). Instead, scripture must be viewed as a historical record of the origins of Christianity, and in this sense as an *indirect* authority. Nor can individual experience provide an absolute authority in questions of truth:

> Individual experience can never mediate absolute, unconditional certainty. At best it can offer no more than a certainty which needs clarification and confirmation in an ongoing process of experience. This subjective certainty does indeed experience the presence of truth and its unconditionality but only in an ongoing process. (*ST* 1:47)

The disputed nature of Christian truth claims thus provides the context in which the Christian theologian works today.

Pannenberg's career, especially in the early years, exemplifies this program. By 1961 his break with Karl Barth led him to reject the appeal to a separate, epistemically privileged "salvation history" (*Heilsgeschichte*) in favor of a search for signs of universal patterns in history that might reflect its divine source. Likewise, his 1963 Christology substituted careful historical-critical work for the traditional account of Jesus as seen through the eyes of faith. Pannenberg's powerful methodological requirement deserves citation in full:

> As long as historiography does not begin dogmatically with a narrow concept of reality according to which "dead men do not rise," it is not clear why historiography should not in principle be able to speak about Jesus' resurrection as the explanation that is best established of such events as the disciples' experiences of the appearances and the discovery of the empty tomb. If, however, historical study declares itself unable to establish what "really" happened on Easter, then all the more, faith is not able to do so; for faith cannot ascertain anything certain about events of the past that would perhaps be inaccessible to the historian.[9]

True to this methodological commitment, the first volume of Pannenberg's systematic theology turns first to the history of the world religions, arguing for the fundamental nature of the human religious impulse on the basis of the early and universal appearance of religious beliefs and practices in human history. For example, atheism cannot account for or support belief in the oneness of humanity and the value of all human being:

> The question arises, however, whether the concept of the unity of humanity as a point of reference for the plurality of cultures and religions does not still have monotheism as its premise. The alternative is not polytheistic religion but an atheistic version of the idea of humanity on the basis of our equality by nature. . . . But is it really possible to establish human unity and equality atheistically? Can we simply presuppose unity and equality as simple facts? (*ST* 1:151)

Once humans have found reasons for looking beyond naturalism for a possible divine revelation in the midst of human history, it becomes natural, even urgent, to look to the world's religions as a locus of this revelation. Yet each of these religions has a historical existence, having been born, developed, and spread through time in response to specific historical and cultural developments. If Christianity is to merit belief on the part of men and women today, it must show that its claims about history, *as incarnated in the life of Jesus and the history of the church*, better explain human history and human experience as a whole than do its competitors:

> Religious perceptions are thus exposed to the question whether they properly fulfill their function of bringing to light the infinite in the finite. In other words, the gods of the religions must show in our experience of the world that they are the powers which they claim to be. They must confirm themselves by the implications of meaning in this experience so that its content can be understood as an expression of the power of God and not his weakness. (*ST* 1:167)

Note that Pannenberg's insistence that Christianity (and all other religions) must establish its credentials is *not* a return to natural theology:

> In this process of experience, and the awareness of God that it brings, we do not have primarily the natural theology of the philosophers. What we have is the religious experience of God by means of a sense of the working and being of God in creation. There has not been a philosophical natural theology from the beginning of creation. But in the history of humanity there has always been in some form an explicit awareness of God which is linked to experience of the works of creation. (*ST* 1:117)

Christian proclamation is not reduced to a philosophical theory, of which Christianity is merely an example; rather, Pannenberg's concern is with the actual events of the life of Jesus. On this basis he seeks in the remainder of the *Systematic Theology* to work out the logic of this event and its implications for one's understanding of humanity, the world, and history.

In Pannenberg's theological method, the key question is whether theology will respond to contemporary skepticism and naturalism by "privatizing" Christian truth claims, relying on subjective religious experiences and appeals to the authority of scripture, or whether it will enter boldly into the debates about what constitutes knowledge, making the best case that it can for the indispensability of theological knowledge. The latter approach presupposes the *Intersubjective Principle*, to which we return in later chapters—the principle that only those assertions should count as knowledge that are able to win support within existing discussions in and between the academic disciplines. This principle implies that theological assertions must have the status of hypotheses:

> Theology is therefore subject to the requirement of scientific integrity which demands that theoretical models should be explicit and systematic. These, and the statements connected with them, then have the form of hypotheses.[10]

After all, "theology deals with the philosophical question of reality and must meet the criteria which apply to philosophical statements" (*TPS* 339). It follows, further, that *criticizability* will serve as a criterion for knowledge, for only those assertions that can be criticized and supported within the context of an organized field of inquiry deserve the appellation of knowledge.

Most crucial here is that Pannenberg accepts *the contested nature of theological truth claims.* In today's cultural context, as we have seen, claims about God can no longer be advanced with epistemic certainty. Believers *may* still experience an inner certainty in conjunction with their belief in God, but this does not justify them in claiming that their religious beliefs are equally as certain as knowledge about the empirical world. Unless we engage in what W. W. Bartley calls "the retreat to commitment,"[11] we must acknowledge that Christian claims about God are indeed contested and open to dispute in the context of multiple world religions and the ongoing advance of science. Theology makes claims about the end of history, about the second coming of Christ, and about the coming kingdom of God—all future claims which remain disputable (*strittig*) until they actually occur:

An important part of this view is that it is only the end of all history which can bring a final decision about all claims about reality as a whole and thus about the reality of God and the destiny of man. Nevertheless, since assumptions about reality as a whole are unavoidable for the lives of persons in the present, it is necessary here and now to work out criteria which will make possible at least a provisional decision between them. Such a decision can be based only on the success or failure of assumptions about reality as a whole, such as are made explicit in religious traditions and philosophical models, to prove themselves in the various areas of our actual experience. (*TPS* 343, trans. modified)

Pannenberg's opus offers a good example of what theology looks like when it is understood to be contentious (*strittig*) and to include within it the question of its own truth.[12] His well-known and influential position moves a quantum leap beyond traditional theologies, which usually attempt to settle the question of their own truth in advance in one of three ways. The best traditional theologies precede their doctrinal conclusions with a prolegomenon that offers reasons to take their core assumptions as true; then, having dealt once and for all with the truth question, they think they can proceed with calmness and assurance to spell out its various implications.[13] Another group, among which conservative evangelicals are perhaps the best known today, frequently offers as prolegomena arguments for the authority of the Christian Scriptures and then, having settled that question, appeals with assurance to that scripture to ground the truth of all further theological assertions. As the widely distributed pamphlets of the famous American evangelist Billy Graham put it: "God says it in His Word. I believe it in my heart. That settles it forever." Finally, the third group—into which a surprising number of systematic theologians fall—simply presupposes the truth of one's own revisionistic system of beliefs without ever pausing to say what one means by this truth or why others should accept it as true.

➤ Theology beyond Established Conclusions: The Model of Charles Sanders Peirce

Pannenberg's theology is based on the fundamental conviction that God has already both revealed *and accomplished* the end of history in the life, death, and resurrection of Jesus Christ. In one sense, history waits only for the final manifestation of that proleptic event. For Pannenberg, one presumes, belief that the end of history was present in Jesus represents the minimal condition for an adequate Christian theology.

But what if one is not persuaded by his arguments for the historicity of the resurrection and the superiority of Christianity among the world religions? For those who remain unpersuaded, a more radical model of theological reflection becomes necessary. At the center of this model lies the conviction that *the life of faith is possible even in the absence of knowing*—for example, knowing that the end of history has already been accomplished in the Christ event. For example, Christian discipleship might be based instead on the belief that a divinely inspired spiritual rebirth took place in the hearts of the disciples, as Edward Schillebeeckx holds,[14] or, more robustly, on the belief that a spiritual resurrection occurred in which the identity of Jesus was preserved "through the Holy Spirit" after his death and experienced by the disciples. A religious life based on these or similar beliefs *hopes* for an end of history where there will be "a new heaven and a new earth" and where "he will wipe every tear from their eyes; there will be no more death or mourning or crying or pain, for the old order of things has passed away" (Rev 21:1, 4)—an end for which, in the beautiful words of Julian of Norwich, "All shall be well, and all shall be well, and all manner of thing shall be well." But such faith is cautious about the transition from hope to knowledge.

Now Pannenberg would be right to protest that hope alone is not sufficient for spiritual practice. And I concur: we should speak instead of an attitude of "hope-plus-faith," that is, a stance of sincere hope for a particular outcome, combined with the sort of religious life that acts *as if* that hope were a certainty.[15] The obligation, moreover, is to continue to look for data and arguments that might make a still stronger case for the reasonableness of faith—or, conversely, that may undercut its reasonableness. Yet, I suggest, this stance is possible even when believers are themselves unsure whether their arguments establish the superiority of their belief position over its competitors.

To show the viability of a critical faith, two further things are necessary. First, it must continue to be a religious stance that is able to impart meaning to believers, manifesting sufficient stability to constitute a religious form of life. I am convinced that a critical faith can meet this "level-one" requirement (see chapter 3). Second, one must develop a workable model of theological reflection appropriate to such a religious life, a model that avoids both the Scylla of dogmatic certainty and the Charybdis of a religious life without content or conviction.

The work of Charles Sanders Peirce, which combines a sophisticated theory of critical inquiry with an underlying commitment to realism, offers a crucial resource for this task. Peirce argued famously that "truth is the character which . . . we may *justifiably hope* will be enjoyed by beliefs that survive however long or far inquiry is pursued or prolonged."[16] This led him, despite (or perhaps because of) his deep religious convictions, to sharply challenge theology, which he claimed "masqueraded as a science while it was, in essence, antithetical to the spirit of science."[17] As Douglas Anderson comments:

> Theology thus embodies all that Peirce resisted: tenacity, authority, closure of inquiry, and absence of growth. It has repeatedly proved itself a danger to humanity, and, as Parker aptly states, theologians are "to be chastised as much for muddying the waters of religion as they are for obstructing the scientific spirit."[18]

Peirce believed that theology was *essentially* exclusive and that its primary task "was to demand adherence to a specific doctrine and to reject, usually in an articulate fashion, any deviation from this doctrine."[19] After all, didn't Peirce claim that "religious truth having been once defined [theologically] is never to be altered in the most minute particular" (*CP* 1:40)?[20]

But on what grounds did Peirce conclude that theology is beyond all reform? Is it not possible to theologize in a manner that corresponds to a more open model of the religious life? Peirce described the religious life beautifully: "If religious life is to ameliorate the world, it must . . . hold an abiding respect for truth. Such respect involves an openness to growth, to development. Thus, as ideas develop through the community of inquirers, they will have a gradual effect on religious belief and subsequently on religious practices."[21] He thus thought it completely reasonable, as Michael Raposa notes, "that certain religious beliefs should be revised or even discarded as a result of new scientific discoveries."[22] But why then believe that theology *could* never be a part of this same ongoing, open-ended process? Hence the theological program that I am defending accepts the opposite conclusion. Peirce is right to insist that respect for truth can lie at the heart of faith, allowing religious beliefs to be revised, and sometimes discarded, in light of new scientific discoveries. But, contra Peirce, *theology can be an intellectual guide to help believers determine when revising or discarding is justified and when it is not.*

I began this section by resisting Pannenberg's claim that the *sine qua non* of the Christian life is the assertion that the end has already been accomplished in Jesus Christ. We began instead to formulate a vision for theology that includes, in a more radical fashion, the possibility of its own impossibility. On this view theologians can engage in research and reflection without presupposing in advance that their research will finally confirm what they hope to be true. For example, one might engage in dialogue with other religious traditions without knowing in advance that the comparisons will favor the superiority of one's own tradition over the others. Similarly, one can engage closely with scientific results, and with the spirit of naturalism, without at present knowing that the best arguments will in the end favor the theistic position.

➤ Theology, Inquiry, and the Nature of Discursive Communities

What are the methodological commitments of this "theology in a new key," and what is the theory of knowledge that lies behind it? In the view advanced here, truth and the ongoing process of inquiry are deeply intertwined. Famously, Peirce held that truth is "the opinion which is fated to be ultimately agreed to by all who investigate"; correspondingly, reality is "the object represented in this opinion" (*CP* 5:407). Or, in his more precise formulation:

> Truth is that concordance of an abstract statement with the ideal limit towards which endless investigation would tend to bring scientific belief, which concordance the abstract statement may possess by virtue of the confession of its inaccuracy and one-sidedness, and this confession is an essential ingredient of truth. . . . Reality is that mode of being by virtue of which the real thing is as it is, irrespectively of what any mind or any definite collection of minds may represent it to be. (*CP* 5:565)

The debate surrounding Peirce's realism and theory of truth is technical, but his basic vision of inquiry is easy to grasp—and compelling. Peter Skagestad gives it powerful expression in his classic, *The Road of Inquiry*:

> To Peirce, knowledge is no longer regarded statically as a body of propositions resembling a more or less finished building, but dynamically as a process of inquiry. Peirce at times described this process as a march forward towards truth as an infinitely distant goal. During this march we never have firm rock beneath our feet; we are walking on a bog, and we can be certain only that the bog is sufficiently firm to carry us *for the time being*. Not only is this all the certainty that we can achieve, it is also all the certainty that we can rationally wish for, since it is precisely the tenuousness of the ground that constantly prods us forward, ever closer to our goal. . . . Science "is not standing upon the bedrock of facts. It is walking upon a bog, and can only say, this ground seems to hold for the present. Here I will stay till it begins to give way." (*CP* 5:589)[23]

All reflection, in this view, inherently brings with it certain norms, as in Jürgen Habermas's famous concept of the "ideal speech situation." In particular, inquiry presupposes *truth* as its regulating goal: all thinking is right or wrong, good or bad, depending on whether or not it leads toward that outcome.[24] (We return to the question of truth in chapter 2.) Christopher Hookway puts the point nicely:

> Since Peirce identifies the truth with what anyone is fated to believe, if she only inquires for long enough, it is natural to conclude that his account of reality depends upon identifying a single fundamental aim for inquiry, that of contributing to the growth of finished knowledge.[25]

In the end, we must credit Peirce with recognizing two of the most basic assumptions of inquiry. First, private claims to knowledge are not enough; validity claims must be "redeemed" through critical discourse. (Habermas, following Peirce, refers to these as *einlösbare Geltungsansprüche*, redeemable validity claims). The goal of the truth-seeker, as Hilary Putnam puts it, is to find "a coherent system of beliefs which will ultimately be accepted by the widest possible community of inquirers as a result of strenuous inquiry."[26] Second, the inquirer must presuppose that inquiry is moving toward a final hoped-for consensus, even while she may be rather skeptical concerning the current results of inquiry. Peirce puts the point concisely: "Undoubtedly, we hope that this, *or something approximating to this*, is so, or we should not trouble ourselves to make much inquiry. But we do not necessarily have much confidence that it *is* so" (*CP* 5:432).[27] Theology, like the other disciplines with which it must be in dialogue, exists in the ever-changing realm in which hope, faith, doubt, and skepticism intersect.

Theology in the Midst of the Sciences

I have intentionally emphasized the inner dimension of critical faith, since the primary level of belief and practice is altered by the inclusion of doubting, questioning, and inquiring within the heart of the religious life. But, as we've seen, the changes do not stop there. The nature of theological reflection concerning this belief and practice is also transformed. The dialogue of theology with the sciences is perhaps the clearest example. It both defines the new methods of proceeding and leads to some of the most important results.

Indeed, the commitment to vital dialogue changes more within theology than at first meets the eye. First, theology's relationship to its own history is transformed. In the fundamentalist impulse there is an immense antipathy toward changing what theologians of the past have stipulated as the "essentials" of the faith. (The same is true of many of the pietist traditions within Europe, as well as of fundamentally creedal traditions, whether Orthodox or Catholic.) If one's primary commitment is to remain faithful to "the truth once given," then of course aiding and abetting revisions can only mean a downward slide from that truth. By contrast, the theology I endorse comes closer to the sixteenth-century *semper reformata*: revisions are a constant requirement for any tradition that wishes to speak to its contemporary intellectual and social context. While costly, they are also necessary.

Second, theology's relation to other religious traditions is likewise transformed. It is possible to be committed both to one tradition and to the study of another; indeed, one can even *express* one's commitment to his or her tradition by studying another. Francis Clooney has formulated this point powerfully in his theses on "comparative theology":

> As faith seeking understanding, however, comparative theology eventually involves the theologian in questions of faith, particularly in finding a response to the other tradition's faith experiences and its "articulation" of the world in scripture. For understanding cannot stop neatly at the edge of experience; nor can a close reading of theological texts ward off the possibility of beginning to see the world in part through the scriptures of that other tradition.[28]

Finally, as we will see in later chapters, theology's relation to science is transformed. Indeed, the principles that motivate work in "comparative theology" are closely related to the core principles of the theology-science dialogue. I know my own tradition only by contrasting it with others, and I can evaluate the reasons on behalf of my own tradition only by imagining how they would be received by adherents of other traditions—or even better, by presenting my reasons and hearing how others actually respond. The same is true of theology's dialogue with the natural and social sciences today. Both areas of study dispute that sharp lines can be drawn between the "inside" and the "outside" of religious belief.[29] The contemporary *religious* context for belief is a radically *inter-religious*, pluralistic context. And the *non-religious* context for belief is science, that is, the specific conclusions of the various sciences on the one hand, and the more general assumptions that underlie them, such as naturalism and empiricism, on the other. It no more makes sense to advance theological truth claims in ignorance of the results of the sciences than it does to argue the superiority of one religious tradition over others without knowing what they claim and what the reasons are to which they appeal.

Before we move on, it's important to pause for a moment to consider two popular but inadequate reasons that are sometimes given for theology-science dialogue. The first runs, *"theology is a science, so it's natural that it be in dialogue with its fellow sciences."* It is true that in Latin theology is a *scientia* and that the treatment of theology as a science was basic to much medieval and Scholastic reflection. It's also true that in the twentieth century Thomas F. Torrance and other significant theologians have defended the notion of "theological science."[30] Most recently Alister McGrath has relied on similar arguments from Torrance and Barth in defending the epistemic status of theological assertions.[31] But an etymology doth not an epistemology make.[32] In *today's* context, the natural sciences are able to proceed in radically different ways and to acquire results with a different status than any theological work. Theologians have no choice but to acknowledge these differences and to defend their discipline in its distinctiveness from the way that theories are tested in the natural sciences.

The second reason runs, *"Christians can and should use science to prove the truth of Christian assertions."* Although I happen to be doubtful that any of the classic philosophical proofs for the existence of God actually succeed as proofs, there is nothing wrong in principle with attempting to formulate philosophical proofs. By contrast, the attempt to provide a *scientific* argument for the existence of God is profoundly confused. Amazingly, one of the most popular portions of the contemporary theology-science discussion in the United States, called intelligent design (or "ID" for short), does exactly this. According to William Dembski,[33] the best *scientific* explanation for the evolution of increasing complexity in the universe is that the universe was created by an intelligent designer. The goal of science, I suggest, is to explain the order that we discern in the empirical world, using fundamental natural laws, traceable causal histories, and replicable experiments where possible. Any moves to levels of argumentation at higher levels of abstraction—any arguments on "meta" levels—are inherently philosophical moves. There is nothing wrong with philosophy, but it is not science. One does not have to be a Kantian to agree that asking about the order or purpose of the whole, or asking for the cause of the whole, or about its origin, means moving from the empirical to the metaphysical dimension.

➤ Should Theology Take the Risk?

The topics we will be discussing raise complex and subtle challenges for theological reflection. Notwithstanding certain errors and overstatements on the parts of both scientists and theologians in the various debates, theologians are by and large correct in attempting to respond to recent scientific developments. Of course, there is always some risk that theology will align itself with a scientific theory that turns out to be spurious. One recalls that theologians in the past did embrace the theological implications of perpetual motion, the ether, physical determinism, and a complete reduction to genes or atoms. One must acknowledge the real danger of making similar mistakes in the future.

But, I suggest, the alternative is worse. The alternative is to put forward and embrace theologies that are based on outdated scientific cosmologies and empirically false claims about the world, rather than basing theological reflection on the best available knowledge we have about the universe. Surely the scriptures of one's religious tradition should not function as a dike that serves to protect one against advances in human knowledge. Therein lie the Dark Ages indeed!

Few pictures of this damaging anti-scientific appeal to authority in theology are more evocative, and more painful, than Bertold Brecht's famous scene in *The Life of Galileo*. Galileo points his telescope at the moons of Jupiter and bids the two papal astronomers simply to observe that some heavenly bodies orbit objects other than the sun. Standing on the roof of Galileo's house in Florence under the starry sky, with the evidence only inches away, the papal astronomers launch into a long discourse, using Aristotle and scripture to prove *a priori* that no heavenly body can orbit any other object than the sun. It follows, they conclude, that the telescope must be a tool of the devil.

Even today one can find theological treatises which contain analogous, albeit more subtle, arguments. But nature has a way of winning in the end. It is far better to accept the risks of aligning oneself with the best human efforts at knowledge, and then when necessary to admit mistakes and move on, than to remain "suckled on a creed outworn." Recall again a later moment from Brecht's play. Galileo is condemned for his heresies and sentenced to house arrest. After the verdict is read, the representatives of the papal inquisition depart. Alone on a darkening stage, condemned for his heretical claim that the earth moves around the sun, Galileo stands for a time in silence. Finally, though, he shakes his fist in the direction of the authorities who have just condemned him, and yells triumphantly, "*Und sie bewegt sich doch!*" ("And yet the earth moves nonetheless!").

➤ Conclusion

What then have we learned about the place of theology among the sciences and contemporary philosophy? Some will say it is a precarious place indeed! Developments outside of theology's control—some of which will later turn out to be mistaken—can undercut classical theological positions, can require radically new ways of thinking about God, and can even cast the credibility of theism as such into question. Yet there are several reasons for saying that this position is not only *not* untenable, but is actually the right place for theology to locate itself.

First, theists are fundamentally committed to the belief that in the end there is only one truth. One of the lowest moments in the history of theology was the advent of the "two truths" doctrine, which held that the truths of revelation may stand in opposition to the truths of observation and empirical experimentation. Theologians respond positively to scientific and philosophical advances because we believe that at the end of the day *all* means of ascertaining truth are means of the self-revelation of God. In the end the many shall become one.

Second, we live and work in this vulnerable place because we no longer accept the Scholastic claim that theology's rightful place is to rule as queen of the sciences. The Jesuanic ethic is the opposite: "He [or she] who would be first must be last of all and a servant to all" (Mark 9:35). The theology that exists in the midst of the sciences is a *kenotic* discipline, from the Greek *kenōsis*, "self-emptying" (see Phil 2:5-8). In the following chapters we will explore in some depth what it means to do theology in the form of kenosis. We will find that the stance that is *most* foreign to theology is to "lord it over" others (Mark 10:42)—to stand, as it were, above the fray of the human pursuit of knowledge and to claim for oneself, a mere mortal, that final position of authority that belongs to God alone. Yet is that not precisely what one does when one dismisses the best results of the human pursuit of knowledge from the standpoint of (one's particular understanding of) divine revelation? Far better to have acted in humility and to have claimed less for oneself than one might otherwise have done, leaving it to history and to the progression of knowledge to vindicate, or to falsify, one's own position in the end.

It is this uncertainty that should make one cautious about Robert J. Russell's advocacy of a *fully* symmetrical "creative mutual interaction" between theology and the sciences.[34] It is true that a metaphysical or theological framework can give rise to scientific hypotheses, or at least to heuristic principles that help guide scientific research programs. Moreover, over and over again in the history of science a philosophical stance has served to orient scientific inquiry. In many cases opponents of one stance have advanced another in its place, arguing that *their philosophy* would produce better scientific work and results. What distinguishes my interpretation of "creative mutual interaction" from Russell's is that it remains merely heuristic, in Webster's sense of the term: "helping to discover or learn; . . . using rules of thumb to find solutions or answers."[35]

So there is room for humility. Yet there is room for boldness as well. Theological voices may be bold because we recognize that human reflection must eventually make the transition from empirical and scientific results to philosophical and metaphysical questions. Critical faith dwells in the region of this transition and is nurtured by its inevitability. Were it not inevitable that the human mind should turn to questions of meaning, value, and ultimate reality, our conclusions here would represent a one-sided victory for science: science would set the parameters for theological reflection, whereas theology could at best offer a heuristic to assist scientists in their work.

What makes science successful is its ability to ask highly constrained questions. Topics are scientific only when they can have an empirical answer; theories are scientific only when they face the bar of experience (either directly, or mediated through other theories) in order to be corroborated or falsified. Nor can "experience" here mean mystical experience; it is that shared realm of intersubjective discourse that we defined in examining Peirce and Habermas above. *Any claim that is not empirically and intersubjectively testable in this way is one that stands outside the sciences.* Such claims are *metaphysical* claims. (Of course, the division need not be permanent: today's metaphysics may be part of tomorrow's empirical science.)

What scientists and philosophers of science discovered in the late twentieth century, though they should have known it from centuries past, is that the spheres of the empirical and the metaphysical are not autonomous. Knowledge in one is incomplete unless one also understands the contribution of the other. Empirical results raise urgent metaphysical questions, and metaphysical positions frame empirical research. Only those who know both sides can sort out the confusions that arise in each. Moreover, many assertions that sound at first like scientific claims turn out upon closer analysis not to be. Those who argue for physicalism, for example, may sound like the consummate scientists. But physicalism is the claim that all things that exist are physical things, which presumably means that all existing things are composed of matter and energy as they are understood in physics, and which may mean that the only real causes are microphysical causes. It doesn't take much reflection to realize that these claims quickly involve one in complex philosophical arguments—arguments of the sort not likely to be published in *Physical Review Letters*.[36]

A full discussion of the real issues therefore moves along an unbroken line from actual scientific results to philosophical questions to metaphysical or theological hypotheses. There should be nothing troubling about this fact. The tight constraints that have allowed humans to gain ever more scientific knowledge of the world beg for closer analysis; yet it's obvious that the conditions of the possibility of scientific inquiry cannot themselves be objects of scientific inquiry. Over and over again, scientific results usher in speculations about the most appropriate metaphysical position for one to take. Indeed, across history some of the greatest and most fascinating—and most productive—metaphysical reflection has taken place at the boundaries of science.

This fact does not by itself win any battles for theology. But it *is* good news for theology, for it provides a rationale and an agenda for those who accept the challenge of doing theology in the midst of the sciences. It encourages us to study the scientific debates deeply enough that we can comprehend the questions that arise at their boundaries. When one does this, one can't help but wonder about the best philosophical views to hold in response. The most rational course of action is then to formulate appropriate metaphysical positions, including theological positions, and to defend them as well as one can. If one pursues this process with all the subtlety it requires—not throwing God immediately into the fray, but following the chain of philosophical questions as they arise in the discussion—then one eventually finds oneself involved in the metaphysical quest. In this broadest of all contexts, I venture to add, the theological response is certainly not *less* profound than many of its competitors.

Religious Truth and Scientific Truth

A Comparative Exploration

W E ARE ATTEMPTING TO HEED THE CALL FOR A CRITICAL FAITH, AND IN the first chapter we began to explore the radical consequences of this call. The critical reader, the kind of reader I've called for in the opening chapter, will however immediately recognize an important concern. If theology is to let the dialogue with science and philosophy be this significant, how will it preserve its identity *as theology*? Will it, can it become merely another *Wissenschaft*, another field of inquiry alongside others? This oft-repeated worry has to do with the methodology of theology: What are its unique methods? What do we know about God, and how is it known? And what is the nature of theological truth?

Clearly this last question must come first, for its answer will guide the inquiry into many of the other topics. Is the truth of theology different from the truth of science? If not, some are afraid that theology will be subsumed, sooner or later, within the sciences. But if it is, mustn't theology by its very nature stand *outside* the discussion among the sciences? These are not simple questions. The literature on theories of truth is vast. One has the sense of wrestling with an issue as complex as the question, "What is God?" Indeed, perhaps the two topics are more closely bound together than is often acknowledged.

Having in the past used analytic methods to address this question,[1] I wish here to explore another approach to the topic. Phenomenology is the field of philosophy that attempts to describe the way that phenomena actually appear, noting similarities and differences between diverse areas of human experience. The comparison with scientific truth provides a particularly auspicious focus for an inquiry into the nature of theological truth. In the sciences, it's often said, one is concerned with the objective world rather than an all-too-subjective universe of religious beings and values, with a clearly specified domain rather than one apparently resistant to all cartographic efforts, and with a method productive of proven results rather than a methodless wandering through perennial (and perennially unanswerable) questions. In the scientist's methodological self-confidence, her knowing how to pursue knowledge she does not yet possess, lies the appropriateness of science as a foil for this phenomenology of religious truth.

The methods of phenomenology free one to describe without having to judge between the types of truth or to arbitrate their relative epistemic merits. (We turn to evaluation at this chapter's end and in subsequent chapters.) At the same time, pursuing the comparison with science helpfully structures our examination of the question of religious truth. We will have to look at the attitudes of practitioners in both areas, at their *modi operandi* in constructing the claims they hold to be true, and at the types of statements they generally make. The "truth proper to science" lies in the type of statement scientists construct, the broader theoretical frameworks they employ, and, crucially, the techniques they use to verify their claims. The comparison will thus predispose us to look at religious belief in terms of the methods, attitudes, and practices of religious persons, extrapolating from these to the nature of religious truth.

Inspired by the phenomenologists' technique of "variation," we will proceed via three contrasting modes of construing scientific and religious truth. I begin with the scientist's "natural attitude," the traditional view of science as a strictly rational practice aimed at objective truth. But the one-sidedness of this picture inevitably gives rise to its opposite, a "hermeneutical" construal of science (section two). This view, by treating science only as subjective human activity, seeks to wed science and religion where the first had divorced them. Still, the strict identification of science and religion gives rise to problems of its own: however "religious" science becomes, however "subjective," it remains a theoretical endeavor in a manner distinct from religion. Consequently, the final comments on the science-religion relation (section three) will involve negating the negation of the traditional view, neither dichotomizing nor identifying their two types of truth. In the final analysis one is led to reaffirm certain traditional distinctions between scientific and religious truth—though, I hope to show, in a manner different from their traditional formulations.

A quick caveat: it is common for philosophers of science to be somewhat suspicious of broad statements about the nature of "science," even to eschew any statements whatsoever about "science" as a whole; students of religion are no less reticent about general definitions of "religion." Such reticence is not entirely misplaced; phenomenological studies have indeed revealed important variants among scientific disciplines and subdisciplines.[2] Nonetheless, one leaves some broad features of both science and religion unnecessarily obscure when one rejects *all* reflection about these phenomena in general. If ours were an age of over-ambitious interdisciplinary work, perhaps one could dispense with all broad comparisons of this sort. But ours is instead an age in which scholars seem to have lost their nerve; scientists retreat increasingly into their specialized work, and seminaries and divinity schools are increasingly refusing to undertake any serious exploration of science as it is actually practiced. (Indeed, constructive theology itself is being sidelined at a number of schools.) In an age of cautious, "safe" academics it may be refreshing to undertake the adventure of some risky comparisons.

A Contrastive Theory of Religious Truth

We begin, then, with a phenomenological analysis of scientific truth as it is manifested in the traditional image of natural science. According to this view, successful science mirrors the way things are; it is characterized by detachment, a thoroughly rational method, and asymptotic progress toward a system of propositions that would correspond, one-to-one, with physical reality. In its nature and mode of disclosure, scientific truth so construed diverges widely from the personal involvement and concern with meaning found in religion.

This analysis portrays scientists as in confident contact with a comprehensible world. There is an apparent paradox here: nature confronts us as other, as something standing apart from us, which is not us; yet scientific study approaches nature with more epistemic confidence than it does the human other. The paradox is only apparent, however, for science's strength lies precisely in its ability to control. Using scientific methods, the domain under study can be closed, excluding forces and entities qualitatively different from the target domain. In accepting the law of entropy as a general law of thermodynamics, for instance, one construes the universe as a closed system, with no ordering influences from "outside." It is the power of scientific theory to admit only that world that can be grasped using quantitative concepts and replicable studies.

A second seeming paradox catches one's attention as well. Science, with its detailed specifications of domain and method, imposes an *a priori* structure on nature. Kant's "discovery" of the forms of intuition and categories of the understanding stemmed from his natural philosophy, his reflection on science. Science enjoys the power of prediction (in solid state physics up to eight significant digits) as a result of the initial focus on the quantitative, replicable features of nature. Once the parameters are set, scientists become the consummate listeners to nature. Heidegger (among others) grasped this fact with reference to Greek science, which was born out of the observation of nature before the concept of experimentation had been developed. *Ta mathēmata* is what can be remembered, the knowable in nature.[3] Nothing is qualitatively changed with the addition of experimentation. In fact, phenomenologically, experimentation only intensifies the same paradoxical form: it involves the move from passive observing to structured observing. The questions are now more carefully posed to nature, and the result is a heightened listening.

Two of the features of science that are brought to the fore by this traditional phenomenological perspective tend to support the traditionally sharp distinctions between science and religion. First, the scientific attitude is said to involve the transition from viewing the world as "ready-to-hand" (participatory understanding) to "present-at-hand" (abstract analysis), and questions about its own status as knowledge are excluded. Science seeks to formulate true assertions about the world. To do so, it abstracts from questions about the mode of being of the questioner and from any features she has that set her apart from other inquirers. The central role of *replicability* means just this: any researcher who can recreate precisely these objective conditions will observe just these consequent behaviors. Out of the *de facto* plurality of life-worlds the scientist seeks to discover a single underlying framework that belongs to every possible observer. Think again of Kant's insistence that his forms and categories (and, in his moral philosophy, the categorical imperative) will apply not just to all persons, but to *all rational beings*. Here is a philosophy of the "they" (*das Man*) *par excellence*!

But, second, this "strength" of the scientific perspective may also be viewed as its weakness. To attain unambiguous access to its domain it must rule out questions that require a different theoretical perspective, as well as self-referential questions. Husserl and Heidegger, Alfred Schutz and Maurice Merleau-Ponty, Julia Kristeva, and Judith Butler have variously argued that this move makes science dependent on an external analysis for clarification of its own concepts and practices. Still, from a purely descriptive standpoint one must admit that, once this domain is established, science can then speak with particular authority about the phenomena it studies. It can "unveil" (*alēthein*) them in a powerful fashion once the limits are set. Of course, there's a cost: what makes a science the best judge of its own field may also make it incompetent to judge the *nature* of its own truths, their proper scope, or their inherent limitations.[4]

Scientific truth, according to this traditional model, is the truth of correspondence, the *adequatio rei et intellectus*. It evokes a picture theory of language, in which scientists create terms for the basic entities in the physical world ("reality as it really is") and utilize mathematical functions to describe the lawlike interrelations among these real things. Prediction is possible because of the accuracy of this linguistic modeling. For example, the equations that dictate the extension of an acceleration curve reflect analogous forces in nature that act on their "real" objects in the same way.

Within this model, what catches the phenomenologist's attention about scientific truth is the striving for mastery. It expresses the will to dominance—dominance through analysis and objectification. To objectify is to put under one's control, whether it be the theoretical control of "saying the truth about something" or the technological control of routine manipulation. This is the opposite pole to the experience of the other as other. In fact, the critics of science frequently criticize this move from their moral (or religious) perspective by speaking of "dehumanizing" the other, reducing her to the status of an object, which scientific theory controls outside the strictures of moral demands.

What, then, is the truth "proper to" science as it has disclosed itself up to this point? To the extent that the scientific attitude takes the form here described, scientific truth is revealed as objective and dispassionate; it is not person-relative but turns instead on the paradigm of impersonal knowledge. The resultant assertions are free from perspectival corruption. They may impose a grid (à la Kant), but this grid is necessarily imposed by *any* rational creature who wishes "really to know" the natural world. Since science strives for true propositions, propositions that mediate between words and worlds, scientific truth can only mean perfect correspondence with the nature of the way things are. It is the seeing of things as they reveal themselves objectively to the observer (whether she has structured the seeing through experimentation or not). It is the truth of disciplined observation, of clear questions that demand clear answers.

The position just sketched provides the phenomenologist of religion with a clear orientation for a *via negativa*, for it gives rise to a point-by-point characterization of religious truth in contradistinction to science so understood. Religious truth, it would seem by contrast, is subjective, passionate, and intrinsically perspectival. The truths of religious explanations are the truths of myth and personal disclosure, not the truths of *logos*. The religious person is *involved*, and her involvement is a matter of ultimate concern to her. Unlike scientific truth, religious truth is inseparable from questions of meaning. It does not share the cognitive goal of re-picturing the world (human or divine) with objective accuracy, but the "meaninged" or semantic goal of understanding the divine (or other conceptualizations of the religious ultimate) in a *personal* manner, that is, as it encounters me and in terms of the call to response that he/she/it imposes on me.

And so on—the contrasts inspired by this *via negativa* can be, and often have been, extended at will. In fact, many of the dichotomies that are used to characterize the religious dimension—reason versus faith, nature versus grace, natural versus supernatural—stem from precisely this same presupposed opposition between science and religion. The reasons given for accepting this "contrastive" theory of religious truth are sometimes heuristic and sometimes essential: some believe that religious truth is most truly characterized by contrasting it to this scientific mode of knowing, others that the religious ultimate can only be described in negative terms such as these. In any event, whether consciously or not, contrastive theories of religious truth usually presuppose a phenomenology of science as objective knowledge of the sort described here.

The Identity of Scientific and Religious Truth

But closer observation of the phenomena of scientific practice strongly challenges the adequacy of the traditional picture. A new face of science has been unveiled by more recent work, which supports, *at minimum*, the compatibility of scientific and religious truth. In fact, we will now explore the case for accepting an even stronger view, which I will entitle the "identity theory" of scientific and religious truth. This more extreme view holds that there is *no* difference in principle between scientific and religious truth, that the two types of truth are ultimately indistinguishable. Defending this view means negating the negation defended in section 1 of this chapter. By tightening to their very limits the phenomenological cords that bind science and religion, we will be able to ascertain where they break—if they do—and why. As I will show, the results provide crucial parameters for the phenomenology of religious truth.

We begin by challenging two misconceptions. First, science is not merely common sense made rigorous, whereas the religious pursuit of truth stands in sharp opposition to the everyday, rational view of the world. Even if one assumed that the physics of Aristotle and Newton simply presupposed the common-sense view of the world of their day—an assumption I would sharply dispute—this can hardly be said of recent work in physical cosmology or quantum physics. Like religious thought, theorizing in science may *begin* with the world as we know it, but it frequently concludes with a world unrecognizable to the non-initiate. Second, scientific work does not exhibit a kind of pure rationality or objectivity that is absent from other forms of human activity, whereas the religious quest transcends, or completely falls short of, the accepted canons of rational thought. Instead, I propose we explore the possibility that both activities are identical, in the sense that *both involve a critical use of hypotheses and doubt within a subjective human framework pervasively influenced by personal, societal, and historical factors.* This "identity theory" of scientific and religious truth can be defended in two separate ways: through the content of scientific statements (the *type of truth* that science grasps), and through the attitudes and activities of scientific researchers (the *means to truth* that they employ). Addressing each separately reveals perhaps unexpected similarities in religious and scientific activity.

Consider first the content of science. It has not proven possible to interpret scientific theories as explanations that obey a certain formal structure and general criteria of adequacy. The physics of special relativity and quantum mechanics have made observer limitations central to the epistemology of science, as well as to its view of reality. Attempts to overcome these limitations through purely objective and universal approaches that negate the effects of observer perspective have not been successful, leaving behind an awareness of the irreducibly pragmatic and perspectival dimensions in human knowing. The "truth" of scientific statements now includes intrinsically perspectival elements: the observer's spatio-temporal frame of reference, her moment and manner of measurement, even the specific why-question that she is asking through her experimental design and theoretical apparatus. A massive literature now treats scientific theories as myths, models, narratives, and stories, and ascribes to them only the truth proper to such accounts.[5]

These new insights have stemmed not only from advances in physics. Equally important have been the attempts to isolate the social sciences as distinct disciplines operating according to their own principles. Thinkers such as Dilthey, Rickert, and Windelband at the end of nineteenth century fought to weaken the grip of natural scientific models on human studies and to establish methods and theoretical structures appropriate to the nature of human existence in the world. Under the influence of Husserl, Alfred Schutz defended an "interpretive social science" inspired by a phenomenology of the life-world, and Maurice Merleau-Ponty worked to specify the relation between subject and object in a manner congenial to the demands of both scientific research and human existence. This research was taken up first into social scientific practice, with the result that it's no longer considered odd to utilize phenomenological methods as a part of one's social scientific work.[6] More recently, the fundamentally hermeneutical nature of the natural sciences has been recognized as well.[7]

These developments constitute an antithesis to the traditional understanding of science as essentially objective and abstractive (section one). In this new view, scientific theories are viewed as one *perspective*, one of many ways humans attempt to construct a coherent, comprehensible world for themselves. Epistemologists might try to argue that there is a greater probability that scientific statements are truer than religious ones. But phenomenologists are interested instead in the mode of manifestation, and here religion and science are identical: both are symbolizing activities aimed at making the world meaningful through the creation of a symbolic universe. Each context has its own manner of speaking or type of "speech acts"; each speech act makes its unique type of validity claim; different validity claims are tested according to different criteria. Jürgen Habermas, for instance, has distinguished "constative," "expressive," and "regulative" speech acts, depending on whether the context is theoretical, expressive, or ethical. Each context has its own distinctive truth within the broader project of human communication.[8]

These theses distinguish this new view of science from the "positivism" that infected the descriptions in section one. Scientific truth can only be elucidated in terms of its social context. As McHugh notes,

> . . . there are no adequate grounds for establishing criteria of truth except the grounds that are employed to grant or concede it—truth is conceivable only as a socially organized upshot of contingent courses of linguistic, conceptual, and social behavior. The truth of a statement is not independent of the conditions of its utterance, and so to study truth is to study the ways truth can be methodically conferred.[9]

We know that religious beliefs about oneself and the world reflect one's cultural and historical setting; so too the beliefs of scientists. We know that the truths of religion are inherently historical;[10] those of science are equally so. Phenomenologically, science must therefore be construed as the totality of the contexts operative in its formulations. Science is our perspectival dictation to nature as much as our response to nature's own speech.

The foregoing analysis begins to indicate the complexity of elucidating a scientific theory of truth. It suggests that scientific judgments are not made true by some sort of perfect correspondence with reality, with objective states of affairs. Rather, scientific truth might need to be reconceived from the standpoint of coherence rather than correspondence. As Kockelmans has written, "[scientific] judgments state how things are as seen from some limited context of meaning or, in the final analysis, from the perspective of the whole of meaning of which we can conceive."[11] It may be that a particular theoretical structure better allows the truth of the world to manifest itself in scientific statements, hence that one structure is "truer" than another. But there are reasons to be skeptical that the scientist actually possesses an eidetic vision of this sort. More likely, if all criteria of evaluation are indeed theory-laden, one can judge the relative adequacy of a given higher-order theory only on internal, coherential grounds. Recall, for example, that experiments are generally suggested by the presently accepted theoretical structure; data are molded by it, conclusions interpreted by it, anomalies explained away by it.

In short, a coherence theory of science means abandoning the belief that nature is speaking in some direct and unmediated sense through scientific statements. In this view, what we call scientific truth just is the coherence within the various sets of conclusions that we call scientific: the coherence of sets of observations with sets of predictions, the coherence of different kinds of theories with one another, the coherence of the sets of beliefs held by practicing scientists.

Hence, once again one would seem to have grounds for treating the cognitive or belief components of science and religion as (more or less) identical. Both are striving for unity, seeking to avoid the cognitive dissonances of incoherence, and neither has direct access to the reality with which it is concerned. If the parallels can be maintained on this level, do they also survive when we shift from the cognitive to the noncognitive components of science?

We have considered the content of science; now what about the activities of scientists? There are good phenomenological reasons to view science not as a purely theoretical endeavor but as a particular species of human activity, one that reflects the perspectives of its participants. A careful study of actual scientific activity is unlikely to convert one to the standpoint of Karl Popper, who famously held that genuine science is a purely rational project involving "conclusive falsifications" of hypotheses and theories. Instead, the pendulum in the philosophy of science has swung away from formal models of scientific explanation and rationality and toward an increasingly pragmatic and institutional view. Emphasizing history and sociology tends to produce instrumentalist accounts of scientific theories, which contrast sharply with the realism presupposed in section one. In this view, interactions with the "world" (as we have pre-formed it through our theoretical parameters) give rise to scientific theories; such theories are no more than predictions of future interactions we will have. Here, once again, parallels with religious truth suggest themselves. Religious experiences, rituals, and socialization usually precede the formulation of beliefs, and beliefs for their part give rise to further attitudes and actions. In both science and religion, the effects of this hermeneutical circle of pre-understandings and expectations invalidate "linear" claims to objectivity.

Science as human activity can be viewed in two different ways, one personal and the other institutional. Faced with the demise of positivistic accounts of science, many conclude that scientific knowledge is personal knowledge; scientific truth, personal truth.[12] In other words, science does not stand completely apart from the researcher's wish to construct a meaningful context for living; instead, it is one of the projects that arises out of his life-world. How can one hypostatize science, as if it were a Platonic form, if science is simply what persons called scientists do? The researching biochemist in the lab does not exemplify some timeless "logic of discovery"; rather, her various guesses and trials are better studied by a psychology of research.[13] For anyone, scientist or otherwise, to hold that a claim is warranted is for him to find its justifications credible, which ultimately involves an internal (even if not arbitrary) "seeing" or "finding." Science, one might say, institutionalizes the mental state of doubt. But—to continue the personalist perspective—judging is a type of skill, commitment to a theory a disposition, the quest for objectivity a passion or prejudice.

Science is also a social activity. Like all other social or symbolic worlds, a scientific world is constructed. An individual is trained according to textbook examples and problem sets, which provide "exemplars" (T. S. Kuhn) of correct answers and problem-solving methods. When a theoretical perspective has amassed a sufficient number of anomalies (incompatibilities with new experimental data or with other firmly entrenched theories), a group of scholars will replace it with a different framework, creating a new research program or subdiscipline if necessary. Historical coincidences, such as the inability of a major theorist to form a "school" or the emergence of an attractive alternate hypothesis, can be as decisive in such shifts as any empirical observation. Factors such as the theory-dependence of observations and experimental data or the difficulty of deciding when recalcitrant data really militate against a given hypothesis make the justification of scientific truths as knotty as that of religious hypotheses. In fact, the decisions can be so complex and highly subjective that Kuhn referred to them as scientific "conversions" four different times in *The Structure of Scientific Revolutions.*[14]

Finally, when we view science as an institution we begin to perceive the extent to which scientific statements express relations of power within the scientific community.[15] Science as "institution" includes the role of textbooks, the editorial criteria of leading journals, and the better ability of professors at top universities to find jobs for their doctoral or post-doctoral students. It involves a social network with its own rites and rituals that fosters a certain view of the world. And it includes the expressions of these power relations as they determine what gets published in *Science* and *Nature* or who presents, and on what topics, at major conferences. Under this perspective, science is one of many social worlds, one of many ways of socially constructing reality, and its truth is the reality that results. To take a historical example,[16] one might wish to say that Galileo predominated over his opponents because his experiments let the world speak as it really is. But it is equally true to say that Galilean science predominated because Galileo wrote in the vernacular, used better rhetorical techniques than his churchly opponents, offered an alternative to a now-outworn metaphysics—and because his worldview was more compatible with the humanistic, mercantile, and Reformation interests of a Europe gradually emerging from the control of the Roman Catholic Church.

In short, in this view one obscures the "truth proper to science" if one insists on describing it in abstraction from such phenomena. The interests of science are inseparable from its truth. Thus the scientist's account of scientific truth might run as follows: "I decide when, where, and how to inquire of nature. On at least three different levels I handcuff nature in order to get it to speak. First, I set the most basic parameters in that I presuppose certain foundational principles of rationality, mathematicizability, and replicability. Then, in choosing the specified realm and the experimental methods of my particular subdiscipline, I set more particular requirements. (The molecular biologist will see nature revealing different truths than the environmental biologist; the cognitive psychologist will discover different truths than the social psychologist.) Finally, I produce an even more specific account of truth through the group of theories that I either accept or view as live options." These restrictions, taken together, introduce a complex variety of subjective factors. Admittedly, they are not as monolithic as a single "seeing as" that some say characterizes all science, nor as specific as Gadamer's claim that "the knowledge of all the natural sciences is knowledge for domination."[17] Still, the interests out of which the truth of science is constructed are highly relative to time, existing scientific institutions, specific powerful individuals, and so forth.

Phenomenologists of religion will have read the previous paragraphs with a wry grin: Isn't religion's truth usually characterized in precisely these terms? Winston King writes of the often imperceptible shift from religion as effort or quest to religion as response.[18] Louis Dupré describes in detail the creation of symbols which, however human, then acquire the weight of the sacred.[19] Eliade proclaims the inevitable transition from the history of religions to the phenomenology of religion. And van der Leeuw's classic phenomenology of religion is based on the manifestation of the divine or transcendent through religious symbols and practices.

Appealing to the view of science described in this section, identity theorists typically conclude that there is no difference in the phenomenology of the truths "proper to" science and religion. Many phenomenologists of religion chronicle both the transcendent intentionality of religious experience *and* the personal and social nature of all religious words, exploring the complex realm of their interactions without dismissing either side. Scientific truth can be thematized using exactly the same two poles. Does our reflection on the commonalities in mystical experience lead us to posit a shared intuition of the divine through the mystical consciousness? Science also, as we saw in section one, contains its moments of waiting and listening. Does our observation of historical and cultural differences among religious phenomena lead us to stress the role of communal norms and practices? Here, too, a scientific model exists, for it's just as difficult to separate the activity and passivity of the scientist. (Recall that their intrinsic inseparability was Kant's fundamental point.) When one interpolates from a finite number of experimental data to a smooth curve, thereby making claims regarding a potentially infinite number of unobserved states of affairs, is one listening to nature, or is one dictating to her? When one "understands" a historical text or event, is one hearing its author or dominating her? Especially in the social sciences, it is impossible to cleanly separate the hypotheses one constructs about human actions from the more intuitive understandings one has of their significance.[20]

Moreover, the dichotomy between religion and science fails from the other (the religious) side as well. In the modern Western context adherence to a religious tradition and its practices is often accompanied by doubts about its truth. This has created a phenomenon that I labeled the "secular believer" in chapter 1.[21] Such believers remain committed to the beliefs and ritual practices of their tradition while at the same time holding them open to (active or passive) doubt. In a dynamic that Richard Dawkins, Daniel Dennett, and their friends have completely overlooked, this means that religious believers may actually evidence a *more* tentative, hypothetical stance toward their beliefs than many scientists do. The scientist may (sometimes? frequently?) be more firmly and devoutly attached to her theories than (some? many?) religious believers are to theirs.

Much can be said about the historical genesis of this surprising reversal. Its causes include both the failure of the modern Cartesian attempt to ground religious truth in the individual's subjectivity and science's perceived role as the authoritative source of truths about the world. Just as crucially, it reflects a certain drawing-together of two very different arbiters of religious truth, theology and the study of religion. I understand theology as religious reflection on the content of *one's own* beliefs, and the study of religion as reflection about religious beliefs and practices that are generally *not* one's own, generally within the context of the social sciences. Theology is therefore reflection from the perspective of religious observance, or at least location, whereas religious studies involves "external" reflection that brackets the question of the truth of the beliefs under study. I am arguing that the secular believer is no longer a person for whom theology (in this sense) is the arbiter of religious truth, but that his or her stance toward religious truth may be equally the product of reflection and work in other disciplines.

For the secular believer, doubt is a central part of the faith. Tillich saw this point clearly:

> This element of doubt is a condition of all spiritual life. The threat to spiritual life is not doubt as an element but the total doubt. . . . [The doubting person] asks for an answer which is valid within and not outside the situation of his despair. . . . [The only answer is] that the acceptance of despair is in itself faith and on the boundary line of the courage to be.[22]

Nor need the doubt about religious truth be confined to passive, passing worries. The believer who admits it as an inevitable concomitant of her faith may also experience doubt at the center of her religious life and actively pursue its insights. The resultant dialogue between the religious and secular perspectives within the individual's life creates an internal tension that becomes central to the dynamics of her faith and religious practice. It is the complex state of possessing religious truth while at the same time questing for truth. Within the context of her experience in the church or synagogue the secular believer may consciously select among received teachings; compare them with the teachings of science, philosophy, and other religious traditions; collect and weigh apparent instances of falsification of her tradition's beliefs; and so on.

Of course, this activity need not be pursued in a disinterested manner, any more than the scientist must be dispassionate about her work. In fact, it may well be that a passionate concern with the outcome is essential to any religious preoccupation with the truth question. Still, the phenomenon of the secular believer shows that a genuine openness regarding the truth of one's own beliefs remains compatible with sincere religious commitment and practice. When combined with the subjective elements in scientific practice discussed above, this fact *appears* to justify an identity theory of scientific and religious truth. Or are the observations in this section, like those in section one, also in need of a corrective?

Compatibilism without Identity

When one analyzes the intentionality of the scientific disciplines, as revealed in the attitudes of their practitioners and the practices of the scientific community, one is struck by the (often unacknowledged) parallels with religious truth. These parallels challenge traditional dichotomies and lead one to speculate about the possibility of identifying the two kinds of truth. Nevertheless, I now suggest, the very attempt to identify them reveals the ultimate untenability of the identity theory. One recognizes that, in the effort to equate them, essential phenomena of both fields are omitted. Correcting for the one-sided emphases in the two preceding sections, therefore, draws our attention to several fundamental differences between the truth proper to the two fields, differences that now emerge as essential. Here I can treat only the most obvious of these.

First, science still involves a theoretical attitude, at least in its intentionality. This attitude may well be influenced by the subjective wishes of researchers and theorists; by their drive for power, hope for a particular experimental outcome, faith in their own theories, or desire to receive tenure. But the nature of the activity requires that one suppress the influence of such factors—whether successfully, unconsciously, or in outright bad faith—in one's publications and lectures. "Objectivity" remains the regulative ideal of scientific practice, at least in the natural sciences.

Not so with religion. Here, beyond the common urge to objectify the divine, the guiding values include subjectivity in faith and response. Clifford Geertz summarizes the fundamental contrasts:

> [The religious perspective] differs from the scientific perspective in that it questions the realities of everyday life not out of an institutionalized scepticism which dissolves the world's givenness into a whirl of probabilistic hypotheses, but in terms of what it takes to be wider, nonhypothetical truths. Rather than detachment, its watchword is commitment; rather than analysis, encounter.[23]

Now these distinctions of Geertz's may err toward the black and white. Whatever theologians and anthropologists may tell them, most religious persons are very concerned about what they believe. Few would be content to replace doctrinal claims with a mere, "I'm feeling religious today." And of course, any account that would neglect the believer's sense of the essence of her faith in favor of moral, political, or aesthetic reductionism is anathema to a phenomenology of religion.

Thus the truth of Geertz's words must be carefully stated, for the distinction has now become quantitative rather than qualitative. Both science and religion share the quest for true belief. Moreover, scientists *may* be passionately attached to their theories as matters of ultimate concern to them. But for religious persons such involvement or engagement—"the assurance of things hoped for, the conviction of things unseen"—is more than an allowable concomitant of religious teachings; it is essential to the religious phenomenon itself. Science, but not religion, can be played with the mind alone. The secular believer whom I described above may well treat her beliefs as conjectures, as Wolfhart Pannenberg has repeatedly suggested, and she may avoid the "immunization strategies" of which Hans Albert accuses theologians. But she will never *rejoice* in the falsification of her hypotheses, as Karl Popper's ideal scientist will.[24]

Second, the scientific endeavor has often been characterized by the sense of a progressive mastery of nature, a piece-by-piece conquest of her secrets. The shifts detailed in section two have weakened this connection by stressing the diversity of scientific motives instead of simply equating science with the will to dominate. (Think of the role of aesthetic, political, and religious motives in the activity of scientists such as Copernicus, Galileo, and Einstein.) The mastery thesis is further weakened by epistemic doubts about whether we really know what is hypothesized in our theories, and indeed whether there is actually any real external world for us *to* possess. Nevertheless, these developments have scarcely removed the attitude of possession from science. The move from realism to instrumentalism, for example, heightens the awareness that theories are retained in the first place because they are useful for our purposes.

By contrast, the religious object is characterized by its *unpossessability*; it remains always beyond all claims made about it. The religious attitude never claims to master the object of devotion, even in those moments of greatest closeness when the mystic believes she is most clearly perceiving the divine. When worship strives after possession, religion crosses the line into the realm of magic. The religious meaning, van der Leeuw writes, is the "last word," yet one that is never spoken:

> The ultimate meaning [is] a secret which reveals itself repeatedly, only nevertheless to remain eternally concealed. It implies an advance to the farthest boundary, where only one sole fact is understood:—that all comprehension is "beyond."[25]

Attentiveness, subordination, worship—concepts such as these struggle to express the sense of encounter with a Something Greater that underlies the religious attitude. Where scientific truth is "for us," religious truth remains "beyond us."

Third, the truth of religion is not found in a specific object of experience but in the *ground* of all experience. In contrast to the scientific mind, the religious consciousness will never countenance the divine as one object among other objects in the world. The resistance to objectifying the divine is legion: Tillich's move beyond ontology to the ground of Being, Duméry's use of the transcendental reduction to speak of the ground of all experience rather than mere objects of experience,[26] the concentration on the meaning of religious attitudes (Louis Dupré), the subjectivism of Hick's "seeing as" or Hare's "bliks," the "neither/nor" of Buddhism's non-dualistic consciousness, and of course the mystical *via negativa* in its many forms.

This difference between religion and science is reflected in the different ways their truths are expressed. "Completed science," if such a notion is coherent, would be a system of propositions that reflected the totality of states of affairs. This ideal could in principle be reached by a gradual accretion of corroborated theories. By contrast, the need to negate or qualify one's statements about the divine increases almost proportionately with their correctness. When "adequate" statements are made about the divine, the believer inevitably insists that they are to be taken analogically, doxologically, maieutically, praxologically, even equivocally or apophatically.[27] There is a sense in which believers will accept *specific* events or doctrinal teachings as adequate, while insisting that, at the more general level, the ultimate truth exceeds all abilities of human language. The appeal to a knowledge beyond words—or to the limiting, self-negating function of parables, myths, and symbols—is the constant theme of the religious teacher.

Finally, scientific activity—and hence scientific truth—remains *sui generis* on account of its method, which in some ways *does* allow humans to move beyond their particular frameworks toward intersubjective agreement. Thus limitations must be placed on the notion, introduced above, of scientific truth as "personal knowledge." Scientific activity may be permeated by individual perspectives and institutional influences on belief change or maintenance. But it's also characterized by significant mechanisms for avoiding, or recognizing and eliminating, errors and prejudices in the construction of theories. Whereas in art and religion, differences in individual and group perspectives, in cultures and cultic practices, add to the richness of artistic and religious truth, the constant goal in science is to transcend perspectival differences. Where perspectives are ultimate givens, as in special relativity or cultural anthropology, mathematical functions or formal taxonomies (respectively) must be found to specify the interrelationships between frameworks.

➤ Conclusion

In the final analysis we thus find ourselves driven back to affirm at least some of the traditional distinctions between scientific and religious truth. The movement of our inquiry has not been strictly circular, however, for some progress has been made. Having discovered the significant overlaps between scientific and religious activity in section two, the four distinctions in section three can no longer be construed as signs of a fundamental religion-science dichotomy, in the sense envisioned in section one. Though one must grant important differences between science and religion, one can do so as part of a nuanced understanding of the two, one that eschews black-and-white distinctions in favor of careful gradations that are more truly representative of the complex realities of the phenomena themselves.[28]

The Contemporary Science *and* Religion Discussion

New Adventures *for* Theology, *or a* Futile Quest *for* Legitimation?

T HE PREVIOUS TWO CHAPTERS HAVE DEFENDED A MODEL OF AN OPEN and engaged theology, a model that brings it into vital dialogue with the best of contemporary philosophy and science. The best way to deepen this vision for theology is to probe it, to expose it to the most searching criticisms one can formulate. Is this really a new adventure for theology, or is it a feeble attempt to legitimize the Christian tradition by making it appear open to the intellectual currents of our day? This is no idle charge; many contributions to the religion-science dialogue in recent years have given the appearance of a Christianity really engaging with the sciences, when in fact core beliefs are not really exposed to the scrutiny of naturalism, physicalism, and the scientific method. In this chapter we must ask: What would it mean for scientists and religious believers to enter into real dialogue—that is, a dialogue that might really be transformative on both sides?

Many of us believe that the growing field of religion-science has helped to relegitimate religion "for an age of science." These claims raise the provocative question: Is the nascent field creating a genuine fit between religion and science, or does it offer merely the *appearance* of a fit? To pose the question immediately raises a dilemma for scholars in this field. On the one hand, as I hope to show, if theologians intend to establish a genuine fit, the demands on them may be rather more radical than they realize. On the other hand, if scholars in this field aim merely to show the *contrasts* between science and theism, then it is not clear what they are advocating that modern thinkers have not long since accepted. In response to this dilemma, I will argue for what I will call a "stage-three" discourse between science and theology, one that seeks to achieve maximum traction between the two fields. The consequences of committing oneself to stage-three dialogue are exciting and, in some cases, radical.

Admittedly, the project also gives rise to a serious fear: What if more is lost than gained in establishing the reasonableness of religious beliefs in part through dialogue with the sciences? Yet, I'll suggest, the alternative is worse. Believers could of course abandon the quest for any rational integration and bridge-building with modern science and philosophy. But the cost is a gradual but inevitable fall into fundamentalism, with disastrous consequences both for society and for religion.

➤ The Challenge of Rationality

The motivation for the science-religion debate should thus be obvious. The contemporary religious believer does not need to follow Karl Barth in proclaiming a loud "Nein!" to any point of contact (*Anknüpfungspunkt*) with the modern world and its discourse. In fact, since the Hellenization of Christianity in its early centuries, a wide variety of efforts at reconciliation have helped to form the core of systematic theology. The present-day dialogue of theologians with contemporary science and with science's underlying assumptions is only the most recent in a long series of such efforts.

But here a concern arises. As we saw in chapter 1, Charles Sanders Peirce, and more recently Jürgen Habermas, have spelled out the requirements of rationality as a set of conditions on intersubjective discourse among the relevant communities of inquiry. This model is based to a significant extent on the discursive practices of the democratic state. It's often acknowledged that democracy is not the most efficient way for humanity to govern itself, and obviously it isn't an infallible way of reaching decisions. Yet democratic systems do have one virtue: there is no *better* way for a human community to reach political decisions. Something similar is true about defining rational argumentation in terms of relevant communities of inquiry. There is no guarantee that the results will be unbiased, unprejudiced, or true. But rational discourse offers our best available means for recognizing and eliminating bias and prejudice and for maximizing our odds of holding true beliefs about the world.

To accept a discursive theory of rationality means to enter into an open community of inquiry to which all have equal access, and in which all participants agree to follow the force of the better argument. To the extent that one declares his religious beliefs "off limits" from this analysis, he in effect refuses to participate. He is like the one who sits at the table, ready to offer criticisms of those to his left and right, but who, when his own beliefs come up for criticism, stands up and moves back from the table, proclaiming that he was not really buying into the rules of this form of discourse. After all, the demand of a "procedural rationality" is that one cannot sometimes accept it and sometimes reject it, depending on one's proclivities at the moment. To say, for example, that one holds his "auxiliary hypotheses" open to criticism, but then to exempt all of one's important beliefs from critical probing, is not really to have accepted the standards of procedural rationality in the first place.

For some years I have been formulating this requirement using the concept of "traction." When the mechanics for race-car driver Michael Schumacher prepare his Formula One Ferrari, they adjust the suspension and the "down force" on the race car such that all four tires will receive the maximum amount of traction. Michael Schumacher was for some years the world's fastest driver because he had the skill to maintain traction between his tires and the race course while driving through corners at unbelievable speeds. Imagine the traction that it takes to slow a Ferrari from 250 kilometers per hour to ninety (that is, from 150 miles per hour to fifty) *in three seconds*. Procedural rationality requires that those involved in "discourse aimed at understanding" also seek to maintain traction for their language with the same passion for traction of Michael Schumacher and his mechanics. To make truth claims that one does not try to substantiate in an open discourse is to lose traction, and hence rational justification, for one's language. It's like going into a skid—an experience that, as most drivers know, is likely to end badly.

➤ The Three Stages of Dialogue between Science and Religion

Let me try to generalize this point. The demands of procedural rationality involve what we might call a "third stage" understanding of the science-religion discussion. In order to explain this third stage, I must first review the first and second stages as they apply to the dialogue between science and religion. The first stage simply involves initiating a dialogue between the methods and theories of these two different activities of the human spirit. To initiate such a dialogue is no simple matter, as one can imagine. The fact that this dialogue exists in our culture, and that it has become important to many scientists and theologians today, already signals significant cultural changes from the earlier model of "warfare" between science and religion. The emergence of stage-one dialogue, then, represents an acknowledgment of the post-Enlightenment context for theological reflection today—an acknowledgment that was resisted, for example, by Karl Barth and his followers, and is still resisted by a very large number of conservative theologians working today. From the standpoint of the later stages in the dialogue, however, a stage-one understanding of theological method is still "too little, too late."

The stage-two science and religion dialogue adds the commitment to withdraw those assertions that are counter-indicated by the overall available evidence. This type of dialogue one associates with the spirit of Karl Popper—or better, perhaps, with the spirit of Popper combined with the greater realism and accuracy of his student, Imre Lakatos. Correcting Popper, Lakatos defended a philosophy of science according to which there may be "crucial counter-evidence," although it is recognized "only with hindsight." There is falsification, but it is dependent on the emergence of better theories that anticipate new facts. Finally, there is a testing of theories against evidence, but this test involves a "reflective equilibrium" (John Rawls) or broad coherence between bodies of theory, rather than an unambiguous falsification of a specific theory by a specific set of data. As Lakatos commented, "It is not that we propose a theory and Nature may shout NO; rather, we propose a maze of theories, and Nature may shout INCONSISTENT."[1]

Consider the picture implied in John Rawls's famous notion of "reflective equilibrium," which has been widely used in epistemology.[2] Instead of deducing conclusions in one field from another field, the Rawlsian approach allows one to retain the two fields as separate and distinct. One then takes the tentative conclusions from both fields and brings them into contact with each other. Since any lack of fit will undercut the rationality of the agent's overall position—she will find herself holding epistemically incompatible propositions—she will be highly motivated to alter her beliefs in one or both fields in order to establish a coherence between the two. Note that, using the Rawlsian approach, she can make these adjustments without needing to treat the one side or the other as authoritative and inviolate. This approach harks back to Otto Neurath's famous metaphor of building a raft in the middle of the ocean. One cannot "ground" one's constructive work upon firm bedrock, for all one really has to hand, as it were, are the various floating pieces and the desire to keep oneself from sinking altogether. So one uses the available pieces to fashion the most viable raft possible.

The notion of reflective equilibrium offers a first picture of what theology will look like when dialogue is given this central role. It is not necessary to make science or philosophy, or even exegesis and the historical-critical method, into the foundation, deriving all remaining beliefs from them. Since such a move would in essence *reduce* theology to these other disciplines, that would not be a proposal for theological method but for the elimination of theology altogether. Instead, it is quite a different suggestion to emphasize radical dialogue between theology and its natural discussion partners: science, philosophy, other religious traditions, and human experience as formulated in the humanities and the arts. Close dialogues of this sort are desirable because it is better to have coherence and consonance between the conclusions of the various disciplines than to have a situation where they stand in tension. Reflective equilibrium begins with this conviction; it adds that a given individual or group should acknowledge the areas where tensions lie and work to find modifications on one or the other side that will help to minimize these tensions.

Those unfamiliar with the science-religion discussion may ask, "But why do you distinguish between stage one and stage two? Is it not obvious that any theologian who seriously engages in this dialogue already accepts the commitment to withdraw those claims that are counter-indicated by the evidence?" Yet in fact the commitment to revise claims that become problematic in dialogue with experts from other fields is *not* accepted by most who participate in the science-religion dialogue. Many who engage in the dialogue care very little about traction. From their publications one has to infer that they are actually embarked on something much closer to a process of self-discovery. They're interested in seeing what light might be shed on their personal beliefs by the discussion with science—perhaps in the way that a Christian might engage in an extended dialogue with a Buddhist, not in order to raise any questions about the truth or falsity of her position, but instead only to come to understand more clearly what she believes as a Christian. (Of course, many scientists in the dialogue are equally inclined to insulate their philosophical assumptions from scrutiny.) In a process of self-discovery the *truth* of one's beliefs is not in question, whereas stage-two discourse is deeply concerned about distinguishing true and false assertions.

Unfortunately, the evidence suggests that much more of the recent theology-science dialogue is more like the early Christian-Buddhist dialogues than one might have suspected—even though the rhetoric used by the authors seems to promise something more. Stage-two discourse in this field is relatively rare.

What then is stage-three discourse? This most demanding type of science-religion discourse embraces the full intent of the Peircian-Habermasian procedural account of rationality. Here one not only expresses the commitment to withdraw those claims that are counter-indicated by the evidence as a whole, but one actually *seeks out* those discursive contexts in which maximum traction between science and religion can be obtained.

Consider the example of historical-critical work on the life of Jesus. In stage-three discourse, the believer in the uniqueness of Jesus—that is, the one who believes that something uniquely revelatory occurred in and through this human life—seeks to construct interchanges with contemporary historical-critical discourse that have the potential to maximize traction and lead to consensus among the relevant experts. There are temptations on both sides, of course. Believers many not hold their beliefs in Jesus' uniqueness open to real scrutiny, and skeptics may derive their conclusions from deep methodological assumptions that they are also not willing to put on the table for debate. (One thinks of the work of the Jesus Seminar, whose press releases have been widely published in recent years.[3] At least some of its members knew in advance that *nothing unique could have occurred* in the case of Jesus, since that conclusion was built into their methodology from the outset.) By contrast, discourse rationality accepts the idea that truth *can* be tested in an "inner-worldly" fashion, even if the resolution is never final. Thus, in the historical Jesus example, stage-three dialogue involves the attempt to find agreement among participants concerning the life of Jesus, even when the resulting agreement may clash with the pre-commitments brought to the table by the participants themselves.

Of course, it may well not be possible to *resolve* stage-three debates in the near term. Such debates are not promises of rational resolution; they represent our best efforts to reach intersubjective agreement. As we saw in chapter 1, Peirce acknowledges that the final convergence may lie in an indeterminate future that is infinitely deferred; his work presupposes an "infinite horizon of intelligibility." This sense of "never final" is crucial to all discourse-based theories of rationality. *And yet our discursive obligations are present-tense.* As Habermas writes, "in communicative action, we orient ourselves to validity claims that we can raise only as a matter of fact in the context of *our* language, of *our* form of life, whereas the redeemability implicitly co-posited points beyond the provinciality of the given historical context."[4]

The examples could be multiplied, but the point should already be clear. In stage-one discourse between science and religion, *nothing* is really at stake. One hopes for a somewhat better self-understanding, but one cannot otherwise speak of real traction. In stage-two discourse, one does face the potential of falsification with fear and trembling. This is the first stage at which one can claim intersubjective rationality—that is, a rationality that is anything more substantial than "faithfulness to one's own object," as T. F. Torrance once formulated it. Only stage-three science-religion discourse, however, represents a full investment in procedural rationality, for only at this level is one actively engaged in maximizing traction wherever possible. At this level, one's own self-conception as a religious thinker motivates the need for diverse groups of informed discussion partners, who alone can provide the feedback necessary to evaluate one's own self-conception; hence one begins actively to seek out such discussion partners and to bring them into dialogue.[5] This truly is post-Enlightenment theology, theology as public discourse, for here *it becomes part of one's own inner theological motivation* to construct and support the communities of discourse that provide this feedback.

➤ The Dynamics of Faith

What effect might stage-two or stage-three approaches have on the experience of faith? Clearly, a faith that is compatible with a stage-three commitment to rationality will diverge from certain traditional models of faith. It will have to be a religious faith that can co-exist with high levels of uncertainty and openness to change. Already, Paul Tillich anticipated this effect in arguing that there can be no true faith without an admixture of doubt: "If doubt appears, it should not be considered as the negation of faith, but as an element which was always and will always be present in the act of faith. Existential doubt and faith are poles of the same reality, the state of ultimate concern."[6] Suffice it to say that, for those who inhabit this perspective—and they are many more than critics of religions such as Dawkins acknowledge—a genuine fusion occurs between faith and the call to a fully public discourse.

In *Dynamics of Faith* Paul Tillich famously wrote, "About the object of our faith, doubt is unavoidable. It is not the enemy of faith but a part of it, to be met with risk and courage. . . . Doubt is included in every act of faith."[7] The reasons, for Tillich, were intrinsic to what faith is. Faith, he noted, always involves the entire personality: "It happens in the center of the personal life and includes all its elements."[8] Moreover, it is aware of the element of insecurity in all deep existential responses.[9] Faith "is uncertain, insofar as it brings finite beings into relation with an infinite reality. The element of uncertainty in faith cannot be avoided, and must be accepted."[10]

These insights led Tillich to recognize the deep interconnections between faith and doubt. On the one side, the skeptic is not completely outside of faith. "Man is that being who is essentially concerned about his being. . . . The skeptic, so long as he is a serious skeptic, is not without faith, even though it has no concrete content."[11] On the other hand, even the theologian is not completely "inside" faith. "Every theologian is committed *and* alienated; he is always in faith *and* in doubt."[12] The doubt implied in faith accepts this bivalence and takes it into itself in an act of courage: "Living faith includes the doubt about itself, the courage to take this doubt into itself, and the risk of courage."[13] Tillich was more cautious about "skeptical" and "methodological" doubt than I would be. But he was unambiguous about existential doubt; it is "the doubt which is implicit in every act of faith."[14] Indeed, this type of doubt potentially applies to *all* human beliefs: "It is an attitude of actually rejecting any certainty."[15]

The dialogical process that gives rise to doubt can in the end produce a deep and profound faith, or it can lead to a final state of non-belief. Between these poles, it can also produce periods of time when one's overall stance vis-à-vis the truth claims of her tradition is no longer one of belief. The notion of the "secular believer" (chapter 1) suggests that there can be a stance of identification with and participation in the life of a religious community even during (possibly extended) times when outright belief is not possible. In previous work Steven Knapp and I have labeled this phenomenon "possibilistic acceptance" and have analyzed it from both epistemic and phenomenological perspectives.[16] Participation in private and communal religious practices and seeking to live according to the community's values, we argued, can continue even at times of great epistemic doubt. (Whereas Christians have long struggled to acknowledge possibilistic acceptance as part of the religious life, Jewish tradition and practice has for millennia stressed the centrality of ongoing observance even in the face of deep doubt and even unbelief.) Rather than being interpreted as a sign of failure, as "sin," these periods of doubt should be seen as inevitable components of the spiritual life for many believers today.

To this point I have focused on the question of faith as it pertains to individuals. But what about the faith of a religious community? In many cases propositional beliefs, creeds, and confessions are intrinsic to defining a given tradition. How can religious communities affirm that doubt is intrinsic to faith[17] without undercutting their very existence? I agree with Tillich that matters of the content of religious belief remain crucial to religious traditions; theology may be dialogical without becoming non-propositional.[18] However, participation in dialogue requires the religious community to acknowledge that its creeds and other traditional beliefs are not absolutes. For Tillich this was the meaning of the "Protestant Principle": creeds and theological theories point beyond themselves to something that lies behind all such formulations, no matter how revered or ancient they may be.[19]

➤ Does Critical Rationality Spell the End of Transcendence?

I have suggested that a religious faith is still possible even for those who endorse a stage-three notion of procedural rationality. Now one might grant that religious *faith* is still possible but charge that religious *content* is no longer possible. This appears to be Habermas's position. The only transcendence he allows for is a "transcendence from within."[20] Habermas's debts to Kant are central to this negative judgment on theology, for they lead him to expect in advance that certain fundamental commitments will not be "redeemable" (*einlösbar*). Indeed, his Kantianism causes him to know in advance, or think he knows, that *all* statements about transcendence depend only on emotion or on fundamental moral convictions.

This quick dismissal should strike readers as strange in light of the speculations that Habermas engages in elsewhere in the same text. Consider, for example, his comment on Schelling's 1809 *Essay on Freedom* (which was, incidentally, the subject of

Habermas's own dissertation), where he explores the contingent creation of all things by God. Habermas affirms, "In order to be able to see himself confirmed in his own freedom through an alter ego, God must delimit himself precisely within this freedom" (*RR* 161), and he insists that this myth "is more than just a myth." Are such statements merely about the conditions of the possibility of human freedom? Can they be reduced to the regulative principle that "no subject, not even God himself, can be truly free without being recognized as free by at least one other subject" (*RR* 161)? Habermas's more-than-mythical reflections at this point do not fully cohere with the Kantian strictures he places upon them. Indeed, at one point he concedes "the evidence of my relation to a theological heritage," even detailing its roots in the Lurianic doctrine of *Zimzum* and the "post-Fichtean idealism of Baader and Schelling" (*RR* 160). Given this confession, is it enough to say that "a philosophy that oversteps the bounds of methodological atheism loses its philosophical seriousness" (*RR* 160)?

Why ought one to affirm "methodological atheism" rather than methodological *agnosticism*, as discourse rationality would seem to require? Why not a methodological position that admits, as Habermas does elsewhere, that certain questions remain beyond our ability to decide them intersubjectively—so much so, indeed, that one cannot resolve them in the direction of atheism rather than theism? I suggest that the thrust of recent philosophy of science is not post- or anti-metaphysical in the Kantian sense, and that discourse rationality does not require an opposition to all metaphysical reflection. Recent science, I will argue, has destroyed Karl Popper's vision of a neat "demarcation" between science and non-science. What one finds instead is an unbroken line: science continually raises meta-questions that it can neither answer nor dismiss. Such questions are demonstrably relevant to the project of science, even though they cannot be resolved by science. (Note that the rhetorical edge of the so-called New Atheists turns on the assumption that they can be.) This result realigns and corrects the "modern" project: metaphysics and theology are constrained by science in a new way, and science is brought back into dialogue with meta-scientific concerns. This renewed dialogue cannot but affect the status of theism today.

The point is certainly not that all meta-scientific questions can be resolved. One expects a sort of surd, a remnant that will continue to tantalize us at the boundaries of discursive reason, neither redeemable nor dismissible. Some semantic content will presumably always lie beyond the pale of philosophical reason. Does not Habermas himself seem to acknowledge this fact when he writes that "philosophy, even in its postmetaphysical form, will be able neither to replace nor to repress religion as long as religious language is the bearer of a semantic content that is inspiring and even indispensable, since this content eludes (for the time being?) the explanatory force of philosophical language and continues to resist translation into reasoning discourses"?[21]

Discourse theory does not require us to dismiss these remnants as metaphysically meaningless or as "merely regulative" in the Kantian sense. Nor need it incline us more toward atheism than toward theism—as Habermas himself seems to acknowledge elsewhere. Obviously, anti-theological judgments cannot be substantiated merely by assuming that all metaphysical judgments are arbitrary! Thus critics are turning to more subtle attempts to close down all discourse about the semantic content of religious beliefs. The most widespread strategy is to argue that the only perspective from which religious language is of interest is the *functionalist* perspective. Metaphysical topics are then admitted to the discussion table only in terms of how such language functions for an individual or within a society (see chapter 15). This remains an arbitrary strategy, however, since the appeal to functional considerations cannot itself be functionally justified without circularity, nor metaphysically justified without inconsistency.

➤ Discourse Rationality and Metaphysics

We can no longer be satisfied with the proclamation that we live in a "postmetaphysical age." That was the experiment tried out in logical positivism from the Vienna Circle to Hans Reichenbach. But it didn't work. The scientific theories themselves led the students of science back into the very domains they once sought to rule off-limits. We have discovered that a continuum exists between uncontroversially scientific questions ("How do you compute the propagation of a quantum mechanical system using the Schrödinger wave equation?") and questions that science itself can no longer decide ("Who was right, Niels Bohr or David Bohm, if their two positions are indeed empirically equivalent?").[22]

These new results require some revision to the discourse-centered theories of rationality of Peirce and Habermas. Discourse rationality is incomplete until it can give an account of *why* humans are not ideally rational, for until you understand what endangers a process, you cannot adequately compensate for those dangers or protect yourself against them. In discussing that part of religion that holds itself aloof from rational assessment, Habermas is convinced that it has to do with the privacy of religious experience. "Philosophy cannot appropriate what is talked about in religious discourse *as* religious experiences. . . . Theology also loses its identity if it only cites religious experience, and under the descriptions of religious discourse no longer acknowledges [these experiences] as its own basis" (*RR* 74–75).

But as we have seen, in the science-religion discussion it is not religious experience as such that causes problems for reason. In this field, authors do not generally appeal to some private religious experience as what motivates them to work to build bridges between science and "something more" that scientific theories cannot express or test. *The movement from science to "something beyond" is motivated not by religious experience but by the scientific questions themselves, which lead one to, and beyond, the limits of decidability from a scientific perspective.* Perhaps matters would have been easier if Habermas had been right, for then knowability and unknowability would map neatly onto the distinction between the public and private spheres, which lies at the heart of liberal democratic thought. Liberal democracy insists on a central role for the private sphere, as long as it remains within the politically imposed limits. In fact, much of what motivates consumers and voters lies in this private sphere: personal beliefs, cultural heritage, and those "lifestyle preferences" that matter so much to individuals. By "lifestyle preferences," I mean choices of food, drink, and sexual expression—the who, when, and how of sexual activity between consenting adults.

If the "private sphere" of religion consists merely in religious experiences that somehow parallel sexual experiences, religion has been nicely domesticated. For what defines the personal sphere is that it eschews any truth claims. Religion as "lifestyle preference" is religion without truth claims, just as one makes no truth claims when she celebrates the Christmas holiday with traditional German foods rather than with traditional American Christmas cuisine.

"Religion" as manifested in the science-religion discussion is *not* primarily about religious experience or "lifestyle preferences." It becomes relevant to the broader discursive community by questions that science raises but cannot answer using its own resources. The resulting type of science-religion dialogue arises out of what we might call "metaphysical discomfort." The antidote to this discomfort is not "postmetaphysical thinking," as Habermas would have us believe. It is rather *a new form of metaphysics and theology*. The theology (or metaphysics) that comports with science must be hypothetical, pluralistic, fluid in its use of empirical and conceptual arguments, continually open to revision. By contrast, the metaphysics that Habermas resists we also should resist, that is, a "unified metaphysical thought [which] . . . transposes solidarity . . . into the identity of an underlying essence" (*RR* 105). But this is just not the sort of metaphysics that recent debate in the sciences compels us to explore.

➤ Conclusion: Religion, Doubt, and Traction

I have sought to sketch the sort of metaphysics that can comport with science. The result of this exploration allows us to return to the question with which we began: What kind of a religion is it that can be satisfied with pluralistic and hypothetical forms of reflection of this sort? Where does this type of religion fall vis-à-vis the distinction between the public and private spheres?

It is not a religion that can be dissolved into the public sphere. Habermas recognizes that a fully secularized religion, a religion that knows itself only through its public-sphere face, no longer serves the functions of traditional religion. On the other hand, I have also argued that a religion that dwells only in the private sphere, where religious experiences are understood as analogous to "personal lifestyle preferences," does not adequately describe the results of our inquiry. The notion of transcendence is not so easily domesticated.

Yet it's also inconsistent with our results to protect the propositions of one's faith by building high walls and ensconcing religious belief within its own unique fortress of truth, thereby closing it off from public examination and criticism. The excesses of fundamentalism in recent years are clear enough proof of the untenability of this approach. One who closes himself up in this way deprives himself of the feedback he needs to ensure the rationality of his own commitments.[23]

For these reasons, I've suggested that the science-religion dialogue offers a new model for religious belief today. At least in its stage-three form, the dialogue fosters a new approach to religious content, one in which religious beliefs are not cut off from other areas of knowledge by carefully constructed walls. The scientific developments of the last few centuries have shown that scientific results will always raise questions that cannot be fully tested scientifically, just as the tip of the iceberg hints at a huge mass of ice below the surface of the ocean. Thus scientists and religionists alike have every interest in getting a clearer sense of the nature of reality as a whole, without being deterred by the worry that they will completely demystify it, dissect it until nothing is left, or reduce all knowledge to physics.

This is what stage-three science-religion discourse entails. The scientist and the religious believer can share the same motivation: to extend human understanding as far as it will go. They do, however, wager differently about how things will come out in the end. Think of the debate about the nature of consciousness. The reductive neuroscientist wagers that in the end humanity will possess an exhaustive understanding of consciousness given in neuroscientific terms. The religious person wagers that the further humans extend our knowledge of the brain, the more clearly we will recognize that something lies forever beyond natural scientific understanding, and thus that the perspectives of the humanities and social sciences remain in some sense irreducible.

How much traction can one actually establish between science and theology? Will efforts to follow the lines from science toward the "something beyond" always lose traction at some point, causing the project to skid off in the direction of fideism? Certainly there is significant evidence that, as one follows the questions upward and outward from core scientific theories, at some point one will begin to formulate hypotheses that are radically underdetermined by the existing evidence. The point of the traction idea, however, is not to make empirical predictions about what percentage of religious belief can be tested. Nor should traction be confused with the patently false claims of Leibnizian rationalists, "intelligent design" theorists, and other natural theologians, whose neat arguments from science to God attract headlines and large followings among conservative religious thinkers. Traction is about an *intentionality*, a quest for feedback, an obligation to maintain contact between religious beliefs and publically accessible data as long as possible. Whether the effort at traction proves fruitful or not will be decided in the course of dialogue with the sciences. It cannot be legislated or presupposed in advance.

This, then, is the "post-Enlightenment" approach to religion. An "enlightened" religion seeks to extend the domain of scientific understanding as far as it can possibly go. Some may wager that the sustained effort to extend knowledge will in the end reveal that the throne of God is empty—however useful theological terms may be for other purposes. Others wager that science will not in the end lead to the demise of theology. If the mystery of reality is infinitely deep, no progression of understanding threatens it. Both groups can embrace scientific techniques and rejoice in the advance of knowledge, working side by side to extend the reach of justified knowledge as far as it will go. The religious dimension is not at risk in this process, I have suggested. It will be with us as long as the quest for knowledge is.

PART TWO

Emergence

Why Emergence Matters

A New Paradigm
for Relating *the* Sciences

IT HAS BEEN SAID, "AS GOES YOUR SCIENCE, SO GOES YOUR GOD." Theologians throughout history have used the best science of their day to help them (re)conceive the nature of God. When it comes to this vital task, the easiest route is, however, not usually the best one. It's tempting to roll over and allow science simply to dictate what one can and cannot say about the divine. But science is not in the business of researching the nature of God; in addition to scientific results, one also needs sophisticated philosophical tools to say anything intelligent about what is clearly not only an empirical matter. (The so-called New Atheists offer a great example of how much nonsense one can write about theological topics when one is ignorant of the relevant philosophical resources.)[1] Of course, on the other side there's an equally strong temptation to dismiss science altogether and "just do theology," as if it didn't matter that humanity has acquired all this revolutionary new knowledge of how the natural world works.

Between the two easy ways out lies a fascinating, and to my mind indispensable task: to wed the best of contemporary science with the most fundamental insights of theology. One of the most significant developments in recent years is the discovery of emergent complexity and the wide variety of new research it has produced. In this and the following three chapters I will present some of these new results and begin to explore their implications. At the center of our inquiry lies a theological question: How should one conceive the divine in a world of pervasive emergence?

Modern science sought to reduce all natural phenomena to matter and the laws of physics. Theologians in response preached a transcendent God separate from the world. But a revolution has taken place in the last decades. Scientists now recognize nature's tendency to produce more and more complex forms of organization, not all reducible to fundamental laws. This new "non-reductionist" picture of the world gives rise to radically different assessments of human consciousness, morality, and spirituality. In these chapters we will trace the sciences of emergence across cosmic evolution—from fundamental physics, through the biological sciences, and on to the emergence of consciousness and religion. I hope to show that they are not opponents to be feared but represent potentially important allies to theologians.

➤ The Concept of Emergence: A First Approximation

The concept of emergence is often presented by contrasting it with two alternative (and still widely held) views. According to *reductionist theories*, the phenomena studied by a given discipline are only scientifically (read: truly) understood when they can be expressed using the laws of a lower-level discipline. When scientific reduction is successful, the phenomena become a special case of the more general explanatory framework represented by those laws. If one seeks to reduce every given level to the level beneath it, one must eventually come down to the fundamental laws of physics, the bedrock of all else.

According to *dualist theories*, by contrast, there are gaps in the relations between the various disciplines, such that the reductionist ideal is impossible. Not only can phenomena of *mind or spirit* not be explained in terms of any lower-level laws, but dualists also challenge the claim that mind depends essentially on any of its physical or material substrates. Thus dualists have classically held that minds are essentially different from bodies and can continue to exist without them. Minds do not rely on the physical energies that sustain bodies and allow them to move; instead they belong to a different ontological order altogether.

Emergence theories attempt to split the difference between these opposing positions. They grant the downward dependence of the reductionists, but they challenge the achievability of downward explanatory reduction. Rather, they maintain that it is a contingent fact of natural history that new levels of organization emerge, which, because they are novel, are not predictable or explainable in terms of any lower-level laws, forces, or particles. Emergence does not justify talk of souls and spirits, but it does help one to make sense of the real causal (and hence explanatory) role of psychological and religious qualities.

It is helpful to supplement this framework, which is the standard way to define emergence theories, with a second one. According to this way of defining the concept, emergence is a theory about evolution. Specifically, it's a theory about how the various scientific disciplines that study cosmic evolution are related to one another. Suppose we order the various scientific disciplines according to the order in cosmic history in which the phenomena that each studies first arose: quantum physics, classical or macrophysics, physical chemistry, biochemistry, genetics, cell biology, anatomy, and so on. Let's label the resulting list using the letters A, B, C, and so forth, to stand for the specific disciplines. We can then number the particular relations between any two neighboring disciplines using the integers 1, 2, 3, and so on, yielding a three-leveled picture of emergence (see Figure 1).

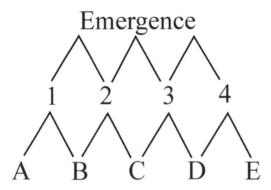

Figure 1: Emergence is not itself a scientific theory. It identifies features shared in common in the transitions between scientific theories at various levels of reality.

As the diagram shows, emergence theory thus becomes a sort of third-order theory: a theory about the relations between the relations between scientific disciplines.

➤ The Re-Emergence of Emergence

A special issue of the *Proceedings of the National Academy of Sciences* explores the principles of self-organization and the formation of complex matter, asking "what are the steps and the processes that lead from the elementary particle to the thinking organism, the (present!) entity of highest complexity?"[2] Complexity, the authors argue, is inherently a systemic function. It involves the interaction between multiple components of multiple kinds and the principles that affect their correlation, coupling, and feedback relationships. The goal of the sciences of complexity is "to progressively discover, understand, and implement the rules that govern [matter's] evolution from inanimate to animate and beyond, to ultimately acquire the ability to create new forms of complex matter."[3] Emergent complexity spans the entire spectrum of cosmic history, "from divided to condensed matter then to organized and adaptive matter, on to living matter and thinking matter, up the ladder of complexity."[4]

This vision clearly forms the core of research programs currently running in most, if not all, of the major natural sciences, from the emergence of classical physical systems out of quantum physical systems, through the emergence of chemical properties and the origins of life, and on up to the higher cognitive behaviors of the great apes. Indeed, Gerald Edelman and Giulio Tononi are not doing anything different when, in their widely cited *Science* article, "Consciousness and Complexity," they offer a theory of consciousness as an emergent property of the brain.[5]

Examples of emergence do not start at the level of life or mind, however; they are already present in scientists' attempts to explain the very earliest stages of cosmic evolution. Classical physics, for example, has been described as emergent out of quantum physics.[6] And recently Stephen Adler has argued that quantum theory itself is an emergent phenomenon.[7] The recent physics Nobel laureate Robert Laughlin drew significant attention to the emergence debate within the sciences by arguing that scientific reduction is a dogma and that his field, condensed matter physics, could be grasped only by using the paradigm of emergence.[8] Among his examples of emergent phenomena are superconductivity, the quantum Hall effect, phase transitions, crystallization, collective instabilities, and hydrodynamics.

Other studies of complex matter in which nonlinearities dominate, such as soft materials, come to similar conclusions. Elbio Dagotto, for example, recently reported the "spontaneous emergence of electronic nanometer-scale structures" in transition metal oxides:

> In complex systems the properties of a few particles are not sufficient to understand large aggregates when these particles strongly interact. Rather, in such systems, which are not merely complicated, one expects emergence, namely the generation of properties that do not preexist in a system's constituents. This concept is contrary to the philosophy of reductionism, the traditional physics hallmark. Complex systems spontaneously tend to form structures (self-organization) and these structures vary widely in size and scales.[9]

Chemists have long held up their discipline as a model of emergence. Pier Luigi Luisi, for example, maintains that chemistry is "the embodiment of emergence" because it studies properties that, although rooted in physical structures, cannot be explained without the help of a new conceptual framework. Chemical properties emerge only in sufficiently complex natural systems, and one requires a level of analysis distinct from physics in order to understand them.[10] Luisi also endorses downward causation: "chemical examples show that emergence must go hand in hand with downward causation—one is the consequence of the other, and the two phenomena take place simultaneously."[11] He adds finally that "life can be seen as a particular kind of emergent property" and "life itself is indeed the most dramatic outcome of emergence."[12]

This new perspective goes under multiple names within specific sciences. "Emergence" is, as mentioned above, only an overarching rubric to describe many different research programs in many different sciences. Molecular biologists speak, for instance, of the emergence of a "network perspective," which is necessary for describing how particular types of chemical reactions are catalyzed by evolutionarily related enzymes.[13] The analogue of metabolic networks in the study of cells is *systems biology*, one of the fastest growing areas in contemporary biology. Hiroaki Kitano describes its core assumption: "While an understanding of genes and proteins continues to be important, the focus [of systems biology] is on understanding a system's structure and dynamics. Because a system is not just an assembly of genes and proteins, its properties cannot be fully understood merely by drawing diagrams of their interconnections."[14]

In cell biology, what was at first merely a way of expressing reservations about purely gene-driven analyses ("epigenesis" or "epigenetic factors") has become a rigorous study of "system-level insights" in its own right.[15] As Kitano writes, "a transition is occurring in biology from the molecular level to the system level that promises to revolutionize our understanding of complex biological regulatory systems and to provide major new opportunities for practical application of such knowledge."[16] And in an interesting review in *Science*, Kevin Laland baptizes the new approach as "the new interactionism," which describes "how genes are triggered into action by environmental events; how they switch other genes on and off; how they guide neurons to build brains; and how learning operates through gene expression."[17]

The new interactionism goes between the horns of the classical dilemmas, "genes *versus* environment" and "nature *versus* nurture." Indeed, these new perspectives may defuse one further classical dilemma: the dilemma between "upward" and "downward" causation. Reductionists have generally held that all causal influences occur at the level of microphysics. These effects, taking place within highly complex systems, are said to account for the deceptive appearance that distinctively biological or psychological causes exist. In opposition to them, idealists and Cartesian dualists protested that there are distinct types of causes, mental causes, which are different in kind from physical causes, are not dependent on them, and which exercise their own form of causal agency in the world. But from the systems or interactionist perspective, the entire dichotomy appears to be mistaken. Causality is "circular." It involves interacting effects between different levels of natural organization, for example, between the microscopic and the macroscopic. This new framework, as Moreno and Umerez note,

> makes it possible to talk properly about the appearance of new kinds of causal relationships. . . . Thus, what enables us to speak in terms of a double causal action—upward and downward—is precisely the conjunction of a circular causality with [at least] two different levels of organization, one of which is constituted by informational components. . . . [This] special, downward kind of causation appears just when very complex (interwoven) meta-networks of recursive reaction networks arise in Nature.[18]

Harold Morowitz likewise denies that the notion of downward causation is speculative, describing it instead as a "key feature" that is characteristic of all biological emergence.[19] One can trace examples of emergence along the path of natural history from the first cells to the great apes.[20] In fact, Morowitz identifies as many as 28 distinct levels of emergence in his monograph, *The Emergence of Everything*.[21] In an article in *Physics Today*, the astrophysicist George Ellis describes the emergent features of quantum measurement, DNA coding, social creations, and economics.[22] And I have not even begun to trace the construal of consciousness as an emergent phenomenon from sufficiently complex brains and central nervous systems.[23] It is basic to the cognitive sciences, to evolutionary psychology, and to traditional social science (psychology, sociology, cultural anthropology) to treat consciousness as depending on its neural substratum but not as identical to it. We return to the topic of consciousness in chapter 6.

➤ What Makes Emergence Scientific?

It is one thing to speculate about emergence as part of a metaphysical theory, and something else to claim scientific support for the framework of emergence. Although I believe such claims are justified, they bring with them unique challenges.

As long as one continues to do science, one attempts to draw the closest possible connections between the set of phenomena that one is studying and the lower-level laws that are available. The scientific study of chemistry is impossible, for example, without its connections to physics. To study the origins of life *means* to try to explain the transition from non-reproducing biochemical molecules to reproducing life forms (and if one could understand life in terms of biochemistry, so much the better). And to understand an animal's behavior scientifically *is* to explain as much of it as possible in terms of the body's morphology, hormone releases, selective pressures, and the like. The quest to explain phenomena in terms of reconstructible, testable causal systems is so basic to the project of science that we could almost use it as *the* defining characteristic of science.

The phenomenon of emergence makes this project more difficult, but it does not eliminate it. If it had turned out to be possible to explain higher-order phenomena in terms of lower-order laws across the scientific disciplines, then science would be in the position fully to achieve the goal in terms of which it is defined. Even if, as emergence theorists believe, the natural world is such that downward reduction is often impossible in principle, the goal does not simply disappear, to be replaced by a happy-go-lucky holism. One can still determine the scientific or non-scientific status of a theory about the world by the continued presence of this goal, namely, to connect the phenomena of one level as closely and precisely as possible with the phenomena at the next lowest level.

Consider two concrete examples. Walter Elsasser, in his classic *Reflections on a Theory of Organisms*,[24] makes the case for the autonomy of biological explanations. Elsasser believes that the "information stability" of living things cannot be reduced to the physico-chemical stability of molecules. Alongside this emergentist manifesto, however, Elsasser is careful to show how the scientific study of life forms is still possible. He does not argue for the untestability of biological theories, for example, but rather for the necessity of utilizing different kinds of tests. It's just that biological causality "cannot be fully verified by the standard procedure of the physicist or chemist," that is, by "measurement followed by mathematical extrapolation, technically called integration, of the equations of quantum mechanics that govern molecular motion."[25]

Moreover, Elsasser gives very precise, empirical reasons for a certain autonomy of biology, which he defines in a precise and rigorous fashion. Thus his fourth chapter demonstrates how an immense number of molecular configurations are compatible with a given set of physico-chemical constraints. Even if the structure and dynamics of all molecules can be understood by applying quantum mechanical principles, "a cell is much too complex to admit of meaningful analysis in such terms."[26] Because of this "combinatorial explosion" (Harold Morowitz), it is demonstrably impossible to compute cell behavior in quantum-physical terms. Likewise, in a later chapter Elsasser describes how physicists study stable systems (those in which each mode of motion is stable) and then come to understand what happens when the system is perturbated. All biological systems, by contrast, are massively unstable. They are, in Stuart Kauffman's beautiful expression, always existing "at the edge of chaos."[27] Hence it is not possible to understand them by extrapolation from stable systems and through computation of each perturbation—which is to say: it's impossible to understand them in terms of physics alone. Elsasser states, "Owing to the amplificatory effect, the ultimate changes are no longer predictable."[28] Elsasser concludes that "the morphological future of such [biological] systems [is] unpredictable on the basis of physics and chemistry."[29]

Finally, Elsasser remains committed to the scientific study of biological phenomena, even in light of this unpredictability. He emphasizes that biological results "cannot differ from any known rule of physics and chemistry."[30] He continues to emphasize the importance of structure (morphology) and function as basic to testable biological theories. And he does not advance biological holism as a way of avoiding tests and experiments, but rather as representing a call for a new type of testability: "if the holistic properties are to be verified experimentally, a different type of experiment from that conventionally used by physicists and chemists is required."[31]

Elsasser thus represents a paradigm example of scientific emergence. Under the influence of this example, Morowitz comments, "emergence requires pruning rules to reduce the transcomputable to the computable. . . . [I]n both Elsasser's approach and [John] Holland's view, biology requires its own laws that are not necessarily derivable from physics, but do not contradict the physical foundations."[32]

Contrast this careful demonstration of how emergence remains a part of the scientific project with the approach to emergence taken by B. C. Goodwin and Rupert Sheldrake. Both thinkers wish to appeal to what they call "morphogenetic fields" and "morphic resonance." Goodwin explicitly refuses to interpret the morphogenetic field in terms of any known forces: "electrical forces can affect it . . . but I would not wish to suggest that [it] is essentially electrical. Chemical substances" can affect it, yet it is not "essentially chemical or biochemical in nature." He is nonetheless certain that morphogenetic fields "play a primary role in the developmental process."[33] Similarly, Sheldrake postulates "patterns of oscillatory activity" throughout the world, which he calls morphic resonance.[34] Resonances are strongest, he is sure, with one's own past, somewhat weaker with genetically similar animals, and weaker still with animals from other races. Apparently, though, some resonance still exists between all living things. The construction of a genuinely scientific theory of morphic resonance looks unlikely, however, since like Goodwin he is loath to tie morphic resonance to any known forces.

Sheldrake does claim that his theory has "testable predictions," though he admits that his predictions "may seem so improbable as to be absurd." For example,

> if thousands of rats were trained to perform a new task in a laboratory in London, similar rats should learn to carry out the same task more quickly in laboratories

everywhere else. If the speed of learning of rats in another laboratory, say in New York, were to be measured before and after the rats in London were trained, the rats tested on the second occasion should learn more quickly than those tested on the first. The effect should take place in the absence of any known type of physical connection or communication between the two laboratories.[35]

Unfortunately, this kind of (alleged) testability is not sufficient to make a theory scientific. It's equally crucial that the theories in question specify their connections with the existing body of scientific knowledge. In addition to meeting this condition, a theory of scientific emergence must provide details, given as much as possible in terms of lower-level theories, that show why a given set of phenomena would be irreducible to those theories. When somebody suggests, as Sheldrake does, that there are both energetic and non-energetic fields, it is difficult to see how connections can be drawn with any scientific field theory.

➤ The Logic of Scientific Emergence

Terrence Deacon offers the clearest expression of the logic of scientific emergence available today. It is therefore valuable to consider his recent proposals in some detail. Deacon begins with the empirical evidence that "complex dynamical ensembles can spontaneously assume ordered patterns of behavior that are not prefigured in the properties of their component elements or in their interaction patterns."[36] In his view, only emergence theories can adequately interpret and explain this type of self-organization.

Not all emergences are identical, however. Deacon is the first to have identified three distinct "orders" of emergence. First-order emergence involves the appearance of new properties in the aggregate that are not present in the individual particles. Deacon draws his primary examples from quantum theory and statistical thermodynamics, though he admits that even simpler examples can be adduced, such as how the properties of multiple water molecules together produce liquid properties. He writes, "Although the nature of the wave and its detailed underlying dynamical realization in each [particular wave] may differ depending on whether the fluid is water, air, or an electromagnetic field, the ability to propagate a wave is a first-order emergent feature they all share in common."[37] As with the other two "orders" of emergence, Deacon is careful to specify exactly the conditions under which this kind of emergence will occur. Thus he argues, for example, that "it is only when certain of the regularities of molecular interaction relationships add up rather than cancel one another that certain *between*-molecule relationships can produce aggregate behaviors with ascent in scale."[38]

In second-order emergence, specific perturbations of a system are amplified, resulting in types of causal effects not seen in the first order. In the formation of snow crystals, for example, the specific temperature and humidity present at each stage of the crystal's descent through the air are "recorded" in the emerging structure of the crystal as it evolves. These features then influence its subsequent structural formation.

The structural features emerging at a given point are amplified, in other words, such that they affect all subsequent crystal growth. These "feed-forward circles of cause and effect" are distinctive of this new type of emergent property. Deacon offers detailed examples, drawing from "self-undermining (divergent) chaotic systems, as in turbulent flow, and self-organizing (partially convergent) chaotic systems."[39] Second-order emergence is also found in the so-called autopoietic systems. This type of emergence works not just by aggregating individual components (say, molecules), but here systematic features play a causal role. Put differently, forms or structures, and not merely particles, become the operative links in the feed-forward cycle.

Third-order emergence shares this feature from the previous order. Yet now what is passed on is *information or memory*, not merely forms and structures. As a result, Deacon argues,

> third-order emergence inevitably exhibits a developmental and/or evolutionary character . . . It occurs where there is both amplification of global influences on parts, but also redundant "sampling" of these influences and reintroduction of them redundantly across time and into different realizations of the same type of second-order system.[40]

The classic example of third-order emergence is the self-reproducing cell.[41] Cells exhibit features not present in pre-biological physical systems. They contain information—specifically, information sufficient for building other cells like themselves. The information is stored within a boundary (the cell wall), which allows the cell as a whole to function as an entity in its own right on which environmental forces act. Because cells can make copies of themselves in ways that pre-biotic structures cannot, the forces of natural selection can begin to operate for the first time. A cell thus becomes a sort of hypothesis about what informational structure will survive and reproduce most effectively in a given environment. If the cell exists in an environment congenial to its existence, it will make more successful copies of itself than will its rivals, and will come to prosper in its ecosystem. Deacon describes this process as "a sort of self-referential self-organization, an autopoiesis of autopoieses."[42] As a result, cells can only be understood through "a combination of multi-scale, historical, and semiotic analyses. . . . This is why living and cognitive processes require us to introduce concepts such as representation, adaptation, information, and function in order to capture the logic of the most salient emergent phenomena."[43]

By introducing the framework of semiotics, derived from the work of C. S. Peirce, Deacon implicitly claims that the cell is an interpreter of the world. It stands in an informationally mediated relationship to its environment. Emergent entities at this level refer to or represent their world. They are themselves hypotheses about how best to survive and thrive in a particular environment. Despite his occasional reticence about anti-reductionist language, Deacon's position clearly stands as a sharp alternative to reductionist analyses of the natural world:

Life and mind cannot be adequately described in terms that treat them as merely supervenient because this collapses innumerable convoluted levels of emergent relationships.
Life is not mere chemical mechanism. Nor is cognition mere molecular computation.[44]

If Deacon is right—and I think recent origins-of-life research, systems biology,
and ecosystems theory all offer empirical support for his analysis—then to understand
life scientifically means to understand it according to different principles than those
that pertain to purely physical or chemical systems. Only third-order emergent processes in evolution have the capacity "to progressively embed [other] evolutionary processes within one another via representations that amplify their information-handling
power."[45] Indeed, the process of emergence does not stop with the first self-reproducing
cell. Under evolutionary selection pressures, natural systems continue to increase in
complexity, discovering ever new ways of "making a living" (as Stuart Kauffman likes
to say) in the world. In Deacon's masterful study, *The Symbolic Species*,[46] for example,
he traces the co-evolution of brains and language or culture. Language use, of course,
remains dependent on a complex brain and central nervous system, but language can
never be reduced to an instinct (Steven Pinker) or a mere byproduct of brain processes.
The two evolving phenomena mutually influence one another. The result is a continual
growth in the complexity of both. For example, Deacon argues, language moves from
the "iconic" mode of representation to a more complex form of reference involving
indexicals, and finally (in *Homo sapiens*) to the rich symbolic modes of representation
that are the bread and butter of human cultural existence.

➤ In Defense of Strong Emergence

One finds in the literature an ongoing battle between weaker and stronger versions of
emergence theory. The more robust version, which I have labeled "strong emergence"
and defended in *Mind and Emergence,* makes two claims. First, new *things* emerge
in natural history, not just new properties of some fundamental things or stuff; and,
second, these emergent things exercise their own types of causal power. Such "downward causation" occurs at many different levels in nature. Strong emergence is a thesis
about the nature of natural evolution.

Of course, interpretations of evolution are fraught with controversy. If evolution is
really "all about the genes," as Richard Dawkins seeks to convince us, then all evolved
structures are nothing more than expressions of this same fundamental dynamic.
However rich and staggeringly diverse these manifestations are, they can and should
still be understood from a gene-centric perspective. If, on the other hand, the dualists
are right, then at some point in the evolutionary process one encounters a radical,
ontological break and mind arises. In this sense dualists remain at heart Cartesians:
one can study the entire physical world from atoms to chimpanzees with the same set
of mechanistic explanatory tools. But as soon as one turns to man and woman, who
alone possess *res cogitans*, a new explanatory tool box is required, one that, they insist,
relies instead on the nature of souls and the eternal Laws of Thought.

In contrast to both views, emergence claims that the story of evolution is one of continuity *and* discontinuity. Continuity first: everything in the natural world is composed of the same "stuff" of matter and energy, and no new substances are added along the way. This means no souls and no personal substances—a difficult entailment for some religious persons. When one pursues the scientific project, one seeks to develop a continuity of understanding to the greatest possible extent. But sharing the scientist's "natural piety" for the world *as it actually expresses itself empirically* also means that one works with whatever explanatory framework best explains the data at present—as long as it is testable and can demonstrate its explanatory superiority over its rivals.

Practicing this natural piety—this commitment to study the world in whatever ways it presents itself to us—means that we are not merely biologists *simplicitur*, much less geneticists only. We are cytologists, systems biologists, botanists, zoologists, primatologists. We are not only molecular biologists and geneticists, but also population biologists and ecosystem theorists. We are interested in the large and complex as much as in the small, in emergent phenomena as well as reducible phenomena. This, I suggest, was the mind set that lay behind Charles Darwin's great breakthroughs. Recall his famous description of the riverbank in the *Origin of Species*:

> It is interesting to contemplate an entangled bank, clothed with many plants of many kinds, with birds singing on the bushes, with various insects flitting about, and with worms crawling through the damp earth, and to reflect that these elaborately constructed forms, so different from each other in so complex a manner, have all been produced by laws acting around us. . . . There is grandeur in this view of life, with its several powers, having originally breathed into a few forms or into one; and that, whilst this planet has gone on cycling on according to the fixed law of gravity, from so simple a beginning endless forms most beautiful and most wonderful have been, and are being, evolved.[47]

➤ Conclusion

What Darwin could only envision in 1858 had become scientific reality by the end of the twentieth century. In one sense, discovering complex systems is just "science as usual." The new systems biology provides causal explanations of natural systems, which are then empirically tested and verified. In another sense, however, emergence represents a new way of doing and understanding science. It is science without reductionism. Now systems of emergent phenomena are understood not only in terms of lower-level laws and processes, but equally in terms of the higher-level systems that constrain their functioning and their outcomes.

The science is complicated; there are many more subtleties in the study of emergent phenomena than we have covered here. But enough is on the table for one to see that the results are potentially of revolutionary significance for our understanding of human religion and religious belief. In the next chapter we explore the role of emergent thinking in the philosophy of biology, and chapters 6 and 7 will consider its impact upon theology.

Emergent Realities

5

The Evolution
of Life *and* Mind

I N MEDIEVAL AND EARLY MODERN PHILOSOPHY THE BASIC STRUCTURES
of the biosphere were seen as static, as given once and for all.[1] Each species was
believed to be eternal, having been directly created by God; were any of them to disappear, the "plenum," the fullness of creation, would be threatened—and with it the
perfection of God. Similarly, consciousness was typically approached "from the top
down." It was associated with *pneuma*, with *ratio*, with *spiritus*, indeed with the *imago
Dei*. By contrast, scientists are today able to study consciousness "from the bottom
up." It's no longer necessary to postulate a timeless substance, an essential substrate
whose powers are responsible for mental functioning. Now, in both biology and the
study of consciousness, a new worry has risen to the surface: Can life and mind be
dispensed with altogether as explanatory categories? Can one say, as Laplace once said
about the God-hypothesis, "I have no need of that hypothesis"?

In this chapter, I shall argue that, although the "bottom-up" study of living systems does not require entelechies or a "vital force," and although the study of consciousness does not immediately presuppose a theory of Spirit or *Geist*, these fields
do not need to be eliminativist. Using the framework of recent emergence theory,
we can now get closer to a non-reductive theory of consciousness than has ever been
possible before. But this breakthrough comes with a price. It turns out that one can
solve the so-called "hard problem"—the famous tensions between first-person and
third-person analyses—*only when one understands the emergence of consciousness in connection with the emergence of living systems over the course of biological evolution*. I turn
first, therefore, to the major interpretations of the evolutionary process, analyzing the
prospects for an emergentist understanding. With these results in hand, we return to
the question of consciousness in quest of a theory of emergent mind.

➤ Major Challenges

My commitment to fallibilism and to critical discourse (see part I above)[2] suggests beginning with the two chief challenges to the emergentist program. The first is top-down causation. Any theological use of emergent thinking seems to require emergent causes, yet some scientists strongly resist the use of such language. They argue that the physical substratum for a set of phenomena either does or doesn't causally determine the outcome. If brain processes causally determine thought, for example, then mental descriptions seem redundant, because the causal (and hence explanatory) work is all being done at the lower level. Those who deny that lower-level descriptions determine the outcome have abandoned the principle of the causal closure of the physical world, which, they charge, is a fundamental presupposition of physical science. Philosophically, this is a complex issue.

The second major challenge to emergence theory represents a major parting of the ways in the interpretation of biology today. The one road—I suppose we should call it the *left* fork—leans toward a physics-based account of both biology and mind, and ultimately to a reductive treatment of religious phenomena and truth claims. In the previous chapter I labeled this the path of *weak emergence*. The other road—the *right* fork, perhaps—defends the possibility of adequate accounts of reality that are not physics-based, that is, accounts in which explanations at higher levels of organization cannot be reduced to lower-level explanations, even in principle (*strong emergence*).

Terry Deacon has succinctly formulated the decision point that divides the left and right forks of interpretation. He writes, "For these reasons it is essential to recognize that biology is not merely a physical science, it is a semiotic science; a science where significance and representation are essential elements."[3] Evolutionary biology is still a natural science. It is not "just a matter of interpretation." And yet, as Deacon rightly notes, it "stands at the border between physical and semiotic science."[4] I believe the study of emergent phenomena supports Deacon's interpretation, and that it offers a key for understanding the phenomena of symbolic language use, and thus the human mental and emotional life. More strongly, I believe that, if we are *unsuccessful* in defending the right fork in interpreting the biological results, we will be unable to defend a non-reductive theory of mind. Conversely, following the left fork in the interpretation of biology entails an unnecessarily physics-bound position in the philosophy (and theology) of mind.[5]

➤ Pre-Biological Emergence

It's important to analyze particular instances of emergence in order to grasp what the emergence of mind might entail. Consider, for example, emergence in chemistry, which encompasses at least two distinct sets of phenomena. The one concerns the formation of equilibrium structures, such as the structure of a crystal, which could continue to exist in a thermodynamically closed environment. The other involves dissipative structures, those that are involved in a continuous energy exchange with their environment. Dissipative structures have attracted particular interest because they exhibit the property of self-organization. Chemists are now studying examples of self-organization, or the spontaneous generation of complicated dissipative structures from less highly organized antecedents.[6]

It is important to note that emergence through self-organization is a bottom-up phenomenon. Nothing in the study of dissipative systems requires one to introduce the notion that the crystals or boiling water are acting intentionally or seeking to carry out purposes, however rudimentary, and no explanation in chemistry directly requires God to make it work. In fact, no teleological language whatsoever is required to understand chemical processes. The reason is that the chemical phenomena are less complex than those we encounter in studying the evolution of living systems. In biology, by contrast, the behaviors of organisms themselves prompt theorists to utilize various forms of purposive language, whether teleological or "teleonomic."

Yet the phenomena of self-organization in chemistry do move beyond the theoretical resources of traditional reductionist and atomistic accounts. It is meaningless to say that the complex patterns that emerge in self-organizing processes are contained in the individual atoms or molecules themselves. Instead, emergent properties must be traced back to the dynamics of highly complex chemical systems. Mathematical complexity theory reveals some of these patterns,[7] and fractals offer a dramatic and often beautiful expression of them.

Paul Cilliers notes that in self-organizing systems, "The structure of the system is not the result of an a priori design, nor is it determined directly by external conditions. It is a result of interaction between the system and its environment."[8] Niels Gregersen adds that the patterns "are informed by an *internal generative program* which is neither the result of an *a priori* design nor an *ad hoc*-construct triggered by environmental factors."[9] In the case of self-organized complexity, large systems contain what he calls an "internal autonomous program which constrains the array of possibilities and itself controls the system-world interactions."[10]

➤ Emergence at the Boundaries of Biology

Various theorists have used the concept of autopoietic ("self-making") complexity in order to give a convincing analysis of the type of emergence that lies at the boundaries of biology. This next level of complexity adds the requirement that the dynamics of the process also produce new internal components, thus leading to new system-world interactions.[11] Among the examples of autopoiesis cited are RNA reproduction, the immune system, neural networks, language systems, and historically self-reflexive agents.

Such systems quickly become non-computational, that is, future states could not be computed even if one had an exhaustive knowledge of their present state and the fastest computer that is physically possible. Note that this non-computability is the *negative* formulation of what turns out to be a basic, and highly significant, feature of biological organisms in their interactions with their environment: the definitive failure of reductionism in biology. Given that organisms have developed new internal programs or informational states that affect their dispositions to respond to their environment, and given that the evolution of these internal states is not directly traceable to (or computable from) inputs from the external environment, a reductive account of their interactions with their environment will no longer be possible even in principle. Instead, the explanations must be given in a theoretical framework that looks a lot more like ecosystems theory. The altered behaviors of the organism bring about changes in its environment that affect other organisms. Their complex responses, reflecting their own internal dynamics, in turn alter the shared environment, and hence its impact on each individual organism, in unpredictable ways. Here we have a "network of interdependency" (Gregersen's term): a set of interactions between part and whole—or, we may now need to say, between individual and group—that is only partly analogous to what occurs in the chemical world.

Writing as a theologian, Niels Gregersen has sought to show that chemical self-organization is compatible with a theistic notion of the purposes of God in creation.[12] I have no doubt that a theological account can be written that incorporates the principles of self-organization and remains consistent with the Christian tradition. The emergence hypothesis takes an additional step, however. The goal of a thoroughgoing emergence approach is to see what happens when one follows the line of emergence *all the way through*, asking both about the "highest" levels of which we are aware and about the nature of a world that displays emergent levels of this sort along the way. In other words, the burning question is not only how the God of traditional theism can be reconciled with the thermodynamics of dissipative systems or with the phenomena of self-organization—such reconciliations are, I fear, all too easy and thus represent too low a standard (see the standard of "stage-three discourse" in chapter 3). Rather, the question is what kind of doctrine of creation—and for that matter, doctrine of God—one might write in response to the fact of the ladder of emergence taken as a whole, a question to which we return in chapter 7.

Toward an Emergentist Theory of the Biosphere[13]

If the emergence hypothesis is correct, at least in broad outline, then the natural world exhibits different kinds of properties at different levels, and different kinds of causation are at work at the various levels. There may be a very large number of such levels, with subtle gradations between them, or there may be a smaller number of basic levels. Note that we must be able to distinguish three or more levels of emergence for my thesis to be correct. For if we could distinguish only two, then the suspicion would be raised that emergence is only a variety of dualism: the world contains only mental and physical properties, only mental and physical causes. But in that case the difference between them (the critic would point out) would represent exactly that "great divide" that so stymied classical dualists such as Descartes. To make sure that the position is not crypto-dualist, we must be able to discern clear and robust examples of emergence within the biological sciences before making any claims about an emergent theory of mind.

The biosphere manifests a fantastic increase in complexity. Life forms absorb physical energy and use it to build complicated structures such as eyes, organs, and DNA strands. They also reflect energy back in the form of complicated behaviors in the environment. Although the second law of thermodynamics always wins in the end—the *net* result is always an increase of entropy in the universe—the principles of life function in the opposite direction. They make short-term inroads in the overall march toward thermodynamic equilibrium.

This fact is significant because most biological processes accomplish an *increase in order*, at least on the short term, whereas what is (thermodynamically) typical in the world is the increase in *disorder*. Note in addition that processes that bring about an increase in order—those that lead to more complex and more highly structured systems—*will generally appear purposive*. The appearance of purposiveness is increased when the purpose-like behavior is manifested in the actions of organisms. This appearance of purposiveness is increased still further when it is the *internal* changes in the biological agents themselves that cause further increases in complexity, as is the case in the autopoietic processes discussed above.

I emphasize again: biological evolution does not directly require purpose as an explanatory category. One may believe that there is a God, a supernatural intentional agent with goals and purposes, but biology does not prove that nature as a whole possesses overarching purposes. So what are we to say about the discrepancy between these two theoretical systems? Drawing from Kant, I propose a theory of *purposiveness without purpose* in the emergence and behavior of organisms. *Purposiveness without purpose* represents a middle instance between the non-purposiveness of chemical emergence and the clearly purposive behavior of intentional (self-conscious) agents. The parts of an organism (or organ or cell or ecosystem) work together for its survival. The organism (cell, organ, ecosystem) does not consciously carry out purposes in the way an intentional agent does. Yet the result of natural selection is that the parts, structures, and functions of the organism work together to maximize its chances for survival. There is a meaningful organization: growth, nurturance, and reproduction are purposively related to the survival of the organism. The new field of biosemiotics in the biological sciences has worked out the "in order that" structure of this relationship of parts, though without reliance on any broader metaphysical notion of purpose.[14]

Biology cannot explicitly introduce conscious purpose into the evolutionary process, since its ontology does not include any entities (short of the higher primates perhaps) of which it makes biological sense to postulate conscious intentional actions. But this does not prevent the ascription of *quasi-purposiveness* to biological agents well prior to *Homo sapiens*. Eventually, there emerged a level at which entities within the created universe became capable of acting according to explicit conscious purposes. At that point there emerged conscious persons who could be affected by and affect other conscious beings, in a manner fully consistent with, though also going beyond, the laws of physics. Yet this evolutionary achievement rests on the shoulders of innumerable gradual developments, much as the eye with its exact presentation of a field of vision is built on the countless varieties of heat and light sensors that preceded it. Thus, there is some evidence, for example, that other higher primates possess a rudimentary theory of mind (call it proto-mentality).[15] The same holds true for virtually every other human capacity. Each one was rehearsed, if you will, tried out in draft form and honed through environmental feedback.[16]As the primates developed more and more complex central nervous systems in response to their environments, they also gradually developed capacities unmatched elsewhere in the biosphere.

If this account is carried through consistently, it allows us to speak of human thoughts and intentions, human symbolic interactions, as a genuinely new level of experience and behavior. And yet, like every other form of activity within the created universe, human thought is *also* conditioned by the regularities of physical law and by the quasi-intentional level of biological drives. Human thoughts are removed from any simple identity with "pure spirit" by their location within an organism which is determined by the various and sundry forms of organismic striving. Traces of these various drives and urges remain in our involuntary reflexes, our immune and limbic systems, in the body's regulation of hormones, and in the release and uptake of neurotransmitters and inhibitors in every synapse of our brains. Much of this complex history of origination is reflected in our DNA, which serves both as a historical overview of how we got here and as a constant reminder that each capacity is built on the foundations of the less advanced capacities of our ancestors.

What natural history teaches us, then, is that philosophers from Plato to Descartes (and many of the religious traditions!) were wrong: *there is no absolute dividing line between mind and matter.* Human cognitive behaviors, purposes, and goals are anticipated in the quasi-purposive behavior of organisms. Dualism is a flatlands philosophy, one that disregards the depth of understanding provided by natural history. But, it turns out, reductive physicalists are no better off. Their error is the mirror image of the dualists' blindness to natural history. If the one group overemphasizes the distinctiveness of human cognition, the other fails to recognize it in the first place.

Emergence represents a *tertium quid*. It suggests a new sort of picture. As organisms have evolved within the biosphere they have exhibited ever new ways of functioning, which in most cases could not have been predicted from the point of view of "lower" stages of development. The lesson here is *gradualism*: living systems first display purposive behavior not found in more simple systems, and then gradually manifest higher degrees of self-monitoring and internal (neural) representations of their environment, until the internalized world of symbols and intentions that we associate with consciousness emerges. Of course, one may wish to speak of human thought in terms of a more robust account of human freedom. But emergence suggests that, *if* such freedom exists,[17] it has to be understood in terms of a developmental story that includes the role of physical laws, biological drives, and the increasing latitude of behavior in more complex organisms—features both shared with other animals and distinguishing us from them. Let me put the point differently. Organisms have a latitude of "choice" or "spontaneity" that increasingly differentiates them from non-living systems as they grow more complex, to the degree that one must, perhaps, finally acknowledge a qualitative difference. In human decision making, this range and quality of choice is manifested in a manner both continuous *and* discontinuous with the stages of development out of which it evolved. In this respect, as in many others, human "mind" can be seen as one particular peak in the evolutionary landscape[18]— both resting on the foothills below it and yet higher in elevation (performance) than anything around.

➤ Rethinking the Role of Form and Structure: Toward a New Theory of Causation

I have argued for an "in-between" status for evolutionary biology. It is concerned with information (semiotics) and with function in a way that physics and chemistry are not; in this limited sense it is teleological in nature. What separates biology from more radically hermeneutical (interpretation-centered) disciplines, however, is the connection of biological information with form or structure. It's crucial to pause a moment to consider the implications of this "more than" status of biology vis-à-vis physics and chemistry. How can we do justice to this difference without projecting onto the biosphere more than we actually observe to be there?

Humans are strongly tempted to parse "purposiveness" using the categories of personal action in the world. You form an intention in your head. You reflect on the best steps for carrying it out. You resolve to act on your intention. And then you carry out the action. Since it does not seem likely that fruit flies and cockroaches go through these steps—they don't have the central nervous system to support such cognitive activity—pre-Darwinian biology ascribed the apparent order in biological development to an "unseen hand" underlying all natural change. This hidden Orderer brought emergence about as we might, were we puppeteers guiding the movements of evolution with invisible strings. But this temptation must be resisted. It involves an unjustified reading-back of human intentions into the biosphere. However frustrating it may be for the natural theologian, the so-called miracles of nature are largely explained by the Darwinian principles of random variation and selective retention, supported by physical law from below and constrained by feedback effects from higher-order emergent systems.

Yet this conclusion does not simply hand victory to a classical Darwinism metaphysics of the sort espoused by Richard Dawkins.[19] The reductionism and atomism that undergirds the Dawkinsian metaphysic is unnecessary and, increasingly, counterindicated by the growth of systems biology. Dawkins's core mistake does not lie in excluding an anthropocentric account of biological development as brought about by the hand of God. Rather, his mistake lies in focusing exclusively on the *material* of evolution, without adequately considering its form or structure. On such an account, all biological structures are merely vehicles for their genes. This makes them (evolutionarily speaking) derivatives of the "interests" of their genes and means to the end of the genes' survival.

By contrast, I suggest placing renewed emphasis on *the causal significance of form*. In classical philosophy, form meant meaningful structure. For Plato, for example, it meant ideational content (the idea of a thing). For Aristotle, it meant the comprehensible nature or essence of a thing. Today, an adequate construal of biology requires understanding both what the evolutionary process builds upon and what it eventually yields. To put it differently, comprehending biological processes requires *both* moving upward from the underlying physical laws and particles *and* moving backwards from what evolution has produced: the semantic or meaning-oriented, symbol-producing nature of human existence in the world. The same informational dynamics that structure our lives is present, albeit in nascent form, in the biosphere and in all living things.

In this view, form or structure cannot be read from the bottom up only, but must also be understood from the top down. Form is not only a complex aggregate of parts but also an informational structure. Biological structures record information and interact with their environments in a process we might call *formal causation*. Of course, individual organisms are not aware of the information as humans may be aware of the content of their thoughts. Yet these structures are responsible for much of what happens to organisms in their environments. We think of the DNA code as information, since it structures (via messenger RNA) the cell and is decisive in the formation of new cells. But *nature* does not know a distinction between DNA and the rest of the cell structure. The DNA is a potential for structure. Cell walls and cell differentiation and proto-organs are structure actualized. To put the point differently: just as the DNA is encoded information, the cell structure is expressed information—as are also the structures of a single-celled organism, a simple plant or animal, or a complicated central nervous system. Ontologically, there is no difference between structure and information; there are only varying degrees of informational complexity. At some point, when the recursive loops become complex enough, the organism begins to monitor its own behavior, leading eventually to the most complex form of modeling yet discovered: the self-awareness or self-consciousness we experience as human animals.

The recognition of the top-down causal (constraining) role of structure means a decisive break from Dawkins's genetic reductionism. When Steven J. Gould began criticizing the reductionist model in the late 1970s, it was because of the nature of structure and environmental impact on structure. He wrote, "Minor adjustment within populations may be sequential and adaptive. . . . Evolutionary trends may represent a kind of higher-level selection upon essentially static species themselves, not the slow and steady alteration of a single large population through untold ages."[20] The building blocks of the cell do not alone account for the cell's development and functioning. Environmental factors and chemical changes at the level of the cell as a whole act as mechanisms to promote the expression of genetic potentials in a sort of "top-down" causation. What's right about the modern synthesis—its ability to account for major changes through a sequence of smaller genetic changes—has been retained. Yet it has been *supplemented* by top-down theories that account for the causal role of biological forms and structures. Complex systems theory has retained this expanded notion of emergent form, which helps to account for broader, more sudden, and nonsequential change in the biosphere.

Earlier I distinguished between the kind of purpose that requires self-conscious intentional choices (call it *purpose proper*) and the kind of purpose that lacks such self-conscious decisions, which I called *purposiveness without purpose*. Similarly, we must distinguish between different sorts of causal forces in natural history. As John Polking-horne has argued, human beings "act both energetically and informationally."[21] In the physical world we encounter only efficient causes. In cases of conscious intentional behavior, we encounter final causes. The point of transition, the point at which both are active without being fully differentiated, occurs with the role of formal causes in the biological sciences.

But, the critic may complain, even if form connotes different things at different levels, why introduce any notion of emergent causative novelty? "Perhaps," he continues,[22] "the argument as you have sketched it involves an evolutionary progression from mechanical regularity to 'purposiveness without purpose' to conscious purposes in human action, but I do not at this point see how this progression requires or even suggests genuine *causal* novelty at any of these stages."

But natural history and the theory of emergence suggest that all causation is *not* identical. Under some conditions causation operates in a highly regular fashion, without distinction among the objects on which it operates. Under other conditions it acquires a recursive structure that produces quasi-purposive patterns of behavior. Under still other conditions it operates on specific objects for specific ends. Using a family resemblance model, we can now characterize these families of causal activity for the first time. We might well speak of them as physical causality, biological or organismic causality, and mental causality.

➤ Mediating First-Person and Third-Person Accounts

We are now in a position to speak of the emergence of mind. Our entire discussion leads us to understand a mental property to be a type of property that evidences a dependence relation on another type of property, the physical (or neurophysiological) state of the organism. This dependence relation has both a synchronic and a diachronic dimension. Mental properties depend on the entire natural history that led to the evolution of an increasingly complex brain and central nervous system, as well as on the physical state of the organism at a particular time. The dependence in question is neither logical nor metaphysical. Rather, the assertion of both a diachronic and a synchronic dependence of mental properties is our best reconstruction of the highly contingent natural history that eventually produced organisms like us. Of course, understanding the dependency relation in terms of natural history represents a firm break with all dualist theories of mind, thereby distinguishing the emergence approach as a separate ontological option in the debate.

Such a contingent, type-type relationship between the mental and the physical also allows one to give a more robust account of the non-reducibility of the mental than the competing accounts provide. However radically different the new kinds of properties brought about at other levels of emergence may be, mental predicates introduce the dimension of the "first personal," which is not present (at least not verifiably so) at any earlier stage in natural history. Those who defend the strong emergentist theory of the mental appeal to certain unique characteristics of the mental in order to defend their claim, such as uniquely first-personal aspects of mental phenomena, the irreducible nature of *qualia*, or the unique and otherwise undefinable nature of "what it is like to be" a bat, an ape, or a person.

These unique features raise an important methodological problem. How are human persons to be studied in a scientific manner, if they and their properties are indeed unique in natural history? One can use objective tests at all previous levels of emergence because there one is concerned exclusively with objects in the world and their behaviors. What happens if, as I have argued, the objects that we call *Homo sapiens* also bring with themselves more complex "internal" properties, such as self-consciousness? How can such qualities be studied in an objective fashion? How can the theoretical perspective of the neurosciences be reconciled with more traditional social sciences such as psychology, sociology, and cultural anthropology?

Each party in the mind-body debate has its own proposed solution to the problem. Reductive physicalists wish to overcome the problem by eliminating the internal dimension, at least in the final analysis. Humans *just are* their set of objective properties. Behaviorists and functionalists wish to overcome it by not making any claims about the internal dimension, even though they do not deny its existence. All that is necessary, they claim, is to study the "inputs" and the behavioral "outputs." What happens between input and output occurs in a sort of "black box" to which we as empirical investigators have no access. Dualists insist on studying the contents of consciousness, yet at the cost of denying that the natural sciences have access to these phenomena. Consciousness is another type of entity altogether and requires, they insist, a "science of spirit" (whatever that would mean) in order to understand it.

But why insist on this dichotomy? I am not convinced that we should settle for any of these three compromises. Why could one not use human behaviors in the world in order to understand the actions of agents, while at the same time presupposing the existence and causal efficacy of mental states? Naturally, an independent realm of essentially mental essences would not be accessible to scientific study. But the use of human behaviors in the world, including spoken behaviors, might well shed light on the internal life of psycho-bio-physical agents, allowing one to formulate and test hypotheses about their subjective experience of the world. As Wilfrid Sellars wrote in a classic essay:

> The conceptual framework of person is not something that needs to be *reconciled with* the scientific image, but rather something to be *joined* to it. Thus to complete the scientific image we need to enrich it *not* with more ways of saying what is the case, but with the language of community and individual intentions, so that by construing the actions we intend to do and the circumstances in which we intend them in scientific terms, we *directly* relate the world as conceived by scientific theory to our purposes, and make it *our* world. . . .[23]

This synthetic and agent-based approach has the advantage of drawing on the way of thinking and type of data to which ordinary language and the everyday interpretation of human behavior also appeal. Because the approach is emergentist and not reductionist, it is willing and able to take humans' first-personal experience of their own agency into account. We know ourselves to be agents. We know ourselves to be able to decide on an action (say, lifting an arm) and then to carry it out. And we know ourselves to be able to tell untruths, that is, to intend one thing and to say or do another. As soon as the prejudice that underlies physicalistic theories of the mental is removed, then it is natural for one to apply these sorts of knowledge in support of one's interpretation of the second- and third-personal encounters that one experiences in the world.

An interesting example of this sort of research is found in the recent work by Richard Davidson. Davidson and his colleagues perform real-time fMRI brain scans. For their subjects they have chosen Tibetan Buddhist monks, individuals who are trained in meditative techniques and who are able to place themselves in a particular subjective state that they have chosen with what appears to be a high level of reliability.[24] This type of research demonstrates that the increased knowledge of the neural correlates of consciousness here achieved could not be attained without using the subjects' highly reliable reports on their mental states. It is a notable, and philosophically extremely important, discovery that the best neural scanning techniques and the most advanced first-personal reporting techniques must cooperate together if we are to increase our understanding of the mental. Or, in Francisco Varela's pithy summary, "a proper scientific analysis of the mind . . . leads to the need for a detailed examination of *experience* itself."[25] A very strong case would have to be made that there is something fundamentally wrong with this approach before one should be willing to give up such an obviously successful way of extending human knowledge of the natural world into the realm of emergent mental states. In the absence of such a case, I continue to endorse such "interactionist" methods as a means both to increase empirical knowledge and to better understand what is the nature of human agency in the world.

➤ Emergence Summarized: The Three Basic Levels

We have briefly surveyed the importance of emergence as a recurring pattern across the range of the sciences. But the strong evidence for emergent phenomena might at the same time present the greatest difficulty to the theory. The nearly thirty different levels of emergence that Harold Morowitz claims to identify, for example, might cause one to worry: What reason do we have for thinking that *any* interesting continuity runs through the immensely variegated examples of emergence that one finds in the literature today? Is there any way to bring order into this chaos?

It depends on what principle one uses in comparing the instances. The principle most often used in the literature—correlating emergence with increasing complexity (of structure, of behavior, of language usage)—is indispensable, since it has the potential to bring a quantitative measure, a metric, to the process. For example, one can measure linguistic complexity in terms of syntactic richness, size of vocabulary, and so forth. At the same time, quantitative measures fail to explain the "breaks" in the process at which qualitatively new behaviors or experiences arise. The very success in establishing quantitative comparisons might seem to rule out *a forteriori* any qualitative characterization of the results. Or, to put it differently, one thereby acknowledges many instances of emergence, but each is *sui generis*.

Beyond summarizing individual examples of emergence, then, we must also look for broad patterns that link together multiple instances of emergence within the natural world. In pursuing this strategy, one loses the more rigorous criterion of a quantitative measure, and yet a more qualitative analysis is necessary in order to discover broader similarities in the natural world. Let us therefore take a step back from the ladder of emergences in order to see whether the individual instances can be grouped together into any larger patterns. I suggest that two such patterns stand out in particular.

The emergence of life used to be treated as a single distinct ontological change: at one point there were only inorganic materials, and at the next (distinct) moment there were life forms. This construal of the living-nonliving distinction has not stood up to recent results. Biochemists are now arguing that, given the structure of the heavy elements, it was not improbable that life would arise on earth. Gerald Joyce and Jeffrey Bada, both at the Scripps Institution of Oceanography in San Diego, define life as "a self-sustain[ing] chemical system capable of undergoing Darwinian evolution." It's likely that life began as a "boundary-less soup of replicating molecules." Only later did the first membranes arise by chance.[26] If the biochemists are right, the boundary between living and nonliving things is much more porous than we thought in the past; the line between them is a hazy one, and motion across it can occur in a gradual fashion.

Still, even if the line of distinction is not completely clear—some characteristics of viruses link them more closely to the nonliving, other characteristics to the living world—there are broad characteristics shared by organisms throughout the biosphere and throughout evolutionary history. Growth and development, homeostasis, reproduction, and controlled energy exchange with the environment are shared features of living organisms. Equally fundamental is the fact that change over time is controlled by a process of evolutionary adaptation. These features are so basic that there is some temptation to call them *meta-emergent properties*.[27] In the end, it may be more accurate to analyze life not in terms of a single moment of emergence, but rather as a sort of family resemblance that ties together a large number of individual emergent steps.

Another broad area of family resemblance has to do with self-awareness. Self-awareness in the biological sense involves not just the monitoring of the external environment (which is too easily confused with perception), but also the monitoring of the organism's own internal states and the modification of its behaviors as a result. The self-reflexivity of this feedback loop has been fruitfully explored by Terence Deacon.[28] Some also distinguish reflective self-awareness from generic self-awareness as a separate area of family resemblance. As the name implies, reflective self-awareness requires the ability to monitor one's own self-monitoring. If the feedback loop of self-awareness is a second-order phenomenon, then reflective self-awareness becomes a third-order phenomenon: being aware of *how* you are aware. Using more strongly mental predicates, we could describe it as knowing that one is thinking, or knowing one's own thoughts, or knowing that one is experiencing certain *qualia*.

➤ Conclusion

We have seen that natural history begins with the world of physics and runs through a large number of stages of emergent complexity, each associated with its own unique qualities, dynamics, and regularities. It is now possible to develop a philosophy of emergence in which the sciences (and meta-scientific reflection) provide the major touchstones. We see in the natural world an open-ended process of increasing complexity, which leads to qualitatively new forms of existence. In these chapters I am arguing that the ladder of emergence leads eventually to the level of the significance and the meaningful use of symbolic language—a level on which ontological reference can occur and truth claims can be parsed.

Among multiple family resemblances, we considered in particular the emergence of life and biological causality; and the emergence of mind (or mental properties), together with the forms of mental causality associated with it. Clearly, there are certain advantages to an emergentist theory of mind. It helps one to criticize reductive ("eliminativist") approaches in the philosophy of mind, allowing one to maintain the reality of mental properties, to include them within the process of explaining human behavior, and even to speak of the "downward" causal influence of mental properties on the actions a person carries out in the world. Yet all these benefits are consistent with affirming the continuing dependence of mental phenomena on the underlying states of the brain and central nervous system. And (in contrast to dualism) the emergent paradigm encourages neuroscientific studies—including study of the neural correlates of consciousness—as far as they can possibly be taken. At the same time, it gives us grounds to predict that these studies will not provide the complete explanation of actions in the world in which persons are agents.

There is a cost, of course. One can't speak of the emergence of a new substance: a soul, metaphysical self, or *Geist*, at least not on the basis of the science alone. But perhaps that is a cost one should be willing to pay. This cost is, at any rate, far lower than the costs that one must pay if one adopts either a reductionist or dualist stance regarding mind and consciousness.

From World *to* Spirit?

Complexity, Anthropology, Theology

A S WITH OTHER SCIENTIFIC BREAKTHROUGHS, THE PHENOMENA OF emergent complexity stand, regardless of whether theologians pause to take notice of them and whether religious believers think they are good news or bad news. Yet it's far better for those who reflect on the nature of the world and God's relationship to it—and isn't that a task that faces every theist?—to include these results in their understanding of the natural order. In the case of emergence, this project is particularly urgent. The philosophy of reductionism, which has dominated much of the history of modern science, constitutes one of the sharpest challenges to all forms of theistic belief. Should it turn out that this "defeater" of Christian (or Jewish or Muslim) theism were based on faulty assumptions about the natural world, that result will naturally be of great interest to all who believe in God.

In every case where science-religion interaction establishes significant common ground, one finds two different forms of theological response: natural theology and the theology of nature. These two responses are exemplified, respectively, in this and the following chapter, in which I will show how the "big picture" of emergence can be supportive of theological conclusions. And in chapter 8 we will watch what happens when the new emergent picture of the world is used as the organizing principle for a systematic theology.

I have organized the presentation in this chapter as a sort of musical quintet, involving players from five different fields: science, philosophy of science, philosophical anthropology, metaphysics, and theology. Lest the reader's attention wander as we proceed through the four movements of the piece, I should state the leitmotif right at the opening: *the contemporary naturalist should be pulled in two different directions by the growth of science.* The sciences suggest nature's self-sufficiency as a closed and coherent system, and yet they also hint at what we may credibly view as a transcendent source for nature. The idea of a transcendent source does not negate science, but it does undercut claims on behalf of the *self-sufficiency* of science.

The task of this chapter is to construct an apologetic argument. But apologetics can only be taken seriously, I suggest, if it in turn takes scientific naturalism seriously. On the one hand, most naturalisms today stand opposed to any belief in an actually existing God. If theists do not address this challenge, they will have no position left to defend. On the other hand, all scientific methods of explanation, and most of contemporary theories of knowledge, presuppose naturalism. To eschew these standards altogether is to cut one's arguments off from the broader communities of inquiry—a move that I challenged in chapter 3.

Nevertheless, the situation is perhaps not so desperate. The "intelligent design" movement notwithstanding, there is no place within science for purely empirical proofs of the existence of God or God's purposes within evolutionary history—nor for the opposite. Science *qua* science simply cannot make pronouncements on the question of the existence of God. Nevertheless, one *can* reflect philosophically and theologically on the biological data and what they might portend. In the next few pages I'd like to undertake that speculative task, controlling the results as much as possible through scientific insights, yet without claiming scientific warrant for all the conclusions. I suggest that the new theories of emergent complexity, as we have been exploring them in the last few chapters, represent an ideal point of departure.

➤ Emergence in Nature

As we've seen, there are numerous reasons for biologists to be cautious about talk of purpose in evolution. Unfortunately, these reasons have sometimes produced a reticence to acknowledge the significance of teleological systems within the biosphere. Recent years have brought renewed study of macroevolutionary patterns, however, and it is now not uncommon to find treatments of organisms and their behaviors as purposive systems. Many biologists now speak of a "directionality" to evolution, frequently correlating it with the increase in biological complexity.[2]

The natural theology to be defended here proceeds in order through three theses. First, analogies between various cases of emergent complexity are strong enough to support emergence as a fundamental characteristic of natural history and emergence theory over reduction as the more adequate philosophy of science. Second, the development of symbolic language in *Homo sapiens* sets in motion a new level of evolution, cultural evolution, which requires forms of explanation that are different from and not reducible to biological explanation. As a species that creates its own open-ended social and cultural worlds, *Homo sapiens* is essentially self-transcending. Finally, I will suggest that this emergent understanding of humanity is fully consistent with a theistic worldview and, as I shall argue, may even be better explained by theism than by its competitors.

Step one of the argument, then, turns on the claim that analogies between various cases of emergent complexity are strong enough to support emergence over reduction as the more adequate philosophy of science and as a fundamental characteristic of natural history.

Recall that emergence is linked to complexity, that is, to the principles of self-organization and the formation of complex systems. Complexity theory asks, "what are the steps and the processes that lead from the elementary particle to the thinking organism, the (present!) entity of highest complexity?"[3] Complexity is inherently a systemic function. It involves the interaction between many components of various kinds and the principles that affect their correlation, coupling, and feedback relationships. The goal of the sciences of complexity, writes Jean-Marie Lehn, is "to progressively discover, understand, and implement the rules that govern [matter's] evolution from inanimate to animate and beyond, to ultimately acquire the ability to create new forms of complex matter."[4] Emergent complexity spans the entire spectrum of cosmic history, "from divided to condensed matter then to organized and adaptive matter, on to living matter and thinking matter, up the ladder of complexity."[5]

Emergence, then, is the hypothesis that reduction, or rather "reductionism," is false. An emergent theory of human thought and action, for example, argues that the reduction of the human sciences to biology or physics is false. A non-reductive theory of religious belief argues that the reduction of religious belief to its psycho-social functions is false. (Of course, one of these emergent accounts might be successful and the other unsuccessful.)

That's the negative pole of emergence theory. What are its positive assertions? Three general claims undergird emergence theory in the philosophy of science. First, empirical reality divides naturally into multiple levels (William Wimsatt). Over the course of natural history, new emergent levels evolve. Second, emergent wholes that are more than the sum of their parts require new types of explanation adequate to each new level of phenomena. Third, such emergent wholes manifest new types of causal interaction. Biological systems are not "nothing more than" microphysical interactions. They include irreducible biological interactions and must be explained in biological terms. Nor are the mental experiences that you are having right now (which may or may not be related to your reading this chapter) "nothing but" complicated brain states. In a real and important sense, one mental state can indeed cause another.

Entire books could be, and have been, devoted to the recent evidence on behalf of these emergent claims. The emergence of living organisms, and the emergence of mental experience, are often listed as the standard intuitive examples of such phenomena. But, as we've seen, emergence is not manifested only at the level of life or mind. It is evident even at the very earliest stages of cosmic evolution. Classical physics has been described as emergent out of quantum physics.[6] Even quantum phenomena may themselves be emergent.[7] In an influential book, physics Nobel laureate Robert Laughlin has recently argued that scientific reduction is a dogma and that many of the key features of his field, condensed matter physics, can be explained only within the paradigm of emergence.[8]

➤ Philosophical Anthropology

What does this commitment to the data as they present themselves say about the animal in whom we are most interested, *Homo sapiens*? The emergentist pursues every bit of common ground that she can discover between humans and other animals—from the common chemical composition and structure of DNA through the mechanisms of cell communication and regeneration, to the development of a central nervous system and brain, to behavioral similarities, to physiological responses. Nerve cell similarities, for example, allow us to learn from electrochemical responses in electric eels. Brain plasticity is similar in frogs and humans. We learn about our own social nature from mirror cells and from the rudimentary "theory of other minds" applied to chimpanzees. Reconciling behaviors among the great apes, and studying mutual care-taking among bonobos, help us understand our own interdependencies more fully. All of these continuities are for the good from a scientific perspective.

Yet humans are also discontinuous with our animal cousins. The significantly larger frontal cortex and more complex anatomy of our brains have produced a mental life and corresponding behaviors that are qualitatively different from those of our closest animal relatives. We are, as Terrence Deacon aptly puts it, "the symbolic species."[9] One difference gives rise to another, in a beautiful cascading effect of exponentially increasing complexity. Our disproportionately large brains give rise to more varied language use and linguistic play. More complex language use in turn produces anatomical changes, such as larger language areas, greater brain plasticity, and more complex interrelationships among the brain regions. This is the famous thesis of the "co-evolution" of human brains and human culture.[10]

Quantitative increases in complexity eventually lead to qualitative differences, the emergence of new types of systems with correspondingly new types of causation. The evolution of human culture is startlingly different from any evolutionary dynamics that preceded it. To put the differences simplistically, this new form of evolution, cultural evolution, is not only Darwinian but also Lamarckian. That is, it allows for the heritability of acquired traits. When you learn to use email—or shall we say, when you become enslaved to your various email accounts—you can pass this knowledge on to your children (poor things!). Most of what is important to us—our language, our knowledge of proper ways to behave, our beliefs about the existence or non-existence of God—is transmitted across generations in this fashion.

So far we have spoken of empirical facts, but now things become somewhat more speculative. For we must ask: What is the nature of human persons, who emerge through the complex interaction of (Darwinian) biological evolution and (Lamarckian) cultural evolution?

In the social world, events without significance are rare. Virtually everything we do either has, or *fails* to have, an underlying valence of meaning. We do not merely grow older; we move through a series of rites of passage. We do not merely use words and encounter objects; we fashion signs in our language and transform objects into symbols of deep judgments about the world (the cross, the flag, even the color of our scarves). The sociologist of religion Peter Berger writes, "Man, biologically denied the ordering mechanisms with which other animals are endowed, is *compelled to impose his own order* on experience. Man's sociality presupposes the collective character of this ordering of reality."[11]

If this quest for meaning fails, "not only will the individual . . . begin to lose his moral bearings, with disastrous psychological consequences, but he will become uncertain about his cognitive bearings as well."[12] Yet building worlds of meaning is not just an individual task. "Society," Berger notes, "is the guardian of social order and meaning, not only objectively, in its institutional structures, but subjectively as well, in its structuring of individual consciousness."[13]

The importance of this quest for meaning for anthropology cannot be overstated: *The construction of meaning is ubiquitous; it plays a role in all that humans do and think.* Nor is it limited to human contexts. One must also find one's sense of self within the natural world as well. Clearly this is no easy task. A famous text by Friedrich Nietzsche clearly expresses the tension faced by individuals in a dark universe: "Once upon a time, in a distant corner of this universe with its countless flickering solar systems, there was a planet, and on this planet some intelligent animals discovered knowledge. It was the most noble and most mendacious minute in the history of the universe— but only a minute. After Nature had breathed a few times their star burned out, and the intelligent animals had to die."[14]

Nietzsche's nihilism reveals the urgency of this highest and broadest human task: *to make sense of our existence as a whole.* Somehow what we know about the physical universe, with its apparently unbending laws and hostile conditions for life, must be integrated into our sense of who we are. The trouble is, conclusions from the physical sciences—whether it's the Big Bang or the emergence of complexity—do not directly prove the existence of God or an "intelligent designer," or for that matter any other metaphysical conclusions about ultimate reality. Yet the quest for meaning does unavoidably confront us with the question: Can one defend an account of this physical world in irreducibly religious or spiritual terms? Can one develop a rational theology of nature? Can the term "God" still do real work, or should we conclude, with Pierre-Simon Laplace, "I have no need of that hypothesis"?

Religion is the attempt to conceive the entire universe as being humanly significant.[15] Religion strives for "the establishment . . . of an all-embracing sacred order . . . a sacred cosmos that will be capable of maintaining itself in the ever-present face of chaos." Berger continues: "Every society is, in the last resort, [persons] banded together in the face of death. The power of religion depends, in the last resort, upon the credibility of the banners it puts in the hands of [men and women] as they stand before death, or more accurately, as they walk, inevitably, toward it."[16]

Put in most general terms, the object of religion is the sacred. The sacred is what stands out from normal life. It is, in Rudolf Otto's famous words, *mysterium tremendum et fascinans,* a mystery that arouses both fear and fascination. The cosmos posited by religion is one that transcends humanity as well as including us. "The sacred cosmos is confronted by [humanity] as an immensely powerful reality other than [ourselves]. Yet," Berger adds, "this reality addresses itself to [us] and locates [our] life in an ultimately meaningful order."[17] The most powerful conceptualizations (and myths and stories) of the sacred are those that neither reduce it to a feature of this world, one quality among others, nor reserve it for a level of transcendence outside of and beyond this world as a whole.

What then of the ideas and beliefs that arise out of the religious quest for meaning? Are the *ideals* that humans strive for—love, justice, compassion—all fictions? Or are some metaphysical beliefs actually *true of the world*? Do the sciences prove that we are alone in a hostile universe, as Nietzsche thought? Or do they offer clues about another possibility: that humans are pervasively preoccupied with religious symbols and practices *because* we live in a universe that is open toward transcendence, a universe that is the product of some deeper cosmic order? Could this deeper order or orderer even have some personal qualities, that is, could it be that it is not *less* intelligent and conscious than we are? Could the existence of this deeper reality be hinted at in the physical world, in cosmic history, and in the inner life of the subjects studied by psychologists, sociologists, artists, and novelists?[18] Could not something of the divine be revealed by studying that animal that struggles with the question of God, ourselves?

➤ Theology

The emergent view of human nature and existence that we have been exploring is certainly religiously significant. It shows that human religiosity is not an absurd reaction to our existence or a sign of infantile irrationality, as some have claimed. Instead, the religious response is intrinsic to human existence in the world.

But now the question arises: Can we know whether any of these religious responses are *true*? Obviously, humans do not just have emotional and aesthetic responses to the universe and the question of its ultimate meaning. Our attempts to construct meaning often come in the form of rather specific beliefs about the universe, about its ultimate origins and final destiny. Are all such beliefs mere projections onto a cold universe, bereft of meaning, by an animal all too hungry for some sense of cosmic purpose? Or are we justified in our hope and belief that some ultimate significance may underlie the process of emergence of which we ourselves are a part?

Agnosticism, Atheism, and Intelligent Design

Of course, one response to this question is agnosticism. We are unavoidably driven to formulate hypotheses about the "before" and the "after," as David Hume puts it. Yet, according to the agnostic, no beliefs of this type have any "traction" in the real world. And if none are testable, he continues, none are rational. Psychologically interesting, perhaps, but of no interest to seekers after Truth.

This tragic view of our human fate is widespread and popular, especially in the age of science. It became increasingly attractive in the modern period, perhaps because of its Byronic tone. Just think of the oft-repeated mantras of the modern prophets of agnosticism. Steven Weinberg famously writes, "The more the universe seems comprehensible, the more it also seems pointless."[19] Jacques Monod's view is even more bleak:

Chance alone is the source of every innovation, of all creation in the biosphere. Pure chance, absolutely free but blind, is at the very root of the stupendous edifice of evolution. The central concept of biology . . . is today the sole conceivable hypothesis, the only one compatible with observed and tested fact. All forms of life are the product of chance. . . .[20]

John Polkinghorne provides a trenchant summary of this worldview (which is, of course, not the view he holds): "All culture, including science, will be no more than a transient episode, but while human society lasts it represents a small island of self-created meaning, around which laps the ocean of cosmic meaninglessness."[21]

One can't help but admire the existentialist's courage. But courage does not, of course, make a position true. From another standpoint, the agnostic's pessimistic rejection of all metaphysical reflection also represents a form of betting against oneself. How will we ever *know* whether it's possible to evaluate hypotheses that go beyond the strictly scientific, unless we engage in rigorous and critical debate on these topics? I made the case for the importance of such debate in chapter 3. Unfortunately, the cultural prejudice of our day militates increasingly against serious discourse between science and theology. During a recent stay in Britain, I listened to a BBC-TV program hosted by Richard Dawkins, who argued that all religious belief is superficial and anti-intellectual, the "root of all evil." Yet scholarly theologians were noticeably absent from the broadcast, and all serious debate on the topic was excluded.

Of course, debate-blocking measures occur from the other side as well. The American "intelligent design" theorist Michael Behe argues that the functions of hemoglobin *could never* be biologically explained. "Each of the steps of the [blood–] clotting cascade," he asserts, "is irreducibly complex. . . . The clotting cascade was not produced by natural selection. . . . That is why I conclude that the cascade is a product of design."[22] Some American members of the intelligent design movement go even further: "Every fact of creation drips with evidence of God as the creator," writes Terry Gray, and "Every time we think or speak about a fact of creation it is either acknowledging God as the creator or denying him."[23]

But surely there must be a region between the cavalier dismissal of religious reflection on the one side and, on the other, direct inferences to God from what science does not know. In between these over-quick responses (one militantly anti-religious, the other undermining science altogether) is a third realm of discourse, one in which religious truth claims can be calmly and rationally assessed. "But," the agnostic may again reply, "rational assessment of such metaphysical claims is just not possible." Perhaps. Yet proving the possibility of metaphysics in advance is certainly a tall order. How will we know until we try? Until one actually engages in the process of examining and comparing claims about the nature of reality—including their consistency with science—it's pointless to make *a priori* claims about what can and cannot be rationally decided. Is it not better to wager *for* the human quest for knowledge, in the broadest sense of this term, rather than deciding in advance that the quest is quixotic?

In these pages, then, I shall argue that the emergent understanding of nature and humanity supports the idea of a metaphysical reality that is not less than personal, a ground of existence to which agency may also be ascribed. The case proceeds in three steps.[24]

1. Emergent Spiritual Properties

I have argued that emergence is a broad pattern shared across the sciences and a genuine macro-pattern manifested in natural history. If each stage of the evolutionary process produces new levels of emergent phenomena, then is it not likely that the level of human culture will produce (or has produced) yet another level? Let's call this the level of spirituality, the emergence of spiritual predicates.

Is this argument sufficient for a doctrine of God? Some theorists have attempted to understand the divine directly in terms of the arrow of emergence. According to what I have called *radically emergent theism*,[25] the divine itself becomes yet another emergent property in natural history—and indeed, presumably, the final one. This is the route taken, most famously, by Samuel Alexander in the Gifford Lectures of 1918–19, published as *Space, Time, and Deity*:

> As actual, God does not possess the quality of deity but *is the universe as tending to that quality*. . . . Thus there is no actual infinite being with the quality of deity; but there is an actual infinite, the whole universe, with a nisus toward deity; and this is the God of the religious consciousness, though that consciousness habitually forecasts the divinity of its object as actually realised in an individual form. . . . The actual reality which has deity is the world of empiricals filling up all Space-Time and tending towards a higher quality. Deity is a nisus and not an accomplishment.[26]

What humans call "God" is just the emergent property of spirituality in the universe. And "God" is simply the universe becoming aware of itself.

Note that Alexander's argument does not produce theism in any traditional sense. In fact, contemporary scientists with a more Buddhist orientation, such as Terry Deacon and Ursula Goodenough,[27] are happy to speak of the emergence of spiritual significance without God.

But, I suggest, Alexander's sort of immediate connection between emergent patterns in nature and metaphysics is too direct. He obviously assumes that emergence is both necessary *and sufficient* for doing metaphysics and theology. But there are reasons to be skeptical of such straight-line extrapolations from science to metaphysics. Scientific results may be necessary for theological conclusions, but they are not sufficient. When one introduces the level of metaphysics—that is, questions of the ultimate source or origin—other conceptual resources are required.

One thing we *can* learn from Alexander. Once one has granted the ongoing advent of new emergent patterns, it is arbitrary to stop the progression with mental predicates. There may well be further levels of emergence—either qualities of which we humans have some inkling, or qualities utterly unknown to us. The Alexander argument for viewing emergence as open-ended thus represents an important ally against reductionism, that is, against the limitation of emergence to the level of human mentality.

We should embrace this argument, noting that it effectively undercuts attempts to limit reality to the (better understood) earlier stages of natural history.

2. The Divine Is Not Less Than Personal

If we are to reach the next level of reflection, we must pause to consider for a moment what it means for some of these higher-order properties, such as personhood, to emerge.

Science—and here I mean to include the social sciences—does not warrant the introduction of souls or other non-natural entities in the world. Nor are the sciences as such capable of detecting and explaining divine action, if it does indeed occur. But even if soul-language is problematic, one is surely justified in moving from the emergence of mental predicates and personal qualities to the language of persons acting in the world. Indeed, would it not be arbitrary to acknowledge the emergence of the sort of psychological and intentional predicates that characterize the human person whilst refusing to acknowledge that form of agency which we all know as the activities of persons? I well remember a major international symposium at the American Academy of Arts and Sciences a few years ago, at which a panel of neuroscientists was chiding philosophers of mind for their doubts about whether humans are really conscious and whether consciousness does anything in the world. "Ascribing consciousness to persons is basic to the practice of neurology in medicine," one neurologist argued. "When a patient shows rapidly decreasing awareness and cognitive functioning, that's a key sign for us that medical intervention is justified." Of course, the physicians insisted, medicine cannot resolve the question of whether their patients have, or are, spiritual souls. But, they argued, to be experts in neuroscience in no way undercuts the belief that one's patients are persons—to the contrary!

How then shall we view persons, if they are more than bundles of mental and psychological predicates (David Hume) on the one hand, yet less than substantial souls or hylomorphic entities on the other? I suggest that language of personhood or "whole persons" serves an indispensable function in comprehending human actions and interactions. When one limits oneself to the neural correlates of consciousness, one can research only isolated mental attributes such as the state of arousal or fear or uncertainty. Electrode stimulation of a particular cortical region (as in the classic experiments by Benjamin Libet) will correlate only with specific behaviors or memories. Such analyses fail to do justice to the realities of our existence as agents in the world—to our wishes, goals, and intentions, both conscious and unconscious. Only explanations that include this emergent level, the level of personal actions and intentions, are in fact able to explain the data available to us, the data of introspection, the data of human behavior, and the data of human cultural production.

Now combine this conclusion with the previous one and notice what results. In step one of the argument, I defended the emergent level of mental properties—the properties of persons in the world—as well as an emergent level of spiritual properties. This result confronts us with the question: Why should we now deny of the spiritual level what we are willing to affirm of humans? If humans can be conceived as persons, why are we so certain that the divine can be no more than a series or bundle of spiritual properties—no more than the world as a whole "deising" itself, as Samuel Alexander put it? Is it not much more natural and reasonable to postulate such spiritual properties as being unified in a being or agent?

Some caution is called for here. We should not be flat-footed literalists. There is no reason to limit our conception of deity to the sort of agency or personhood that we know through the various human and animal agents which we encounter in the world. A wide variety of metaphysical models are available, and they are significantly different. Patristic beliefs about the trinitarian God, with their reliance on the Greek notion of substance, are not identical to theologies of emanation or to perennial philosophies or to "Ground of Being" theologies. Classical philosophical theism is not identical to panentheism, the belief that the world is located within the divine although God is also more than the world (see part III). But what all these models share in common is the conception of the religious object as more than merely a bundle of emergent properties; and surely they are right to do so.

So, if emergence leads us to speak of a higher kind of agency than our own, what *kind* of agency might it be? In some traditions the spiritual level is conceived as *less than* personal. Think for example of the metaphysics of karma, which is understood as a force that works more as natural law than as personal agent. (Of course, actual Hindu religious practice is also deeply influenced by *bhakti*, the practice of devotion to a personal god or gods.) But surely, once we have granted that natural history has produced personal agency of the sort we know in our own actions, we should not expect that the next higher level, the level of spiritual properties, would be characterized by a *lower* form of causality, a causality analogous to natural law. Is it not more reasonable to conceive of the religious object, the divine, as everything that human persons are—and presumably infinitely more?

In short, the irreducibility of person-language, combined with the open-ended nature of the emergence hierarchy, induces us to use language for the divine that is not-less-than-personal. It suggests a divinity that is not inferior in agency to human agents, but rather one that infinitely transcends all forms of finite agency—a creative divine, and hence, perhaps, a providential God as well.

3. Religious Experience, Revelation, and the Established Religions

Science is not sufficient for metaphysics or theology. One should resist any straight-line extrapolations from scientific emergence to a metaphysical theory of deity as the sum of all emergent spiritual properties. Yet, *some* inferences can be drawn. We have so far discovered two. First, if there are emergent mental properties, it makes sense to speak of the personality or character that produces these patterns, and hence of the persons who *have* the properties that we detect in their actions. Second, as we saw, if there are emergent spiritual properties it also makes sense to speak of the nature or character of the reality or being that produces the patterns that we detect. Since it is incoherent to imagine that the ultimate ground or spiritual reality is *less than* what it has produced, and it clearly isn't merely a human person, we are justified in conceiving it as supra-personal. In short, we have discovered reasons to make the transition from finite agency to transcendent agency, at least in this carefully circumscribed sense. In the argument's third and final step, I will argue for an analogous transition from metaphysics to theology.

I now assume that one is justified in conceiving the metaphysical ultimate as not-less-than-personal. One may well be skeptical of divine incursions into the physical order, and hence of physical miracles as traditionally conceived. Yet a world that is "upwardly open," in the way that emergence theory describes it to be, might at its most complex levels manifest *something* of the influence of the divine. If any sign of more-than-personal divine activity exists, where might it be recognizable as such? Two possibilities come immediately to mind: individual religious experience, and the putative revelations of the divine recorded in the sacred scriptures of the great world religious traditions. In the experience of mystics through the ages lie shared observations and insights that, as Wordsworth put it, "disturb [us] with the joy / Of elevated thoughts; a sense sublime / Of something far more deeply interfused. . . ." Given the vagaries of human experience, and the fallibility of subjective reports of which we are only too aware, the philosophical force of these "intimations of transcendence" may be limited. Still, if a self-revealing divine agent exists, it is hard to dismiss the possibility that something of this being may be manifest in the inner life.

What of the second route—the various sacred scriptures after which so many have molded their lives, and the traditions of reflection to which they have given rise? Of course, the hypothesis of a not-less-than-personal divine can be explored in a purely conceptual fashion. We can enquire whether it is consistent, coherent, and better justified than its rivals. But it can also be explored historically. We can study the documents that claim to be the histories of divine self-revelation, the records of the putative interaction of God and humanity.[28] Here other sorts of terms become relevant to our enquiry, terms more reminiscent of theological debate and religious practice—terms such as Spirit, pre-existence, self-revelation, creation, providence; terms such as grace, sin, and salvation; but also terms such as Atman and Brahman, *moksha, sunyata,* and co-dependent origination.

I do not share the optimism of the Oxford philosopher of religion, Richard Swinburne, whose many books attempt to construct a ladder of reasoning step by unbroken step from purely philosophical considerations to Christian theological conclusions. Instead, I have argued that enquiring into the locus, or loci, of divine self-revelation offers another means of proceeding, that it is also reasonable to look to the putative histories of divine revelation to see what patterns may emerge there. If the conceptual arguments of the metaphysicians regarding the divine nature are to be taken seriously, as I have sought to show, then the accounts that claim to record the self-revelation of God may serve as important sources of material as well. Especially where patterns of belief and value emerge across these traditions, they merit our close attention.

But here Reason falters. It is a tall mountain that we have ascended, and I must sound a note of caution. At about this point, it seems to me, unaided reflection starts to lose its bearings, and the ascending path of speculation begins to disappear into the clouds. (Which is not to deny that many have climbed confidently onward, armed only with the ropes of purely *a priori* arguments.) Just consider the difficulties that now arise. The claims of the various religious traditions conflict. The primary sources are heavily redacted by later communities. Even within the various traditions, specific beliefs are contested. Cultural and historical differences threaten incommensurability. And subjective factors increasingly color one's own assessment of the data. Rationality begins to lose its footing, and even metaphysicians must proceed with caution, if at all.

One may have strong reasons to establish a primary location within a particular tradition of religious practice, as I find my primary location within the Christian tradition. Still, the obscurity of the topic and the depths of the disagreements between religious traditions call for caution when one reaches this point in the argument. Boldness, a quality needed when we left the relatively safe fields of accepted science and began the ascent of metaphysical reflection, can now become a liability. And when it comes to beliefs contested between Jews, Christians, and Muslims, even more humility is required. Christians in particular—the boldness of whose truth claims in the past has produced crusades, inquisitions, and pogroms—would do well to emphasize the present limitations on knowledge. "For now we see in a mirror, dimly, but then we will see face to face" (1 Cor 13:12). We *hope* for a culmination of humanity's quest for knowledge of God, rather than a sort of sacred agnosticism. We hope for confirmation of our sense that we are not alone in the universe. Yet the hope for future confirmation cannot become the battering ram of religious apologetics, knocking down the walls of opposing religious traditions. "Now we know only in part; then we will know fully, even as we have been fully known."[29]

➤ Conclusion

I have argued that emergence theory sheds new light on natural history and the relationships between different levels of phenomena in the world. It also encourages one to recognize the unique qualities of human beings, yet without denying our closeness to other animals and our interconnection with nature as a whole. The ladder of natural emergence first led us to speculate about the emergence of spiritual properties, and then, taking the metaphysical leap (the *salto mortale*?), to postulate a not-less-than-personal spiritual reality or ground. I maintain that these results are fully consistent with a theistic worldview and may even be better explained by theism than by its competitors.

Science therefore does not undercut the belief that this rich and diverse natural order may reflect an intentional act of creation. Science certainly constrains our beliefs about divine action, but it does not eliminate the possibility that a Creator is engaged at least with humanity, and perhaps elsewhere in the universe as well. Thus, it turns out, it is dogmatism, not science, to claim that personal agency and meaningfulness are foreign to this universe. If the present argument is successful, one is fully justified in looking to the resources of the existing religious traditions in order to understand the upwardly open process of emergence as it is manifested both in the natural world and in the cultural realms of art, literature, and philosophy. Perhaps we are, after all, at home in the universe.[30]

Theological Reflections on Emergence

From Emergent Nature to the Emerging Church

IN CHAPTERS 4 AND 5, WE EXPLORED THE NEW CONCEPTION OF AN emerging universe. And, in the previous chapter, I outlined a natural theology based on the concept of emergence. But sketching such an argument is only the opening to a series of challenging theological questions, not the substitute for them. If emergence is in fact a fundamental feature of the natural world, as I am arguing, then one wants to know what an emergent theology would look like if fleshed out in detail. Where is it consistent with traditional notions of God, and where do the two concepts diverge? Could it meet the criteria for a distinctively Christian theology; that is, could it show sufficient continuity with the Christian Scriptures, the Christian faith experience, and the traditional emphases of theologians through the ages? All of these concerns fall under the overarching challenge that science raises for theology: Can belief in a divine reality be reconciled with the world as we have now come to know it through scientific study?

The goal of this chapter is not to prove the rational superiority of an emergent theology to all other theological options—how could one do that without a full discussion of the competing positions? Indeed, given the necessary brevity, it is not even possible to trace all the different ways in which this theology overlaps with and diverges from the other major options in the Christian tradition. Our goal must be a much more modest one: to show how a theology that is responsive to the insights of emergent complexity might address the standard loci of systematic theology, and to ask whether these new responses are consistent, coherent, and convincing.

Once one accepts the methodological commitments laid out in the preceding chapters, a broad spectrum of scientific theories becomes relevant for theological reflection. Among them, those theories that concern the nature of human persons particularly deserve theological attention (see chapter 6). To the extent that emergence theories support a position on the nature of human consciousness, their interest spans not only the natural and human sciences, but theology as well.

The reason is significant: any theory of human agency, emergent or otherwise, is bound to have important consequences for theology. After all, anyone who speaks of God as an "agent" implies that this agent is somehow analogous to human agents. Moreover, one implicitly evokes the concept of agent whenever one appeals to the notion of divine action (though some theologians seem strangely reticent to acknowledge this fact). If there are divine actions, then obviously the divine must be understood as the agent of those actions. One does not speak, for example, of the actions of karma. Karma is a lawlike regularity that has a moral dimension. It entails that actions of a certain sort will have causal effects. An agent, by contrast, is one who initiates and carries out her own actions.[1] Moreover, God is universally understood by believers as an agent who is worthy of worship. But the practices of praying to and worshiping the ultimate reality are valid only if the ultimate reality has attributes that render it worthy of this extraordinary behavior, which include not only moral attributes but also cognitive attributes such as autonomy, rationality, intentionality, and so forth. The practice of worship implies the belief that God is the sort of agent who possesses *at least* all the positive qualities humans have as person-agents (and presumably others as well), and possesses them to the highest possible degree.

Which position one takes on consciousness, mind, or spirit in humans will have a major effect on what one will be able to say about the nature of God.[2] If we are unable even to give a coherent account of what it is to be, think, and act as a human agent, for example, our odds of making sense of a divine agent are pretty slim. Conversely, if we can develop an adequate account of human agency, then the door is at least open for theologians to specify the ways in which God as divine agent is like human agents and the ways in which God is distinct from them.

➤ Radically Emergent Theism and Its Less Radical Competitors

The metaphysical label that best describes the methods and results of complex systems theory is *emergent monism*.[3] This position denies that reality is primarily to be characterized as *either* "physical" *or* "mental" or, for that matter, as simultaneously both. Reality manifests itself at various levels, and at each level it is (to the best of our knowledge) as the sciences particular to that level describe it to be. Moreover, these various levels—and thus the objects and properties particular to each—arose one by one over the course of cosmic evolution. At one point reality was physical. Later it was both physical and biological. And, on at least one planet, there are entities that are simultaneously physical, biological, and mental. "Higher" (that is, later) entities, causes, and properties are dependent on the "lower" levels out of which they have arisen.[4] Hence thought and other emergent mental properties are dependent on neurophysiological states but not reducible to them.[5] In earlier works I have offered a detailed defense of an emergent view of human agency, that is, the view that human agents emerge based on the presence of complex physiological structures but subsequently exercise a "downward" causal agency of their own.[6]

Our task now is to formulate an emergent theology that is both consistent with this view of agency and adequate to the Christian tradition. Immediately a difficulty arises, however. The view of God that maximizes similarities with the emergent view of persons—let us call it *radically emergent theism*—conflicts at a number of points with basic tenets of the theological tradition. For example, Christian theology has traditionally taught that God pre-existed the world, created it *ex nihilo*, guides its development in some way, and will be involved in bringing about its final culmination. The best way to deal with these tensions is first to present them in their strongest possible form and then to expand the range of what might count as emergent theology.

The obvious starting point for the emergent thinker is to draw the strongest possible analogy between the divine agent and human agents (see the previous chapter). If the mental side of human existence is emergent from a complex physical system (the brain and central nervous system), yet remains dependent upon it, and if divine subjectivity is understood on analogy with this result, would one not also have to construe the divine as an emergent property of the physical world? Radically emergent theism holds that at one time there was no God, only the physical world, and that God is gradually emerging in the process of natural history. On this view, "the divine" is another emergent property of the universe, alongside life and mind, gradually appearing as the universe reaches certain stages of complexity. This was the position taken by Samuel Alexander, for example, as in the passage quoted on page 95 above.[7]

Certainly, radically emergent theism offers the closest possible parallel between divine and human agents. Yet note that *accepting the results of emergent complexity does not compel one to endorse this particular conclusion*. One can agree that the most plausible contemporary account of human agency involves the emergence of mental phenomena from brains interacting with their environments, while still insisting that this account does not exhaust the nature of the divine agent. For example, an emergent thinker can hold (as I do) that God was present from the very beginning as the Ground of all things, and that the essential divine nature remains unchanged throughout cosmic history, even if many aspects of the agency of God—God's actual responses to actually existing beings—are only gradually manifested as the universe proceeds to develop life, consciousness, and spiritual experience. Let's call this the *moderately emergent view* of the divine nature.

A moderately emergent theology of this type, combined with the use of emergent vocabulary in describing human subjectivity, gives rise to some significant parallels with the process theologies of A. N. Whitehead and Charles Hartshorne. Both views stress the emerging, responsive nature of the divine experience. Also, both views posit two "poles" within the divine: an antecedent nature, pre-existing the cosmos, which is responsible for its creation, and a consequent nature, which arises in relation and response to the creative activity of humans and other living things within the world.

One should not criticize radically emergent theists merely because they have reformulated theology in light of a new systematic principle. Rather, the real question concerns the *manner and extent* of one's use of this principle. Should one follow the lead of the emergent theory of human mentality *all the way*, deriving one's doctrine of God directly, even exclusively, from its principles? Or can one endorse an emergent anthropology while supplementing it with other principles on the way to a complete doctrine of God? It turns out that there is in fact a wide variety of ways in which a theology can be emergent, ranging from more or less unmodified traditional theologies with slight colorings of process, all the way to views so radically divergent from traditional theism that one is hard-pressed to call them "theologies" any longer.

Clearly, not all of these views accept the strong conclusions of Samuel Alexander's radically emergent theism. Some accept those modifications of traditional theism that are necessary to bring it into line with emergent insights. Seeing a plausible emergent theology developed, complete with Christology, ecclesiology, and the rest, may help to allay the suspicions of those who are worried that talk of emergence will inevitably compromise Christian theism. Conversely, those who are skeptical that *any* plausible form of theism can still be found—say, because of the tensions between traditional theism and contemporary science—may be encouraged to encounter a more progressive view of theism that at least tries to respond to the perspective of emergence.

➤ The Two Sides of God

In order to produce a significant emergent theology, I must assume that the argument for the viability of Christian theism in chapter 6 is sound. But what form of theism will it be? Clearly, there is a painful incongruity between the focus on emerging systems and the notion of an unchanging, self-sufficient God who is supposed to express the divine nature in a ubiquitously interrelated, constantly emerging world. Turning to a moderately emergent theism opens up a number of more fruitful options. For example, God could be full and complete in God's own nature, and fully relational within God's self, prior to the creation of any world at all (classical trinitarian theology); or God could have an eternal nature and a *potential* for relation, but only actualize that relation fully in the context of God's relationship with a created world.

I admit that, in choosing between these two options, I am strongly influenced by the biblical picture of the relational and responsive God. I cannot do the exegesis here, other than to note that the responsiveness of God seems to be an important theme both in the Hebrew Bible and in the New Testament.[8] We have good reason to resist any positions in systematic theology that tend to undercut the two-sidedness of the relationship with God that occurs in actual historical moments of encounter. A theology of genuinely two-sided relations entails real effects on God: the divine experience is different after the encounter than before. This stance thus inclines me toward the second of the two views.

In the view I wish to defend, God fulfills a number of roles that are not direct products of God's personal nature. The world as contingent is ontologically dependent on God as its non-contingent ground. The world as finite in time is dependent on a being with no beginning in time. The world as a mixture of good and evil (of positive and negative moral attributes) depends on a ground which is goodness itself. And the finite world must be included within the all-encompassing infinite (as Hegel showed in his *Logic*).

It is difficult but not impossible to encompass both personal and non-personal functions within a single doctrine of God. Minimally, one has to conceive God's nature as having two sides or "poles": an antecedent (pre-existing) pole, which represents God's eternal and unchanging nature, and a consequent pole, which emerges in the course of God's interaction with the world. Process theologians have done an effective job of constructing a sophisticated philosophical theology that elaborates "dipolar theism," and I have sought to supplement their accounts by drawing more heavily on the tradition of German Idealism, especially the work of Schelling (see chapters 9 and 10 below).[9] A dipolar theology allows one to conceive God both as the ongoing Ground of emerging processes *and* as responsive to the entities that emerge within those processes. The adequacy of this basic framework for theology is presupposed in what follows.

➤ "God with Us" and Two Modes of Doing Christology

It is time now to consider the features of a distinctively Christian theology. There is only one way to make this transition: to establish conceptual links between the philosophical theology sketched to this point and Christology, the doctrine of Christ (see also chapter 13). The goal is not to survey the entire field of christological options, but only to provide an example of the sort of Christology that would be consistent with an emergent theology. And if it is to be a Christian emergent theology, one must pay particular attention to the biblical texts, first as they describe the nature of God, and subsequently as they convey the narrative and teachings of Jesus of Nazareth, who was called the Christ.

From a Christian perspective, the personal or "consequent" nature of God represents "God with us." To conceive God in this way is to attempt to understand God in God's identification with the world. It is to think of God in terms of a love that embraces creation, that is willing to "come alongside" humanity and other living things, to identify with us, to suffer with us. (Think of the description of God's Spirit as *Paraclete* in the Gospel of John: the one who comes alongside.) For an infinite God to enter into relation with finite creatures in this way is for this God to have emptied Godself of certain divine attributes (since an all-powerful, always-acting God would leave no place for separate agents to freely initiate independent actions on their own behalf). The Greek word for this self-emptying is *kenosis*. Hence the Christology compatible with this position will be, above all, a kenotic Christology.

The question is: How far is this kenosis, this "coming alongside" and suffering with, to be extended? When does belief end and metaphor take over? Let me describe the possibility in terms of a series of "what ifs." What if divine action involves more than a passive responsiveness to the world and human experience? What if God took some initiative in the process? Indeed, what if God responded to the dogged concreteness of human experience—our need to comprehend general truths via individual experiences—by making Godself known in particular persons, or even, possibly, in an especially clear way in one individual?

Some people experience no hesitation in the face of this possibility and are ready to move on to the next step in the argument. But others find themselves not quite able to develop the belief that this has happened, even though they view it as an attractive possibility, and even one that they could make the focus of their religious faith. In earlier publications, Steven Knapp and I have described this response as a *possibilistic faith*: the response to a compelling possibility that one can accept and live by, even while lacking the requisite historical proofs that it has actually occurred.[10] For those who orient their values, and even their lives, in the mode of possibilistic acceptance, what is indispensable for Christian theology is not historical proof of the uniqueness of Jesus, but rather some way to conceive the Jesus event as involving an act of God. Believers and possibilists alike require an understanding of "God in Christ" that would involve a two-way relationship between God and this individual person, expressed through acts on the part of both.[11] That is, the account needs to speak of actions that Jesus performed and attitudes that he manifested toward God that helped to constitute his uniqueness before God, as well as of actions that God performed that helped to make the Jesus event revelatory of the divine nature.

An Emergent Theology in Outline

Christian theologians have always drawn on the conceptual frameworks or philosophical systems available in their day. True, scripture and traditional affirmations (for example, the creeds) constrained the answers that were given, and theologians returned again and again to a central set of questions (the questions of Peter Lombard, the major systematic loci of Phillip Melanchthon). As the modern era progressed, however, and as new scientific knowledge emerged, many theologians came to believe that the philosophical frameworks that had once guided systematic theologians were no longer adequate.[12] The story of modern theology is the story of finding new answers to the traditional questions in light of things humanity has learned over the last several hundred years.

I agree that there is a core set of topics that a Christian theology is expected to address: Christology, pneumatology, ecclesiology, eschatology, and so forth. But the scaffolding—the organizing framework that one uses to respond to these questions—is not given once and for all; theology is "always reformed, always reforming." It remains valuable to see how the use of new frameworks and organizing principles affects the answers one gives to the classic questions. Hence I would now like to ask: What would a systematic theology look like if developed out of the context of emergent thinking? How would one be inclined to respond to the traditional loci using the framework of emerging systems?

Consider the following responses to nine of the traditional loci.

1. The Doctrine of Creation

The whole range of scientific data concerning emergent systems can be incorporated in the doctrine of the created world. It is not the place of a theological doctrine of creation to replace science, but to acknowledge its findings.[13] Thus all scientific detail on emergent systems in evolution found elsewhere in this book and in other publications[14] becomes relevant to a revised doctrine of creation.

Emergent thinking represents a sort of upwardly ascending arrow, since it is hard to avoid the meta-scientific questions that it raises. Is there a further stage of emergence beyond the level of mind, such as spirituality or spirit? Is mind utterly without precedent, or does emerging mind reflect something of the nature of whatever Cause preceded the Big Bang and helped to produce it? If mind is not a strange anomaly in the universe, but somehow reflects the nature of its ultimate Source, could it be that the Source also includes other personal qualities—or, at least, that it is not-less-than, personal, as I argued in the previous chapter? If so, might that Source, *qua* personal cause, not also have intentions regarding the evolution of the universe, and might it sometimes act in such a way as to further those purposes? The fusion of emergent systems and belief in a Creator God, I have argued, represents the strongest available answer to these questions.

2. The Doctrine of God

As I will argue in more detail in part III, the doctrine of God that best allows belief in divine action to be synthesized with modern science in general, and with the sciences of emergence in particular, is panentheism.[15] Panentheism is frequently defined as the theological view that the world is in some sense contained within God, although God is also more than the world.[16]

In chapter 6, I suggested that it makes sense to move from the emergent levels of consciousness—intentionality, self-awareness, rational reflection, artistic creativity, and the like—to the notion of spirit. Given the multiple levels of causality defended in earlier chapters, this could mean that one is justified in speaking of the causal activity of spirit in connection with the phenomena of consciousness. Although I once thought otherwise, I now doubt that one can locate this type of causal activity as a further stage in natural history, merely by extrapolating further from the causal activity of organisms and from more rudimentary forms of mental causation. Higher-order causal activity in nature may well help to give an account of the causal activity of God, but it is not by itself sufficient for that purpose.

Note that panentheism is consistent with most of the traditional attributes of God.[17] No major modifications need to be made to traditional understandings of divine wisdom, goodness, love, grace, mercy, long-suffering, righteousness, or veracity. The doctrines of divine omnipotence and sovereignty do however need to be modified, insofar as panentheism implies that God has freely chosen to limit God's *a priori* omnipotence in order to allow other free centers of conscious agency to come into being. Features of the created world that might have been otherwise, such as certain of the laws of nature, represent free divine decisions. But if God is to remain consistent with God's own nature, God is now constrained by those decisions, which means that God's present power is further limited. Even more clearly, the doctrine of God's immutability can no longer be asserted of God unequivocally. The primordial nature of God is indeed unchanging, but the personal responsive side of God is genuinely emergent, in the sense that it comes to encompass new experiences as it enters into new relations with creatures.

Panentheism allows one to draw inferences both from God to world (for example, *imago Dei* arguments) and from features of the world to the nature of God. For example, I have elsewhere defended the panentheistic analogy as a means for comprehending God's relationship to the world.[18] The panentheistic analogy suggests that the relationship of God and the world is in some ways analogous to the relationship of our minds and our bodies. "Mind" is not merely a part of the body, and "mental" means more than the brain taken as a whole. Yet mind is also not totally separate from the body. Similarly, panentheists do not conceive of God as outside of or separate from the world. Rather, we understand divine immanence in the strongest possible sense, such that relatedness to the world becomes (and for some panentheists, always was) an essential part of the divine-being-in-relation.[19]

3. The God-World Relation and Divine Action

We return to the divine action debate in more detail in part IV, but a first sketch of the position is essential here. Several decades of work on the divine action question have resulted in some very clear constraints. Doctrines of creation have always held that, if God exists, God must be viewed in some way as the ultimate source of the natural world. Yet a world that is to provide a stable context for intentional action will need to possess its own integrity and order. On the one hand, if one wishes to preserve the doctrine of providence, one must retain the language of a divine lure. On the other hand, if one moves from that conclusion to affirming a divine manipulation of physical events and human decisions, such that God sometimes directly brings about results in the natural world without the mediation of natural ("secondary") causes, the problem of evil becomes insurmountable (see chapter 15), for there are innumerable events in the world that a benevolent God would presumably prevent if free and able to do so. Furthermore, as we will see below, if we imagine that God can suspend natural law at will, both the integrity of the natural order and the significance of human action are called into question.

Negatively, to say that complex phenomena like life or mind lend themselves to theological explanation is to say that they cannot be given a reductive explanation in terms of lower levels of "natural" functioning, which is exactly what emergence says. But it isn't as if God gets into the picture for the very first time when one particular level (say, thought) emerges from the levels that preceded it. The beauty of panentheism is that, if it is right, the energies at work at the physical level are *already* divine energies, and physical regularities are already expressions of the fundamental constancy of the divine character (as Eastern Orthodox theologians have long taught).[20] Thus I believe that panentheism brings an indispensable framework to the study of emergent systems, for if the world remains within and is permeated by the divine, then it is possible to speak of divine purposes and goals being expressed even at the stage at which there are no other actually conscious agents. Even the lawful behavior of the natural world can now be an expression or manifestation of the divine character or intentionality.

Because physical phenomena do not function with anything we can identify as "focal" or direct purpose, we may speak of them as manifesting only God's "autonomic agency," just as the actions of our own bodies are divided between autonomic processes and focal intentions. For the panentheist, the regularities of natural law represent the autonomic or, as it were, habitual operation of divine action apart from God's specific or focal intentions. By contrast, should God sometimes consciously influence conscious thought processes in humans or other animals, we would speak of these as focal divine actions.

As organisms evolve and begin to behave in more complex ways, panentheism allows one to speak of a category of divine action that is not merely autonomic—that is, not completely explicable as a mechanical result of God's autonomic agency—but that nevertheless stops short of focal purpose. We can speak of the central features of the biological realm as reflecting the divine character and influence without claiming that kidneys or amoebas themselves possess the goals of functioning as they do. After all, actual purposes can be predicated only of purposive beings. A colony of bacteria functions in a purposive manner without possessing actual purposes. The colony behaves *as if* it really desired to nourish itself and grow, but it does not desire growth in the conscious way that you might now desire a glass of orange juice.

Herein lies the crux of a theological interpretation of the natural world. Like physical regularities, emergent biological regularities reflect the divine character. Yet here, because organisms also behave in a purposive manner, there is a place for speaking of divine influence in principle. The influence in question must be intermediate between the conscious influence that is possible in relation to conscious beings and the apparent impossibility of influence (outside of natural law) in physics. If biological organisms are indeed more than machines, and if it is correct to ascribe drives, strivings, and non-conscious goals to them, then there is room for influence on these goals.

The idea here is to try to understand what are the distinctive forms of influence or causation that one finds in biology but not in physics or chemistry, and then to ask whether they offer room, in principle, for divine influence. If biological explanations are ultimately law-based in the strong way that physical explanations are, then there will be no room for divine influence. If they exhibit causal influences analogous to the way that one thought can (non-nomologically) influence another, then there will be room in principle.

Scientists have only recently broken away from the dream that biological phenomena could be derived from the laws of physics. Only recently have some begun to argue that information can exercise an emergent causal role. Could it be that biological information, or information from even higher levels of organization, could function as a form of divine influence, as Arthur Peacocke and others have argued?[21] We do know that the behavior of all biological systems, from genes to complex organisms, is influenced by broader environmental factors. Could this provide an opening for a broader sort of "top-down" influence? It's now widely acknowledged that form (structure) is crucial to biological explanations. Could a neo-Aristotelian version of "formal causality" be developed that might be of both biological and theological interest?[22] These remain speculative but important openings to reflection on divine action in dialogue with the sciences.

4. Christology

Emergent thinking links most naturally with a kenotic Christology, that is, a doctrine of Christ that emphasizes his voluntary self-emptying in the sense of Philippians 2. According to kenotic Christologies, Jesus remains both a revelation of the nature of God and an exemplar for humanity in a no less profound sense than in classical theology. In this Christology, Jesus actualized a potentiality that each human enjoys as one who is made in the image of God, living a life of perfect devotion to God and acknowledging the true relationship of creature to Creator in every thought and action. Panentheists believe that all are located within the divine presence in no less a sense than Jesus was. But gaps remain between what God wills and what we will. This is the core insight of the doctrine of sin. By contrast, according to Christian belief no such gaps existed in the life of Jesus. He alone perfectly lived a life of perfect union with God.

In the more liberal forms of emergent theology one finds affirmations of the resurrection of "the Spirit of Christ," but not a physical resurrection of the individual man Jesus. The act of God that produces the resurrection raises the Spirit of Christ, the Spirit or Counselor "whom the Father will send in my name, [who] will teach you all things and will remind you of everything I have said to you" (John 14:26). Because of this act of God, after Jesus' death the "mind of Christ"—Jesus' surrender of his will to the Father's will, for which God "highly exalted him" (Phil 2:9)—remained available to his disciples and later to their followers in the church.

Some readers will not be able to form a belief in the continuing personal existence of Jesus, whereas others will insist upon the physical resurrection of Jesus and hence his continuing existence as a person. I will not be able to resolve that debate here. Note, however, that in either case one may still believe that the divine power and presence is manifested whenever a person adopts, internalizes, and thereby shares in the "mind of Christ"—the mind of the one who prayed, "not my will, but Thine be done" (Luke 22:42). Allowing the will of God to work in one's own actions and "mind" can produce a mode of being in which not the individual human ego but the divinely intended outcome is decisive (Phil 2:5). To be "in Christ"—Paul's favorite description of the mode of Christian existence[23]—means to subordinate one's own will to the will of the divine, echoing Jesus' basic prayer, "may your will be done" (Matt 26:42; compare with Matt 6:10).

What is attractive about this approach to Christology is that it already incorporates the divine act into Jesus' God-consciousness. It is not as if there were a description of Jesus' will and actions on the one hand and, on the other, a separate metaphysical superstructure of divine intervention added on top of it. Instead, to describe the historical Jesus as I have done *just is* to give an account of divine involvement. In virtue of continually subsuming his will to the divine will, Jesus caused his actions to become *part of* the divine act. There are not two actions, but one. Jesus manifests the divine power by subsuming his will to God's. At the same time (or for the same reason, or in virtue of the same act), God used Jesus to manifest the divine will and bring about the divine intentions.

This fusion of human and divine is what was right about traditional "two-natures" Christologies and the traditional doctrine of "incarnation." It is just that emergent theologians now locate the fusion in *shared action and attitude* rather than in some *a priori* ontological story. As process theologians describe divine action as "the lure of God" (Lewis Ford), and as traditional theology refuses to separate the act of God and the revelation of God, we too might understand God to be genuinely revealed through human agents who seek to submit themselves to God's will.[24]

For some, it is easiest to think of this as a series of "what ifs." What if God, by an intentional divine self-limitation, chooses to bring about God's purposes in the world only through the actions of worldly creatures? And what if a particularly clear model, or *the* uniquely clear model, for this kenotic revelation comes in the self-submission of Jesus to what he called "the will of the Father"?[25] Finally, what if Jesus' acts of intentional self-submission are matched not by an impersonal and undifferentiated transmission of divine energy, but rather by an equally personal and specific act of acceptance and guidance on God's part?

Naturally, there are more liberal positions than the one I have defended here, positions in which the entire Jesus narrative is understood as a series of purely human events, with no divine act involved. I have not shown that the biblical and historical evidence *requires* a stronger sense of divine action than in the more liberal readings. Instead, the goal here is to show that another view is also possible: that the Jesus event—and by extrapolation, other events in the natural world—can also credibly be understood as representing one or more divine acts. And out of this combination of human and divine emerges a combined act or series of actions which Christians call the revelation of God in Jesus Christ.

5. Pneumatology

The understanding of Spirit is central to emergent theology. Insofar as they accept the emergence of mind and spirit within evolutionary history, these theologies diverge from panpsychist and panexperientialist positions, which make Spirit an inherent element of the world from the beginning. We likewise eschew all dichotomies between Spirit and matter or between Spirit and body, following the lead of emergent theories of human personhood. Even if the divine Spirit precedes all creation, every manifestation of Spirit in the world depends essentially on the evolutionary process.

Nor can the divine Spirit be a timeless entity standing immutably outside the flow of cosmic history. The divine spirit—by which I mean that aspect of the divine being that correlates with the spirit of which we have knowledge in ourselves—must also be temporal, the emergent result of a long-term process of intimate relationship with beings in the world. In this view, then, Spirit is not a fundamental ontological category but an emergent form of complexity that living things within the world begin to manifest at a certain stage in their development. A theological corrective must be made to the "straight emergence" view, however. The Spirit that emerges corresponds to the Spirit who was present from the beginning, and this Spirit's actions—both its initial creation and its continual lure—help bring about the world and its inhabitants as we know them. Insofar as this emergent theology remains panentheistic, it holds that the physical world was already permeated by and contained within the Spirit of God long before cosmic evolution gave rise to life and mind.

Gone, in this view, are Spirit-body dualities and those claims for immutability that stem from the world of Greek metaphysics, which once served as the philosophical authority for theology's fundamental categories. No place remains for an initial creation of humanity with the dual substances of *res cogitans* and *res extensa*. Aside from this change, many of the attributes that theologians commonly associate with Spirit can still be affirmed. It is just that these qualities now become features of ever-changing entities in the world, rather than necessary features of an unchanging substrate from which the world's qualities are drawn.

6. Anthropology

In light of the foregoing points, it is clear that the doctrine of anthropology will play a larger role than in many traditional theologies. As we saw above in connection with the knowledge of God, emergent theology begins with an understanding of human beings as bio-cultural agents in the context of evolutionary history. Our bio-cultural existence gives us some initial understanding of the nature of God as agent, though it must then be "corrected" to be appropriate to the role of God as the ground and destiny of all things. In other words, emergent theology (like other forms of dipolar theism) includes two stages: the stage of deriving what can be known of the divine agent through our own experience of agency (the consequent nature), and the stage of modifying that understanding in order that it can be appropriate to the nature of a creator who preceded the universe as a whole (the antecedent nature).

This corrected view of God in turn contributes an essential element to anthropology. Emergent theologians will never deny or overrule what is revealed of human nature through the study of biological and cultural evolution. They will however supplement that understanding by including the perspective of the *imago Dei*, the image and nature of God. By taking this step, theology inevitably adds a normative dimension that natural science by itself could never supply. Natural science tells us who we now are and how we have come to be this way. But theology, by viewing humanity from the standpoint of a perfect creator, holds out a standard for what we *should* be, as creatures made in the image of God. For Christians, this model is inherently christological. It involves emulation of the one who was fully human insofar as he was fully related to God.

When panentheism is developed in a manner consistent with emergent thinking, human thought or intention appears as (at least) a three-level phenomenon, with a distinct type of divine influence corresponding to each level. First, since thought is built upon the enduring regularities within the one physical cosmos, it (like everything else) reflects the constant character of the all-pervading God. Given the framework of panentheism, we may view these regularities as an expression of autonomic divine agency. Second, like other forms of activity in the biosphere, the human neurological system is not *only* conditioned by the autonomic or natural-law level, but also by the quasi-intentional level of biological drives and goals. It is thus open to the sort of biological influence or constraint described above. Finally, if human consciousness is indeed an emergent property of our complex neurophysiological structure, then humans (and perhaps some other animals) also exercise a distinctive form of causation: conscious agency. This would in principle allow God to influence our thoughts and motives at the same mental level that other persons influence them, even though the means would be rather different. A full theological account could then describe the modes in which God influences these emergent intentional systems (persons) via the sphere of human-divine interaction which we call the realm of spirit, including personal religious experience, culture, art, philosophy, and theology itself.

7. Ecclesiology

The church is defined, as formerly, in terms of those who follow Christ and live "in Christ." But the church, like all finite things in general, is an emergent and emerging reality. Thus the original horizon of understanding cannot control all present understandings of the church, its founder, and its role.[26] Because Jesus remains the exemplar of *kenosis*, the reports on and early interpretations of his life and teachings remain crucial. But such an exemplary role will not quite manage to support the doctrine of the "plenary inspiration" of scripture, as if the context of the origination of the church were by itself sufficient to determine its actions today. Christians are continually confronted with new situations and ideas never before encountered by humanity or the church, and believers must respond to them with new forms of the self-emptying that Paul thinks of as the mind of Christ: "Have this mind among yourselves, which is yours in Christ Jesus" (Phil 2:5).

If the church is an emergent and continually emerging community, it shares a situation and fate with all of humanity. Emergent theologians refuse to separate God from the world in the interest of preserving the divine purity. Hence, for similar reasons, they decline to fundamentally separate the church from the world. The church must be distinguished by behaviors that mirror the nature and being of God, as well as by a corporate identity that seeks to emulate the personal identity of the one who said, "not my will, but Thine be done." A fitting theology for the emerging church will seek not to be more than human, but to be human in light of that toward which humanity is being lured; not to be anti-scientific, but to find through science some intimations of the nature of God; not to be anti-intellectual, but to be more insightfully intellectual; not to eschew human moral reflection and striving, but to incorporate that striving within a theistic framework; not to be world-transcending, but to embrace a world that is in turn embraced by God.

8. Soteriology

An emergent theology will begin not with a specific narrative of fall and redemption, but (as Paul Tillich began) with the structural difference between God and creation, between infinite and finite, between perfect and imperfect. As we saw in considering anthropology, emergent theology embraces the descriptive account of the human being but supplements it with a normative account of how humankind will look when it is true to its nature as *imago Dei*. This structural difference, and not the primordial myth of an original offense and punishment, provides the basis for introducing the concept of sin. The narrative of the fall remains indispensable for its symbolic functions but is not doctrinally foundational. As Tillich also saw, the structural difference between infinite and finite is mirrored in an intense existential experience of sin. Not only with our minds do we conceive of the structural difference between God and ourselves, for every human being knows *akrasia* (weakness of will), self-centeredness, and the inability to do as one wishes to do (as potently described by Paul in Romans 7).

An emergent theology cannot endorse an absolute dichotomy between the "old man" and the "new man," of the sort sometimes presupposed in the Pauline doctrine of salvation. Emergence thinking is anti-dualistic, seeking always for the continuities that underlie even the appearance of radical novelty in the world. We no longer need to divide the world into two sharply opposed camps, the reprobate and the redeemed. Rather, the doctrine of salvation now takes on a structure closer to the traditional doctrine of *sanctification*. The new self, the mind of Christ, is continually emerging as individuals align their wills with the will of God. Such an alignment is a matter of *degree*. The process of living more and more of one's life in greater and greater conformity to the will of God is a gradual and never-ending process.

Clearly, this approach to soteriology represents some revision of traditional Christian teachings. There are greater or lesser costs associated with any revision of the tradition. This is one in particular that we should be more than willing to pay. In its day, the dichotomy of "you're either in or you're out" contributed to an understanding of the church that separated the lives of Christians much too sharply from the lives of other persons. Sadly, it continues to do so today. Ascribing to an individual the eternal state of "being saved" may have fit well within the mostly atemporal framework of pre-modern metaphysics and anthropology, but it accords poorly with the insights into pervasive process and change that we owe to emergence theories.[27] The understanding of the church as a collection of redeemed individuals, ontologically distinct from all others, also produced a view of the relationship between Christianity and other religions, particularly Judaism, that should strike us today as deeply morally disturbing.

To comprehend the cosmic process of emerging spirit in its full richness and complexity, one must draw on every available source, including all the world's religious and wisdom traditions. The thought that God would reveal the divine nature only and exclusively to one people or group, who subsequently enjoy a state of blessing and closeness to God not matched by any other individuals or groups, represents a triumphalism inappropriate to a kenotic Christian self-understanding. In the history of the church this triumphalism also served to justify the most atrocious of actions. The entire picture ill accords with the self-emptying of Jesus, whose "mind" is to be the example for his church.

I find no place within emergent theology for substitutionary atonement, ransom metaphors, or the focus on the need for a sacrifice to propitiate the wrath of an angry God.

9. Eschatology

According to Wolfhart Pannenberg, the end of history already took place in the death and resurrection of Jesus Christ (*prolepsis*), such that the outcome is already certain. Eschatology is not less important for emergent theologians, though they are likely to view precise predictions of the final outcome as rather less certain. We affirm that God set the process of emergence in motion, intending that the creation would take on higher and higher levels of complexity, and hence more subtle and intimate relationships with the divine, thereby allowing more and more of the nature of God to be experienced by the creation. Still, the present understanding of the process of emergence does not provide much information on the ultimate culmination of this historical process, in which God brings all things to Godself.

Nonetheless, were history merely to end with the "heat death" of the universe, it would be rather difficult to conceive what God might have intended by creating these emergent processes at the outset, only to allow them to be condemned in the end to ultimate futility. Why would God engage in relationship with this world—a relationship that on our view affects the very being of God—if the whole process will one day simply evaporate into nothingness? It is the impossibility of resting content with such a response that intensifies the hope of Christians (and others) for a future of the universe in which God becomes "all in all."

Panentheism fits naturally in such an eschatological perspective. John Polkinghorne has argued that only at the end of time can we conceive of a state where all things are within God and God is all things.[28] I disagree with his contention that such a panentheistic closeness must be confined to the end of history, but I do concur that panentheism presupposes a *telos* in which the world conforms more and more fully to the divine character.

How fully will the eschatological hope be fulfilled? How fully *should* it be fulfilled? Many hope at present not only that God will preserve what is most valuable in the human race (and the world as a whole), conforming it more fully to God's character, but also that those whom they love will be preserved in something like their present state (including, in Polkinghorne's view, perhaps even the family pet!).[29] Many cannot imagine existence without something like their present body, so they hope that it too will be preserved or in some sense replicated. At what point do these hopes become the projection of the only way of life we know, and to what extent are they theologically supported? How much of what you currently know as your identity could disappear before the anticipated future state becomes so dissociated from you that it is no longer reasonable for you to long for it?

According to classic versions of process theology stemming from Whitehead's *Process and Reality*, the only thing one can reasonably hope for is "objective immortality," that is, that all of one's thoughts, feelings and individual reactions will be preserved eternally in the unchanging and unending experience of God. Marjorie Suchocki has sought to extend Whitehead's thought so that it can include also subjective immortality, the continuing existence of the individual subjective principle.[30] Whether or not Suchocki is successful in integrating the hope for subjective immortality with process eschatology, she has correctly seen that the eschaton must be conceived in such a fashion that it remains relevant to individual agents in the present.

The key point to underscore about eschatology is the epistemic point: we do not know the universe's final fate. We find ourselves immersed in a process of continual emergence that evidences tendencies but does not produce final certainties. One need only consider the staggering and unexpected developments in technology over the last, say, twenty years, such as the growth of the world wide web, or the dismal failure of the alleged science of futurology, to realize that the novelty and uncertainty of cultural evolution far exceeds the capacity of human reason, or even imagination! Epistemic humility is a virtue in all branches of theology. In the field of eschatology, this virtue becomes a necessity. "Dear friends, now we are children of God, and what we will be has not yet been made known. But we know that when he appears, we shall be like him, for we shall see him as he is" (1 John 3:2).

➤ Conclusion

We have seen how particular positions on human subjectivity point toward particular theories about the nature of God. Construing the human person as an emergent result of the evolutionary process will therefore have deep effects on one's theology. I have sought to do justice to those effects by outlining a new emergent theology and showing how it might respond differently to nine of the major loci of traditional theology. At the same time, the science-theology debate is a two-way street, involving what Robert Russell calls a "creative mutual interaction." One's theology also affects one's view of human nature, one's interpretation of the scientific results, and one's beliefs about the long-term fate of the universe.

Humans live in a world of pervasive process, a world historical to the core. Each of our distinctive attributes is the result of millions of years of evolution. In us, the evolutionary process has produced self-conscious, reasoning, questioning creatures. We are the animal that has begun to pose to itself metaphysical questions—questions about the universe's ultimate origin and final fate, and questions about the meaningfulness of our own existence. The strangeness of our plight stems in part from the realization that we may have emerged from an origin radically different from ourselves. This is true if we as conscious beings are the products of unconscious physical laws and blind forces, but it is no less true if we as finite beings owe our existence to infinite conscious Spirit.

The Christian tradition is based on the daring wager that the latter option is true. But if we are the products of a conscious creative choice and not the results of a random process alone, then our Creator cannot *also* have emerged through evolution in the same way. This means that, in the midst of a world of pervasive emergence and decay, we set our hopes on the existence of One whose purposes span the Before and After. Here, in this grey realm between the permutations of matter and the becoming of Spirit, and in a dialectic of knowledge and hope, lies Christian faith and Christian proclamation.[31]

PART THREE

Panentheism

8 *An* Introduction *to* Panentheism

IN PUBLICATIONS OVER A NUMBER OF YEARS I'VE DEFENDED PANENTHEISM as a natural outcome of certain crucial developments in modern philosophy, as a framework for speaking of divine action in the context of modern science, and as a response to specific conundrums within Christian systematic theology. Reviewing these publications, however, has made me think more deeply about the most basic question: How can one make an effective case for panentheism with a discussion partner who is skeptical about this theological program?

The simple definition of panentheism is the view that the world is in some sense "within" God, although God is also more than the world. The *Oxford Dictionary of the Christian Church* defines panentheism as "the belief that the Being of God includes and penetrates the whole universe, so that every part of it exists in Him but (as against pantheism) that His Being is more than, and is not exhausted by, the universe." Arthur Peacocke, a panentheist, thus speaks of God as "the circumambient Reality in which the world persists and exists," quoting the famous passage from Augustine's *Confessions* (VII, 7):

> I set before the sight of my spirit the whole creation, whatsoever we can see therein (as sea, earth, air, stars, trees, mortal creatures). . . . But Thee, O Lord, I imagined on every part environing and penetrating it, though every way infinite: as if there were a sea, everywhere and on every side, through unmeasured space, one only boundless sea, and it contained within it some sponge, huge, but bounded; that sponge must needs, in all its parts, be filled with that unmeasurable sea: so conceived I Thy creation, itself finite, full of Thee, the Infinite. . . .[1]

A more technical, and now classical, definition is provided by Charles Hartshorne:

> God is not just the all of "other" things; but yet all other things are literally in him. He is not just the whole of ordinary individuals, since he has unity of experience, and all other individuals are objects of this experience, which is no mere sum of its objects; moreover, his identifying "personality traits" are entirely independent of any set of ordinary actual individuals whatever. To be himself he does not need *this* universe, but only *a* universe, and only contingently does he even contain this particular actual universe. The mere essence of God contains no universe. We are truly "outside" the divine essence, though inside God.[2]

Hartshorne grounds the "more than" in divine subjectivity: because God comprehends all things into the unity of a single divine awareness, and none of the things or subjects comprehended by God does the same thing, God must be more than any of the objects comprehended. But there are other, more traditional ways to construe the "more than" as well. For example, Joseph Bracken has shown a sense in which Aquinas's talk of the ubiquity of God amounts to a sort of panentheism. Since the effect of divine causality is to communicate existence to creatures, God is present to creatures in the most intimate way possible: in their very existence or being. Aquinas holds that "the mover and the thing moved are together in the act of movement, that is, there is nothing intermediate between them." He also maintains that "creatures are in God insofar as they participate in the act of being which belongs by nature to God but which can be extended to creatures in proportion to their finite essences."[3]

I have previously argued[4] that numerous strands in post-Cartesian metaphysics point in the direction of panentheism. Specifically, I attempted to show the weaknesses in Spinoza's immensely influential "dual-aspect monism," according to which the-world-as-mental and the-world-as-physical are extensionally equivalent (see chapter 9). Spinoza's dual-aspect theory admits that we can view the one universe now as a collection of ideas, now as a collection of particles, even though in the end only the one world exists. This theory does not provide an adequate place for the *activity* of thinking, as one can see when one examines the series of criticisms of Spinoza's view running from Lessing, Jacobi, and Mendelssohn to Kant, Fichte, and Schelling. Only when the active agent of thought is included can one do justice to the mental. When applied to God, this criticism tells against Spinoza's famous equation, *deus siva natura*. For God is not adequately conveyed by the idea that contains all other ideas (Spinoza's *idea ideae*).[5] God must also be the agent or consciousness that thinks this idea. Since the world cannot at the same time be that which thinks the world, God must be more than the world.

Similar arguments have been made (by Schleiermacher,[6] Schelling, and Hegel, among others) from the idea of the infinite. What is infinite must include the finite, otherwise the infinite will be limited by that which lies outside it and hence no longer infinite. At the same time, as infinite it must also be more than the finite that it includes. Thus the essential infinity of God will require both that God include all other things within the expanse of the divine nature *and* that God as essentially infinite should be more than any of the finite things or sets of things contained within the divine being.[7]

In recent years scholars have advanced a variety of reasons that might lead one to adopt panentheism. Consider this typology of some of the central options:

- One might hold that classical philosophical theism, "supernaturalistic" theism, or traditional theism is no longer viable, without being convinced that atheism is the most compelling answer.
- One might be convinced that panentheism is more compatible than traditional theism with particular results in physics or biology, or with common features shared across the scientific disciplines, such as the structure of emergence.
- One may be convinced of the truth or preferability of a particular metaphysical position (for example, process philosophy, German Idealism); and panentheism either lies closer to, or is actually entailed by, that metaphysical position.
- One might hold that panentheism can do a better job at preserving certain religious beliefs than classical theism can. So, for example, one might argue that viewing the world as within God allows for the development of an adequate theory of divine action, whereas classical theism, if it succeeded in avoiding deism, could only support an "interventionist" theory of divine action.
- In the process of searching for a mediating metaphysic between Western and Eastern religious philosophical systems, one might come to believe that panentheism provides the most convincing available answer.
- One might find panentheism religiously more viable or more attractive than the alternatives. Some have argued, for instance, that traditional Christian theism is burdened by unanswerable objections such as the problem of evil, whereas panentheistic theologies are able to avoid these objections.
- One might be convinced that classical theism has unacceptable ethical or political implications, while panentheism does not have these implications.

The recent debate, however, reveals a rather remarkable breakdown in the actual arguments for and against panentheistic theologies. In order to understand what kind of a debate is involved in pro-and-con discussions concerning panentheism, it is helpful to step back from the heated exchanges concerning panentheism over the last few decades and to attempt a few summary observations.

First, a quick survey of the literature reveals that panentheism is advocated much more often by philosophical theologians than by systematic or biblical theologians. The term is used most frequently by authors who are wrestling with connections between theology and other disciplines: science, metaphysics, ethics and social-political philosophy, or the contemporary cultural context. The shared argument among these authors runs something like this: "Theology faces some serious difficulties when it enters into interdisciplinary debates, and traditional doctrinal language has not been effective in responding to these difficulties. By contrast, a panentheistic understanding of the God-world relationship is able to make connections with other academic fields. Until we find a conceptual structure that does a *better* job of addressing these problems, we are justified in turning to panentheism as a framework for making sense of God-language in the face of its detractors. Even if this move involves some revisions vis-à-vis traditional formulations, it is a cost one should be willing to pay."

Second, a survey of many contemporary arguments will reveal how difficult it is to express shared criteria for deciding the panentheism question, for even the most rigorous argument in one category may fail to interest those whose motivation stems from another field or set of questions. Likewise, thinkers who are swayed by one or another criticism *against* panentheism are sometimes unmoved by even the strongest arguments in its favor. For some, the steps that panentheism takes away from traditional Christian formulations already constitute sufficient reason to reject it.

Perhaps the best case for panentheism, then, would be a cumulative one. It goes something like this: because there are so many difficulties and dissatisfactions with classical theism today, and because panentheism offers a more attractive response to various (theological, philosophical, ethical, social-political) difficulties, it provides the more compelling overall model of the God-world relation. A cumulative, multi-faceted defense of this sort, we argue, shows that recent work on panentheism constitutes a vital research program in theology,[8] one that brings important new resources to unresolved philosophical and theological debates. If I can show that panentheism opens up new solutions to theology's contemporary difficulties, and if classical philosophical theism is not able to do the same, then one will have reasons for pursuing the panentheist option.

In this introductory chapter, I can only develop one or two specific arguments in any detail. I thus limit myself to laying out two of most important defenses of panentheism, one stemming from developments in the modern "metaphysics of the subject" and the other from the theory of emergence as presented in part II. Combined with other arguments elsewhere, I believe these two arguments are sufficient to advance panentheism as a very serious option within constructive theology today.

➤ On God and Persons

Theologians in the twentieth century were particularly drawn to person-language. Rarely do recent defenses of the continuing relevance of theism in today's intellectual climate or "in light of modern science" explain the God-world relationship in terms of interacting substances, for example, as one might have done in the fourth century. And contemporary philosophers, though they have worked in detail on the problems of personhood, have made scant use of the concepts of *hypokeimenon*, *hypostasis*, and *substantia*.

Instead, when theists attempt to explain why theism should still be viewed as a live option, they most often have recourse to language about persons. God's nature, theists argue, is not less than personal, even though it is also infinitely more. God is a person-like agent, a not-less-than-personal agent, who forms intentions and acts in the world. For trinitarian theologians, the divine being consists of three personal centers of activity, and in these person-like relations *ad extra* God lures and apprehends the world. Indeed, person-based arguments are sometimes even used against panentheists: panentheism must be false, it's sometimes said, because we humans really are persons—agents who engage in personal relationships and who initiate personal activity within the world—whereas panentheism would render us merely "parts" of some larger, impersonal divine whole.

Unfortunately, however, "person" is not a self-explanatory category. Although the Latin term *persona* first arose in a context in which the metaphysics of substance was dominant, it has today largely lost contact with that particular context of origin. Indeed, one of the major reasons for panentheism's significance as a theological resource, I suggest, is that the "panentheistic analogy" provides a rigorous way of specifying what we mean when we apply person-language to God—a sort of rigor too often lacking in discussions of God and personhood.

In the struggle to re-establish a credible theory of personhood after the demise of substance-based theories, modern thinkers have turned to the natural sciences, sociobiology, and evolutionary psychology; to social sciences such as psychology, sociology, economics, and cultural anthropology; to history, literature, and the arts; and, of course, to metaphysical and theological reflection. Among the lessons that this modern "quest for the person" teaches[9] is that no simple appeal to an alleged "common-sense theory of the person" will suffice for rehabilitating the God-world relation. Contemporary deconstructive treatments of personhood alone, for example, are probably sufficient to undermine "common-sense" language about persons (especially the personhood of God!). For additional evidence, one need only consider the radically different understandings of personhood across the world's cultures and religious traditions.

Theologians in the Western traditions have typically maintained that the closest analogy for the relationship between God and humans is the person-to-person relationship, rather than the relation of impersonal forces or deterministic causes. "God relates to us as one person relates to other persons," it is often said, even if God remains infinitely more than "just a person."

Yet it's one thing to use the notion of personhood as an intuitive starting point, quite another to treat the assertion, "God is personal," as all the philosophical basis one needs for determining God's relation to the world. When theologians leave unexplained the sense in which God is personal, has intentions, or relates to the world in a personal fashion, these holes are not filled simply by turning to biblical theology for data on the God-world relationship or by providing a historical survey of the various things doctrinal theologians have said on the topic through the ages.[10]

If one were satisfied with this mode of proceeding, one might well have no motivation for developing a panentheistic theology. The trouble, however, is that the expression "relating to us as persons," especially when applied to God, merely expresses a desideratum. It's the place-holder for an answer, not the answer itself. Gesturing in the direction of personhood is not enough. Theology faces serious theoretical objections, and new conceptual work is necessary to answer them.

Central Moments in the Modern Philosophy of the Subject

The dawn of the modern period in the West coincided with a growing sense that inherited notions of the God-world relation were in trouble. Philosophers and theologians began to give new explications of what it means to be a person in the world—and what it would mean for an infinite God as Ground and Source of all that is to interact with the created world. Indeed, almost as soon as one formulates the question about personhood, one recognizes that the history of modern thought has been a continual attempt to find a metaphysics adequate to express what is meant by "personal being."

Descartes fired the opening salvo by sharply distinguishing persons from all other living things (a move that placed him solidly within the Aristotelian and much of the Scholastic tradition). Famously, he divided the world into *res extensa* and *res cogitans*. Body and mind are essentially different, and the human being consists of both. It is *res cogitans* that we first and fundamentally know ourselves to be.

Unfortunately, this turned out to be an unstable attempt at a solution. The mind-brain interaction proved impossible to specify conceptually in the Cartesian context—surely the pineal gland was not going to suffice! The problem was so intractable that one of Descartes's early followers, Malebranche, was driven to pay the extremely high ransom of occasionalism to avoid it. Perhaps at every instance where mind-body interaction should occur, God directly intervenes to cause the expected changes. For all Leibniz's brilliance, his metaphysical solution was no less expensive. Windowless monads contain all their properties essentially, such that an infinite intellect who knew your individual concept or "haecceity"[11] could predict all your actions. According to his doctrine of pre-established harmony, God chose the world in which all tendencies of monads would be coordinated perfectly, producing the fortuitous appearance that you are responding to the words on this page and that I am affected by the comments you send to me. The British Empiricists, quick to abandon a sinking ship, managed to jettison the notion of human substance altogether, settling finally (in David Hume's philosophy) for a view of the human subject as a "bundle of perceptions" without a discernible principle of metaphysical unity.

Kant provided a philosophically viable way of thinking of the self *sans* Cartesian dualism (albeit with some new dualisms of his own). As William James comments wryly, "At first, 'spirit and matter,' 'soul and body,' stood for a pair of equipollent substances quite on a par in weight and interest. But one day Kant undermined the soul and brought in the transcendental ego, and ever since then the bipolar relation has been very much off its balance."[12] The cost of Kant's move was to make each of the constitutive elements of the person primitive, rather than giving them a metaphysical grounding. On his view, there is input to the human knower from we-know-not-what (Kant called it *das Ding an sich*, or just "x"). Two forms of sensibility and twelve categories of the understanding, he held, are necessarily imposed by sentient beings on their perceptual input, though why this should be the case cannot ever be specified, even in principle. And the result is our experience of other persons and things in the world—the whole human world of experience that we inhabit, the only world we will ever know.

Nonetheless, one thing Kant did realize more clearly than anyone before him: basic to any metaphysics of personhood is an active principle, the activity of unifying diverse experiences into a single whole, which Kant called "the transcendental unity of apperception." To be a human subject is to transform a series of variegated inputs into the core experience of "thought by me" or "felt by me." Interestingly, Augustine had already recognized this phenomenon, as in the passage in the *Confessions* in which he speaks of an extended "present" of attention that is able to experience a temporally extended progression of musical notes as one single melody.[13] But Augustine, according to Kant, lacked an adequate "transcendental" framework for exploring the conditions of the possibility of being a subject, a uniquely human person. Certainly the German Idealists from Jacobi to Hegel went further in working out such a "phenomenology" than had any other thinkers in the Western tradition. An excellent example is Schleiermacher's collection of lectures on dialectics, in which the subjective experiencing and the objective "what is experienced" became the fundamental categories, from which he derived central theological conclusions such as the categories of *tranzendenter Grund* (God) and *Welt*.[14]

Clearly something new was afoot here. For the first time, major steps were being taken from the thing-based ontology of substances toward an ontology of living subjects. It turned out, however, that the entire furniture of metaphysics had to be rearranged. One simply can't get to subjects if one starts with substances in the sense of the Aristotelian tradition. As Hegel famously wrote in *The Phenomonology of Spirit*, being first had to be reconceived as subject (*Sein als Subjekt*). Contemporary theories of personhood—divine *or* human—ignore these developments at their peril.

Whether because of the horrors of German political history or because of the opacity of the German language, English-speaking philosophers and theologians have only partially appropriated the conceptual developments stemming from the explosion of thought between Kant and Hegel. In those few decades (say, 1770 to 1830), the ontology of personhood was rewritten and new foundations were established for a metaphysics of the subject. Fichte's *Science of Logic* (*Wissenschaftslehre*), for example, tried to defend a consistent version of "subjective idealism," the view that all things and all forms of change stem from the self-unfolding subject or ego. But this program, it turned out, faces an insuperable dilemma. Beginning with the finite subject leads (at best) to agnosticism about God, since God as absolute subject would stand outside of or above the dynamics of the developing self as presented in the *Science of Logic* itself. Yet beginning with the creative act of an infinite subject leads to agnosticism about *humans*, since the philosophy of subjective idealism could then no longer explain the process by which the finite ego—its own core principle—comes to be.[15]

By contrast, Schelling's early "objective idealism" followed Spinoza in beginning with the notion of the Absolute. His early attempt, although massively influential, ultimately failed, however, because the idealist principle of pure subjective activity—the synthetic activity of conscious awareness—cannot be derived from a starting point from which it is absent.

Already by 1802 Hegel realized that the answer to these dilemmas could only lie in a fusion of the insights of subjective and objective idealism. According to his own "dialectical idealism," *the activity of the emerging subject produces reality* in an iterating, dialectical process. In this process the subject is repeatedly confronted with an "other" (*das Andere seiner selbst*) and overcomes the difference in a new synthesis that both transcends and preserves (*hebt auf*) their difference. Thanks to this principle of dialectical movement, Hegel's core achievement, the old metaphysics of substance was finally replaced with a new metaphysics of subjectivity. In the new view, being has come to be understood as subject. The idealist theories of the structure of subjectivity now play the role that substance once played in understanding personhood, with no less sophistication and with greater success.

➤ From "Being as Subject" to Panentheism

Here is where panentheism enters: *this new framework for conceiving personal being, which was developed during the modern period from Descartes to Hegel, turns out to necessitate a rethinking of the God-world relationship.* One can't merely tack the new metaphysics of subjectivity onto the old metaphysics of substance with its separate notions of God and world.

Interestingly, Descartes had already seen that the substance idea was pointing in a different direction than the Scholastics had thought. In the *Principia* he wrote, "By substance we can understand nothing other than a thing which exists in such a way as to depend on no other thing for its existence. And there is only one substance which can be understood to depend on no other thing whatsoever, namely God."[16] Spinoza picked up the hint, appropriating it in a far bolder fashion than Descartes ever did. His *Ethics* is an extended argument for the claim that it makes more sense to say that *there is only one substance.* All things are then merely modes or affections of that one substance, that is, manners in which its infinite essence is expressed. Among the infinite attributes of the one whole, which Spinoza called *deus siva natura*, are thought and extension. If thought and extension cannot be separate types of substances, *à la* Descartes, they must be distinct aspects of the One (hence, again, Spinoza's "dual-aspect monism"). To every mode in the world corresponds an idea, and just as the modes proceed upward in an interlocking hierarchy to the physical totality that we call nature as a whole, so also the hierarchy of "ideas of ideas" proceeds upwards to the interlocking whole that he called God. For Spinoza the two are identical: *deus siva natura*—God, that is, Nature.

The trouble is that Spinoza was unable to conceptualize the principle of activity. Of course, he asserted that ideas were both active and passive, and he spoke of nature both as fact (*natura naturata*) and as activity (*natura naturans*). But he did not recognize that there must be a center of agency—what Kant called the "transcendental unity of apperception"—to serve as the unifying force behind any center of conscious experience. It is fascinating to observe how the commentaries of Spinoza's three most important interpreters prior to Kant (Lessing, Jacobi, and

Mendelssohn) gradually tug the Spinozistic system in the direction of an active unifying principle.

Were Spinoza to have added the transcendental unity of apperception, however, he could not have maintained the strict pantheism for which he is so famous, the complete unity of God and Nature. One can indeed speak of the whole of nature as corresponding to the idea of all ideas, but in order to preserve the attributes of both thought and extension one must then also add, above and beyond the totality of facts or ideas, *the active principle of thinking* that conceives all of those ideas. Note, however, that this active principle cannot be identical to the world, or to any part of the world, if it is to be able to form an idea of the world. It can only be an entity that is more than the world, that transcends it. Had Spinoza followed out the logic of his own position in this fashion, he would thus perforce have become a panentheist.

The critical literature on Kant, Fichte, Schelling, and Hegel describes how Spinoza served as a formative influence on each of these thinkers. All four of the core figures in the modern theory of the subject accepted some form of the transcendental unity of apperception. Hence all of them, tacitly or explicitly, accepted this modification of Spinoza in the direction of panentheism: Kant in the latter part of the first *Critique* and in the *Opus Postumum*, albeit in aphoristic form; Fichte in his contributions to the *Atheismusstreit* and especially in his later philosophy; Schelling most clearly in the essay, *On Human Freedom*; and Hegel throughout.

One other advance characterizes these four thinkers: the movement away from a medieval "metaphysics of perfection"—God understood primarily in terms of the logic of the most perfect being (*ens perfectissimum*)—to a new focus on the implications of divine infinity. Again, if space allowed, we could trace the influence of Spinoza's understanding of infinity on all subsequent modern thought about God.[17] The net result of these developments, seen perhaps most clearly in the work of Fichte and Hegel, was the insight that the infinite God could not exclude the finite. Two mistakes in particular were identified. Fichte showed in an early essay that God could not be conceived of as an infinite person.[18] Either God would be absolutely infinite, and in that case not limited by (hence not in relationship with) any other subjects, or God would be a person in relationship with (hence limited by) other persons, and hence not infinite. Hegel later argued that an infinite that stands over against a finite to which it must then be related is not truly infinite (*das schlechte Unendliche*). *The truly infinite includes the finite within itself.* If God is to be truly infinite, then God must include the world within Godself. As Hegel showed, this inclusion can be conceived without eliminating either the agency and essential finitude of created beings *or* the infinity and agency of God. The panentheism that results understands the finite world as logically contained within the infinite God. As this brief history shows, it arises as the inevitable byproduct of the modern theory of subjectivity. Put differently, the same approach to subjectivity that first managed to comprehend the distinctiveness of personhood also entails panentheism as the basis of the God-world relation.

The Panentheistic Analogy

As it turns out, these two major strands in the history of philosophical theology—the concepts of the infinite and the perfect—tend to link with monistic and pluralistic understandings of reality, respectively. In *The Problem of God in Modern Thought*, I tried to show that these two separate families of concepts—infinity-based ultimate unity, and perfection-based irreducible pluralism—help lay out the terrain on which modern theology moves. When one emphasizes the complete perfection of God, one has reason to separate all created, less-than-perfect beings and objects from the divine, because the perfection of God would be compromised if God took into Godself other objects before they had been sufficiently cleansed (sanctified) from their imperfection (sin). Much of the history of Calvinism exhibits the refinement of this logic. By contrast, the logic of the notion of infinity ultimately excludes anything that might be "outside" the infinite—all must be included within it.[19] The emergence of panentheism in the nineteenth century reflects the increasing influence of the concept of the infinite.

As neat as this conceptual division may appear, there are theological reasons to suspect that neither of the two approaches can stand on its own. On the one hand, a strong monism leaves inadequate place for individual difference or for the integrity of creation—precisely the criticism raised again and again against Spinoza's philosophy. On the other hand, a sharp distinction between God and world has led in the modern period to deism and to the apparent impossibility of divine action.[20]

What to do, then? When two factors are both desirable yet neither can stand alone, one looks to the possibility of combining them. Admittedly, the rules of metaphysical debate tend to push one to choose one option or the other in the interest of simplicity and systematicity. But must we consent to this pressure? Sometimes the conjunction supplies the better answer; sometimes the position that's more adequate to the data is the one that is less simple. Perhaps, among the options, the best is the one that preserves both the essential, eternal nature of God and the essentially temporal process of God's relations to others. Herein lies the continuing attraction of "dipolar theism" as it has been defended by process theologians over the last decades. Dipolar theism is the view that God consists of two natures: an "antecedent" nature, which is fixed and unchanging, and a "consequent" nature, which is fully responsive to the world and arises only in interaction with it.

What happens when we return with this result to the question of God's relation to the world? Earlier we found ourselves pulled between the monism of Spinoza's "one substance with many modes," and the separation of God and world based on the demands of divine perfection. Dipolar panentheism suggests a more dialectical answer: not unity or difference, but unity-in-difference. The world is neither indistinguishable from God nor (fully) ontologically separate from God. Univocal language breaks down here, as it often does when we try to express dialectical relations. Arguably, one of the great weaknesses of the line of thought from Whitehead to Hartshorne was to advance dipolar theism with insufficient emphasis on the dialectical nature of the relationship. A Hegelian (or Peircean) revision of process thought would retain the "two-ness" of the two poles in God but would attempt to add as a third moment the movement of relation between them. The resulting trinitarian form of process theology represents a fascinating new research program, to which we will return in due course.[21]

The more abstract (metaphysical or logical) presentation of panentheism is not for everyone. Some will wish for a paraphrase that uses metaphors or analogies. But what kind of metaphor could express the truth that the infinite must comprehend all finite things? Highly concrete metaphors—for example, the world exists in the womb of God—are evocative but too specific to be of broad theoretical interest. For a truth of this generality, one would need to make use of the most general metaphors that language offers.

Herein lies the justification for the central metaphor of panentheism—the "in" metaphor—which is built into the very etymology of this position (panentheism = all-in-God). "In" is a metaphor—an expression that defines or explains by identifying non-identicals—because it ascribes spatiality to God (at least in God's relation to the world), even though God as the Creator of space cannot be intrinsically spatial. Indeed, that the "in" is used metaphorically should be obvious from the fact that panentheists use it in two different directions—the world is in God, and God is in the world—whereas in mundane spatial relations this is impossible. The pie can't be in the cupboard and the cupboard in the pie at the same time! Like the tensions that are created by all living metaphors,[22] this tension drives one beyond any literal interpretation of the two-fold "in." It is not difficult to paraphrase the fundamental claim being made by the metaphor: the interdependence of God and world. The world depends on God because God is its necessary and eternal source; without God's creative act it would neither have come into existence nor exist at this moment. And God depends on the world because the nature of God's actual experience depends on interactions with finite creatures like ourselves.

Thus an analogical relationship suggests itself: the body is to the mind as the body-mind combination—that is, human persons—is to the divine. The world is in some sense analogous to the body of God. God is analogous to the mind which dwells in the body, though God is also more than the natural world taken as a whole. Call it the panentheistic analogy.[23] The power of this analogy lies in the fact that mental causation, as every human agent knows it, is more than physical causation and yet still a part of the natural world. Apparently, no natural law is broken when you form the (mental) intention to raise your hand and then you cause that particular physical object in the world, your hand, to rise. The panentheistic analogy therefore offers the possibility of conceiving divine actions that express divine intentions and agency without breaking natural law. On the panentheistic analogy, there would be no qualitative or ontological difference between the regularity of natural law conceived as expressing the regular or repetitive operation of divine agency and the intentionality of special divine actions. We return to panentheism's picture of divine action in part IV.

Emergence, Reduction, and Complexity

If one is to speak of the divine at all, one must speak analogically—even though all finite, human analogies are inadequate to the infinite God. If one chooses to speak, one will wish to use the best analogies available, while openly acknowledging their limitations. After all, isn't it appropriate to take the highest level of emergence one can find and to apply it, limitations and all, as a model for the divine nature? The strength of the panentheistic analogy is that it takes the highest level of emergence known to us and uses it as a model for the divine reality. The highest level we know is the level of human personhood: the emergence of mind (or mental properties) from the most complicated biological structure yet discovered, the human body and brain.

My thesis with respect to emergence and panentheism is simple: emergence provides the best available means, for those who take science seriously, to rethink (that is, establish a new conceptual basis for) the immanence of God in the world. Where emergence seems to make God too immanent and not transcendent enough, there are reasons internal to the emergence argument itself to correct it back in the direction of transcendence.

It is widely acknowledged that during the modern period the emphasis on God's transcendence of the world merged with the growing power of naturalist explanations to break the delicate balance between transcendence and immanence that theists had established in previous centuries. Unfortunately, it turned out that, if God is transcendent and the world is fully explained by natural law, there is no place for any divine involvement in the world. Naturally, theists still wanted (and want) to affirm that God is omnipresent, aware of and responding to the world. But—and this is the point that theologians continue to fail to see—the conceptual basis for these claims, which had undergirded divine-action claims in the Patristic and medieval periods, gradually collapsed under the pressure of modern science and modern philosophy. Conservative evangelicals and fundamentalists have responded by encouraging us to ignore or contradict modern science. But that is an answer that we should not be willing to countenance. Instead, one should accept the firm results of modern science (though not necessarily the random speculations of off-duty scientists such as Richard Dawkins) and look for a new conceptual basis, or a rediscovery and renewing of older conceptual resources, for asserting the immanence of God. Like other authors, I find panentheism to provide the most adequate means available, and particularly in the combination with emergence that I will call *emergent panentheism*.[24]

Arthur Peacocke has already nicely described the way in which emergent systems represent a sort of nested hierarchy: parts are contained within wholes, which themselves become parts within greater wholes, and so forth. Martinez Hewlett diagrams the relationship as shown in Figure 1.

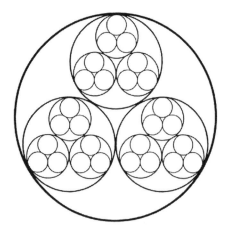

Figure 1. The "embedded systems" description of the natural world.

Figure 1 suggests that the emergence concept is a viable means for expressing the relation "in" or "is internal to." If the same structure could be applied to God's relation to the world, it would comprehend the world as internal to God—precisely the sort of intimate connection of God to world that the theological doctrine of immanence has traditionally offered. Indeed, the connection is closer than is often recognized. For example, note that the terms "in" or "internal" are used metaphorically by emergence theorists as well. What emergence actually offers, put in more formal but less evocative terms, is the set-inclusion relation, $\in$, which is read "belongs to," "is a member of," or "is an element of." This is a relation of logical inclusion rather than (primarily) one of location. Conceptually it's much closer to the (Hegelian) argument, sketched above, that the finite must be included within the infinite. Emergence thus represents a powerful answer to misgivings about the preposition "in."

Note that the nature of the "in" or self-inclusion relation changes as one moves up the hierarchy of complexity in nature. As long as one remains within the nested hierarchies that constitute actual objects in the world (Figure 1), the "in" is indeed locative: atoms are in molecules, molecules in cells, cells in organs, organs in organisms, and so forth. By contrast, organisms are "in" an ecosystem in a rather different sense. Consider the further differences introduced by the statements "William is in the army," "Vermont is in the Union," "her love is in her heart," "we live in community," and "no man is an island; all persons exist in society."

This diversity of usages is important for understanding those complex emergent properties that we collectively call "the mental." The diversity suggests that one doesn't have to be a dualist to account for the relationship of thought to the brain and central nervous system. Conceptually, the mind-brain relationship counts as yet another instance of emergence, albeit a unique one. The increasing complexity of neurophysiological structures over the course of evolution has given rise to an emergent level we might call mentality. Thoughts, intentions, and wishes are complex properties emergent from the brain—influenced by, but not reducible to, their physiological substrate. In a fashion both analogous to and yet different from previous levels of emergence, the brain and central nervous system give rise to mental qualities that are dependent on the brain as a whole and yet qualitatively different from it.

Cells represent a real explanatory level within science because they possess properties not ascribable to the molecules that compose them and because they exercise causal powers that one cannot ascribe to their parts. Likewise, what we call "the mind"—the sum total of mental properties associated with a given organism or person—possesses properties not ascribable to neurons and ganglions, properties such as hoping to win a chess game or comprehending general relativity theory. And mental occurrences such as thoughts and wishes exercise causal influence on each other and on bodies, which make them irreducible components in any adequate causal explanation of the world. Consider, for example, to what extent the surface of the earth must today be explained in terms of the intentions of agents.

➤ Using, and Limiting, the Panentheistic Analogy

To understand the mental as an emergent property is not sufficient for comprehending God's relation to the world, but it may be a necessary step in the process. Consider the tension between mind as property and mind as object. To conceive of mind as an object invites dualism, since (as Descartes argued) an object that is nonphysical, immaterial, not composed out of parts, and not located in space and time must be a very different kind of thing altogether, which he called *res cogitans*. (Think also of the Aristotelian-Thomistic concept of the soul as the form of the body.) Given the dangers of such a dualism, one is tempted to speak only of mental properties: complex, emergent properties predicated of the brain as an object. Certainly there is no problem locating brains among the furniture of the universe and "parsing" them in terms of our knowledge of the physical world. Yet "physicalizing mind" doesn't remove all the tensions either, for mental properties are so radically different in kind from the object that is said to produce them that linking the two (brains and consciousness) remains the "hard problem" of neuroscience.[25]

The same tension arises in applying the notion of emergence to God. If applied directly—that is, in analogy with cases of emergence in the natural world—emergence theory would suggest that "God" or "the divine" is an emergent level or property within (or "of") the natural world. In chapter 6, I labeled this view *radically emergent theism*. In this theology there is no substance or thing that is God. Rather, "deity" is a quality that *the universe* comes to have increasingly over time. This emerging quality of spirituality is imagined to feed back onto the world, in the way that mental phenomena affect physical states in the world. God does not exist in any literal sense, but there may be an increasing "deification" of the universe over time.

In his classic but underappreciated *Space, Time, and Deity*,[26] Samuel Alexander defends radically emergent theism in this sense. As he writes, "God is the whole world as possessing the quality of deity. Of such a being the whole world is the 'body' and deity is the 'mind.'"[27] Alexander's theology endorses a God who is in the process of coming to be: at one time there was no God, and now—to put it strangely—there is only partly God. God is radically dependent on the world:[28] this "finite God," he writes, "represent[s] or gather[s] up into its divine part its whole body."[29] Alexander accepts, one might say, a verbal notion of God: the deity "deisms," and these "deisings" are things that the world does (*nota bene*: the atrocious neologisms are Alexander's). The world is the subject of these actions. It does them, but what the world does is to deify itself. God is verb only, as in the famous book by Rabbi David Cooper, *God Is a Verb: Kabbalah and the Practice of Mystical Judaism*.[30] God does not create the world. The world "deises" itself.

Now it is possible that Alexander offers all that can reasonably be saved out of traditional theism. But I believe that conclusion would be mistaken. Theists have certainly meant to attribute divine properties to an actually existing being or Ground of Being rather than to the physical cosmos. Although radically emergent theism is an option, it's not clear that it's the only one. Suppose instead that panentheists comprehend "divinity" not merely as an emergent property of the natural world, but also as a quality of one who is also an agent, whom we call God. The logic of emergence allows for this move, but it does not require it. Put differently, God can be understood on analogy with properties such as "reproduction," "life," or "thought," which we ascribe to cells, organisms, and minds, respectively. But there are good reasons to think that the properties generally associated with divinity—eternality, perfection, love, justice, and the role of Creator and Source of all that is—are different in kind from such intra-mundane properties. How can God be Source of all things and yet at the same a thing or agent that arises in the course of the history of the cosmos?

It is this conundrum that has forced many panentheists to accept a form of ultimate or theological dualism. We remain dissatisfied with Alexander's treatment of divinity (or, as we might say today, spirituality) within the context of the finite universe and the sciences that explain it. Instead, we make the move to metaphysics, postulating a broader framework in which the cosmos exists and which helps to sustain and explain it. God is, for us, the Source and (we hope) the ultimate culmination of this cosmos, the Alpha and the Omega, the Force or Presence within which all is located.

Emergence is therefore a conceptual structure, born in the crucible of the sciences, that can lead to the category of divinity or spirituality as an emergent property in evolution. But emergence is not in the end adequate to fully explain this property. Emergence propels one to metaphysics, and metaphysical reflection in turn suggests a theological postulate, panentheism, above and beyond the logic of emergence. Emergence helps with models for thinking about the relationship of world to God (for example, the nested hierarchy model in Figure 1), and it serves as a constant reminder of the radically different sorts of inclusion relations found in the natural world. Panentheism then provides a means for incorporating these inner-worldly relations into an explicitly theological model. Emergent panentheism thus represents a more appealing means for thinking of God's relation to the world in comparison with the older models that are associated with classical philosophical theism.[31]

From Substance *to* Subject

Rethinking Spirit *in the* Modern World

HOW SHALL WE COMPREHEND SPIRIT IN THE MODERN WORLD? THIS question forms a key point of contact between philosophy and theology. But it also raises urgent—and difficult—issues for contemporary theologians: How can the transcendence, the otherness, of Spirit be thought of today in light of our ever-increasing knowledge of the law-governed nature of the natural world? What's the relation between Spirit and spirit? Between spirit and body? Between spirit and personhood? These questions bear on most of the central concerns of Christian theists today. They deeply affect how systematic theology is done and the conclusions it reaches. Their impact is deepest when it comes to the task of integrating the various assumptions about spiritual matters into a unified pneumatology, a systematic doctrine of the Spirit. How can one think together of the vastly different functions of Holy Spirit: the Spirit of creation, of life, of redemption and sanctification, of understanding, of freedom?

In these pages, I will attempt to lay out the conceptual background for a constructive Christian engagement with the question of Spirit in the modern world. Because the systematic question is so crucial, I will also sketch a systematic position of my own on the theology of the Spirit. That philosophical concepts and criticisms play such a major role in this project already expresses an important assumption. In the contemporary context, concepts and insights that do not emerge directly out of systematic theology but have their origins elsewhere—in philosophical debates, in the sciences, and in other religious traditions—have become crucial to the task of formulating a Christian theological understanding of Spirit.

Three topics in particular will demand our attention: "postfoundationalist" approaches to pneumatology, idealist theories of the nature of subjectivity, and panentheistic insights into the God-world relationship.

➤ Reflections on the Spirit in a Postfoundationalist Vein

I suggest that we are today witnessing a renaissance of (the possibility of) a new language of Spirit, a possibility that has been closed since neo-idealism went out of vogue in the 1920s. Two factors in particular have opened the door again for links between science, philosophy, and pneumatology: the demise of positivist theories of knowledge, which labeled Spirit-language "literally meaningless," and the continuing need for metaphysical interpretations of contemporary scientific developments.[1] Rather than encountering a philosophical world antagonistic to all such questions, theologians today are finding discussion partners in philosophy departments who are handling issues which are at least analogous.

At the same time, and for related reasons, interesting new developments in the theory of knowledge have opened the doors to a genuinely postfoundationalist theology. Postfoundationalism's more flashy cousin, postmodernism, is much in the air these days (sometimes reducing pollution, sometimes adding a haze of its own). I am not convinced that one needs to completely embrace the more extreme "poststructuralist" theories of language that often march under the postmodern banner: the view that all signs are arbitrary and that the idea of referring to the world is merely a linguistic construct. Nor do I accept the often related charge that constructive Christian theology always commits the sin of "metanarrative" and should therefore be abandoned. By contrast, the claims of postfoundationalist theorists are both clearer and less extreme.[2] They assert merely that theories do not require grounding in a more foundational discipline (type of evidence, observation) in order to pass as rational and to be viable candidates for truth. Thus, for instance, a doctrine of the Spirit does not need a foundation in a universal philosophy of Absolute Spirit in order to have intellectual credibility.

This changed theory of knowledge is very important. At best, it liberates one in a single stroke from the great "yes or no" debates on whether theologians should ever consort with philosophers—debates that we know only too well from the early Barth and from the Barth/Brunner debate in the 1930s.[3] One can now discover, and profit from, points of contact without finding oneself "unlawfully wed" to or enmeshed in the service of idols. The postfoundationalist climate thus fosters theories of the Spirit that are coherence-based, eliminating the need to draw back from distinctively Christian language. Instead, the goal can now be to spell out the logic of interlocking sets of beliefs without first having to establish their probability according to neutral standards. This makes it possible to maintain the truth-directedness of God-language, summoning all the relevant rational resources at our disposal, while at the same time acknowledging the historical conditioned nature of Christian claims and the plurality of other options that are open to believers today. I view these developments as a renewed invitation for theologians to engage philosophers and scientists without fear of hegemony. They serve as the inspiration for what follows.

➤ Beyond Substantivalism

Early modern doctrines of creation assume that there must be a "space" outside God "in" which created substances could be located. Since space and time were understood as an objective framework—something like a big box into which events or objects might be placed—there seemed to be no problem with God creating this big box somewhere and then making a bunch of substances to place into it. Unfortunately, this picture now appears to be physically incorrect. Time is not an absolute quantity but depends on the inertial frames of the observers. Likewise, the geometry of space is transformed by the mass (or energy) of objects, such that in an important sense the space of the universe comes into existence along with the objects themselves.

And there are equally grave theological problems. On this model, it becomes difficult to express the way in which God is present in the world (which may help to explain the headaches theologians have had in trying to make sense of the various modes of God's presence). How can God be present to the believer if one substance can never be internally present to another? Perhaps, some thought, God's omnipresence could still be preserved by asserting a God who perceives the physical world from every point in space simultaneously. Yet locating God at every point in space, while it does provide a pretty good vantage point (God won't miss much), doesn't express the intimate presence and mystical interiority of which the biblical writers and mystics wrote.

Moreover, it's not clear that a substance-based picture can capture the vivifying presence of the divine *ruach* of the Hebrew Bible, the One who is life-giving Spirit. The moment that this breath is withdrawn, say the Hebrew writers, there is no more life, for no separation between the life and the breath can be thought. In fact, "presence at every point in space" doesn't even seem to be the right *category* for describing the person-to-person presence asserted by the biblical documents. Can omnipresence really do justice to the existence of *subjects*, and specifically to the sense of enveloping personal presence reflected in the biblical texts: "Even before there is a word on my tongue, Behold, O Lord, Thou dost know it all. Thou hast enclosed me behind and before, and laid thy hand upon me" (Ps 139:5-6)?

Equally worrisome, recent science has made the notion of divine action more problematic than it was in the pre-modern context. Unlike modern physics, Greek and medieval physics required constant attention from a divine agent, since the world order needed to be maintained at every moment.[4] They also needed some being who would supply the highest goal toward which all things strive, since the understanding of motion included the final cause toward which things move. As long as the goal of perfection had to be imparted to the system to make the physics work, a most-perfect being (*ens perfectissimum*) was almost a *physical* necessity.

By contrast, we now live in an age that has come to accept a very different view of the physical world. A basic assumption of many modern physicists is that physical systems are closed to causal interventions from outside (the principle of the conservation of energy). This closure has led to a several centuries-long struggle to rethink what divine action in the world or miracles could mean (see part IV below). It will still be possible, I believe, to conceive of the active presence of the divine Spirit in the world, but not using the vocabulary of separate and sometimes interacting substances. It is fair to say that theologians today continue to struggle to formulate a theology of Spirit that is both theologically and scientifically adequate.

➤ Theology in a New Key

I wish now to argue that the new freedom—the freedom that emerges after moving beyond substance-based theologies[5]—does not mean eschewing theological reflection altogether. This is not the freedom to abandon the quest for a conceptually consistent Christian position on the nature of Spirit, nor a freedom from the obligation, so clear to our forebears, to specify fully what one means by the Spirit of God. These tasks remain. Instead, what we have is the freedom to explore new and more appropriate models of what "Spirit" might fundamentally be. Let's call it the difference between *responsible* and *relativistic* pluralism.

Relativistic pluralism occurs when one employs whatever metaphors or analogies for Spirit are useful at the present moment, without concern for the consistency of one's various models. Think of it as the theologian's own variant on situation ethics.[6] Situation ethicists denied there were any overarching ethical principles to guide behavior from situation to situation. This conclusion left the individual actor with maximal freedom to act in each situation in whatever manner seemed best to him or her at the time. In the 1960s, this approach struck many readers as a pleasant escape from the restrictive guidelines and parental mores of the previous generation (an especially useful liberation when the question of sexual freedoms was at stake). Our more jaded eyes easily see the difficulties with such freedoms. We now recognize more clearly that in social environments dominated by a particular power group the exercise of unmitigated freedom too easily licenses oppression without a bad conscience.

Could it be that something similar occurs with the situational use of theological models, which *also* sometimes masquerade as having total freedom from conceptual restrictions? At first it was exciting to be freed from the need to pay attention to underlying conceptual structures. The productivity of this freedom is evidenced in books like Sallie McFague's *Metaphorical Theology*,[7] for models for God like parent, friend, and lover do indeed help to open up the theological imagination. Today, of course, a thousand such flowers bloom. Isn't it time to take a step deeper and look for a more adequate *shared conceptual framework* for talking of the divine Spirit, a more systematic pneumatology, within the context of a responsible pluralism?

Of course, it will have to be a framework that enables models to grow rather than blocking all creativity, and it must be a framework that also supports religious practice. Creativity and practice require some open-endedness, since contexts change. Nonetheless, appropriate Christian language about the Spirit is not fully unconstrained. Various parameters guide the constructive theologian: biblical scholarship, insights from the tradition, scientific progress, ethical and political principles. We can be pluralistic in our theologies of Spirit, to be sure, but we can also do so within the context of intellectual virtues such as conceptual coherence, rigorous systematicity, and attention to the conceptual underpinnings of what one is asserting.

➤ Resources

What kind of holistic principle can serve as the central concept for a philosophically informed (though still postfoundational) theology of Spirit? If substance metaphysics doesn't provide the principle, what will? It is often said that what theology needs is a *personalistic* rather than an object-based framework. Where then will its specific content come from? Necessarily, biblical language and the history of theology must contribute. Yet they're not sufficient by themselves. Since others have written in detail on the resources of biblical language and historical theology, I propose to focus here on the specific conceptual resources arising out of the history of modern philosophy. What kind of pneumatology begins to emerge when one brings the tradition into contact with these resources?

Of course, one can't speak of the resources of modern philosophy for addressing the problem of divine Spirit without granting that there *is* a distinctively modern problem of God in the first place. After all, the term "resources" presupposes that there is a challenge *for which* these thinkers' contributions are helpful. I thus break rather sharply with the otherwise informed and intelligent treatment of modern theistic thought in William Placher's *The Domestication of Transcendence*.[8] One quickly realizes that Placher's "resources" are only used for "*correcting* some of the errors of modernity by learning from some earlier theology."[9] Thus, for example, he takes recent process theology as a negative example "of continuing the seventeenth-century project of trying to get clear on the categories we use to speak of God, to subject the divine to the structures of human reason, and thereby, I believe, to domesticate the transcendent."[10] Of course, if one sees no need to reflect on the categories she uses for speaking about God, then clearly she will hold that the specifically modern discussions can only lead theology astray. But I would have thought that one would wish to get as clear as possible on how God can best be conceived—not only in light of the shortcomings of modern secular thought, but also as a requirement of Christian faith and practice itself.

1. From Substance to Spirit

The most important single change in modern thought was the movement from substance to spirit. During this period, "spirit" came to be defined not as a special case of a more general category (substance), but as a foundational ontological principle in its own right—and even as *the* foundational ontological principle. Aristotle had developed a notion of substance that owed its motion and its *telos* to a highest substance. St. Thomas endorsed a plurality of finite substances that owe their existence to the divine being who is Being itself. And Spinoza, the culminator of the substance tradition, spelled out its logical requirement by allowing for only one substance, of which all things (and thus all persons) are modes.

The key modern resource for the theology of Spirit is the switch from substantivalist thinking to a subject-based ontology. During this period the Spirit came to be linked in the first place with human subjects and with their experience. This is a tremendous transformation from the medieval period, where the Spirit represented an objective metaphysical principle, tied closely to principles such as order, appropriate place in the hierarchy of being, goal-directedness or universal teleology, and the ontological separation between God and world ("'your thoughts are not my thoughts,' saith the Lord"). The importance of the shift cannot be overstated. Hegel, who, like the owl of Minerva, came later and began to grasp the full philosophical significance of events that had already transpired, labeled it the epochal shift from a philosophy of substance to a philosophy of Spirit:

> On my view, which can only be justified by the presentation of the system itself, everything depends on grasping and expressing what is true not as *substance*, but just as much as *subject*. . . . Living substance is, moreover, that Being which is in truth *subject*—or, what amounts to the same thing, which is in truth real only insofar as it is the movement of positing itself (*Sichselbstsetzens*) or the mediation of "becoming other" with itself.[11]

In his discussion of Hegel's *Logic,* Marcuse comments, "From the knowledge of being as movement and of this movement as 'relation to itself' (*Sich-verhalten*), [Hegel] constructs not only the doctrine of being and essence, but also the doctrine of the concept. The entire ontology is nothing other than a concrete pursuit of the fundamental modes of being, understood as 'relation to itself,' throughout the basic regions of what exists."[12] The highest and fullest expression of this self-relating movement is Spirit.

This is a radical shift indeed! The Spirit, which in the Middle Ages had served as a *principle of demarcation* between the human and superhuman, the natural and supernatural, now became the *principle of unity* between the two, the basic principle of all being. We exist as Spirit and pervasively in Spirit. Spirit now becomes the basic ontological category, that which unites all living things.

2. Spinoza and the Spinoza Tradition

I have argued elsewhere[13] that the clearest place to observe the collapse of the substance paradigm and the emergence of its successor is in the Spinoza tradition. By the Spinoza tradition I mean the 100 years of debate and controversy about Spinoza's philosophy, beginning with his death in 1677 and continuing through the emergence of the new philosophies of Spirit in the wake of Kant's *Critique of Pure Reason*. Spinoza should not technically be credited with a direct role in the new metaphysics of the subject, since his *Ethics* still espouses a classical theory of substance. But the culminator of a tradition is in one sense the parent of what follows, and Spinozism does represent the culmination of substance metaphysics. Following a hint in Descartes's *Principia* (I, 51), Spinoza realized that, strictly speaking, there could only be one substance, that is, one thing "that is in itself and is conceived through itself" (*Ethics*

E1def.3). All other things are then, strictly speaking, merely modes of one single substance (E1def.5) that, as we saw, he called "God or nature." Spinoza correctly recognized that it follows that "whatever is, is in God, and nothing can be or be conceived without God" (E1P15).

In this view, then, a personal substance is not really a substance any longer. Personal substances are actually just modes with particular sorts of characteristics. It's true that it may be the essence of a living thing to "strive to persist in its own being," a universal characteristic which Spinoza called *conatus* (E3P7). It's also true that Spinoza was a dual-aspect monist, holding that the one reality is truly understood by using the attributes of both mind and body. But although this theory moved modern thought beyond Descartes's dueling substances (*res cogitans* and *res extensa*), it failed to grasp what is unique about spirit. Dual-aspect theories make three assertions: there is *the order of thought*, which consists of a nested series of ideas of ideas of ideas, and so on; and there is *the order of things*, which consists of modes containing modes containing modes, and so forth; and there is (allegedly) a perfect correspondence or matching relation between them. But postulating two separate "orders" with a one-to-one correspondence between them falls short of comprehending the nature of that active principle that we call spirit. Consciousness, the dynamic of a self-unfolding Spirit, is still missing.

Contrast Spinoza's position with G. E. Lessing's philosophical theology. It was Lessing's controversial reliance on Spinoza which gave rise to the famous "Spinoza Dispute" in the middle and late eighteenth century, one of the formative influences on German Idealism as well as on Schleiermacher and the birth of modern theology. In *The Education of the Human Race,* Lessing already posited a plurality and a movement in God based on self-understanding. God's unity "must be a transcendental unity which does not exclude a sort of plurality." He must have "the most perfect conception of himself, i.e. a conception which contains everything which is in him."[14] This divine self-conception is then mirrored in humans, who share a subjectivity that seeks to rise toward the divine:

> And why should not we too, by means of a religion whose historical truth, if you
> will, looks dubious, be led in a similar way to closer and better conceptions of the
> divine Being, of our own nature, of our relation to God, which human reason would
> never have reached on its own?[15]

Major advances in the understanding of Spirit emerged as the Spinoza Dispute flamed during the subsequent decades, especially at the hands of its two most famous protagonists, Jacobi and Mendelssohn. On the one hand, Mendelssohn, like Spinoza, suggested that any adequate theism must understand the world as internal to God, *whether or not* it also posits a world outside of God. On the other hand, in contrast to Spinoza, he attributed to God consciousness, intentionality, and agency. His reason is important. God must be capable of representing to himself (*sich vorstellen*) all finite things, together with their moral qualities, beauty, and order. God must also give preference to the best and most perfect series of things. This active role for God suggested a theory of subjectivity that could be applied *both to God and to finite subjects*, pointing at the same time (and for the same reason) beyond Spinoza's pantheism toward panentheism:

> [For both theist and panentheist] I, a human, a thought of the divine, will never cease to be a divine thought . . . hence [the two positions] are distinguished only by a subtlety that could never make a practical difference . . . : whether God let this idea of the best group of contingent things shine out, roll out, stream out—or with what picture should I compare it? (since this subtlety can't be described other than with pictures); whether he let the light shine away from him like lightening or only illumine within? Whether it remained a spring or whether the spring flowed out in a stream? . . . Fundamentally, it is a misinterpretation of the metaphors that transforms God too pictorially into the world or places the world too pictorially within God.[16]

3. Kant and the German Idealists

Without doubt, the breakthrough in the movement from substance to subject occurs in Kant's *Critique of Pure Reason*, and specifically in the notion of the transcendental unity of apperception:

> There must, therefore, be a transcendental ground of the unity of consciousness in the synthesis of the manifold of all our intuitions, . . . a ground without which it would be impossible to think any object for our intuitions. . . . There must be a condition that precedes all experience, and which makes experience itself possible. (A106–7)

> The abiding and unchanging "I" (pure apperception) forms the correlate of all our representations insofar as it is to be at all possible that we should become conscious of them (A123). . . . An understanding in which through self-consciousness all the manifold would *eo ipso* be given, would be *intuitive*; our understanding can only *think*, and for intuition must look to the senses. I am conscious of the self as identical in respect of the manifold of representations that are given to me in an intuition, because I call them one and all *my* representations, and so apprehend them as constituting *one* intuition. This amounts to saying that I am conscious to myself *a priori* of a necessary synthesis of representations. (B135)

These texts defend the necessity of postulating an "I" that accompanies every perception of a given individual—precisely that aspect of Spirit that's missing in Spinoza's account. Spinoza knew that one has to be able to speak both of a series of ideas and of a world of things (modes) that the ideas either correctly represent or fail to represent.[17] But Kant was the first to insist that the real mystery lies in that sense of ongoing personal identity that accompanies every one of my perceptions and by virtue of which each perception is *my* perception.[18] Arguably, it was the mystery of this transcendental unity of apperception that suggested to Kant the need to write a second critique (on practical reasoning) and later a third critique (on imagination and judgment), because (arguably) Kant's discovery of the role of self-consciousness in *theoretical* knowledge launched him on a phenomenological exploration of the practical and aesthetic dimensions of this same "transcendental" self.

Without doubt, it was this very mystery of the subject that exercised Kant's first great follower, Fichte, in his gradual development of a *subjective idealism* through the various drafts of the *Wissenschaftslehre*. Indeed, the mystery of subjectivity is probably the leitmotif of Fichte's entire philosophical project (see chapter 8). Schelling then continued the struggle to grasp the nature of subjectivity. Like Hegel, he combined the question of the subject's knowing with the ontological question of what is and the theological question of the highest being:

> Since [this knowledge of the infinite] encompasses the intuitions of the individual as well as the thought of the general, it encompasses the unity of the general and specific, of thought and being, of infinite and finite. The infinite *knowledge* of the absolute is at the same time the *being* of the absolute. With this we reach absolute idealism.[19]

Yet Schelling's form of idealism refused to let the logic of the absolute stand in the way of divine freedom. Especially in the "Essay on Freedom" (*Freiheitsschrift*) of 1809, and perhaps better than any before him, Schelling placed a new stress on the centrality of will, of freedom, and of the irrational (or transrational) moment in the life of the subject. The focus on freedom follows also from a consideration of what is required if self-revelation is to be possible:

> Now a free being is free in the sense that it does not have to reveal itself. To reveal itself is to act, and all acting is a self-revelation. In order to be a free being, it must be free either to remain with its mere ability [to act], or to make the transition to action. If this transition were made with necessity, [God] would not be what he really is, namely free.[20]

Eventually these struggles gave rise to the birth of the first full phenomenology of spirit, Hegel's *Phänomenologie des Geistes*, with its famous manifesto of the shift from substance to spirit:

> With the attainment of such a conception, therefore, self-consciousness has returned into itself and passed from those opposite characteristics. . . . Its object is now the category . . . become conscious of itself. Its account with its previous forms is now closed; they lie behind it in the forgotten past; they . . . are developed solely within itself as transparent moments. . . . Throughout all these moments self-consciousness holds firmly to that simple unity of self with objective existence which is its constitutive generic nature.[21]

There is much to say about the modern theory of the subject, the continuities with Greek and medieval thought, the breaks with those traditions, and the significance of this paradigm shift for theology. Here I can emphasize only the most fundamental point. With the wisdom that only hindsight can bring, Peter Strawson boiled down the rich distinctions of the German Idealists to the fundamental contrast between the first-person and the third-person perspective.[22] To be a person is to be a being that can be characterized from *both* perspectives. Yet first-personal terms are not translatable without remainder into third-personal (scientific) accounts. Since Strawson, other analytic philosophers have continued to analyze the unique features of a subject-centered ontology (though most would turn over in their graves before they called it that). For example, Thomas Nagel, in the process of reflecting on "what it would be like to be a bat," argues analogously that there is an irreducibly first-personal dimension involved in being a human subject.[23]

We have just observed the emergence of a new understanding of spirit or subjectivity in modern thought. Included in this new concept are at least five key features: spirit as the active principle of thought; self-consciousness; freedom; a principle of individual identity through time; and a notion of person that includes both the physical and the mental aspects of human existence and their interrelationship. There is much here that is of value for theologians.[24] Yet, surprisingly, theological reflection on the Spirit often contents itself with what is in essence a pre-modern notion of the personal, for instance with Spirit as an attribute of the one divine substance. Then, when such substantival ways of conceiving of God prove to be inadequate or lead to skeptical conclusions, theologians are tempted to throw up their hands and declare that Spirit just can't be grasped by the human mind. Pluralism then takes over, and multiple metaphors replace concerted efforts toward a unified pneumatology.

4. Schleiermacher

Assertions of the death of pneumatology are premature, however. Let's go back to one of the formative figures of the turn to the subject, and a thinker who was in the first place a theologian. (We'll return to this same theologian in chapter 13.) Schleiermacher clearly exemplifies the shift from substance to spirit, and many of the tendencies that "the father of modern theology" bequeathed to his children have multiplied in influence along with the number of his offspring.

In the *Speeches,* Schleiermacher linked religion with the Spirit, and the Spirit with the realm of the subject's experience. The core of the *Speeches* is intuition and feeling, the two "combined and inseparable" (73),[25] and the object of religious feeling and intuition is the infinite. Herein lies the theme of religion: not to ask how things appear to our eyes, "but rather in and for the universe" (80), since religion arises in the subject's "instinct for the universe" (*Instinkt fürs Universum,* 114). Religion is first and foremost a perspective (*Ansicht,* 118) that the subject takes. For example, a miracle need not be construed as a contradiction of natural law. It may have a natural explanation, but it is at the same time "the immediate relation of an appearance to the Infinite, the Universe" (117). This is emphatically not a God-of-the-gaps position, finding God in the "unexplainable and foreign" (117). Instead, it is a way of seeing the trans-natural in all natural things, the infinite in and through the finite.

The Spirit moves always upward, seeking to understand the infinite; and religion lives in the "infinite nature of the Whole, the One and All" (51). In my view, a single claim underlies the whole of the crucial second speech:

> All finite things exist only through the determination of their boundaries, which must be "cut out" (*herausgeschnitten*) out of the Infinite. Only in this manner can anything within these boundaries itself be infinite and formed on its own.[26]

This is the *sine qua non* for the doctrine of the Spirit: "Nothing individual [can] be separated, except insofar as it is arbitrarily cut out [of the one Whole or Spirit] in time and space."[27]

For Schleiermacher, then, the differentiation of individuals (the *principium individuationis*) is subsequent and secondary to the one unity of/in the Spirit. We are, as it were, cut out of the one all-encompassing whole. The problem is no longer how to constitute the unity of humanity with God, but rather how to understand in what respect humans are *other* than God. Note also that Schleiermacher here sets up Spirit in contradistinction to mind or rationality. For the *Sturm und Drang* thinkers, like the Romantics who followed them, Spirit is on the side of emotion, that which is pre- or anti-rational. In a famous passage, Wordsworth thus construed the realm of Spirit as "the sense sublime / Of something far more deeply interfused, / Whose dwelling is the light of setting suns, / And the round ocean and the living air, / And the blue sky, and in the mind of man" ("Tintern Abbey"). Similarly, the metaphors of Spirit that Schleiermacher preferred were those of the lover and the baby carried in the arms of a loving parent. To the extent that something is of Spirit, it is known prior to and beyond any rational cognition.

It is not uncommon for theologians to distinguish Schleiermacher's early position in the *Speeches*, where the concept of God occurs in the context of a sort of pantheism (or better, panentheism), from the later work in *The Christian Faith*, where the links with traditional theism and dogmatic theology are much more pronounced. But to separate the two works too sharply is a mistake. Isn't the sense of absolute dependence, at root, another expression of the primacy of Spirit as the all-encompassing medium of our existence? Indeed, God-consciousness as the systematic principle of Schleiermacher's mature theological reflection functions primarily as a hermeneutical principle that allows him to draw multiple inferences from a basic monism of the Spirit. The logical movement of Schleiermacher's theology is from the fundamental unity of Spirit to an initial differentiation between infinite and finite spirit, and from thence to (at least identifiable paraphrases of) traditional Christian doctrine. Schleiermacher's later work is thus an attempt to take an essentially undifferentiated ontological principle, one which is for that reason anomalous or even "savage," and to "domesticate" it in a manner consistent with the institutional church and the existence of communally expressible doctrines—to dress it up and take it out into public, so to speak.

But, as critics have often noted, the domestication is only partly successful. Clearly, a tension remains between the Romantic side of Schleiermacher's thought and the more differentiated conceptual formulations that he attempts in his later doctrinal work. It would be fine if Schleiermacher had simply discarded his earlier position as youthful enthusiasm. But, if (as I've argued) that's a misinterpretation, then the later doctrinal formulations must be viewed as much more provisional than is commonly held. In this view, they become snapshots of a continuously flowing reality, a process that has already moved on by the time that we have formulated it (compare this to Whitehead's *Adventures of Ideas*). The same tension between the ever-flowing "one Spirit" and any expression of it, built into modern theology by Schleiermacher, runs straight from him through the intervening years and into the theological present, as students of nineteenth and twentieth theology know all too well. In the words of Peter Hodgson's famous book, the "winds of the Spirit" blow as they will (John 3:8)—not despite, but *because* of the fact that it is the one Spirit that blows in every case. Herein lies the appropriateness of Langdon Gilkey's baptizing the task of contemporary theology as one of "naming the whirlwind"—even if we don't actually succeed at "taming the whirlwind."[28]

5. Closing with Hegel

Against a certain widespread prejudice in Anglo-American circles, I have narrated the modern philosophical resources for the theology of Spirit as culminating with Hegel. Few critics of a "metaphysics of the subject" today seem to understand the amazing synthesis of Greek, medieval, and early modern motifs that his theory of subjectivity achieved. *Human* subjects may slip far below the full self-awareness that Hegel presupposed—for reasons that Marx, Durkheim, Nietzsche, and Freud were later to bring painfully to our attention. But if the highest being (or Being itself) is a *personal* reality, full self-consciousness and a sense of spiritual unity are precisely the features one would expect it to have.

I must express one hesitancy, however. Ironically, Hegel may be guiltier of domestication than the German Idealists who preceded him. For example, Fichte in his later work moved beyond the self-assertive Ego (*das Ich*) as the unifying principle, finding again in the undifferentiated One or *das absolute Ich* the ultimate principle. Hegel made the attempt to again wed Spirit and Rationality after they had (as he might have said) tragically fallen into opposition in the work of Schleiermacher, Fichte, and Schelling. In his philosophy Spirit becomes the ultimate principle of rationality, the reason why "the Real is the Rational." The result, as readers well know, is a universal necessity: all events occur according to the necessary unfolding of reality in and toward absolute Spirit. Even creation, according to the *Philosophie der Religion*, must be a necessary creation. The ineluctable movement toward self-consciousness must be consummated according to very concrete steps. Ethics, social theory, politics, indeed art and religion as well, must all find their precise places as they are *aufgehoben* (transcended-yet-preserved) into the final dialectical unity.

This stress on rational necessity represents, I believe, an excessively conservative overreaction to what Hegel presumably saw as the antinomian tendencies in Schleiermacher and Schelling. Hegel's attempt to wed the Enlightened Kant with Romantics like Schelling appears to the more skeptically minded as an impossible marriage, one that impoverishes both parties. If there is any domestication, surely it is here. What should one then conclude? Does it spell an end to any modern philosophy of Spirit if Hegel's synthesis (and others like it) fails? Undoubtedly their failure leaves one with a less rationalist understanding of Spirit. It also raises roadblocks in the path of any proposed union of philosophy and theology—at least any as tight as that which Hegel claimed for his own work. But if this is the actual situation, then we are better advised to work at the humbler connections than to dismiss the language of Spirit altogether.

➤ The Case for Panentheism

What relevance do these historical developments have for a theology of the spirit or Spirit today? Clearly, dualist theories of the person—theories that treat spirit and body as two separate substances—must be avoided, since spirit has superceded substantival thinking. Out of the remaining alternatives on the relation of body and spirit, the strongest option from a theological perspective is psychophysical unity: spirit and body are not two substances, nor is the one reduced to the other, but both are dimensions of the one existing person.[29]

Persons consist (in part) of complicated physical systems, yet what they are is something more than can be analyzed or explained in physical terms. In humans, subjectivity arises out of a very complex set of interactions that includes the human body, its brain, and its interaction with its environment. The subjectivity that we call "spirit" is an emergent phenomenon insofar as it's not reducible to the physical system that gives rise to it. Hence *personhood* is best understood as an emergent level of reality.[30] Emergence here must be understood in an ontological sense. With the advent of subjectivity or spirituality, a new type of property and activity is present, one that needs to be analyzed in its own terms and not merely in terms of the lower levels that preceded and gave rise to it.

Such a view stands opposed to reductionist theories of the person, which claim that a sufficient explanation of human persons can be given in terms of the underlying neural structures, or biochemistry, or even quantum-physical events.[31] Put differently, the modern philosophies of spirit are essentially anti-reductionist, since they maintain that the vocabulary of spirit is necessary to account for some of the vital dimensions of human personhood—and presumably for whatever that overarching unity is that makes of the moments of an individual life a single spiritual unity. The study of mental phenomena thus plays a particularly important role in grasping what is particular to personhood. Still, psychophysical unity implies that consciousness or spirituality must be understood in connection with the body in which they are manifested. This perspective encourages scientists and theologians to work together toward understanding persons and their interactions in ways that do not negate the concerns (or the basic methods) of either approach.

Now we are ready to turn to the question of divine Spirit. Theological terms are introduced "from below" when they are expected to help explain the data of science and human experience in the world. We find in the world levels of increasing complexity. One of these levels is that of personhood as just described. At the same time, humans are not "pure spirit." Indeed, much of what defines our humanness has to do with the struggle between—or, in happy cases, the smooth synthesis of—the physical, psychological, and spiritual dimensions of human existence. (One thinks of Paul's descriptions, in Romans and elsewhere, of the conflicts between *sarx* and *pneuma*.)

If the spiritual side of personhood is emergent, then a spiritual being that transcends the world will have to be introduced as a *higher* experiential or ontological level—indeed, for theists, as the culminating level—above the level of embodied spirit that characterizes human experience. The mistake of positions like vitalism and pantheism was to introduce God too early, at too low a level (say, at the level of a basic life-principle), rather than at, or above, the highest level of which we are aware, the level of consciousness. By contrast, if one introduces God-language in complete abstraction from what we know of the human spirit and human personhood, one is bound to fall back into the dualism from which we have just escaped—either the dualism of spirit and body, or a complete dualism between the human and divine spirit which threatens to erase the *imago Dei*.

How are such dualisms to be avoided? I suggest that one can apply something like the theory of levels worked out in this chapter and in part II, at least during the "from below" phase of a theology of Spirit. The theory of levels led us to conceive human spirit as embodied mental functioning. The goal of an experientially based theory of Spirit, then, is to apply this same relationship between various levels to the understanding of the divine Spirit and the God-world relation.

We thus begin by speaking of God not as disembodied but as (voluntarily) embodied Spirit.[32] Note that this argument concerns the *introduction* of language about the Spirit of God. It has to do with the context of discovery and not yet with the final theoretical context (which may include, for example, a fuller trinitarian vocabulary). In the preceding chapter, I used the panentheistic analogy as a means for introducing God-language "from below."[33] Just as *spirit* stands for the dimension of personal being that we only find in conjunction with highly complex physical systems such as the human body, so God can be introduced as that spiritual identity, presence, and agency that we come to know out of the physical world (the universe) taken as a whole. Recall that panentheistic theologies maintain that the world is within God, although God is also more than the world. Each human being is a center of identity that, although involving the identity of a body, *also* functions as a spiritual unit, that is, a unity having intentions, thoughts, and desires that do not apply to the body taken by itself. Likewise, God as an agent has knowledge, intentions, and plans that *go beyond* anything in the world. The analogy suggests a purely philosophical reason for resisting pantheism: it is not clear that it allows us to conceive of the divine as agency.

Toward a Theology of Immanent Spirit

Let's see what further conclusions we can derive from this analogy. This line of argument reflects the interdependence of systematic and biblical theology defended above and the commitments to integrative theology described in part I. Inspired by the biblical and theological traditions, one develops a systematic conception of person-hood, one that pertains both to the divine and the human persons, and *then* corrects this conception based on insights drawn from our present context. Taking the notion of personal (or person-like) subjectivity or agency as truly basic for our understanding of God, let's first try to think of God as a person analogous to us, and *then* correct this notion in all the ways that are necessary.

Individual persons are not separate from their bodies. They are not essentially disembodied souls that had the bad luck to be locked within bodies. Bodies are crucial to human agency in the world. The input that we receive as embodied agents is critical to the experiences that we have, and hence to the persons that we become. At the same time, we are also more than our bodies, which are physical things that are studied by physiologists and neuroscientists.[34] We include a center of subjective experience. We are essentially subjects. Still, we only know subjects as *embodied subjectivity*. For example, an essential part of what it is to be a person is to exist in community (family and other social units). Yet community relies on embodiedness and would be incomprehensible without it.

How else can we grasp what it means for God to be personal except based on this, the only understanding of personhood that we have? What happens when we explore the analogy further? Clearly God cannot have a particular body (though the doctrine of the incarnation, traditionally understood, teaches that it is possible for at least one person of the triune God to be embodied). But suppose that God were related to the whole universe in a way at least vaguely analogous to our relations to our bodies.[35] The universe would then become the focal point of God's agency.

When the world is understood as ontologically "outside" God, then any actions that God takes within the world must represent interventions from outside into the world's order. This model of God as a sort of foreign agent intervening into an independently existing order raises numerous problems. If the creation (and its Creator) were perfect from the start, why would it have to be "fixed" in this manner? Are regularities within the world to be understood as representing a causality independent of God, one that functions all on its own? Would it not be far better theologically to view even inner-worldly causality as (in at least some sense) a manifestation of divine agency? How could these divine interventions be known at all by humans if they came from completely outside the order that we inhabit?

On the panentheistic analogy, there would be no *qualitative* or ontological difference between the regularity of natural law and the intentionality of special divine action. Put differently, this view denies that only the latter should count as divine action and not the former. Instead, natural laws, when viewed theologically, will count as descriptions of the predictable regularity of patterns of divine action. The fact that our universe exhibits the physical regularities it does could be taken as a surd, a brute fact needing no further explanation (atheism). Or it could be attributed to an original act of God, by which God "set the clock in motion" and then let it run on its own (deism). Classical theology held that the continuing "concurrence" of God is required to keep things ticking along. Panentheism stands closest to classical Western theism in this affirmation, yet it draws an even closer link between physics and theology. Since

God is present in each physical interaction and at each point in space, each interaction is a part of the divine being in the broadest sense, for it is "in him [that] we live and move and have our being" (Acts 17:28).

Natural regularities within God's universe, then, would be roughly analogous to autonomic responses within an individual's body—the things that one's body does without conscious interference or guidance. In one sense, such behaviors are still one's own "actions," even though they occur through the body's operating in a regular or autonomic manner and one thus performs them unconsciously. For instance, one can become conscious of particular actions that the body normally carries out automatically (by concentrating, for example, on breathing in and out—a process you were presumably not thinking about before reading this sentence, even though you were still performing it). The breathing example does suggest a difference, however. Theologically, we must conclude that God, being omniscient, would *always* be aware of God's autonomic or habitual actions within the universe.

Yet this theological interpretation of natural regularities as (autonomic) divine actions does not rule out *conscious* actions that God might undertake. In fact, the analogy with human agency actually creates the expectation that God would also consciously pursue certain ends, just as human agents also engage in actions that they perform consciously and with particular intentions in mind. How we are to understand such "focal" divine actions and how belief in them could be compatible with the institution of science—these are questions that demand careful attention. For now, the point is only to argue that divine action, which is obviously not an issue for atheism or deism, is better addressed within the context of panentheism than in the philosophical context presupposed by classical Western theism.

At the same time, the panentheistic analogy also suggests that God as personal should be *more than* the universe. Put differently, God's consciousness or awareness is more than the world created and sustained by God. This means that there's no need to question God's transcendence of the world, which is fundamental to biblical theism. As the scriptures suggest, God continues to be aware of all that occurs within the world and to value and judge it. But now God's relationship to the world is much more intimate than can be conceptualized on any externalist or substance-based model.

Corrections to the Panentheistic Analogy

I have argued that panentheism makes a better systematic model to use in dialogue with the biblical and theological traditions than does the substance language of the classical theologians. But the method I've proposed now requires that we allow the tradition to correct this model as necessary.

The first correction involves survival of the death of the body. The traditional picture of God includes God's pre-existence of the world as its Creator, and God's existence subsequent to the world as the one who establishes a new heaven and a new earth. So God must be a being who *can* exist separate from the world. This means that the creation of the world does not need to be viewed as necessary, either in the form of a rational necessity (Hegel) or as an automatic emanation from God (Neoplatonic thought). Nonetheless, when God *has* freely decided to create a world, God stands in a relationship to it as close as our relation to our own bodies. God is no more outside God's creation than we are really disembodied spirits who happen to inhabit (or be trapped in!) our bodies during some period of time.

Further, note that if we can assert this survival of God apart from the world, the panentheistic analogy (now used in the opposite direction) gives us some reason to hope that through God's power we too will enjoy a state of presence with God after the death of our bodies—which is the message of hope expressed in the New Testament teaching of the resurrection of Jesus. The hope lies in this: that as Christ has overcome the sting of death (1 Cor 15:55), so also believers will be given a new heavenly body "like his glorious body" (Phil 3:21). Belief in salvation includes the sense that he has gone "to prepare a place," and the eschatological hope is that "I will come again, and receive you to myself; that where I am, you may be also" (John 14:2-3). In *God and Contemporary Science,* I discussed two correlates of the panentheistic analogy. First, it allows one to understand lawlike behavior in the world as an expression of the *autonomic* action of God in this "body," which is never fully separate from the divine Spirit that animates it. Second, it provides a way to understand *focal* divine agency, namely, as those events in the world that express divine intentions in a particularly sharp or clear manner. Both correlates express the assumption that the problem of divine action becomes much less intractable when God is not understood as a separate agent located outside the world but rather as embodied in the world (though also transcending it).

Once we have gotten this far (but only then) it becomes possible to think more directly about the nature of the divine Spirit whose nature is reflected, however dimly, in our own. Here we reach, at last, the distinctively theological moment: to drop the limitation to empirical experience and reflect, to the limited extent that we are able, on the nature of God "from above."[36] Theological reflection "from above" is *also* justified by the non-reducibility of emergent levels. Recall that each new level (physics, biology, psychology) requires its own explanatory categories and its own unique level of analysis; and each one introduces surprising new characteristics that could not have been anticipated from the lower level alone. Analogously, we find that the divine agent must be characterized not only in psychological (human-spirit) terms, but also in terms of a level of pure Spirit that transcends the universe as a whole.

At this point classical theological concepts also come into play. God is not contingent but necessary, not mortal but eternal, not finite but infinite. As such, God serves as the Ground of the world, and the world in turn must be understood as grounded in God. (Note that the metaphor of grounding is not spatial, though it is consistent with the structure of panentheism.) What is the nature of the one who grounds? According to the logic of the concept, the infinite, though first arising out of the notion of the finite as its counter, must encompass the finite within it while at the same time infinitely transcending it. Infinite Spirit may include personal predicates and qualities within it, but as such it is also more than personal—trans-personal. This is one reason why traditional theology was right to maintain that God consists of three divine persons rather than that God is *a* personal being.

Let's pause for a moment to look back over the terrain we have traversed. How has the original context of discovery been transformed by this more systematic reflection on the nature of divine being? The notions of Ground, infinity, and necessary existence are new to the theological level of analysis and would not be predictable from within the empirical world alone. Likewise, the way that the divine infinity partially relativizes personal predicates when applied to God could not have been predicted from the lower level.

What happens to the God-world relation? In one sense the panentheistic analogy also has been corrected. Is the world "in" God in the same logical sense that the finite is "within" the infinite? Well, this may work for the divine Spirit and the world (compare this with the inclusion relationship that characterizes panentheism), but certainly one would not say that the human body is "in" the human spirit in the same sense! "Spirit" is a holistic level of description for what is most characteristic of the living, thinking, feeling human person. Spatial metaphors don't finally do justice to the unitive nature of this phenomenon. The body is "in" the spirit in the sense that the living human body *qua* physical system has its identity, its locus, and its *telos* "in" the spiritual life that is the highest expression of its identity (and in an additional sense that will emerge out of the discussion of Levinas below). It's true to speak of the world as "contained in" the divine—but only in the sense that the divine is omnipresent within it, and in the sense of ontological dependence: no finite thing would exist at the next moment were it not for continuing divine concurrence.

In summary, we might say that a "pneumatology from below" expresses the way in which the concept of divine Spirit is arrived at within the context of modern thought, whereas "pneumatology from above" is the attempt to rethink that content from a theological perspective. Or, to put it differently, pneumatology involves a two-fold transformation of our own experience of spirit: (1) we extrapolate from the qualities of spirit known through the natural world and through encounters with other human persons, augmenting them to the level appropriate to divine Spirit and (2) we seek to conceive the nature of Infinite Spirit based on our experience as embodied agents.

Neither of these routes provides a direct basis for understanding God in Godself. One response to this limit is simply to throw up one's hands. God is a complete mystery, and nothing whatsoever can be said truly of the nature of the divine. But whatever skeptical or post-modern reasons there may be for taking the ineffable way out, there are Christian reasons for resisting the "complete mystery" response. The Christian belief is that God has in some ways made Godself known. The line of ascent upwards towards an understanding of the divine nature certainly has its limits when it is drawn from the human side—just as the line of *moral* ascent towards Godlikeness is questioned in both Jewish and Christian traditions. But God has broken down the dividing wall (Eph 2:14), making known the divine nature and plans that had been hidden since the foundation of the world (Eph 1:9ff.). Now, a "salvation economy" (*Heilsökonomie*) cannot be grasped without also grasping something of the character of the One who acts to bring about the divine will. Any attempt to draw a sharp distinction between the way God *reveals Godself to be* for purposes of salvation (as in the language of revelation, the economic Trinity, God at work in the world) and the way God *really is* in God's own nature (the immanent Trinity, God *an sich*) would raise serious problems of reliability. For surely God cannot reveal the divine nature falsely given the character of God as understood by the Christian tradition.

➤ Infinite Spirit, All-Encompassing Spirit

Spirit or subjectivity thus constitutes the overarching connection. In one sense, it bridges the gap between human and divine. And yet *only* in one sense, for the distinction between the human and the divine must *also* be thought. One crucial means for expressing the difference between God and humanity in modern theology has been the concept of infinity.[37] "Infinite" is a privative. It seems to say that the infinite subject must be *absolutely other* than finite subjects. Only one entity can be absolutely infinite, the necessary source or ground for all that exists. Thus modern thinkers have conceived of God as infinite Ground, the condition of the possibility of all finite or contingent things.

Yet there is also a wrinkle, which Hegel expressed more clearly than any before him. An infinite that excludes the finite is "the bad infinite" (*das schlechte Unendliche*), and not "the true infinite" (*das wahre Unendliche*) at all. Such an infinite is not unlimited in the strongest sense, inasmuch as it is limited by the finite that lies outside it and is other to it. The true infinite, Hegel realized, must therefore include the finite as a part, while at the same time retaining within itself the distinction between infinite and finite.

This famous Hegelian insight alone, even apart from other compelling arguments, would be enough to raise panentheism to the forefront of theological attention. Panentheism asserts that all things are encompassed by the divine being, while God is also more than the set of all finite things. This is closely analogous to the claim, sketched in the last section, that the finite must be contained within the all-encompassing Infinite. Whatever is finite must be a part of the infinite whole without losing its distinctiveness from that which grounds it.

It may be sufficient for a dialectical philosopher merely to note this logical similarity and logical difference, but theologians are charged with understanding more concretely what these terms mean. The *difference* between God and world is a major theme in the Hebrew and Greek Scriptures. It finds perhaps its most powerful expression in the doctrine of creation. All finite things are traceable back to a free and unconstrained act of the Creator. They continue in existence only because of God's sustenance of the world. No contingent thing would exist without God's ongoing concurring will at each new moment. Numerous other theological doctrines stress the difference between God and world, including the doctrine of God's absolute goodness or moral perfection, and the doctrines of sin, salvation, redemption, and sanctification to which it gives rise.

Unfortunately, theologians have not fared as well in conceptualizing the *other* half of the puzzle, the *not-otherness* of God and God's creation.[38] Traditionally, the major reminder of this truth has been the *imago Dei*. It would be interesting to explore the various ways in which the *imago Dei* has been parsed out—consciousness, will, freedom, rationality, sociality or communality, self-transcendence—and to ask what precise model of the "other and not-other" each one assumes about the divine-human relationship.

The present theology of Spirit offers an attractive contemporary answer to the question of this "not-other." It turns on *combining a panentheistic understanding of the God-world relation with a richer theory of the nature of the spirit/Spirit shared by humans and God.* This positive theory of immanent Spirit allows one to conceive of the similarities between God and creation without abolishing the differences that remain.

What happens when the dynamics of subjectivity are combined with the interpenetrating (perichoretic) dance of finite and divine Spirit? A new two-sided movement emerges that deserves a closer look. Human thought begins with the movement upwards, which (thanks to the spiritual nature shared by God and creatures) allows one to move conceptually from finite things to the all-encompassing Infinite. But what about the task of conceiving finite things from the perspective of the Infinite? What about making sense of the divine being "from above"? As Emmanuel Levinas notes, in one sense it's true to say that the infinite is incarnated within the finite, since the infinite is thought by the finite.[39] The thought of the Infinite is part of the content of finitude. Indeed, Levinas continues, this thought is the most basic thought for the finite, since it is prior to all that the finite knows and is. At the same time, the thought of the Infinite is the one thought that by its very nature goes beyond the finite's comprehension. The finite is given the thought of something that is its source, its being, its perspective or definition—and yet this "other" is by definition incomprehensible for it. This is the paradox of divine Spirit.

This powerful paradox suggests a dual role for infinite Spirit. On the one hand, it represents the all-encompassing framework within which the individual Spirit "lives and moves and has its being." On the other hand, the Infinite is present as a thought within the finite mind, present yet ungraspable, present in its absence or—perhaps better from a Christian perspective—revelatory in its elusiveness. Divine Spirit confronts the thinking subject with what Levinas calls "the more in the less"—the task for thought that it can never fulfill. "The Infinite affects thought by devastating it and at the same time calls upon it; a 'putting it back in its place' it puts thought in place. It awakens it."[40] In this case the unthought is no peripheral thought. What teases the mind at the edges of consciousness is at the same time what suggests itself as the ground of consciousness itself.

Let me put this point even more strongly. One encounters here importantly two different "in" relations or subsumption relations—*the idea "in" human consciousness of an Infinite Ground "in" which consciousness itself lives and moves and has its being*—two "ins" that appear to exclude one another. And yet they are for pneumatology two halves of a single dialectical whole, which represents the constitutive condition of consciousness itself.

I have argued that panentheism most successfully thematizes this two-fold "in" in the God-world relation. Because panentheism emphasizes the immanence of God to a greater degree than classical theism, it helps reduce the problems associated with the transcendence—and thus foreignness (or at least *perceived* foreignness)—of God. Of course, theologians should not pretend that even panentheism's greater stress on the immanence of God will overcome the widespread resistance to grounding the human subject in a divine source. The reason is that most of the modern history of the subject has involved the self-assertion of the subject, and hence its independence from any sort of grounding relation. It would not be an overstatement to say (as Louis Dupré has so convincingly shown)[41] that the subject came to be taken as the sole source of meaning and value in the modern period. As *causa sui*, as self-constituting, and as the creator of all things that it values (hence, of all things that *are* of value), the modern subject has taken itself to replace both Creator and created in the traditional view—to have abolished Absolute Subject altogether.[42]

For the modern subject, and equally so for the postmodern (post-)subject, Spirit is set free from any metaphysical parameters and allowed to roam freely, immersing itself fully in the self-creating enterprise which is its natural birthright. What makes Levinas's position so significant is that it confronts the *causa sui* perspective from within. In Levinas's reading, the subject still finds itself preoccupied with the notion of an Infinite Other. Reading backwards historically, one finds signs of this continuing preoccupation with an infinite ground even in those modern philosophers (for example, Fichte) in which the self-grounding of the Ego is most pronounced. This, I have argued, is the key opening for a theological doctrine of the Spirit today.

➤ Theology Anthropomorphized, Anthropology Theologized

What are the costs of this new opening? We saw that in the late medieval and early modern periods the Spirit of God was held to be ontologically transcendent of yet present to the world. Two major modern developments in particular—the Kantian critique of metaphysics and the strong focus on immanence in Spinoza's philosophy—then led to philosophies of the Spirit that challenged the separateness and transcendence typical of the earlier models. In the nineteenth century, skeptics (paradigmatically, Nietzsche) claimed to complete the movement by dismissing all trans-human or trans-natural reference whatsoever for God-language. By contrast, I've argued that the language of the Spirit still has the resources for retaining both the immanence and the transcendence of God when it is understood within a panentheistic framework.

It is not quite so easy, once Spirit has become a shared framework in the sense here described, to distinguish as precisely between the transcendent and immanent dimensions of Spirit.[43] The reasons have to do both with the philosophy of language and with the nature of Spirit itself. In the philosophy of language, what may have been lost is the sense that one can describe transcendent realities in a language that is *fully appropriate to its object,* that is, a full transcendent language. Human language simply cannot be purged of its "merely human" sources in culture, historical epoch, and personal experience. Without pausing to list the various epistemological grounds for the irreversible co-mingling of human and divine, I suggest that attempts at regaining the purity of God-spawned language appear to have fallen short. (We return to this theme in chapter 13.) Depending on one's orientation, one may call it, following Yovel, "the adventures of immanence" or, with more ominous overtones, "condemnation to immanence."

It is an age, we might say, in which one can no longer hold Feuerbach at arm's length.[44] Feuerbach's thesis was that language about God is really language about the human species. It projects our wishes, aspirations, and self-understanding onto an empty heaven. Now Feuerbach clearly overstated his thesis. No amount of evidence of correlations between human desires and needs on the one hand and theology on the other would suffice to establish the *direction* of influence. Just as statistical correlations in the social sciences require background assumptions in order to decide what causes what, so some prior theoretical assumptions must be used to decide which realm (the human or the divine) is prior and which is the product of projection. Feuerbach employed assumptions that reduced God-language downward, while Hegel and more conservative theologians reversed the assumptions, reducing anthropological language "upwards." The battle will continue over *which* discipline, anthropology or theology, should trump. Here to stay now, however, is the relation of mutual dependence between them.

The ambiguity of the *imago Dei* thus mirrors the primordial ambiguity of the task of theology itself. We speak of a God whom we know only through our own experience in and reflection on the world, yet we conceive of this God as also transcending the world in the essential divine nature. As Jürgen Moltmann writes,

> Whatever the "image of God" means in particular instances, in every case that which represents God and corresponds to God, and that in which God recognizes the divine self, is intended. Humans beings are the image of God on earth insofar as they correspond to God and represent the invisible God in the visible world. Humans beings are the image of God on earth insofar as God recognizes the divine self in them as in a mirror.[45]

This epistemic situation, which I claim is intrinsic to theology, is mirrored ontologically in the doctrine of Christian panentheism. The necessary fit between *what* we know and *how* we know it is an important bulwark for the position. We are embodied persons whose only knowledge of agency comes in the context of a spiritual or mental "self"—a self that acts through the medium of a body and perceives all that it knows of the world through this same medium, but that is in some sense also "more than" its physical existence and the physical medium in which it exists. Yet the God whom we know in this fashion and under these constraints is one who by nature transcends the world and created it freely. That God is one who encompasses all created things within the single divine presence. No spot of creation is external to the divine, thus our very existence plays itself out within the one divine Being.

Just as it is unlikely that *a*-theological arguments will ever prove that *no* transcendent being exists to bear the predicates attributed to it, it's also unlikely that theological arguments will prove the existence of this transcendent being. Thus, Feuerbach's best efforts to the contrary, God's existence remains a live option. The failure of proofs on both sides has left theologians without the ability to show the extent to which God-language is rooted in direct divine revelation. I have in the past challenged sharp distinctions between the "inside" and the "outside" of faith communities.[46] If correct, this means that many of the ambiguities that exist in contemporary thought and society are ambiguities in which Christian thought participates as well. No evidence requires one to eschew claims for the existence of God, but the best evidence does force one to admit that language about God is also language about ourselves. If, as the tradition maintains, a transcendent Spirit inspires theological reflection, then it is equally true that the Spirit does so out of and through human embodied experience in the world. The result is theological language that points toward God at the same time that it just as clearly expresses much about the speaker, her background, her culture, and her intellectual milieu.

In the Christian tradition, the Spirit has always connoted the presence of God in the world. In John's gospel, Jesus says, "I will ask the Father and he will give you another Counselor, the Spirit of truth, to be with you forever. . . . But the Counselor, the Holy Spirit, whom the Father will send in my name, will teach you all things and will remind you of everything I have said to you" (John 14:16-17, 26). This is a kenotic Spirit who does not take center stage but remains the Spirit of Christ. Only in the ambiguity of Jesus' absence can the Spirit be present (John 16:7). The ambiguity of the Spirit's leading is necessitated by the mode of its speaking: the Spirit will "prove the world wrong about sin and righteousness and judgment" (16:8). Thus when the Spirit "guides into all truth" (16:13) it is a different sort of presence, a more muffled presence, an internal guidance—the still, small voice which, often as not, does not wear its source on its sleeve.

➤ Conclusion

What do these results mean for talk of Spirit today? It's possible to engage in studies of the human spirit which are purely descriptive, or purely political, or purely meta-phorical, and which eschew theological concepts altogether. But we have also traced the outline of another possibility: a language of spirit/Spirit that is in dialogue with the great modern philosophies of Spirit as well as with the anti-metaphysical and anti-theistic thinkers of the last century or so. What emerges from this study is a clear picture of the close correlation between studies of the human and the divine Spirit. The same correlation that led to Feuerbach's projection critique also led to the rich works in theological anthropology of this century.[47] The result is an understanding of spirit/Spirit that is not opposed to theological reflection but rather a guide to the form it must take today.

More specifically, the constructive argument of this chapter involved reappropriating (and thereby transforming) idealist theories of the subject and of divine subjectivity. The resulting position did not begin "from above" by presupposing a doctrine of the Trinity. But it does stem from the attempt to do justice to the monistic, dualistic, and trinitarian moments in any adequate theory of divine Spirit.[48]

In one sense the view is monistic, because there remains an important respect in which God is one. All that exists, being dependent on God, is included within the divine presence in a unified fashion. Unfortunately, strict pantheism casts both the existence of God and divine personality into question. Thus the only sufficiently radical way in which the monistic element can be appropriated within Christian theology is within a *panentheistic* context.

The view is also dualistic. There is something deeply right about the distinction between God as the Ground of Being and the personal side of God that develops in the process of God's interaction with the universe, a distinction developed in different but complementary ways by Whitehead and Tillich. It is here that the resources of idealist theories of the subject come into play: the Other remains of constitutive importance in the development of subjectivity.

Finally, the view is trinitarian because only a God who enters into relationship with other subjects as genuine others to Godself could be the sort of personal God that we find in the Hebrew and Greek Scriptures. The moment of mediation has been variously presented: in the classical trinitarian theology of Father, Son, and Spirit; in the theories of self-consciousness of German Idealism and neo-idealism; in recent process variants;[49] in liberation theology; and in various modified forms among liberal theologians of our day.

Reflections of the sort explored in this chapter often raise fears of the "subordination" of Christian systematic theology to a foreign power or to a sort of philosophical foundation-building. I wish thus to conclude by emphasizing again the negative theological moment that still confronts theologians when we speak of the Spirit of the living God. It remains possible to incorporate this negative moment without tacitly assenting to a "crucifixion of the intellect," a demand that reflection cease for the sake of faith. In the *Dialectics,* Schleiermacher emphasizes the role of limit language in talk of God, for reasons that are not fideistic in nature. Talk of spirit, whether human or divine, implies an intrinsic "unavailability to analysis" that places an inherent limit on all language about God. Likewise, Levinas has argued powerfully that the spirit of the other is that which recedes infinitely from our grasp, while retaining its ethical call upon us.[50]

Nonetheless, it remains possible, and perhaps *spiritually and ethically* necessary, to reflect systematically on the God whom one is encountering in the sacraments, in the scriptures, in the corporate experience of the church, in other religions, and in the world. After all, interpretations of the biblical texts and the Christian tradition are closely wed with broader models of the sort we have discussed, and reflection aimed at consistency and systematic coherence remains central to the activity of theology and to living of the religious life. Hence we end where we started—by acknowledging our irreducibly pluralistic context, which leaves behind philosophical foundations while at the same time encouraging the ongoing quest for ever-new models of the Spirit today.

The Becoming *of the* One Who Always Was

Toward a Trinity *in* Process

> Religion is the translation of general ideas into particular thoughts, particular emotions, and particular purposes; it is directed to the end of stretching individual interest beyond its self-federating particularity. Philosophy finds religion, and modifies it; and conversely religion is among the data of experience which philosophy must weave into its own scheme. (A. N. Whitehead)[1]

NEITHER PHILOSOPHERS NOR THEOLOGIANS HAVE EVER REALLY BEEN satisfied with the division of labor with respect to God. Theologians at their best have held to the goal of conceptual rigor. Still, they have often felt shackled by the foreign demands of the discipline of philosophy, which were often perceived as conflicting with beliefs from the very tradition with whose preservation they were charged. Philosophers, by contrast, have expressed impatience with the (to them inexplicable) concern of theology to preserve the merely contingent beliefs of a religious tradition that seemed hopelessly arbitrary and dogmatic. Standard criteria for turf separation—for example, systematic theology is characterized by particularity and philosophical theology by generality[2]—generally fail to satisfy either side.

No area of this discussion has been more disputed than that of the doctrine of the Trinity. Is it a necessary result of reason? An arbitrary, even contradictory belief left over from doctrinal squabbles nearly two millenia ago? A faith insight allowing for philosophical explication but not proof? A model useful in different ways within theology and metaphysics? Because of the centrality of the questions it raises, the debate surrounding the Trinity offers a particularly effective test case for establishing the lines between philosophy and theology. Moreover, because of its associations with Scholastic metaphysics, and particularly with the thought of Thomas of Aquinas, it becomes a crucial locus in the dialogue between "classical" and process theology. At the same time, the dispute is so laden with past misunderstandings and conceptual confusions that one wonders initially whether perhaps no progress whatsoever can be made here.

Process thought stemming from Whitehead can play an important role in this discussion. This is partly because process thinkers have subjected substance-based metaphysics, and in particular the static categories of medieval, perfection-based language about God, to keen critical scrutiny. But it is also because of the specific dilemma with which Whitehead struggled. Is God non-temporal and non-personal, a category of the ultimate but not in fact an actual entity, or is God personal and temporal?[3] This dilemma, I shall argue, represents one of the most basic issues, if not *the* most basic conceptual issue in the history of the modern thought about God. Whether or not we side with Whitehead's own attempt at a rapprochement, and with the concepts of entity and person on which it rests, we dare not fall beneath his level of understanding of the problem.

In this chapter, I defend a version of a "Trinity in process" that attempts to mediate between the usual positions in classical and process theologies. If the argument is successful, it will cast doubts on the widespread assumption that these two schools of thought are intrinsically opposed. The key element of my proposal is a distinction between the *necessity* of a three-fold division within God on the one hand and, on the other, the *contingency* of God's free self-revelation, including God's revelation as Father, Son, and Holy Spirit. Under this view, the particular trinitarian form that God's self-revelation has taken in the Christian tradition[4] is a result of God's response to free human decisions and to the (non-determined) development of the world. Nonetheless, the Trinity that God has been revealed to be is at the same time an expression of a structure or potentiality that was present in God's nature from the start.

➤ Theologians in Dialogue with Neo-Process Thought

In Whitehead's own day, the key issues in the debate with Christian theologians concerned matters such as orthodoxy, submission to the pope, and faithfulness to the creeds.[5] These are not (obviously) the burning loci of controversy in the confrontation between Christianity and the academy today. Through a series of steps that we can only mention here, science and epistemology since Whitehead's day have discarded most of the vestiges of positivistic empiricism, non-creedal Christianity has gained significant ground, and even conservative theologians speak increasingly of multiple models of God.

With the failure of Kant's twelve categories (and those of his competitors) to live up to their alleged necessary status, and with their transformation at the hands of twentieth-century philosophers into multiple conceptual schemes and "ways of worldmaking,"[6] the delineation of the realm of the metaphysical by means of the distinction "necessary/unnecessary" has become untenable. In its place, we need to turn again to Whitehead's own insistence on pluralism and on the preliminary nature of all knowledge. After all, several different models can be useful for interpreting the world—and the God-world relationship. This fact points toward a "pluralistic metaphysics," which implies (*inter alia*) multiple "models of God."[7] What is interesting for our purposes is that this shift does not make an appeal to Christian content irrelevant—quite the contrary. For now the source of beliefs is less important. What counts first and foremost is their fruitfulness as models in various explanatory and theoretical contexts.

A third transformation should be mentioned (even if it cannot be fully argued here): the movement from Whiteheadian orthodoxy to neo-process thought. Some major rethinking of Whitehead's doctrine of God has taken place. A variety of theologies now exist that are informed by Whitehead without exactly following his own theological speculations. This descriptive claim is also a normative one: a Trinity in process only becomes a live option once the strictures of orthodox Whiteheadianism are removed.

And it is right that they be removed. I agree with Neville that Whitehead's exact doctrine of God "cannot be sustained in critical scrutiny."[8] This is why trinitarian thinkers—and not only they!—should be encouraged to rethink Whitehead, to propose modifications in key Whiteheadian concepts, and to explore alternative process conceptualities. The mark of a process thinker has never been orthodoxy. Given Whitehead's own views, "orthodox Whiteheadianism" is probably an oxymoron. Thus the term *neo*-process thought in my heading, which connotes and encourages a movement beyond the stage where consistency with (even the basic tenets of) Whitehead's thought served as the criterion of adequacy. Indeed, one might well argue that there never was such a stage, that from the very beginning Whitehead's readers and followers were rethinking fundamental points.[9]

If we were not working now in the context of neo-process thought, one key assumption of my argument would probably seem unpalatable: the tenet that atomism is not finally adequate as a theory of individuality. Of course, Whitehead was never an atomist in the traditional sense of the term. There are a number of aspects of his thought that go beyond atomism. He clearly holds, for example, that the whole of the actual occasion is more than the sum of its parts.[10] Likewise, the objective immortality of all past occasions in God is more than the "objective" content of these occasions themselves, since God also values them in his appropriation. So Joseph Bracken is in one sense extending a Whiteheadian principle when he argues that we have to ascribe to societies a non-reductive reality, a reality that is not reduced to the parts of which they consist. He speaks of the "key point on which I differ, if not from Whitehead, at least from some Whiteheadians. That key point is that communities (or, in Whiteheadian language, structured societies of a particular complexity) exercise an agency which is not simply reducible to the agency of their constituent actual entities. The whole, in other words, is more than the sum of its parts. . . ."[11] A similar point has been argued repeatedly in the biological sciences and the philosophy of science under the heading of the doctrine of emergent properties[12] (see part II). The proposal that follows might be seen as a contribution toward a neo-process theology. If a structured society cannot exercise agency, then God as three-in-one will probably be unthinkable from the start.

➤ God for Us, God with Us

The starting point for Robert Neville's theology is the argument that "everything determinate needs determination."[13] Before this point there is no God, nothing determinate whatsoever, but only sheer indeterminacy (which is indistinguishable from sheer nothingness). No specific theological conclusions, and much less a concrete doctrine of God, can be developed, he thinks, until the primordial selection of basic metaphysical principles has taken place *ex nihilo*.

I wish to proceed "backwards," as it might at first appear, that is, from the opposite end from which Neville (and Hegel, with his pure undifferentiated Being) begins. Where does the trinitarian doctrine begin, and what is its immanent "logic"? The chief interest of the classical theological doctrine of the Trinity was to think of God's real involvement with humanity. If God is eternally tri-personal, then it will be possible to speak of a divine life, a divine community, analogous to our own. From all eternity, God will have included within Godself a (self-)giving and receiving, a choosing and being chosen, a begetting and a being begotten—and some process of mediation between these two poles. According to the classical view, the eternal Son is identical with an individual human being, Jesus, at least in one of his natures (since Jesus' human nature is not taken into Trinity itself). God's involvement with humankind in the form of the incarnation of the second Person reduces the gap between God and God's creation. Human history can now be understood only in conjunction with, or as a part of, salvation history.

Notice how this closeness between God and humanity raises the possibility of a reduction of God *to* humanity. The danger is two-fold. A full reduction would make the very existence of God a projection of human wishes, human aspirations, or the happenstances of human reason. The other danger of projection transpires through an illicit transposition of human categories onto the divine. The divine "otherness" may be lost when we characterize it too fully with human predicates, construing the trinitarian God as a group of persons on the model of a human society. God would then exist only *pro nobis*, for us, reducing the divine nature to the product of God's interactions with creation and nothing more.

The need, then, was to correct for an overly anthropomorphized understanding of God. So the starting point—namely, attempting to think "God with us, God for us"—was supplemented conceptually with the notion of "God in and of Godself." That is, the classical doctrine of the Trinity avoided reductionist tendencies by insisting on an eternal nature in God that remained unaffected by interaction with humans. Alternatively, the entire trinitarian structure itself was understood to precede all interactions with the world.

But can an approach that begins with thinking about the self-revealing God use that very same framework to theorize about God apart from all revelation? Can the "Trinity of revelation" be projected backwards to a trio of divine persons before the foundation of the world? Or must we *change* the underlying basis if we wish to speak of "God in and of Godself," appealing no longer to God's own self-revelation but rather to purely conceptual considerations? It will be my argument that success in specifying the transcendent divine nature is not best guaranteed by an immanent Trinity of Father, Son, and Holy Spirit, understood as the mirror image of the economic Trinity, though now extrapolated into God's essence apart from any interaction with the world. Where then *are* we to start the effort to think about the "hidden" side of God? And why conclude that the resulting structure will still be trinitarian?

➤ A Meditation on the Infinite

The most effective entrée and guideline for conceiving this otherness of God is, I shall argue, the finite-infinite distinction. This might seem a questionable starting point for a neo-process theology, given Whitehead's insistence that "it belongs to the nature of physical experience that it is finite" (*PR* 345). He speaks here of God's consequent nature as being "determined, incomplete, consequent, 'everlasting,' fully actual, and conscious," but never actually calls it infinite. Still, Whitehead's position is too ambiguous, as Lewis Ford has shown,[14] and his flirtation with the concept of the infinite too great, for one to rule out all connection between process thought and the theory of the infinite. What is it, then, about the concept of the infinite that makes it ineliminable for an adequate theism? A brief meditation, inspired by Descartes, may help convey the role that this concept has to play; the rest of the chapter wrestles with its significance for trinitarian thought.

"When I turn my mind's eye upon myself," writes Descartes in Meditation 3, "I understand that I am a thing which is incomplete and dependent on another and which aspires without limit to ever greater and better things" (VII, 51).[15] This is the Cartesian original intuition: I am finite. We know our finitude immediately through our dependence on an "other" or others outside ourselves. This starting point can be expressed philosophically, psychologically, biologically, existentially. In its various guises, it has been called a fundamental intuition, a logical truth, as well as conceptual, analytic, and *a priori*. What these various labels have in common is the insight that no additional evidence needs to be called in on its behalf. The intuition of finitude is, I suggest, the first and the basis for all subsequent reflection on God and on ourselves.

Now for the second step. I am finite; I am *not infinite*. Insofar as it occurs without argument and *appears* to rely on negation alone, the transition from intuiting finitude to an intuition of the infinite has a good claim to immediacy. The original intuition—I am finite—gives rise immediately to the idea of *something without limits*. To be aware of finitude is to have, however implicitly, the idea of the infinite. The two are equiprimordial—if indeed the idea of the unlimited is not actually the more primitive of the two. Insofar as I can only intuit limits against the (assumed) backdrop of an unlimited whole, perhaps my sense of dependence already implies the prior idea of something that is independent. *How* to think of this is a matter for later reflection. For now, I suggest only that the idea of the infinite arises as the natural and inevitable counterpart to the intuitive awareness that we as finite beings have of our finitude.

Like the original intuition, this idea also has an immediate link with our being in the world. We could deepen it by developing a philosophical anthropology or phenomenology based on types of the experience of the unlimited.[16] Since the idea of the unlimited arises directly out of our immediate intuition that we are finite, it already suggests a religious side to human existence—as long as "religious" is taken in a broad sense and as neutral (at this point) on the question of the existence of a divine being or beings. The reciprocal relationship between human finitude and the idea of the infinite helps to define human existence, even before full theoretical explication. "Finite being," with its implicit contrast to infinity, thus becomes a general term for our ontological status as beings with limits.

It is easier to grant the intuition of the infinite when one acknowledges what it does *not* prove. If (as I think) the ontological proof is not rationally compelling, the idea of an infinite being does not entail its actual existence. Neither does it entail an actual comprehension of this infinite.[17] Focusing on the original emergence of the idea of the infinite gives us reason to assert an ontological link between finitude and infinitude, even if no clear content for the idea of an infinite God can yet be formed.[18] However rich the notion of the infinite may be as an intuition, then, it will underdetermine philosophical debate. Still, if the intuition is admissible in the sense presented, it can help to sort out the conceptual frameworks that attempt to think about the nature of God in Godself. Further, without being a "proof" of theism, it does help to foster our understanding of theistic beliefs, and may even provide a source of *prima facie* evidence as we consider signs of "God with us" that point in the direction of an infinite being.

Once the ideas of the finite and infinite are given, certain implications follow with greater or lesser immediacy. For example, if the idea of an infinite is granted, then by its nature it will be prior to the idea of the finite.[19] If this argument is valid, it will reverse the order of presentation above. The infinite will be prior to the finite in everything except the order of discovery. Infinity is not understood by negating a boundary or limit, that is, negating the finite. Instead, all limitation first implies a negation of the infinite. Further, it could perhaps be shown that the infinite is the condition of the possibility of the existence of finite things. This would give it a type of transcendental status, reminiscent of Kant's regulative ideas. It would be in part an *a priori* idea, rather than just the product of experience.[20] But enough has been said to suggest how the progression from intuition to philosophy proper might proceed. Let us therefore break off the meditation here. In a moment it will be clear what role this originary intuition has to play in the search for a Trinity in process.

➤ Thinking with Whitehead beyond Whitehead

Is it possible to identify the infinite with God in some way, or would this link raise insuperable problems? An individual being, it seems, cannot be infinite, for to be *a* being is to exist alongside other beings and to be limited by them. Yet God can fulfill the functions of primordial envisagement and concrescence, responding to the world at all moments, it seems, only if God is understood as (in some sense) an actual occasion like others. How then could we think of a dimension in God that is not in itself a feature of a personal being?

And yet this is precisely the modification of Whitehead that recent process thought has been pursuing as the most profitable. As Cobb puts it: "My own judgment, informed by Marjorie Suchocki, is that we need to reflect more radically on the undeveloped insights of Whitehead about the profound difference between the one nontemporal actual entity which originates conceptually and the many temporal actual occasions which originate physically."[21] More concretely, "in *some* respects the everlasting concrescence of God must resemble temporal succession as well as genetic succession, and in some respects it must be profoundly different from both."[22]

This suggestion of Suchocki and Cobb is the one I wish to pursue in the remaining pages of this chapter. But first we should pause for a moment and survey the lay of the land. What are the major alternatives that are open to a neo-process theology? The range of available options looks something like this:

1. *Dipolar theism*: The unchanging or eternal (antecedent) nature of God is supplemented by a responsive (consequent) side. The one represents the essential nature of God, the other the responsive nature. The responsive pole could be conceived as a single, eternally concrescing actual entity (Whitehead), or, since it must evidence a high level of continuity, as a personally ordered society of actual occasions (Hartshorne).[23]

2. *Classical theism*: Although God may have both essential and responsive sides, the more important is God's essential nature. The responsive side may either be subordinated to the essential, or (in more extreme views) even dismissed as not actually a part of God's nature at all. Traditional theists are worried that trying to make room for God's becoming in history may marginalize or eliminate certain essential properties and perfections.

3. *All the significant divine properties are necessary*: Whatever emerges on the responsive side could be treated as merely contingent. According to this view, one is free to draw conclusions and to theorize about God as revealed in interaction with humans. However, everything that one says remains under the aegis of God's contingent pattern of self-revelation, and therefore the theoretical conclusions tell us little or nothing about the internal nature of God. That is the task of *a priori* metaphysics. Gregory Boyd, for example, who concentrates primarily on Hartshorne, holds a view of God "as eternally social, as alone actually necessary, and as actually infinite while nevertheless being open to contingent expressions of this antecedent necessity," a view that, he tells us, "fulfills all *a priori* requirements and retains the advantageous elements of both the classical and neoclassical views of God, while avoiding the difficulties of both."[24]

4. *God as power of the future*: The eternal pole, by contrast, might be dropped from the picture completely. This would make God fully responsive. If Whitehead was wrong in separating God and Creativity, and the two are to be identified instead, then this responsive God would have to be located entirely in the future (Lewis Ford).[25]

5. *God as society of persons*: God could be understood as a collection of occasions of some sort. Clearly it is not very satisfactory to treat God as a mere aggregate, yet it

may also raise insoluble problems to think of God (or one pole of God) as personal. In *The Triune Symbol*, Joseph Bracken drew a distinction between the three divine persons as "personally ordered societies of occasions" and the one God as a structured society (or society of sub-societies) in Whitehead's sense.[26] In a later book, *Society and Spirit*, he generalizes the concept, thinking of Whitehead's societies as "structured fields of activity for their constituent actual occasions."[27] A field has a certain unity in itself, and yet it is able to encompass other fields or occasions within it. This notion allows for the sort of inclusion relation that is conceptually necessary for an adequate doctrine of the Trinity. In particular, it can serve as the conceptual basis for *panenthe- ism*, the inclusion of the world within God: "While all finite entities exist in God and through the power of God, they are ontologically distinct from God in terms of both their being and activity."[28] We return to these themes below.

6. *God is not a being*: The very idea of God being "a being" at all could be cast into question. This would involve some fundamental rethinking, obviously, since the belief that God is a being has been a leading assumption in many theologies and is the position taken by Whitehead at many points in *Process and Reality*. By contrast, God as the "power of the future," in Ford's sense, would not be "a being" at all. If we pursue this possibility, it will be necessary for us to say *what* God *is not* insofar as God is not a being; for example, following Ivor Leclerc, being itself, the good, ground, or the infinite per se. This route may be a difficult and rocky one. Yet it is the one to which I believe one is propelled when the question of God is formulated in the manner so far explored.

➤ Romanticism and Process Theology

It is at this point that we can profitably supplement Whitehead's reflection with the work of the nineteenth-century thinker whose philosophy may stand the closest to Whitehead's: F. W. J. von Schelling, the so-called philosopher of Romanticism. In general (see chapter 9) there are resources in the German Idealist thinkers that are, I believe, crucial for a viable trinitarian theology today. In the rich tradition from Kant to Hegel, as I've argued elsewhere,[29] the work of Schelling's middle period stands out as a philosophical basis for trinitarian thought.

A helpful list of the significant parallels between Whitehead and Schelling is already available.[30] As Antoon Braeckman notes, (1) Schelling defines the imagination as "the activity whereby the infinite is unified into the finite, or as the act through which the many become one." Yet this is exactly how Whitehead understands Creativity. For both, nature itself is creative activity, *natura naturans*, and things are identified through their own creative advance. (2) In both, there is creative advance. Nature is an agency that, "by developing itself, constitutes an evolution toward ever more complex instances, i.e. towards human consciousness in the end." (3) In both, this process functions by means of "internal causation." Each actual entity becomes itself through its own process of concrescence. Likewise, Schelling holds that the organism produces or "constitutes" itself.

But instead of developing further links, let us turn immediately to the major difference. Both philosophers center their work on a mental principle, one of activity, feeling, and valuation. But, "in Schelling the paradigm of this basic structure is given by the *self-conscious* Ego, whereas Whitehead's paradigm is an *unconscious* experience."[31] In other words, Schelling's idealist theory of consciousness would seem at first to rule out any final rapprochement of their positions. Is not the core of Whitehead's view that the primary units are atomistic moments of experience or awareness, actual occasions which synthesize their predecessors and pass immediately into a state of objective existence (objects for other awarenesses) as soon as their subjective moment of concrescence has passed?

Much could be said about the mistakes and misinterpretations in Whitehead's famous chapter on "The Subjectivist Principle." Whitehead was not enough of a scholar of Idealism (as Braeckman shows, he admits to only secondary knowledge of the literature) to differentiate between Hegel's overly absolutistic theories and the more cautious claims of Schelling's writings on divine freedom and potency. Thus he was not able to appreciate how the subjective inclusion relations of Schelling's dipolar theism could avoid the heavy-handed laws that Hegel attributed to the rational development of *Geist* (Spirit). Yet these resources supplement Whitehead's own thought at what may be its weakest points. Basically, I suggest, Whitehead never found an adequate principle to account for the continuing identity of awareness and valuation of conscious beings through time. Moreover, God remained in certain ways an exception to Whitehead's own principles. Something like Hartshorne's early correction of Whitehead—viewing God as a personally ordered society of actual occasions—was necessary to overcome the difficulties. Yet by the time one has made the necessary corrections, be they Hartshorne's or others, one has already moved beyond an atomistic theory of consciousness, and hence beyond the conceptual limits of a *strictly* Whiteheadian framework.

The differences notwithstanding, it is fair to say that what Hartshorne calls a personally ordered society and Bracken a structured field of activity, Schelling calls a center of self-consciousness. The main difference is that, for process thinkers, there is a level *beneath* self-consciousness which is taken to be in some sense fundamental. Thus Bracken argues against Hegel that objective spirit is present at all levels of nature, even where self-consciousness is missing.[32] At the same time, using the concept of field, he also uses Hegel against Whitehead to argue that societies of occasions have a real identity as individuals; *the construction of identity is not just "from below" in an atomistic sense.* The later chapters of his *Society and Spirit* offer a trinitarian view of God according to which each of the divine persons is understood "as a succession of actual occasions" which form an "objective unity as one God" in the form of a "structured society."[33]

The starting point, then, for a synthesis between process and idealist thought is, as Bracken has seen, thinking of societies of actual occasions as fields (or something like fields), which have their own reality. They are not ontologically derivative, in the sense of being reducible to the actual occasions they include, but are characterized instead by a reality that can only be described from the perspective of the whole.

What happens to the theory of actual occasions when the emphasis is shifted from part to whole?

➤ Is God a Subject?

This move brings us to the transitional question in our analysis. Is God then subjective *an sich*, apart from or prior to any relationship with the world?

Schelling argues that God is *potentially subjective*—that is, must be thought as possessing the structure of subjectivity. However, God is not actually subjective, in a sense analogous to existing human subjects, until God interacts with an other. From the standpoint of philosophical reflection, then, before the foundation of the world it makes sense to speak only of a structural potentiality for subjectivity in God.[34] In order to have such a potential, it must be a complex structure, one with multiple elements or "moments." From the standpoint of theology, of course, something else happens. Additional considerations are introduced via the concept of revelation, which incline us to view the structure as enough like human consciousness that we can and must speak of it as subjectivity. Such a move can be made only by appealing to the four dimensions or facets of subjectivity: life, movement, consciousness, and responsiveness. The task in the following section, therefore, will be to evaluate the theological proposal that I develop here, in order to decide whether it has the components necessary for speaking of a divine subjectivity independent of the world. Does it make sense to speak of an actual divine community prior to the creation of the world of finite occasions?

As we've seen, Whitehead translated the "eternal will of God" as used within Christianity into the "consequent nature" of God.[35] But, as has often been pointed out, he was inconsistent on this matter. Whitehead often treats God generically, as "the principle of limitation" or concretion.[36] At other points, however, he does not include God among his lists of categories and principles at all, but treats God as a single individual. Even where God *is* understood as a being, it is clear that in many ways God must be an exception to the nature of other beings (in contradiction to the principles at, for example, *PR* 319, 205f.).

The traditional way of construing the problem is first to treat God as *a* being, then to specify ways in which God is *different* from other beings, and finally to introduce some sort of principle of analogy to draw the two together. I find this approach philosophically problematic, in part because of the difficulties with specifying the analogy in a way that does not reduce to equivocity. But what can be offered in its place? Let us begin more radically, dismissing the notion of God as *a* being completely (at least at the start) and trying to specify what might remain. At the end, I believe, we will discover similarities strong enough to justify reintroducing most of the traditional theological categories. But first we must wrestle with the *other* dimension of the God question, for the idea of infinite being examined above stands in tension with the idea of *a* being, which means one who is limited by other beings. Recall that Plato treated God as the *archē*, the source, the good itself,[37] a doctrine that Plotinus appropriated in his own way when he made the One the center of his metaphysics of ascension and participation. Aquinas likewise saw that God would have to be "being itself" (*ipsum esse*). What was it that these thinkers saw and that Schelling elevated to the center of his doctrine of God?

God as Ground and the "God above God"

For a philosophical theology motivated by Schelling there will be three moments in God:

1. *Infinite Creative Ground.* I first construe the One or being itself as Infinite Creative Ground. The notion of *infinity* expresses the absolute lack of limitation and, by implication, the nonexistence of any other being or thing that might do the limiting. The idea of *Ground* hints at the connection with the finite things which we (as finite beings) know to exist; that is, in some way this infinite dimension must serve as the ground of what exists. Ground is preferable to "cause" in order not to confuse the notion of finite causes with this ultimate ground. (As Kant argued, our ordinary category of cause depends on the context of empirical experience.) As Ground of the finite, as we saw above, the infinite precedes the finite and serves as the condition of the possibility for the existence of anything finite whatsoever.

Finally, we speak of it as *Creative*, because it grounds the many and makes them one. Through it the many become one. It's what makes the universe a *uni*verse, not a multiverse. Whitehead speaks of creativity as the "ultimate which is actual in virtue of its accidents" and can be characterized only through them: "In the philosophy of organism this ultimate is termed 'creativity'; and God is its primordial, non-temporal accident" (*PR* 7). Creativity in Whitehead, like the infinite in much of the Western tradition, is indeterminate and as such unknowable. It is the potential for creative development, not the dictator of the outcome of this process.[38]

Now where, conceptually speaking, is this Ground to be located? There are three possibilities: a Ground is outside of God, which is God's foundation; a Ground is within God in some sense; or the Ground is identical to God. The first seems impossible. A god would not be God, in the sense that the tradition has maintained, if dependent on an external Reason. Nor can the consequent nature of God simply *be* the Ground, since it itself is the result of interactions with the world. Hence, I suggest, we should speak of a Ground *within* God. And this obviously entails that we must work with a multiple, as opposed to monistic, picture of God.

The inclusion of Ground within God may at first seem easier to accept than that Creativity would be a principle included within divinity (in the broadest sense of the word). At any rate, process thought has tended to separate Creativity and God.[39] But this move unfortunately misses the fundamental and apparently unavoidable tension between God as ultimate principle and God as *a* personal being. The reason to think that the tension may be unavoidable is that the history of Western philosophy seems to represent (as Ivor Leclerc has argued) a profound and long-lasting vacillation between these two approaches to the term "God."[40] "Simply choose one or the other," one is tempted to say. Yet it appears that any theistic metaphysic will be flawed precisely in its dismissal of the one side or the other.

The result is inescapable. As long as one wishes to advocate both God as ultimate principle and God as a personal being, one must incorporate both ideas within one's conception of God. As Schelling writes,

> As there is nothing before or outside of God he must contain within himself the ground of his existence. All philosophies say this, but they speak of this ground as a mere concept without making it something real and actual. This ground of his existence, which God contains [within himself], is not God viewed as absolute, that is insofar as he exists. For it is only the basis of his existence, it is [God's] *nature*—in God, inseparable from him, to be sure, but nevertheless distinguishable from him. (7:358f.)

Divinity must include the ground of being as well as the highest personal being. The two cannot be posited as separate: the ground of being cannot exclude the highest being, nor can a being be God without including the ground of being within itself. However, since God as ultimate principle and God as person stand (in certain respects) in opposition to one another, they cannot simply be asserted simultaneously side by side—*unless* we think of them as in some way mediated by a third moment. The two must be conceived as combined, yet they cannot be identical. Here we have, I submit, the central challenge to philosophical theology. Theology must be trinitarian because *both* of these ideas are essential to an adequate theory of God, and because both can be predicated of God simultaneously only through the mediation of some third principle. (See the comments on the doctrine of Spirit in the previous chapter.)

2. *Consequent.* Because we know ourselves to be finite, we know that finite things exist. Thus we know that the infinite Creative Ground has a consequent. Like the notion of cause and effect, the relationship of Ground and Consequent is a reciprocal one: consequent requires ground, and ground is unthinkable without consequent. As finite, the world both requires God and cannot be identical to God.

Note that by "Consequent," Schelling does not first mean the consequent nature of God, but the world, the "other" to God, that results from God as Ground. Schelling also insists that the world results through a free divine creative act, but we will not be able to explore the strengths and the obvious difficulties of this notion here (for example, how can a Ground carry out a free act, if God is only personal as actually self-conscious?). The important point is that the finite world represents a genuine other to its infinite ground.

3. *Mediation.* Can one remain satisfied with this dualism, or must one, as I suggested above, think of it as a three-fold structure? Can the Ground and its Consequent be thought

> Here at last we reach the highest point of the whole inquiry. The question has long been heard: What is to be gained by [Schelling's] initial distinction between being insofar as it is basis (*Grund*), and being insofar as it exists? For either there is no

common ground for the two—in which case we must declare ourselves in favor of absolute dualism; or there is such common ground—and in that case, in the last analysis, the two coincide again. (7:406)

As is well known, Schelling's answer is the responsive (self-conscious) nature of God, the God who encompasses both the divine Ground and the world of finite beings that results from it. God encompasses the world without becoming identical to it or swallowing up its genuine otherness. This insight makes Schelling one of the earliest explicit panentheists in modern thought. (As far as I know, his 1809 use of the phrase "*pan + en + theismus*" is the first instance of this term.)

The relationship between Schelling and Whitehead on this question remains remarkably close. On the one side, if there is at present something finite "within" God that did not always exist, then God must be in a sense different from before; and if this finite dimension is in a state of becoming, then God also *is* (in this particular sense) as becoming or process. Conversely, the "other" side of God—the absolute in its limitlessness, or as the ground of being—remains always self-identical. This pair of terms (ground, and consequent or result) best expresses the two sides of divinity: the sameness and difference, God's position "above" creation, and yet God's intimate involvement with it. For Schelling, the divine self-consciousness is just the union of these two moments. It is the result of God's experience of the world. Similarly, if less clearly, Whitehead saw that the consequent nature could be analogous to the human experience of creativity and valuation, and still guarantee objective immortality to past actual occasions.

Thus Schelling became a trinitarian philosopher, arguing for a unification of Ground and Consequent in the divine self-consciousness, which is the appropriation of both without overcoming their difference. "All existence must be conditioned in order that it may be actual, that is, personal, existence. God's existence, too, could not be personal if it were not conditioned, except that he has the conditioning factor *within* himself and not outside himself" (7:399). Division, Schelling adds, is the condition of God's own existence *qua* personal (7:403).

I suggest that the philosophical question on which this unification turns is one's position concerning the nature of divine experience. There is a way to think of divine self-consciousness (and in a related sense, human self-consciousness) that avoids Whitehead's worries about subjectivity. If the divine is conscious, then it is conscious in a three-fold way: of itself as Ground, of its product, and of the relationship between self and product. God as conscious of the world clearly incorporates the world without abolishing God's distinction from it.

The position just sketched is called clearly *panentheistic* in the sense I have advocated in the last two chapters. This position was apparently unknown to Whitehead.[41] The reason has to do perhaps more with Whitehead's lack of familiarity with the tradition of German Idealism than with any inherent incompatibility between idealism and process thought. In my framework, *panentheism emerges out of the dialectic between the infinity and the finiteness of God*. We have already discovered a dialectical relation between the absolute as ground and the personal God as consequent. A similar relationship of difference-in-sameness characterizes God's relation to the world, which is construed neither as external to God (for what could be external to infinity?) nor as identical to God (since the predicates of the absolute certainly cannot be predicated of us as individuals). According to Schelling, *if an ultimate principle is to be (adequately) thought* at all, it must be thought out of the unity of the finite and infinite: "Until our doctrine acknowledges such a power in God, or until it grasps the absolute identity of the infinite and finite" (8:74), there is no place to speak of the personality of God. Schelling's insight is that *freedom* provides the best means for thinking through the relationship of infinite and finite. "Freedom," he argues in *The Ages of the World*, "is the affirmative concept of unconditioned eternity" (8:235). As Marjorie Suchocki has written of the God-world relationship, the key is that "the occasion can become itself and more than itself in God. The occasion is linked into the concrescence of God, even while remaining itself. Thus the peculiarity obtains that the occasion is *both* itself *and* God: it is apotheosized. As a participant in the divine concrescence, it will feel its own immediacy, and God's feeling of its immediacy as well."[42]

➤ The Transition to Systematic Theology

To the point we have considered primarily philosophical resources for conceiving a Trinity in process. These thinkers have helped to clarify what it means to say that there is process and development within God, although the whole of God is not conscious.[43] God is clearly not a single actual entity like any other, and yet important analogies remain between human and divine development and experience. The first step was to leave behind a strict atomism, which takes all larger groupings as mere societies or aggregates, in favor of an ontology based on the principle that there must be wholes that are greater than the sum of their parts (under atomism there *could* be no greater whole than that encompassed by the parts). The chief share of the work was then performed by the notion of infinity and Ground as developed in the philosophy of Schelling. Along the way we have noted the ways in which this view requires a modification of Whitehead's thought and have suggested why such changes represent an advance.

The argument to this point has sought to satisfy philosophical theologians. What I write in closing must satisfy systematic theologians, whose concerns are not automatically addressed by a viable philosophical theology alone. Even if the three moments sketched above survive the scrutiny of philosophers, it does not yet follow that they will correspond with what the theological tradition has meant by "Trinity." The Ground within God is not conscious. Further, the consequent is the world as a whole, not (as in traditional theology) the Son, and it contains *many* consciousnesses. Finally, unlike the theological Trinity, divine consciousness seems to pertain only to the third moment.

The point of contact between the two turns on the question of the transition from philosophical to systematic theology and the relationship between them. Like many systematic theologians, I have maintained, against absolute monism, that God is multiple. Further, I have tried to show that a dualistic theory of God is insufficient, that some third moment is required in order to mediate between infinite and finite, ground and consequent. The position is thus clearly trinitarian in at least this minimal sense. (Incidentally, one does not need to worry about larger numbers: beyond three, God would just be a society, hence, an aggregate).

Nonetheless, I have not claimed that a line of reflection will lead all the way to the three-fold God of the Christian tradition. A gap remains. To this extent Thomas Aquinas was right: there is no question of a complete transition from the philosophical to the theological Trinity. A switch in perspectives remains necessary—the switch that Barth and Jüngel have labeled that from "from below" to "from above." It must rely upon an observation drawn from salvation history: God has revealed Godself as Trinity, and has acted in a trinitarian manner. Only the actual history of salvation, and not *a priori* metaphysical speculation, can supply knowledge of what God's free self-revelation encompasses, if it is to be truly free.[44] Indeed, only a brief reflection on the historical dimension of the Christian religion is needed to see the inevitability of breaking with and moving beyond abstract speculation. Even if, as I've argued above, a "moment" of God's being encompasses humanity, and even if it could be shown that this relationship requires God's incarnation in a single human being,[45] it would take historical and not metaphysical arguments to make the case that Jesus represents the best candidate for this honor. Thus no more should be expected from philosophical reflection than a general indication of God's relationship to the world and humanity. The rest is contingent on free divine choices and the happenstances of human history.

Still, my claim is somewhat stronger than that made by Boyd, which is discussed above. Necessarily, God would reveal Godself as Trinity. How can this be, though, since I have already argued that Father, Son, and Spirit are not necessary? What is necessary about the three-fold-ness of systematic theology, and why is it not, as Lewis Ford argues, purely a matter of contingency?

The answer lies, again, in panentheism. *The panentheistic structure is inherently trinitarian.* Here we return to the theological reflection earlier in the chapter. There I presupposed the premise of "God with us." To think about the presence of God theologically *means* to think of God in God's identification with the world, and this identification we might call the second person of the Trinity. Yet if God were totally absorbed in the world, God would lose all separation from the world. In becoming purely immanent, God would become finite. Recall that we found the infinity of God to be a necessary part of God's nature. To become purely immanent would therefore mean to cease to be God. What is it, then, that remains separate or "beyond" the world? Clearly God, and yet a different part or aspect of God: God in (and as) the first person.

Finally—though this may be somewhat harder to see—there must be God in and as the relationship between first and second person, God as the power that relates these two persons and unifies them; and this we call the third person. It may be that we will not be successful at describing the nature *and the necessity* of the Spirit's mediating work in the detail with which contemporary systematic theologians (especially Pannenberg, Moltmann, and Jüngel) have attempted it.[46] But even philosophical theologians can see that the *type* of mediation will be one that philosophers have too often shied away from: one of love. Even those who cannot follow all the details of Schelling's position can espouse the basic insight of his trinitarian philosophy. The division allows that the two

> should become one through love; that is, it divides itself only that there may be life and love and personal existence. For there is love neither in indifference nor where antitheses are combined which require the combination in order to be; but rather . . . this is the secret of love, that it unites such beings as could each exist in itself, and nonetheless neither is nor can be without the other. Therefore, as duality comes to be in the groundless, there also comes to be love, which combines the existent (ideal) with the basis of existence. (7:408)

But the structure just described is not the same as the actuality of it. Or, the economic does not equal the immanent Trinity. It had to *happen* to be real. And, Hegel notwithstanding, it had to happen through the free reaction of God to the world. This is why pure reason could never derive the persons of the Trinity *a priori*, even though panentheism helps us to say something about their Ground.

Is the immanent or the economic Trinity prior? It depends on which question one is asking. If you mean philosophically, that is, if you raise the question of logical priority, then the immanent Trinity is prior. If you mean salvifically, then the economic Trinity is. I am tempted to put this conclusion somewhat more radically: there *is* no immanent Trinity. The extrapolation from *deus pro nobis* to *deus in esse*, God *an sich*, is always arbitrary. Beyond God's actions in history there is only the *potential structure* that we explored above, the sort of structure accessible to pure reason.

Let me put the point differently. Just as it supplies a different metaphor for understanding the God-world relation, so panentheism also brings a different metaphorical emphasis to discussions of the Trinity. Here the central ideas are participation, embracing presence, and redemption in and through the one whole, rather than redemption as making that which is not God to be more god-like. Historically, humanity first knew God's love for the world by God's free decision to create. What God created was not outside of God but remained inside the divine, permeated by the divine. Here is a deep mystery: all is God, hence in one sense all actions are God's, yet we too are agents—made in the image of God, free, moral, and responsible. In this view, there is room within the one overarching divine presence and causality for independent units of activity to arise and to exercise a relative autonomy.[47]

What is true of the doctrine of the God-world relation is true even more so of the inner-trinitarian relations. The former comes first in the order of knowledge and is easier to understand. The latter comes first in the order of being. As we are separate agents and yet still caught up within the one divine presence, so the three divine persons are separate centers of activity which together constitute the unity of the trinitarian God. Panentheism finds an analog to God's own interpersonal relations in the relationship between God and world, just as it finds an analog to God's relationship to the world in our own relationships to our bodies.

Traditional trinitarians accept that Father, Son, and Spirit enjoy an equal participation in the divine nature, since each participates in the one Godhead. Then, at some point, God chose to create a world outside Godself. By contrast, trinitarian panentheists endorse the participation of the created order in God in a manner that is at least analogous to the co-participation of Father, Son, and Spirit in the one Godhead.

Of course, again, *every* analogy used in understanding God must also be negated as soon as it is applied to God. Trinitarian panentheism recognizes three central disanalogies. First, the three divine persons who constitute the divine unity are divine in their very nature. The distinctions between the divine essence and human essence that we explored above hold for our relations to *each* of the divine persons. Thus our participation within the divine presence is not due to our nature but rather to the grace of God. Second, the three divine persons together constitute what it is to be God. God *just is* this tri-unity. By contrast, human thoughts and actions do not, taken together, constitute the divine. God existed before there was any world and would still continue to exist if the universe collapsed into a single infinitely dense point (the "Big Crunch") and were no more. Our existence within the divine is, again, a gift of grace from God. Finally, every action of the trinitarian God reflects the full moral perfection of God: giving, accepting, glorifying. In fact, the singular beauty of the Christian doctrine of God lies in the incredible richness of the inner-trinitarian life. Here the contrast is obvious: no reader of these lines takes his or her thoughts and actions as models of moral perfection. Only divine grace could make possible the audacious assertion that God allows agents such as ourselves to exist within the being of the divine. In many classical models of the God-world relation, God could be present to humans despite the morally abhorrent things that humans do. But most have resisted locating sinful humans *within* the divine. In fact, in many theologies God must withdraw the divine presence as a sign of displeasure or judgment. For panentheists, however, God's grace is so unlimited that God is able to embrace even the darkest of human actions within the very being of God, revealing them to be what they are, yet without affirming them.

Christologically speaking, in this view Jesus becomes the exemplar for humanity in a no less profound sense than in classical theism. He actualized the possibility that each human enjoys as one who is made in the image of God. He lived a life of perfect devotion to God, acknowledging the true relationship of creature to Creator in every thought and action. We are within God, and in that sense present to God, no less than Jesus was. But he alone perfectly lived a life that reflected his locatedness within the divine. We are within God, but Jesus is fully God, yet without ceasing to be human.

I said above that one caveat had to be added to the claim that our thoughts and actions do not constitute the divine. It is an insight that we owe to process theologians, although I believe that the framework of panentheism first supplies the means for truly incorporating this insight into Christian theism. Nothing we do influences or changes the essential nature of God, and God could have existed with no less perfection without us. At the same time, however, it's true that our actions do affect the responsive nature of God: that "part" of God that emerges out of God's response to the universe and to humanity. This process insight—that a responsive God is greater, is more fully God, than a dispassionate God-above-history—beautifully summarizes a deep underlying motivation of panentheism. God is the all-embracing presence. We live and move and have our being within that Presence. God continually responds to our thoughts and actions with all the perfection of God's character, and that interweaving of our action and God's response of grace yields an overall whole that is richer than either would have been on its own. This is the miracle of creation and of history: that God would deign for it to matter to God that we, in all our frailty, would have existed, and, even more miraculously, for the result of our existing and interacting with God to be truly good. Herein lies the eschatological hope and the eschatological promise of Christianity: that, in the end, God will be able to say, "Behold, it was good, yea it was very good."

➤ Conclusion

Whitehead says at one point, in contrasting the philosophy of organism with philosophies of the absolute, "One side makes process ultimate; the other side makes fact ultimate" (PR 7). At too many crucial points in *Process and Reality*, his philosophy is dualistic rather than dialectical: "In our cosmological construction we are, therefore, left with the final opposites, joy and sorrow, good and evil, disjunction and conjunction—that is to say, the many in one—flux and permanence, greatness and triviality, freedom and necessity, God and the World" (PR 341).

I have argued, in effect, that for a process system to be trinitarian it must make both fact *and* process ultimate, both primordial envisagement and resulting actuality, both ground and consequent. But these pairs are incompatible. They can only both be ultimate if they are mediated in some way. It is this, above all, that points us in a trinitarian direction: that the step of mediation is included in the very essence of the position. Many shy away from the word "dialectical" because of Hegel's overblown claims on its behalf. Nonetheless, we find in the third moment—philosophically speaking, God's panentheistic appropriation of the world as God's other; theologically speaking, God's salvific and self-sacrificial love for the world—the core and completing moment of the trinitarian understanding of the divine nature.

"Open Panentheism" and Creation as Kenosis

11

IN THE PREVIOUS THREE CHAPTERS, I HAVE ADVANCED A FORM OF Christian panentheism, the belief that the world remains in some sense within the divine, even though God also transcends the world. In the twentieth century, at least, panentheism is usually connected with the work of Alfred North Whitehead and his followers, especially Charles Hartshorne. But, in contrast to many process theologians, I find myself compelled also to defend the doctrine of creation *ex nihilo*—the belief that there has not always been a world, and hence that the world is not co-eternal with God. Instead, in this view both the creation of the universe and the details concerning *how* it was created involved free divine decisions. To make these assertions is to endorse the radical contingency of ourselves, of our world—and indeed of the existence of any world whatsoever.

The combination of these two different sources gives rise to an intriguing mediating position, which I shall call *open panentheism*. This theology has a deep affinity with the work of Clark Pinnock and other "open theists" or "free will theists,"[1] though it draws more fully on process resources than most of these theologians do. Open panentheism is closely linked to process theism in a number of respects.[2] Both conceive of God as involved more deeply in the temporal flow of history than classical theism was willing to countenance. Both acknowledge certain limitations on what God can do and know (though, as we will see, for rather different reasons). And both think more rigorously than most classical theists did about what is entailed in the use of agency language to describe God and divine action.

Open panentheism seeks to build further on these foundations. It recognizes that deeper ties bind process and open theists than is often acknowledged. On the one hand, process thinkers have formulated urgent problems that open theists must address, problems that may be unanswerable without an increased reliance on process thought. On the other hand, there are resources within classical Christian traditions that can be brought to bear on contemporary challenges to the doctrine of God. Because of these natural linkages, I hope to show, the debate between process and open theism offers some of the most important resources for constructive theology today, especially with regard to the God-world relation.

➤ Cosmology and the Tug toward Process

To speak of the God-world relation is to move onto Alfred North Whitehead's terrain: cosmology. A cosmology must be scientifically informed, but it is also inherently metaphysical. Scientific results and the scientific method thus provide indispensable points of reference and constraint for all work in philosophical cosmology.

Cosmology treads highly contested ground. One group of authors—roughly those in Whiteheadian orbits—writes in defense of process cosmologies. Another group, often bitterly opposed to the first, approaches cosmology using traditional theological categories. Can there be an intersection between them: a panentheistic cosmology deeply influenced by process thought, yet still ready to endorse an initially free creation out of nothing?

Most metaphysical cosmologies maintain that there is some ground or source for all that exists. This ultimate reality then grounds the universe, or, if there are multiple universes or "cosmic epochs,"[3] it grounds the entire series. Let us call the set of all cosmologies that accept this assumption *ground-of-being cosmologies*.[4] So, for example, theistic cosmologies affirm that the observed universe does not contain its ground, its reason for existing, within itself. It is not self-sufficient but depends on and expresses a deeper level of reality. Theists then go on to affirm that this deeper reality from which the cosmos stems and which it reflects is more adequately described as personal than as non-personal. More exactly, we understand this Ground to be *supra*-personal, that is, not *less* than personal. Arthur Peacocke presents a classic argument on behalf of this standpoint:

> Does not the very intimacy of our relation to the fundamental features of the physical world, its so-called "anthropic" features, together with the distinctiveness of personhood, point us in the direction of looking for a best explanation of all-that-is in terms of some kind of entity that could include the personal? Since the personal is the highest level of unification of the physical, mental and spiritual of which we are aware, it is legitimate to recognize that this Ultimate Reality must be *at least personal*, or *supra-personal*—that is, it will be less misleading to attach personal predicates to this Ultimate Reality than not to do so at all.[5]

Note the core tenets of even a minimally theistic cosmology that distinguish it from its competitors. It's more coherent to construe the origin of the universe as an intentional act of creation, Peacocke argues, than to conceive it as emanating in automatic, necessary, or impersonal fashion from its ultimate Source.

The theistic hypothesis generally requires not only that God give rise to the existing universe in a personal fashion but also that God continue to interact with it in a mode that is not-less-than-personal.[6] The increasing strength of scientific explanations has made defending this claim rather more difficult today, however. Of course, one can separate one's beliefs about divine action from one's scientific beliefs, but it looks increasingly difficult, if not impossible, to integrate science with the framework of classical (Hellenistically based) theology. For example, persons, if they are interpreted within the static framework of enduring substances and essences, must lie outside the purview of scientific explanations, which focus on the dynamics of continuously changing, interlocked causal systems.

Static ontologies bring with them other difficulties as well, as we have seen. For instance, certain classical models in philosophical theology described the divine nature such that it would be impossible for God really to know the world in such a way that God could respond to the evolving thoughts and needs of individuals. Thus if one follows the early chapters of Aquinas's *Summa Theologiae*, one must conclude that God cannot know existing creatures as individuals, in all their contingency, but only the eternal forms or universals that they instantiate as this or that *type* of thing. How then could God know or respond to any contingent fact about any creature? Since the contingent facts about us are the things we hold to be most valuable about ourselves (the sort of character we develop over time, the fundamental convictions that we hold, our most intimate relationships), it would appear that God cannot have the sort of knowledge of us that would be required for personal interaction with us.[7]

It is the limitations of the models upon which classic theologians relied—those of substance-based metaphysics, hylomorphism (that is, individuals as combinations of form and matter), and atemporal theories of being—that point many of us toward the understanding of God in process theology. If God is dipolar, then the antecedent nature of God could serve the function of eternal grounding that we discussed above, and the consequent nature of God could then be involved in the sort of person-like interaction with creatures in the world that is crucial for theism. Only with a doctrine of God rich enough to include both poles, I suggest, can one understand the divine both as the ground of being and as an existing being (*der Grund des Seins* and *das höchste Seiende*).

➤ The Challenge from Science and the Philosophy of Religion

Different theological models approach the God-world relationship with rather different sets of assumptions, arguments, and priorities. All of these models, whether they lean more toward process or toward classical theology, bear the burden of providing answers to a significant set of objections. Indeed, the biggest challenge to any contemporary notion of a God who interacts with the cosmos may well come not from philosophical skeptics but from the sciences. Since scientific and philosophical objections set the context for constructive work, it is here we must begin.

The first set of objections arises as a directly scientific argument, and physics here plays the leading role. The construction of theories in physics has traditionally presupposed what philosophers of science call the "causal closure of the physical," which holds that the universe as a whole is a closed system of matter and energy, immune to any causal influence from the outside. But as the work of Alexander Vilenkin and others shows,[8] there are now attractive cosmological models in which a universe can be produced by other universes and can give rise to offspring universes of its own. Lee Smolin's evolving universes model allows for the same sort of inter-universe effects, as do some cosmological models arising out of string theory.[9] Moreover, few, if any, actual physical systems *within* the universe are thermodynamically closed. Of course, it is sometimes fruitful to work with mathematical models which represent idealized systems that are causally closed. But the actual systems that one hopes to model (either subsystems within this universe or the universe as a whole) don't meet the conditions of these idealizations.

What happens if one follows the lead of these considerations and gives up the causal closure of the physical as an ultimate framework for scientific cosmology? This move immediately changes the landscape for theological cosmology. For example, the hold of a strict naturalism, with its in-principle denial of all outside causal influences, is thereby loosened. It now becomes possible *in principle* to conceive some sort of divine influence or "lure" on entities within the universe.

Although this is a significant recognition, it's not the end of the road. A great gap lies between conceptual possibility and probability. Two other factors in particular constrain the space within which theological cosmologists can work, one drawn from science and the other from the philosophy of religion.

First, many of the types of actions traditionally attributed to God, if they occurred, would clash with the practice of science as we know it, if not transforming it into something altogether different. The most difficult case involves direct supernatural interventions that would produce physical states different from those predicted by the laws of physics. Even if the community of experimental physicists could never catch God red-handed, as it were, merely knowing that a physical system could at any instant begin acting in a manner completely inconsistent with natural law because of a divine intervention would be enough, I fear, to undercut the practice of science.[10] I argued in part I that it's better to avoid holding theological positions which, either directly or by implication, clash with the practice of science. After all, science represents the most rigorous form of knowledge currently available to humans. It would be very unfortunate if being a theist meant having to reject that knowledge and the methods that produce it. Moreover, however great the veracity of divine words, it's not clear that theology as a form of human reflection has the epistemic strength to stand against the carefully tested and verified conclusions of science. Thus theists should at least seek to avoid affirming positions on divine action that clash head-on with the scientific method and the specific results of the sciences.

It turns out that there are at least some ways to understand God's influence on creatures within the world that do not undercut science or make it impossible. If God exercises an influence on agents in the world but does not overwhelm or replace their agency (for example, by working as an exception to the natural order), then the scientific study of the world is not rendered futile. Some of the most interesting work at the intersection of theology and science today lies in this area (see part IV). There are good reasons to think that God could guide history according to the divine purposes, including God's involvement in the Christ event, without our having to say that God breaks natural laws. Even more strongly, I suggest that only collaborative work between open theists and process theologians can help us to formulate the needed account, since it lies at the intersection of these two theological movements.

As David Ray Griffin has powerfully shown, claims about divine action are also limited, and perhaps just as strongly, by the problem of evil.[11] Steven Knapp and I have argued that God's limiting God's own interventions into the natural order—acting persuasively on those entities capable of responding, rather than coercively—might be justified by the greater good that could result from this divine self-limitation.[12] For instance, God's self-limitation (*kenosis*) might be the only means for allowing independent finite agents to arise within the universe and for developing complex forms of rational and moral agency. But a self-limitation applied in some cases and not in others—say, a God who allows one person to suffer without intervening to change the situation, yet steps in to reduce the suffering of another—raises the specter of either injustice or inconsistency. No existing response by open theists seems adequate to this charge, and the costs of a rationality-stultifying appeal to mystery are, in our view, too high.

Here one might also recall that Griffin maintains that a freely self-limiting God would still be morally responsible for the suffering that occurs, since this God would be metaphysically capable of eliminating the suffering. He also questions whether the idea of divine self-limitation is even conceptually coherent. Clearly the theodicy that Knapp and I have developed from the standpoint of open panentheism relies crucially on divine self-limitation. How successful our response to Griffin can be depends essentially on the effectiveness of our defense of open panentheism.

➤ Open Panentheism

The dialogue with process thought has helped bring to the surface two major challenges to open panentheism. First, one wonders, is the notion of a self-limiting God coherent, and is it sufficient to address to problem of evil? Process theologians have argued that, if God is metaphysically capable of alleviating suffering and does not do so, God is culpable for the results. Second, is the notion of an initial creation "out of nothing" coherent? It turns out that the answers to these two challenges are related and mutually enrich each other. Open panentheism, I will argue, offers the most convincing overall response, in that it draws most effectively on the insights of both process theology and open theism.

All panentheists believe that creaturely agents are located "within" the divine. But how should we conceive this "within"? Clearly it must involve more than just spatial location, since it would be absurd to locate God at some particular point within the universe and make God absent from others. Insights developed in the work of the neo-Whiteheadian thinker Joseph Bracken offer a powerful response to this challenge.[13] They nicely supplement the arguments developed in the previous three chapters. As Bracken has seen, it is easier to conceive that God would create other centers of activity within the divine being if God's eternal nature *already* consists of multiple, non-identical centers of activity. Surprisingly, this natural kinship between panentheism and trinitarian thought is too infrequently acknowledged.

Process panentheists depart from classical panentheists regarding the aseity and immutability of God: the understanding of God as self-sufficient and unchanging. Eastern Orthodox theology is deeply panentheistic, for example, and yet strongly resistant to a temporalized God.[14] As I argued in *The Problem of God*, there is reason to worry that, in trying to meet the "perfection" standards of Greek metaphysics, the theological tradition has asserted qualities of God that are not appropriate to a biblical theism. Charles Hartshorne saw that theology had been crippled by these Hellenistic assumptions and thereby kept away from its own deeper logic and insights. Whiteheadian process thought, for him, represented a call for theologians to return to a more appropriate picture of the divine nature.

The God-world relation, Hartshorne rightly saw, is dipolar. For present purposes, dipolarity need mean nothing more than that God is related to the world in two modes: as its eternal Ground, the source of all its possibilities; and as the Infinitely Related One, the One who internalizes and unifies all experiences within the world, bathes them in infinite love, and transmits them back to other experiencers in the form of the divine lure.[15] It is no more difficult to conceive of God as both Ground and Responder when God is understood in trinitarian fashion as a community of persons (that is, person-like fields of force or influence). Creation is free. It manifests God's love. Yet God was not constrained or metaphysically required to create. Advocating such a metaphysical constraint actually *decreases* the free responsiveness and relatedness, which its advocates are seeking to safeguard.

As soon as one conceives of God as including multiple centers of activity, however, one has introduced a greater disanalogy between human (and other) agents on the one hand and the divine agents on the other than many process theologians (such as David Ray Griffin) would allow. As soon as one speaks of the divine as the all-encompassing field of activity, as Bracken does—and especially if one introduces the notion of the *infinite* field of the divine—one has said something different than that God is the "chief exemplification" (*PR* 343) of the same metaphysical principles that pertain to all other agents.

Open theists have consistently maintained some such ontological difference between God and other agents, and I think they have been right to do so. For example, human agents differ from the divine in their nature: finite, not infinite; existing contingently rather than existing in all possible worlds; sometimes placing their own limited interests above the divine rather than being by nature perfectly good. Finite agents need a community (and, indeed, an entire world-system with the consistency of regular laws), whereas the community of divine persons does not intrinsically need a context outside itself. In short, the divine has ontological self-sufficiency that no finite, contingent creature can enjoy. It is sufficient for God to be internally related to Godself in order to exist, but no finite creature exists as a result of being internally related.

One can find other ways to express this crucial insight. For example, the divine nature is pre-given. There is (to paraphrase Thomas Nagel) "something it is like to be divine." By contrast, human subjects do not have a pre-given nature. We are "thrown" (Heidegger's *Geworfenheit*), in us "existence precedes essence" (Sartre), or we define ourselves in interaction. We are genuinely free, insomuch as we may choose to be like God and to conform our character to the divine nature, or we may choose to act as if we were *causa sui*. That much, I think, each human being can recognize phenomenologically. Apparently it is essential for the free development of human character that there be a world of other subjects and other things for us to relate to, so that we then "choose this day whom [we] shall serve." Without this fundamental existential choice, it appears, finite agents could not experience the personal and intellectual evolution that we require to become rational, moral agents in the image of the divine. Indeed, one could put the point even more strongly: we are *constituted by* our freedom-in-thrownness. But the divine nature is not so constituted. For Whitehead, for example, the primordial divine nature does not change over time. This necessity—that we are constituted by free, finite relatedness whereas God is not—represents perhaps the deepest disanalogy between human and divine nature.

The Kenotic Doctrine of God

The doctrine of *creatio ex nihilo*, many process thinkers have argued, stands in some tension with the assertion that God is intrinsically love. Wouldn't God need *always* to be related to some world, as a necessary expression of the unlimited divine love? Moreover, if relatedness is an essential quality of the divine, how could there ever be a time when God was not related to an Other?

Traditionally, theologians have responded to this charge of inconsistency by arguing that God is always *internally related within the divine being*. God has always existed as three persons in divine community.

Although I am drawn to this trinitarian response, I think we must admit that belief in the Trinity is not by itself sufficient to defang the objection. It does make a difference that God's love be expressed *ad extra* at some point. Only if God creates real agents outside of God's self—not automata who acknowledge the deity because they must, but agents who freely love God—only then would it be clear that the divine relatedness is more than self-love. The divine love is most fully manifested in real relatedness to agents who are "other" to God: finite in comparison with the divine infinity, and morally limited in contrast to the One who is essentially good.

So why doesn't this mean that there must always be a world as long as there is God? This is process theology's most pointed question to open theism—one that calls for some serious reflection on the part of advocates of creation *ex nihilo*.[16]

For open panentheists, inter-personal relations within God play an essential part in answering this question. The divine essence can be love, even prior to creation, only because the divine exists always as community.[17] Indeed, we understand God's relation to creation, and God's act(s) of creation, *as love* in part by extrapolating from the inner-divine relations. At some point this love was manifested *beyond* the inner-divine relations. At some point the God whose nature is love became internally related to others as well. Like orthodox process theologians, open panentheists affirm that the world is taken up into—indeed, could not exist apart from—the divine being. But, they add, the divine love is manifested just as deeply in that God, not needing to create anything at all, nonetheless created a world of finite beings and processes. The love that is extended from God *ad extra* toward entities who are other than God is even more profound if there were no necessity for God to create *and hence creation was a free act*, than it would be if God were of necessity always accompanied by some world.

Although this particular result is highly reminiscent of the work of open theists, I suggest interpreting it in the context of Bracken's process theology, which we began to consider above. Bracken begins by postulating that God has existed eternally as a trinitarian field of forces, as tri-personal identity. Each aspect of God is personal, or more-than-personal, and together they constitute "a single unbounded field of activity."[18] Open panentheists add that at some point God freely chose to share the divine life, creating finite centers of activity within the space of the divine being. As Bracken writes, "the world of creation is the result of a free decision on the part of the divine persons to share their divine communitarian life with creatures."[19] That is, the divine love manifested, or spilled over, into other centers of activity through an unconstrained divine decision. More strongly than Bracken, though, I would emphasize that finite, created centers of activity, although still contained within the one all-encompassing divine field, differ from God in their essential nature: we are finite, not infinite; we exist contingently, not in all possible worlds; we place our own limited interests above the divine or highest interest, in contrast to the One who is perfectly good by nature (*ens perfectissimum*).[20] Perhaps this is just a difference of emphasis. I stress the difference between finite and infinite (and so also the other divine attributes), whereas Bracken stresses common metaphysical principles that pertain to both types of entities.[21] But even if "difference of emphasis" is the right term, the difference is vital.

The christological concept of *kenosis* or self-emptying (see Phil 2:5-9) offers a particularly powerful means for conceiving this act of creation by a God who until that time was unlimited in power and unconstrained in action. According to a doctrine of "kenotic creation," creation is itself a kenotic, relational act. God freely limited God's infinite power in order to allow for the existence of non-divine agents. This self-limitation is best understood as a self-emptying, insofar as God chose to limit or "empty Godself of" qualities that would otherwise seem to belong to the divine essence, such as omnipotence or the unlimited manifestation of divine glory and agency.[22] We might therefore label the resulting position *open kenotic panentheism*.[23]

Once the world exists, God's experience develops in real interaction with the world. At this point—that is, subsequent to the moment of creation—open panentheists embrace the bulk of what process thought teaches about the God-world relation. God is conceived as combining both an eternal, primordial divine nature and a consequent nature. All possible states of affairs and all "eternal forms" exist primordially in the mind of God. In Michael Lodahl's nice phrase, "the Spirit of God [through Jesus Christ] is identified as the possibility of God that brings the real into emergent being in the world."[24] God offers initial aims to every creature at every moment, and creatures freely choose their responses. God invites creatures to participate in God's own creative activity within the world, resulting in what Lodahl calls *creatio ex creatione* and Paul van Buren describes as *creatio ex amore*. In either case, we become *created co-creators* with God (Philip Hefner).[25] The consequent nature of God then incorporates into the divine experience all the experiences of all beings within the world at every instant. God in relation to the created world manifests love to the highest possible degree because God experiences (that is, incorporates into the divine experience) all the joys, pains, and sorrows of all created things at all times, and then offers back to them a continual leading "for the common good."

I have argued that this picture is fully compatible with the doctrine of creation out of nothing. But it matters deeply *why* open panentheists assert the *ex nihilo*. In my view, this phrase expresses the deeper insight into the nature of creaturely existence before God. As David Larson notes, it "captures and expresses the almost overwhelming amazement that there is anything at all," the "radical contingency" that characterizes our experience in the world—indeed, that characterizes the existence of our world as a whole.[26] Catherine Keller's recent sortie into the deep provides a powerful picture of the God-world relationship in light of this radical contingency.[27] In the context of mythological language (*bildhaftes Denken*), "chaos" and "ocean" help to express what might have preceded the moment of creation, hence what "material" God might have worked with to produce order out of chaos. But in the more rarified language of metaphysics, creation out of *nothing whatsoever* more powerfully conveys the most radical contingency of created things: they exist out of no necessity of their nature, but only in and through their relationship with the final Ground.

The hypothesis of a kenotic creation out of nothing serves as a crucial component in the mediating position of open panentheism. This view accepts the process insight that a God who is love must exist eternally in relation, yet it locates that relatedness already within the divine nature itself *as a model for* God's subsequent relatedness to all things. God then freely creates space within the divine life for other selves or entities. These others are like God in that they too are centers of activity; hence creation is, as the tradition has held, *imago Dei*. Humans may represent the *imago Dei* in certain distinctive ways: for example, in that we are *conscious* of our relatedness (think of it as a sort of relatedness in the "second degree"). It would also appear that we freely emulate the divine nature, or freely resist the lure of God, with a much greater range of choice than is available to other animals. Nevertheless, we exist contingently and might not have existed at all, just as (according to *ex nihilo*) the universe of which we are parts also might not have existed. The creation of both ourselves and the universe, being completely free and unconstrained, was a sign of God's grace, that is, of God's eternal character.

➤ Conclusion

Open panentheism retains many of the features of biblical theism that open theists have emphasized, including creation *ex nihilo* and the free self-limitation of God. At the same time, however, it also draws deeply from the springs of process thought. Open panentheism may be trinitarian, and yet, as the volume on *Trinity in Process*[28] shows, there are a number of viable ways for process thinkers to be trinitarian thinkers. Likewise, in this view the being of God is not metaphysically identical to the being of finite actual entities in the world. But this fact does not need to pose a problem for process theologians. Few, if any, process thinkers actually accept a *full identity* between finite actual occasions and the divine actual occasion or occasions. Indeed, I suggest, the "chief exemplification" of the metaphysical principles *cannot* be identical to just one among the many exemplifications of these principles.

Given the deep consonance between process theology and open panentheism, it may just be that the doctrine of creation *ex nihilo* represents the final stumbling block. I have suggested that—once one grants real relationality within the divine being, a relationality that awaits only the free divine choice to be manifested—one has undercut the alleged necessity of an eternal cosmos for process thought, opening the door to creation *ex nihilo*. Both open panentheism and process theology are strengthened by constructively combining their conceptual resources in this manner.

PART FOUR

Divine Action

Natural Law *and the* Problem *of* Divine Action

PHYSICAL SCIENCE, IT APPEARS, LEAVES NO PLACE FOR DIVINE ACTION. To do science is generally to presuppose that the universe is a closed physical system, that interactions are regular and lawlike, that all causal histories can be traced, and that anomalies will ultimately have physical explanations. Unfortunately, the traditional way of asserting that God acts in the world conflicts with all four of these conditions. It presupposes that the universe is open, that God acts from time to time according to particular purposes, that the ultimate source and explanation of these actions is the divine will, and that no earthly account would ever suffice to explain God's intentions.

Moreover, one faces a certain threat of equivocation when one speaks of both God and physical objects as causes. It would at first seem that the meaning of "cause," used at once in reference to a chemical catalyst and to God's upholding the universe, diverges so widely that the same notion shouldn't be used to express both claims. Only if one can provide some broader account of what features chemicals and providence share in common as causes can one make sense of Jewish, Christian, and Muslim claims for divine action in the world.

The problem of divine agency is therefore one of the most pressing challenges theists face in an age of science. Christians and Muslims in particular have traditionally been committed to a robust account of the actions of God or Allah within the natural order. But how can one attribute events to the causal activity of God if science is based on the assumption that any given event is part of a closed system of natural causes? What conceptual framework might allow believers to acknowledge the power of science without reducing the divine to a "God of the [few remaining] gaps"—or to utter passivity? I assume, because one can hardly deny, that science has been massively successful in explaining events in the natural world. What causes most of the effects we observe in chemistry and physics is not up for grabs, and well-attested scientific explanations are not just "one story among the rest." This is not to deny that scientific conclusions are always preliminary. They remain open to revision, and some will be falsified. Still, the fact that a given theory will possibly be revised in the future does not imply that it stands on the same level as all other accounts of the phenomenon on the market today.[1]

This chapter brings together the work on emergence in part II with the theology of panentheism that I defended in part III. It begins the three-part defense of divine action that I offer in this and the following two chapters.

➤ Questioning Determinism and Causal Closure

The problem is not just that scientists happen to have a preference for non-divine causes. Far more seriously, many have argued that the physical sciences must presuppose the principle of *causal closure*. A core principle of physics is the principle of the *conservation of energy*. Predicting the dynamics of physical systems in classical physics presupposes that the total energy of the system remains constant. (Of course, thermodynamics allows for calculating the evolution of systems that are far from thermodynamic equilibrium.) It is still generally assumed that the total energy of the universe remains constant, although there are cosmological models that do not make this assumption. If one cannot establish values for the increase or decrease of energy in a system, one cannot compute many of its fundamental physical parameters and behaviors.

When one combines these various requirements, one obtains the principle of causal or physical determinism. As William James notes, determinism "professes that those parts of the universe already laid down absolutely appoint and decree what other parts shall be. The future has no ambiguous possibilities hidden in its womb: the part we call the present is compatible with only one totality."[2] This determinism of physical causes involves the claim that the physical state of the world at a given time determines the physical state of the world for all future times. It is thus a *modal* notion. It denies that it is even physically *possible* that the present state of the world should give rise to more than one future state of affairs.[3]

Physical determinism is fundamentally a claim about causality—the claim, namely, that all that happens is a necessary effect of antecedent efficient causes. At the same time, it claims that all physical occurrences are lawful. The universe is such that a given set of physical events can give rise to only one successor set. All versions of determinism accept the *ontological* thesis that the state of the universe up to and including the present time t determines the universe's state in subsequent moments. Obviously, if what happens at time $t + 1$ is determined by the physical state of the world at t, no place remains for divine action.

The challenge for theists is compounded by the fact that the ontological thesis usually begets an *epistemological* thesis: that future states could be predicted if one had enough knowledge of the past and present. Its most famous version is expressed by Laplace's claim that all future and past events could be predicted from a complete knowledge of the present:

> An intelligence which knows at a given instant all forces acting in nature, as well as the momentary positions of all things of which the universe consists, would be able to comprehend the motions of the largest bodies of the world and those of the smallest atoms in one single formula, provided it were powerful enough to subject all data to analysis. To it, nothing would be uncertain; both future and past would be present before its eyes.[4]

Thanks to the appeal that many scientists make (albeit tacitly) to this epistemological thesis, debates about determinism frequently turn into claims about what is physically possible, leading to another set of challenges to theists. It is physically possible, in a broad sense of the phrase, that a divine agent exists—a being with no body who is different in kind from any entity in this world. But, it seems, the actions of such an agent could not be known scientifically because, if God acted, all the scientific observer would detect would be anomalies in causal sequences in the physical world.

Yet scientific critics of theism often draw a harsher conclusion: the existence of a divine being is not just unknowable but physically impossible. Only physical things exist—things composed out of the mass and energy studied by physics—and God is not a physical thing. If the strict interpretation is correct, theism and physicalism are incompatible. I will argue in a moment that physics does not *require* either of these two interpretations. Nonetheless, modern science has generally presupposed one or the other. By and large, the stricter view has predominated.

It is on these grounds, for example, that the "new synthesis" in evolutionary biology is often taken to represent a serious challenge to theism. Evolution, it is said, requires that no outside causal force can affect the development of more complex systems and life forms. Random genetic variation and selective retention through the environment are, outside of physics-based causes, the only allowable causal determinants of the evolutionary process. For its part, theism requires that the development of life be intended by God, so that God is in some sense responsible for the outcome.

Some Christian biologists, most notably Arthur Peacocke, have argued that God could have initiated a process of cosmic evolution that God knew would lead to the development of conscious life, without any other direct influence required on God's part.[5] But this response faces a serious dilemma: either the development of life would have to be a necessary consequence of the Big Bang (which does not seem likely, given the quantum uncertainties involved), or God would have had to be ready to intervene, and perhaps actually *have* intervened, in order to bring about conscious life and to preserve it once it existed (which would contradict the "hands-off" position). At first blush, then, it looks like a stand-off: evolution appears to be incompatible with theism, and divine providence—God's action in the world subsequent to creation—with evolution.

➤ Needed: A New Theory of Causation

The challenge I have just sketched requires theologians to do some fundamental rethinking on the topic of divine action. The inherited tools and concepts are no longer adequate, it appears, to make sense of divine action in an age of science. To put it bluntly, the theologian seems to be faced with an uncomfortable choice between two alternatives: either God acts as the Divine Architect only, creating a finely tuned machine and leaving it to function in a consistent manner somehow expressive of its Designer; or God becomes the Divine Repairman, whose imperfect building of the machine in the first place requires him, like a refrigerator repairman, to return from time to time to fix errors he made the first time around. Though not impossible, it is certainly no easy task to develop an alternative perspective that allows one to speak of a "different but epistemically equal" system of divine causes alongside the network of scientific explanations, one that is co-constitutive of physical events in the world.

Many attempts have been made to respond to this challenge. Some have found an opening in quantum indeterminacy.[6] Perhaps, they argue, the physical world is fully lawlike, and even physically closed *in the specific sense that the total amount of energy remains constant.* But quantum physics, at least on the Copenhagen interpretation, reveals a world that is both law-governed and ontologically indeterminate: unobserved subatomic events do not have a precise location and momentum, and probabilistic laws leave some room for chance. How much of an opening does quantum physics create for divine action? It does seem significant that quantum mechanics allows for multiple outcomes given the same initial conditions, insofar as this fact seems to leave room, at least in principle, for top-down influences (more on this below). Nonetheless, "stochastic" or probabilistic laws are still laws. Perhaps they do not determine each individual case, but they do reflect a physical determinism that pertains to the overall system. Also, the laws say nothing about agents, much less free agents; hence they cannot themselves provide the stronger sense of counterfactual free action that theists appear to need to make the case for divine action.

This lack has led some thinkers to posit a separate realm of mental causation over against the world of physical causes. Among these non-physical types of causation are the "agent causation" of Richard Taylor[7] and the ubiquitous divine causation ("double agency") of Austin Farrer.[8] In these views, mental or divine causes affect outcomes without introducing new energy into the physical world. Certainly views of this sort leave room for full human and divine agency. Unfortunately, they do not integrate easily with physical science as we now know it, and some versions actually contradict physical descriptions of the world.

What then of human agency? Do humans not enjoy freedom of will: "The stick moves the stone and is moved by the hand, which again is moved by the man"?[9] Theists have often argued that as long as humans are free, God could act in the world. After all, if humans can break the chain of physical causality, couldn't God do so all the more? But free will may be less of a trump card than it appears. The dominant view within philosophy has been *compatibilism*, the view that physical determinism is compatible with human agency and moral responsibility.[10] The American legal system, for example, holds individuals responsible if they intend and then carry out an illegal action (say, murder), *even if* the intent was somehow determined by prior causes. According to compatibilists, agents' actions express their character traits. It is irrelevant whether these traits, and consequently the actions themselves, are determined by antecedent causes. Perhaps the "sense of being free" is just mistaken; after all, even a fully determined will could still (falsely) imagine itself to be free. Finally, many scientists argue that neuroscience presupposes (and some would argue that it has already proven) that the only causal agency is physical. Aside from brain states and the body's responses, there *is* no "actor" to be found.

Clearly, it is an urgent task for theologians to provide a clear account of what they mean when they assert that God acts as a causal force within the world. *To succeed at this task we need nothing less than a new theory of causation.* This chapter offers a first sketch of such a theory. The argument presupposes that dualism is mistaken and then seeks to show that, nonetheless, *not all causes are physically reconstructable causes.*

The argument divides into three main parts. I first concede that the threat of equivocation cannot be overcome as long as one's theory of causality includes only physical and divine causes. The gap is just too wide. By contrast, if we find evidence within the natural world of vastly different types of causes, one can perhaps extend the line to include transcendent causal influences as well. And in fact the study of the natural world *does* reveal vastly different types of causal activity, from classical Newtonian causality to gravity to the influence of quantum fields to the "holistic constraints" found in integrated systems—and on to the pervasive role of mental causes in human life, as in your comprehension of the sentence, "Please stop reading this sentence!"

Of course, the objection naturally arises: Are not all natural causal forces ultimately explainable in terms of the laws of the underlying physical reality—unlike divine causes, which are said to issue from a transcendent and free source? In the following sections I marshal the diverse evidence and arguments that point beyond classical notions of physical causality. Taken together, they now encourage us to accept that the genus "cause" includes types of influences other than mechanistic ones.

The final section draws together the results of the earlier sections in support of a systematic theory of divine action. Emergent causal levels, reflecting the hierarchical structure of the natural world, help to elucidate the nature of divine action, though they are not identical to it. The differences that remain between natural and divine causal influences do represent a continuing burden to theists in an age of science. Given an adequately broad theory of causation, however, the burden may be bearable.

This is a high-stakes debate for contemporary theologians. Traditional formulations remain attractive, but they face conceptual objections that some fear are insuperable. Can a scientifically acceptable concept of emergence be developed that will "re-enchant" the world, allowing us to speak of it again as the ongoing handiwork of God? What corresponding changes may be necessary on the side of theology? Can we again find a way to affirm the divine, as Wordsworth once did, in "the light of setting suns, / And the round ocean and the living air, / And the blue sky, and in the mind of man"?

➤ The Framework of Emergence Revisited

As we saw, experts have identified as many as twenty-eight levels of emergence.[11] For simplicity's sake, however, one could speak of four major transitions in the natural world that evidence the phenomenon of emergence: (1) quantum physics to macrophysical systems and chemistry, (2) chemistry to complex biological organisms and ecosystems, (3) the brain and central nervous system to the phenomena of consciousness or "mind," and (4) the emergence of spirit within the natural order, including the question of its ultimate nature and origin. Scientists and philosophers will be able to understand the emergence of life, mind, and spirit only if they succeed in developing a broader conception of causal influence based on emergent levels in the natural world. That broader theory of causality, *mutatis mutandis*, can in turn contribute toward a more adequate notion of God's causal activity in the world.

As a first step in developing a constructive theory of causality, recall the early stages in the development of the concept of emergence. Aristotle's biological research led him to posit a principle of growth within organisms that was responsible for the qualities or form that would later emerge. Aristotle called this principle the *entelechy*, the internal principle of growth and perfection that directs the organism to actualize the qualities that it once contained in a merely potential state. In this view, the adult form of the animal *emerges out of* its youthful form. Aristotle insisted that at least four different kinds of cause are necessary to explain this emergence: "material" causes, or the ways that the matter of a thing affects it; "formal" causes, which operate through the form internal to the organism; "efficient" causes, which work between objects to move or change them; and "final" causes, which pull the organism, as it were, toward its final *telos* or perfection.

Aristotle's influence on Hellenistic, Islamic, and Western medieval philosophy cannot be overstated. Through Thomas Aquinas, who directly adopted his theory of the four causes,[12] Aristotle was brought into the center of Roman Catholic theology, a place he continues to occupy among both conscious and instinctual Thomists to the present day. Thus Aquinas insisted that every event involved not only the efficient cause (what physicists would speak of today as *the* cause of an occurrence), but also the formal and material causes, that is, the influence of the matter and the form on the outcome. Baptizing Aristotle's theory of "final causes," he also introduced the notion of the overall purpose of God as one of the causal forces in every event, thereby making divine causal action a component in every action. Aristotle—or, more generally, Greek natural philosophy—also remained surprisingly dominant in early modern medicine, biology, and geology. In fact, biology was in many respects still under the influence of something like this paradigm when Darwin began his work.

It is true that some contemporary theologians have attempted to preserve this "final" type of causality in some form. One of the most sophisticated representatives is Wolfhart Pannenberg. In *Theology and the Kingdom of God*[13] he adopts something like Aristotelian final causality, speaking of the power of the future as a causal constituent in every event.[14] A similar adaptation of final causality is visible in Lewis Ford's "lure of the future,"[15] a notion that he develops from Whitehead. Thomistic overtones can also be heard in theories of divine action that distinguish between primary and secondary causality—indirectly in the work of Austin Farrer,[16] and more directly in the writings of David Burrell.[17] Such defenses of "future causality" in one guise or another cannot quickly be dismissed as metaphysical non-starters.[18] Nonetheless, they have not won broad acceptance, presumably because modern scientific practice has in general been *defined by* its exclusion of final or future causes from valid scientific theories.

Note that there are ways of introducing divine causal influence other than the Aristotelian-Thomist strategy. One thinks of theologies of process and theologies of emanation. The doctrine of emanation, at least in its most famous (Neoplatonic) form, defends the emergence of the entire hierarchy of being out of the One and the movement of finite beings back up the ladder of derivation to their ultimate source. This Neoplatonist model, of which more orthodox theologians were always skeptical, allows for both a *downward* movement of differentiation and causality and an *upward* movement of increasing perfection. Ultimately, it was argued, diminishing distance from the Source will lead to a final mystical (re)unification with the One. Unlike static models of the world, emanation models allow for a fluid movement downward and upward through the various species, as well as between the physical, psychological, and intellectual spheres. In those cases in which the emanation is understood in a temporal sense, as with Plotinus, the theory of emanation provides an important antecedent to doctrines of biological or universal evolution.

➤ Building the Case: Causal Problems in Quantum Physics

It is often said that the development of quantum mechanics has transformed our understanding of the causal connections in the world. In one sense this is true. Quantum physics countenances types of causal influence utterly foreign to Newtonian physics. In another sense, I will argue, quantum physics does not actually move beyond the framework of physical causes in such a way that it solves the puzzle of divine causal action—at least not until it is supplemented by a broader theory of emergence.

Consider, for example, the position of Werner Heisenberg.[19] Heisenberg tried to explain the Copenhagen interpretation by taking a basically Aristotelian view of quantum mechanics, arguing that quantum potentials are not fully actual but require the agency of an actual observer to become concrete. In this interpretation of the collapse of the wave function, the observer acts as a sort of final cause, pulling a certain potential state into actual existence. Note that this view reverses the standpoint of classical (Newtonian) physics, which requires that the subject ultimately be explained in terms of physical laws.

For the Copenhagen theorists in general, when a definite measurement is made of a quantum system, the resulting macrophysical state results from two things: the pre-existing quantum-physical probability distribution and the scientist's decision of what, when, and how to measure. Indeed, on this view the subject's role may even be the primary one. The "world" is merely potential until the moment of observation, at which time the conscious observer resolves it into an actual state. The most extreme form of this position—the form propounded in some of John Wheeler's writings—holds that the entire universe may have existed in a state of quantum potentiality until the moment when the first observer (human? animal?) emerged, at which point the universe was *retroactively* resolved into macro-physical structures such as stars, planets, and the like. (This would be an example of the "Strong Anthropic Principle.") At one point Wheeler even applied this logic backwards as far as the creation of the universe:

> Is the very mechanism for the universe to come into being meaningless or unwork-able or both unless the universe is guaranteed to produce life, consciousness and observership somewhere and for some little time in its history-to-be? The quantum principle shows that there is a sense in which what the observer will do in the future defines what happens in the past—even in a past so remote that life did not then exist, and shows even more, that "observership" is a prerequisite for any useful ver-sion of "reality."[20]

The debate between the various interpretations of quantum mechanics has not yet been resolved. Indeed, there is reason to wonder whether it could ever be resolved physically. It's therefore in part a philosophical debate and one, as it turns out, that is deeply influenced by metaphysical assumptions about causality. Interpretations pull in several different directions. Those who insist that explanations of the world must be given exclusively in terms of physical causes strongly resist the Copenhagen inter-pretation, which depends in part on the causal activity of a conscious observer—even if abandoning Copenhagen means a certain loss of parsimony. It may *seem* like ontological exuberance of the worst sort to assert, with DeWitt, that "our universe must be viewed as constantly splitting into a stupendous number of branches" and that "every quantum transition taking place on every star, in every galaxy, in every remote corner of the universe is splitting our local world into myriads of copies of itself."[21] But many have held that the "many-worlds" theories represent a cost one should be willing to pay if it turns out that they are the only way to interpret quan-tum mechanics in terms of physical causes alone, so strong is their commitment to avoid appeals to observer- or intention-based causes (that is, final causes).[22]

But what about the everyday evidence that subjects do play an irreducible part in the causal chain? This evidence inclines one to interpret the collapse of the wave func-tion in the measurement event as a sign of the causal role of the observer—as a number of leading theorists have in fact maintained.[23] Instead of multiplying worlds unneces-sarily, these theorists argue, one should see quantum mechanics as a (the?) point at which the explanatory story begins to require non-physical, or even mental, causes.

Thus the quantum physicist Carl Friedrich von Weizsäcker[24] argued that quan-tum physics was a sort of vindication of Kant's dualism, his sharp separation between the kingdom of causes and the kingdom of means and ends. This was also the view taken by Eugene Wigner and his followers. Wigner used the quantum revolution to argue that "the minds of sentient beings occupy a central role in the laws of nature and in the organization of the universe, for it is precisely when the information about an observation enters the consciousness of an observer that the superposition of waves actually collapses into reality."[25] Interestingly, one of Roger Penrose's arguments against many-worlds theories also appeals to subject-based considerations. He calls them "zombie theories of the world" because "the continual branching of the world and the threading of my own consciousness through it would seem to result in my becoming separated from the tracks of consciousness of all my friends."[26] Penrose insists that one needs an adequate theory of consciousness *before* one can make sense of the many-worlds interpretation, at least in its "many-minds" forms.

Of course, there are also serious objections to observer-based interpretations of quantum mechanics, objections that draw out its counterintuitive nature.[27] Still, the fact is that during most of the twentieth century physicists found themselves forced to entertain very un-Newton-like forms of causality, including essentially nonphysical causes, in order to explain the anomalies of the quantum world. Indeed, quantum physics has recently challenged classical notions of causality in yet another way. "Entangled particles" are pairs of particles emitted from a common source that preserve certain symmetries even when widely separated in space. For example, measuring the spin of one entangled particle will instantaneously cause the other to exhibit the corresponding spin—even if the two particles are ten kilometers apart at the instant of measurement. Because no causal influence can be propagated faster than the speed of light, these results suggest a radically new type of influence or connection.[28] So-called entanglement phenomena have been cited, for example, as evidence for holistic conclusions. Even mainline physicists such as Henry Stapp find in them signs of an overarching interconnection of all things:

> The principle of local causes asserts that what happens in one spacetime region is approximately independent of variables subject to the control of an experimenter in a far-away spacelike-separated region. . . . The statistical predictions from which this result follows . . . have been experimentally tested and confirmed. Bell's theorem shows that no theory of reality compatible with quantum theory can allow the spatially separated parts of reality to be independent.[29]

In a more extreme vein, Stapp's comments have led Ken Wilber to claim that entanglement experiments provide increased justification for the holism of the Eastern traditions:

> It is common among the "new-paradigm" thinkers to claim that the basic problem with science is that, under the "Newtonian-Cartesian" worldview, the universe is viewed as atomistic, mechanistic, divided, and fragmented, whereas the new sciences (quantum/relativistic and systems/complexity theory) have shown that the world is not a collection of atomistic fragments but an inseparable web of relations. This "web-of-life" view, they claim, is compatible with traditional spiritual worldviews,

and thus this "new paradigm" will usher in the new quantum self and quantum society, a holistic and healing worldview disclosed by science itself. . . . The problem, in other words, was not that the scientific worldview was atomistic instead of holistic, because it was basically and generally holistic from the start. No, the problem was that it was a thoroughly *flatland holism*. It was not a holism that actually included all of the interior realms of the I and the WE (including the eye of contemplation).[30]

Wilber's speculations go far beyond what most physicists would be willing to conclude. Still, the founders of quantum mechanics were the first to stress that whatever ontology will finally do justice to the results and theories of quantum physics will be radically different from the everyday picture of reality that we are used to in the macrophysical world and, for that matter, in traditional philosophy. Clearly quantum physics requires some radical rethinking of inherited notions of causality in science.

Psychological Causes

Classical physics holds that all causal forces are ultimately explainable in terms of the laws of the underlying physical reality. If this view is correct, it will raise insuperable problems for any appeals to divine causes, since they are said to issue from a transcendent and free source. But there is another area of science, in addition to the one just examined, that suggests the inadequacy of reductionist physicalism. If there are genuinely psychological causes, then there is at least one type of causality that stretches beyond physical causality. If so, it would appear that the genus "cause" may include species of influences that can't finally be parsed in terms of physics.

I have already noted the four major transitions in the natural world that evidence the phenomenon of emergence. In the case of the emergence of consciousness from the human brain and central nervous system, the evidence for another form of causality is perhaps intuitively the most compelling. Obviously the social sciences (psychology, sociology, anthropology, and so forth) assume that humans are causal agents and that our thoughts, wishes, and intentions make a difference in the world. But in the last few decades the natural sciences of the human person—neurobiology, primatology, cognitive science, evolutionary psychology—have also begun to acknowledge the realm of the mental as an emergent phenomenon. The main difficulty today, I suggest, no longer lies in showing the irreducibility of mental phenomena to physical laws, but rather in demonstrating that mental phenomena can have "downward" causal effects on the body and the world (which will be necessary if one is to speak of God's effects on the world).[31]

What emerges in the human case may not be a separate mind or soul. Instead, it is a particular *psychosomatic unity*, an organism that can do things both mentally and physically. Although mental functions supervene upon physiological structures, mental and physical attributes are interconnected and exhibit causal influences in both directions.[32] To say that human persons are psychosomatic unities is to say that we are complexly patterned entities within the world who evidence diverse sets of properties and causes operating at different levels of complexity. A living body and a functioning brain are *necessary* conditions for personhood, yet the irreducible gap between the third-person vocabularies of the neurosciences and the first-person vocabularies of psychology and intuition suggests that they are not *sufficient* conditions. Personhood is not fully translatable into "lower-level" terms. Persons evidence causal and phenomenological properties (*qualia*) that are uniquely personal.

Studies of the human person must be multi-dimensional because persons are the result of causal influences that operate at the physical, biological, psychological, and perhaps spiritual levels—levels that, although interdependent, are not mutually reducible. In particular, psychology does not need to be at war with the experience of human actors in the world on the question of mental causation. There are genuine mental causes that are not themselves reducible to physical systems on which they depend. As Theo Meyering writes, "macro- and micro-causes may be simultaneously operative at various levels of reality without mutual causal rivalry and thus without necessarily excluding each other."[33] The causal history of the mental cannot be told in physical terms alone because the outcome of mental events is not fully determined by phenomena at the physical level. The subjective states of experiencing joy or being self-conscious have an irreducibly mental component. Such phenomena exercise a type of causal influence that includes but is also *more than* the physical and biological states on which they supervene.

Now, a critic may object that talk of mental causes is like returning to occult causes in the physical world or "vitalist" causes in the biological world. But, she continues, scientists stopped appealing to such causes because they recognized that the realms of physics and biology operate in a fully law-like manner—a recognition derived directly from explanatory successes in these sciences.

But how analogous are human persons to rocks and cells? Can our behaviors be exhaustively predicted and explained in a "bottom-up" manner, even in principle? I have argued that we have good evidence to think not. Indeed, the hierarchy of the sciences itself offers evidence of principles that are increasingly divergent from "bottom-up" physical causality.[34] Causal explanations based on selection pressures play a role in the biological sciences (from cell structures through neural systems to ecosystem studies) that is different from the causal explanations of fundamental physics, just as explanations appealing to intentions as causes play a role in explaining human behavior that is without analogy at the level of cell biology.[35] Top-down causal effects are present at multiple levels, though the nature of the "wholes" that influence the behavior of parts varies across the levels. The structure of DNA, for example, contains a record of the top-down action of the environment on cells and organisms through evolutionary history, and gene expression is environmentally influenced throughout ontogenesis. Similarly, in all intentional systems such as human action, the goals in light of which agents act and interpret their actions must be said to have a causal influence on their actions.

➤ Double Agency and Divine Persuasion

Our argument to this point has important implications for theology. It suggests that divine action claims are not equally defensible at all levels of the natural world. Claims that there may have been a divine influence in causal histories involving intentional agents must be assessed differently than claims that God has altered a purely physical chain of events. It is more plausible to maintain that God influences human moral intuitions and religious aspirations than to argue that God fixed the broken plumbing system in one's house (unless one *also* calls a plumber to come and do the repairs!). One reason for the difference is that we do not now possess, and may never possess, laws of human behavior. In contrast to natural scientists, social scientists can at most ascertain broad patterns of human response, and even these evidence a virtually unlimited number of personal and cultural exceptions. Within the human realm, it seems, uniqueness and idiosyncracy are the norm. No laws are broken when we speak of an individual action in a non-standard way—indeed, this is almost what we *mean* by an individual action! If human action is indeed non-nomological, divine causal influence on the thought, will, and emotions of individual persons could occur without breaking natural law. If (and only if) downward mental causation is a viable notion, God could bring about changes in individuals' subjective dispositions without negating the laws that we know to hold in physics and biology.[36]

But what kind of causal influence would this be? The great British philosophical theologian Austin Farrer developed a sophisticated account of divine action, which he called the "double-agency" view.[37] In this view, every action in the world includes a causal role for one or more agents or objects in the world (the "secondary" causes) and a role for God as the "primary" cause of what occurs. Kathryn Tanner summarizes and defends something like Farrer's position:

> The theologian talks of an ordered nexus of created causes and effects in a relation of total and immediate dependence upon divine agency. Two different orders of efficacy become evident: along a "horizontal" plane, an order of created causes and effects; along a "vertical" plane, the order whereby God founds the former. Predicates applied to created beings . . . can be understood to hold simply within the horizontal plane of relations among created beings.[38]

Such a view of action implies that God's action in the world should be understood as something more like divine persuasion. Responding to Tanner, Tom Tracy concludes:

> There are, therefore, important respects in which the free acts of creatures can be regarded as God's acts. If we deny that God is the *sufficient cause* of the creature's free acts, we can immediately go on to affirm that God acts with the infinite resources of omnipotence to *guide* those choices by shaping the orienting conditions under which they are made. In untraceably many, varied, and subtle ways, God continuously

brings to bear the pressure of the divine purpose for us without simply displacing our purposes for ourselves. God's action goes before our own, preparing us (in spite of ourselves) for the unsurpassably great good that God has promised us.[39]

The approach I have taken does alter how God's causal agency is said to contribute to human actions in the world, at least in comparison to classical views of divine action. In most classical views, God's decision to bring about an effect in the world was taken to be sufficient for that effect to occur; no concurrence of any finite person or object was required. In this view, by contrast, God must persuade the agent in question to act in a particular way for the event to occur. This, again, implies a special role for mental causes, understood as instances of emergent causality within the natural world that are dependent on the causal laws of biology but not reducible to them. Intentional agents can be convinced or persuaded, whereas (as far as we know) rocks cannot be persuaded to act on their own—no matter how good the arguments. Though it limits the efficacy of the divine will in the world, I nonetheless believe that this position is sufficient to sustain a viable and scientifically acceptable form of theism for today's world.

Consequently, theists do not need to imagine that God brings about human actions or physical events by divine fiat alone. Divine causality is better understood as a form of causal influence that prepares and persuades. On the one hand, this result makes it much more difficult to conceive a divine influence on rocks or other purely physical systems apart from the laws and initial conditions established by God at creation. On the other hand, it does continue to ascribe to God a crucial causal role in "luring" humanity (and, for all we know, perhaps other biological agents as well) and in influencing the interpersonal, moral, intellectual, and aesthetic dimensions of human personhood. The resulting position emphasizes the genuine openness in history. One cannot *know* in advance that God will bring about the ends that God desires to accomplish,[40] although one can know that, if God is God, the final state of affairs will be consistent with God's nature. In all of these respects, there is an obvious affinity of this view with process theology's understanding of the God-world relation.[41]

➤ Evolution as a Test Case

Evolution represents a particularly difficult test case for this theory of divine causal influence. On the one hand, the standard model has (until recently) required that the evolution of life be solely a product of a process of random genetic mutation, where the environment selects for the fittest individuals. On the other hand, any theist who wishes to avoid deism must assert that God in some way uses the process of evolution to bring about the divine creative intent (for example, conscious life, persons, salvation history).

In most of biological evolution, conscious beings are not present to be influenced, so the exact type of mental processing found in humans cannot be employed. Note, however, that other animals exhibit forms of cognitive processing that may well be sufficiently similar. Moreover, the recent synthesis of biology and information theory appears to extend the scope of these kinds of causal influence down to more primitive biological organisms, and perhaps even to all living systems. The dimension of information became central in biology following the discovery of the genetic code that is responsible for the in-forming of the cell and organism as a whole. Recent work has interpreted biological structures (morphology) and the organism's interaction with its environment as a series of processes involving the storage, use, and exchange of information—a sort of cybernetic or semantic version of Aristotle's formal causes. Even nutrition has been construed as the ingestion of highly structured (informationally rich) matter with low-information energy as a byproduct.[42]

This thinking of information and causality together has several explanatory advantages. For example, it is necessary to combine the two concepts in order to make sense of epigenetic effects—"top-down" causal influences—in developmental and cell biology. The data now show that a two-way interaction occurs between the DNA of a cell and the cell as a whole. Since particular proteins in the cell function selectively to cause particular segments of the genome (that is, particular elements of genetic information) to be expressed, the determining influences are top-down as well as from below. In a similar manner, social behavioral studies in primatology show how the broader environment pervasively influences the development of the organism without contradicting genetics. The effects of broader systems or wholes are indispensable parts of the complete biological explanation. Thus Steven J. Gould writes, "Minor adjustment within populations may be sequential and adaptive. . . . Evolutionary trends may represent a kind of higher-level selection upon essentially static species themselves, not the slow and steady alteration of a single large population through untold ages."[43]

The informational approach clearly opens up significant parallels with information processing in the sphere of mental activity. No biological laws are broken if complicated biological systems such as the brain give rise to emergent mental properties, and if these properties in turn constrain brain functioning. Since most cognitive activity concerns information retention, retrieval, and processing, it is natural to understand mental causation as involving the interplay of informational and biological causes. But the interplay of informational and biological causes does not occur only in thought. To take such a position would be to fall back into dualism rather than understanding mentality as emergent in complex biological systems. In fact, *wherever* form or structure influences biological process—and such influences are pervasive in the biosphere—one can speak of informational causation (in the sense of Dretske's "structuring causes" but not generally as "triggering causes"). [44]

Although I do not think that the scientific study of evolution provides unambiguous evidence of final causality,[45] it does seem that informational or "morphological" factors play a role in causal explanations of evolutionary emergence. Developing forms, be they protein structures or anatomical structures, combine with genetic (bottom-up) and environmental (top-down) influences. Together these three causal factors represent the three major determinants of biological evolution. The eye of faith may see final causality—ultimate purposes that pull the whole process toward its final *telos*—but scientific biology can neither confirm nor deny such claims. Scientifically, one can speak of the purposes and intentions of the various agents who evolve and act within the biosphere, but to speak of the purpose of the process as a whole always involves the transition to metaphysics or theology.

What of that transition? Once one has shown the compatibility of evolution and conscious mental causation, as I have attempted to do here, one can at least begin the process of attempting to reconcile evolution with theism. The first step in the argument was to establish sufficient parallels between downward causal influences in biology and mental causation, allowing the credibility of the latter to be established without recourse to a dualistic theory of mind. I argued that information theory in biology helps to accomplish this goal. The next step is to see if one can construe divine influence on psychological processes in a way that is somewhat analogous to mental influences on biological processes. Here, however, a greater degree of difference must be acknowledged. By definition, God cannot just be a cause alongside others in the natural world in the way that mental causes can. Nor does an infinite divine being belong to the finite causal order in the way that persons do. Nonetheless, the information model, understood within the framework of emergence theory, at least allows for divine causal constraints on the aspirations of persons in a way that does not abrogate the functioning of natural law. No physical laws are broken if there is an imparting of information from a divine source to conscious human agents.[46] The type of influence is at least formally analogous to the chemical effects that are produced when an agent shifts her attention from one object to another, which are everyday occurrences. By contrast, a direct divine intervention to change the chemistry of a cell would be a troubling miracle.

➤ Toward a Theory of Emergent Causality

Let us now attempt to put these various resources together into a single theory of emergent causality. The challenge for this project stems from the fact that explanations in the physical sciences today depend primarily on efficient causation. That is, the success of modern science seems to have been based on its preference for explanations given in terms of traceable and reconstructable causal histories in the natural world. In the inherited view, any talk of form, matter, or purpose becomes causal only when it is reduced to those activating forces that directly or immediately activate change in a physical object. A causal process is a linear chain of events, each of which causes its immediate successor.

The challenge that philosophers and theologians face now is to sketch a new theory of causation. But how is one to reintroduce talk of formal and final causes alongside the efficient causes that are the bread and butter of modern science? The grounds and motivation for the argument must be based on the changes that have occurred as science has moved further and further from the once regnant ideal of universal reduction to physics. Resources for the new approach can be found, *inter alia*, in entanglement phenomena in quantum mechanics, mental causes in psychology, information theory and epigenesis in biology, and the structure of emergence that appears again and again as one climbs the ladder of complexity in the natural world.

Causal relations *up* the emergent hierarchy are uncontroversial, since they rely on efficient causality. The slogan of early modern or "Laplacian" science might be expressed as: "causes propagate upward; explanation, and hence ontology, reduces downward." The Laplacian model of scientific explanation involves explaining complex behaviors (or the behavior of complex bodies) in terms of fundamental forces acting on their constituent parts. It might *look* mysterious that a cell can divide and divide again or that amoeba can engage in what looks like goal-directed behavior. But once one has understood the biochemistry of cell division, the catalytic effect of enzymes, and the basic genetic architecture and functioning of the cell, no unanswerable questions remain. The aggregation of these myriad physical particles and forces tells the complete causal history of cell functioning. With this bottom-up account in place, no other causal story was necessary. Or so it seemed.

But emergence has shown that upward propagation of causes is *not* the whole story. The state of the whole—the whole chemical system within which particles interact, the whole cell, the whole organism, the whole ecosystem, the brain as a whole—affects the behavior of the particles and the causal interactions that they have.

This view is not without its opponents. Thus Carl Gillett argues that no actual downward causal forces are involved. "All individuals are constituted by, or identical to, micro-physical individuals, and all properties are realized by, or identical to, micro-physical properties."[47] Likewise, certain branches of complexity theory, including the work of complexity theorists such as John Holland[48] who use the word emergence, also allow only upward causation, although they do grant that something new and unpredictable (at least in lower-level terms) emerges. We might speak of these positions as involving at most *weak emergence*, emergence without downward causation. By contrast, I argued in part II that the phenomena allow for, and may actually require, the notion of a downwardly propagating causal influence—a view I've called *strong emergence*.

➤ Conclusion

I opened this chapter with the most compelling area, the relationship of the mental to the physical. To make the position as minimally controversial as possible, I have not posited a separately existing substance called soul or mind, but only the existence of mental predicates. Physicalists construe mental phenomena as properties of a physical object, in this case the brain, whose microphysical causal properties are sufficient to account for the effects that we call mentality. In opposition to the physicalist interpretation, I argued that the explanatory power of mental causation—for example, the ability of our ideas and thoughts to cause bodily movements such as speaking, walking, or raising an arm—is great enough that the limitation of causal forces to the microphysical level is unjustified. The onus is on those who would deny any causal efficacy to the emergent level of mentality.

I then turned to the question of evolution. At first blush it looked like a war to the finish. Evolution appears incompatible with theism, and divine providence or action in the world seems incompatible with evolution. Thus one must ask: What is the rational response to a problem that cannot be solved either from the bottom alone (that is, through genetics and biochemistry), or from the top alone (that is, by negating biology and imposing a theological answer)? One looks for a means to bring several different disciplines together to solve the problem—not by making them identical (which is false) or treating them as incompatible (which is inadvisable), but by placing them in a dialectical or systematic relationship. Specifically, the contradiction is overcome if what evolution demands and what theology requires are not contradictory but complementary.

It turns out, I suggest, that the best overall explanation is obtained when one pursues this hypothesis. Contemporary evolutionary theory forbids vital forces or causal influences from outside. Fortunately, theism requires only that the product of the evolutionary process reflect the divine intention to create rational, moral creatures who can be in conscious relationship with the divine. This *might* have occurred by God's initiating a process that God knew in advance would necessarily produce such creatures without the need for any further divine guidance—though the scientific picture today makes complete pre-determination seem unlikely. In the case of evolution, however, it proved possible to find an analog to the downward causation that we experience in conscious volition. According to the analog, God could guide the process of emergence through the introduction of new information (formal causality) and, in the case of sufficiently complex organisms, by holding out an ideal or image that could influence development without altering the mechanisms and structures that constrain evolution from the bottom up (final causality).

I close with three limitations to the argument I have sketched. First, science cannot provide unambiguous evidence for final causality. Finality language is irreducibly metaphysical or theological. Scientific explanations of biological phenomena must still be sought within the framework of evolutionary biology, and the conclusions and constraints of that discipline are not short-circuited by the broader theory of causality I have defended. Second, the framework of guided emergence is not the same thing as the control of the evolutionary process that traditional theists once defended. Guidance via the informational content of the whole or the goals of conscious agents in the world—agents whose goals may also extend beyond the world as a whole—is not a form of efficient or determining causation; in the end it is closer to the lure-like nature of final causality in Aristotelian philosophy. But it *is* sufficient to provide an updated version of what was once meant by divine providence, albeit without the omnipotence and predestination claims that often undergirded this doctrine.

Finally, the informational final causes that I have explored do not "prove God," for one can still do adequate science without introducing them. Advocates of "intelligent design"[49] or "irreducible complexity,"[50] by contrast, put forward evidence that they think should convince non-theistic scientists of the inadequacy of their position. In order to convey the epistemic ambiguity intended by my position, one might better say that there is a "quasi-purposiveness" in nature. In chapter 5 I called this, following Kant, *purposiveness without purpose.*[51] The Kantian parallel suggests viewing such assertions as having an "as if" status: the biological world develops *as if* it were being guided by a divine hand. Of course, one might believe something more theologically and argue for more metaphysically. But for purposes of the discussion with science, all one needs to show is that scientific conclusions do not require one to speak of this guidance as a mere fiction, and this, I believe, the argument has accomplished.

13

Actions Human *and* Divine

Toward a Panentheistic-Participatory Theory *of* Agency

THE NOTION OF DIVINE ACTION ALREADY PRESUPPOSES A DIVINE AGENT (or perhaps more than one), and hence some theory of agency. For this reason the word "agent," when applied to God, must mean at least *some* of the things that it means when applied to human beings and other agents who act in the world. If it doesn't, the use of the term is a complete equivocation, and a theology of divine action is rendered impossible from the outset. Strangely, though, theologians have so far paid scant attention to what it means to speak of a divine agent.

Agency represents one of philosophy's most fascinating problems. As a concept, it implies a number of features—spontaneity, intentionality, freedom, creativity, novelty—that are not easily domesticated by philosophical reflection. As we will see, the conundrums of agency arise in a generic manner *whenever* one attempts to give an account of what it is to be an agent or to exercise agency. Not surprisingly, the problems are not *reduced* for those who wish to speak of divine action. Certain views of agency make it impossible *a priori* for a divine agent to act in the world. Other views render God's agency possible, but unfortunately at the price that it supersedes that of all other agents, so that humans become puppets, mere instruments of the divine purposes.

In these pages, I will argue that the challenges of divine and human agency can be overcome only by a *participatory* account of finite agency. This thesis will require me to draw crucially on the classical theological notion of participation, in order to show how an action can be both the act of a finite agent and at the same time an act of God. We will discover that the only way to make this ancient concept work in the modern context is to construe the relationship of God and world panentheistically, building on the conclusions from part III above.

Two thinkers in the modern period are particularly indispensable for comprehending the relationship of humans and the divine in such a way that the dual agency we are seeking becomes possible. Alfred North Whitehead developed the most theologically open philosophy of agency of the twentieth century, and Friedrich Schleiermacher thought more deeply than any other modern theologian about how humans, encompassed by and within the divine presence, could still exercise distinctive agency of their own. Thus their work is indispensable for constructing a panentheistic-participatory theory of agency.

➤ Divine Action in the Natural World

First, however, recall the general status of contemporary claims about divine action in nature. After all, it's one thing to suggest that God "lures" humans (or nature as a whole) toward the good (see chapters 6-7), and quite another to construct a systematic theological account of divine action. An account of divine action must also do justice to what science has come to know about the structure and evolution of the cosmos and of the agents within it. How can one conceive divine action within the cosmos given the lawlikeness of the physical world, the increasing complexity of the biological world, and the conscious agency that we have found to be indispensable in the world of human actors? If the history of the cosmos does reveal a gradual "becoming conscious" of the spiritual nature of the universe and its Creator, in what sense was that spiritual dimension present and efficacious from the start? Is there some sense in which the same God is present and active in the world in different ways during the different periods and at the different levels of cosmic evolution?

It is easy to formulate several *unsatisfactory* ways of interpreting the suggestion that God affects the physical world. On the one side, there are problems with supposing that God is constantly performing physical miracles by communicating divine purposes to rocks and plants and animals, thereby directly causing them to behave in ways they otherwise wouldn't. On the other, theism is only viable if talk of divine action is not completely futile. Divine action can't just be empty religious rhetoric for occurrences in the world that are in fact fully explained in natural terms. Recent work in the religion-science discussion—one thinks especially of the Vatican/CTNS volumes edited by Robert J. Russell—suggests a more adequate approach: specific features of the physical world must be shown to be compatible with, and even best explained by, the creation of the world by God. For example, one can argue that lawlikeness and regularity reflect the enduring character of God. Big Bang cosmology is consistent with the creation of the universe by a conscious intelligence. And the Anthropic Principle, which holds that many variables are "fine-tuned" for the production of intelligent life, suggests a possible structuring of the universe for the evolution of consciousness. Note that none of these features depends on an intervention of God into the physical order, yet each does reflect the sort of universe one would expect if the theological picture sketched above were true.

The most difficult area in discussions of divine action over the last forty years or so has been biology. Standard Christian accounts of God's causal activity in pre-human life such as creationism either clash with evolution or fail to specify a conceptual framework that would make sense of this alleged divine activity. A notable exception is the work of process thinkers such as John Cobb Jr., David Griffin, Charles Birch, Joseph Bracken, Ian Barbour, and John Haught, who have given perhaps the most convincing and robust account of divine agency in the biosphere.[1] But these accounts come at the cost of panexperientialism,[2] which is a cost that some are not willing to pay.

By contrast, fundamental physics does not seem to offer any openings for divine influence (with the possible exception of quantum indeterminacy—a lengthy debate that I will not reopen here).[3] If one asks about matter, that is, about causation prior to the emergence of life, the answer must be that whatever divine input or organization may have been at work must have been built in from the beginning. Nothing in our understanding of physics suggests the possibility of subsequent direct divine influence over solid state physics or physical chemistry. If panentheism turned out to be untenable then, in my view, one would have to grant that deism is true at least up to the emergence of life.

Biology offers some reasons to break with a purely physics-based view. We found an informational element in biology, involving the roles played by form, structure, and function, which brings with it certain distinctively new features (see chapters 5 and 12). Moreover, the biological order anticipates in certain specific ways the kinds of purposes that one finds more fully expressed in mental phenomena. To avoid anthropomorphism, in chapter 5 (and again at the close of the previous chapter) I used the Kantian concept of *purposiveness without purpose*. *If* one grants that God can play a causal role in influencing thought, *and* if one grants proto-mentality in the biological sphere, then one might expect to see divine causal agency, appropriately limited, at levels in the natural history of life prior to the emergence of conscious beings. But how is such causal agency to be conceived—especially if, like most theologians in this field, one is committed to giving an account that is neither interventionist nor occasionalist? Theologians today are correct, I believe, in eschewing answers that imagine God introducing a new form of energy into the physical universe or directly causing deviations in the motions of created entities. But if one accepts this limitation, in what sense can God be said to exert a causal influence on or within creation?

It's against the backdrop of these challenging questions that we turn to the question of divine and human agency. I will argue that only by drawing on the conceptual resources of the philosophy of (human) agency will we be able to conceive what divine agency might be, and only on the basis of *combining* the two will we be able to return to the daunting question of God's action in the natural world.

➤ Agency in Whitehead and Schleiermacher

Whitehead and Schleiermacher are indispensable for contemporary constructive theology in part because they offer particularly helpful theories of agency. In order to make use of their work, we must first understand the different problems with which each was wrestling. Schleiermacher, for example, was fascinated by the problem of the enduring "I," the subjective unity of apperception. Along with the other German

Idealists, he contributed to a thoroughly dialectical philosophy that conceived of God, world, and other subjects in light of the self-constituting activity of the subject and her experience. Whitehead, as is well known, was a panexperientialist who used the resources of philosophical atomism and the doctrine of internal relations to construct his own account of agents. The result was a comprehensive metaphysical system based on agents or "actual occasions" as the fundamental units of reality. With breathtaking vision, Whitehead's metaphysics applies a single, (more or less) consistent concept of the becoming and perishing of agents across the entire spectrum of existence, from the smallest particles up to God as the Comprehensive Experiencer and Universal Influencer.

If Schleiermacher is the nineteenth-century advocate of a systematic theology that remains in constant process and change, Whitehead is the champion of the same ideas among twentieth-century philosophers. Whitehead's philosophy is equally experience-based, since it is "the endeavor to frame a coherent, logical, necessary system of general ideas in terms of which every element of our experience can be interpreted."[4] His is not a metaphysics of process that itself stands above process. Rather, he realized, the world of continual process demands a metaphysical system that is never closed, never reaches its end, never attains certainty. As Whitehead puts it in *Process and Reality*, "Metaphysical categories are not dogmatic statements of the obvious; they are tentative formulations of the ultimate generalities" (*PR* 8). To be dogmatically Whiteheadian makes as much sense as being a "supply-side" Marxist (or being insanely rational).

Whitehead defines agency in terms of the creative synthesis of the "many" of input data into the "one" of the agent's experience at some moment. Agency is exclusively present-tense; once the synthesis is accomplished, the agent passes out of existence *qua* agent, although the results of her synthetic activity now become available to other agents. Of the three elements of Whitehead's Category of the Ultimate (the one, the many, and creativity) Anna Case-Winters writes,

> A closer look reveals their fundamental dynamism. The many and the one continually flow into one another in the creative process. Wherever there is a unity achieved, it is in fact an incorporation of multiplicity, a complex unity embracing contrasts. It does not remain a closed unity, but it becomes in its turn a datum of experience for the multiplicity of actual entities. Each droplet of experience entails a new integration of multiplicity into a new unity.[5]

Schleiermacher, for his part, inherits and appropriates the core concept of German Idealism, the idea of the synthesizing subject. In the background of his work stands Augustine's notion of the enduring subject or soul. His immediate predecessor, Kant, had taught that each subject is presented with a manifold of percepts and synthesizes them into the relative unity of experience. Kant's argument that one must posit a subjective unity to unify the diversity of perceptions and to account for the activity of synthesis remains among the most compelling passages of the *Critique of Pure Reason*. Indeed, there are unmistakable parallels between Kant's account of this synthetic process and the theory of concrescence that underlies Whitehead's meta-physics of actual occasions.

Fichte also contributed to the powerful theory of agency that we owe to Schleier-macher. Fichte was modernity's great champion of the self-constituting subject, a cen-ter of pure activity that synthesizes both itself and its world. Schleiermacher may have opposed Fichte on a variety of points in the 1790s (for that matter, he was still resisting some of Fichte's views thirty years later). Nonetheless, during those early years, Schleier-macher appropriated Fichte's notion of the synthetic activity of the subject as the basis of the experienced world, and it remained a framework notion for the rest of his life.[6] Schleiermacher insisted that the subject's activity serves as a necessary condition for any adequate account of experience, *since the subject and the world are together responsible for the individuality of each person's experience.* As Herms writes, "In its mediated reciprocal relationship with the world the self finds itself pre-given, without mediation, as reality."[7]

Like Whitehead, Schleiermacher realized, far better than most of his contempo-raries, that *the particularities of individual experience* are crucial to an understanding of agency. General theories of the subject stand in permanent tension with the unique-ness of each individual's experience of the world.[8] It is no exaggeration to say that the focus on individuality and experience serves as one of two basic motifs that run through his entire opus.[9]

These similarities notwithstanding, at least three important contrasts separate Schleiermacher and Whitehead on our topic, namely, the relationship between the moment of creativity or autonomy and the general (as is were) structural features of agency. First, as noted earlier, Schleiermacher did not claim to possess knowledge of a metaphysical subject. The subject remained for him, as for Kant, a transcendental postulation, a condition of the possibility of morality and freedom. Whitehead well recognized the contingency of all metaphysical reflection. We owe to him, as I have argued elsewhere, the idea of "metaphysical hypotheses." *But metaphysical hypotheses are not the same as transcendental postulates.*

Second, Schleiermacher postulated an enduring agent, a subject whose creative activity extends over many moments of time. (For him, as for Kant, the whole of time precedes its division into moments, whereas for Whitehead temporal moments are primary.) For Whitehead, by contrast, what common sense calls an agent or person is actually a society of actual occasions, a construct built up out of moments of experi-ence that are metaphysically basic.

Finally, Schleiermacher presupposed a sharper contrast between human agents and the natural world; agency is what makes humans unique. Whitehead's metaphysic, by contrast, makes this contrast merely a matter of degree: everything that exists in the world has experience and "prehends" other actual occasions of experience.

➤ Panentheism: Human Agents and the Divine Agent

Our discussion would be difficult enough if the problem were limited to finite agents. But, in fact, both Whitehead and Schleiermacher held that human agents exist in interaction with the divine. Indeed, finite agents owe to God much of what is most fundamental to their agency. We turn now to the theological problem of agency.

For both thinkers, an individual's relation to God is constitutive of her individuality. For Whitehead, as Case-Winters notes, "God has particular relevance to each creative act and is therefore, for each, the 'initial object of desire' establishing the initial phase of each subjective aim."[10] Schleiermacher does not similarly imagine an input from God at each moment of concrescence. For him, human subjectivity is a reality extended over time, so that God's influence does not need to be constant. But God's role for the authentic individual is no less dramatic. As Giovanni Moretto notes, "for Schleiermacher authentic individuality is born that moment in which a determined consciousness of Transcendence begins and the finite is united with the Infinite."[11] Nor is the individual self ever muted out in the process: "One who has found oneself again," the *Speeches* assert, "can discover the living God more clearly than others can."[12] Note that the individual's power, although crucial, is never the power of absolute spontaneity or self-sufficiency. It is always a "power appropriated (*angeeignet*) from the universe."[13]

Both thinkers reject all models of the God-world relation that would make the two external to one another and thus only externally related. Whitehead's doctrine of the internal relations of God to each actual occasion is well known. Previous actual occasions are immediately present to each new occasion as "data," and each occasion values those data in a unique way. As Marjorie Suchocki writes, "Internally, every actual entity is a confluence of creativity as it unifies the discrete manyness of its past into the unique unity of itself."[14] Among the many possibilities available at any moment are the possibilities that God values and makes available to the entity. These are not merely abstract possibilities, however. Because God is an agent who responds specifically to events in the world, God holds out to each occasion a specific valuing of its possibilities, a specific recommendation for its becoming. Likewise, Schleiermacher's understanding of the immediate presence of the divine to each subject remains an equally fundamental commitment in his thought. One thinks of the sense of the presence of the infinite in the *Speeches* and the feeling of absolute dependence in the *The Christian Faith*. (We'll return to these works in a moment.)

What is crucial is that both of these thinkers construe the relationship between human and divine agency in a panentheistic fashion. Both presuppose that the divine reality is indispensable for explaining the experience of finite agents in this world. In one sense the existence of the universe is inseparable from that divine reality, although God is not simply identical to the universe.[15]

Of course, one also finds some rather major differences between these two thinkers. Whitehead tries to conceive the divine agent according to the same metaphysical principles with which he conceives all other agents—except that God never perishes. If the world is "within" God in this view, there is a related sense in which the world is "within" *every* actual occasion at the moment of its becoming. In marked contrast, the Schleiermacher of the *Speeches* sometimes does not even seem to conceive of the ultimate as an agent at all. Instead, the Infinite (*das Unendliche*) is the "whole" or the "Universe" (much in the sense of Spinoza's philosophy), rather than a person or actor. At those (admittedly rare) points where Schleiermacher does not treat God as an agent and does not attribute agency to the universe, he stands closer to pantheism than to panentheism.

These two views of God cannot be bridged. They are simply different. Let's therefore step back from Schleiermacher and Whitehead for a moment and clarify the panentheistic theology that I presuppose in what follows.[16] One might treat this exposition as a sort of thought experiment. If the God I am describing exists, could that God exercise agency in the world without abolishing all finite agency?

I begin with a larger quotient of difference between God and world than Whitehead is ready to admit. As in part III above, I conceive of God as a not-less-than-personal reality whose existence and essential nature are not contingent on the existence of a world, even though God's actual experience is. In this view, God freely created the world. The world and the creatures who inhabit it are essentially contingent, and not only each individual but also the cosmos as a whole might not have existed. As long as God can be conceived as a divine community of persons, prior to and apart from creation, the metaphysical requirement that persons exist in a society of interrelation can still be met.

What do we learn about divine agency from the idea of a "kenotic" act of creation—and, for that matter, the ongoing act or acts of such creation—by a freely self-limiting God (chapter 11)? Although finite agents are by their very nature only semi-autonomous, the divine agent becomes less than fully autonomous only because of a prior decision to self-limit its creative activity in order to allow other autonomous centers of activity.[17] This thesis contrasts with Whitehead's view that God, as the highest occasion, is eternally limited by other agents. For Whitehead, the existence of a world of occasions is a metaphysical necessity for the existence of God. As a center of activity, God is always already responding to the concrescences of other occasions. Sherburne puts the point emphatically: "apart from the experiences of subjects there is nothing, nothing, nothing, bare nothingness."[18]

This view of God that I have just outlined, which remains widespread in Christian philosophical theology today and which underlies this book as a whole, raises the challenge to be addressed in the remainder of this chapter and in the following one. How can one construct a theory of agency adequate both to the God "in whom we live and move and have our being" (Acts 17:29) *and* to our more mundane, everyday experiences as human agents? Can Schleiermacher and Whitehead help us here?

➤ Toward a Theology of Participatory Agency

Process theology offers a robust and differentiated account of the divine participation in the becoming of each entity. The divine input is emphatically not limited to human agents, for God contributes to *each* moment of becoming of each occasion within the universe, without coercing the outcome. The orthodox Whiteheadian account presupposes an atomized theory of time and *panexperientialism,* that is, the view that every physical object is its own center of experience. What options remain for those of us who fall short of being orthodox Whiteheadians, perhaps because we cannot endorse these two premises? Is there any other way to conceive of an action both as the act of a finite agent and as an act of God?

I suggest that the introduction of panentheism changes the framework for discussion in important ways from the divine action problem as found in classical theism, and that these changes are indispensable for solving the problem. For panentheists, *every* action, since it takes place "within" the divine, represents an act of God in some sense. The challenge is to integrate this conclusion with the existence of real, robust, finite agency. Traditionally, theists have been committed to three different types of occurrences in the world:

- natural regularities in the world of the sort that physicists study, which are not the products of direct (intentional) action either by humans or by God;
- free actions initiated by human agents, which are not determined either by natural regularities or by God;
- direct influence by God on the world—on the minds of humans, on the actions of other living things, and perhaps also on the outcome of strictly physical processes.[19]

Sorting out these various modes of influence, I suggest, requires a partnership between two different kinds of intellectual specialization. We turn to systematic philosophers for help in finding a conceptual framework adequate to the challenge, and to scientists in order to understand what kinds of causal agency are exercised at different levels of the natural world. My argument for a panentheistic-participatory theory of agency thus proceeds in three steps.

Step 1: Schleiermacher's Contribution to the Theory of Participation

Participation is an inherently dialectical notion. Applied to God and creatures, it expresses the creature's dependence on God for existence (through creation), for ongoing being (through ontological participation or *creatio continua*), and for agency (as in the double-agency doctrine in Thomas Aquinas). One thinks in particular of the Neoplatonic theories of participation, which crucially influenced medieval theology and early modern metaphysics.[20]

These theories must then be enhanced by a theory of language that mirrors the dialectical structure of the ontology of participation. Central to this view of language is Samuel Taylor Coleridge's description of symbols. The symbol is that unit of language that "always partakes of the Reality which it renders intelligible."[21] For Coleridge, a symbol "is always an essential part of that, of the whole of which it is the representative."[22] There is no way around this requirement. If one affirms the participation of each part in a broader whole, adequate language about reality must also participate in the reality that it describes. In short, an adequate theory of participation requires a close fit between a philosophy of language, a theory of agency, and a theology, each of which mirrors the other two. *This is the challenge that any successful theory of divine action must meet.*

Schleiermacher's theory of participation in the first edition of the *Speeches*, while often implicit and clearly not complete, provides some crucial components for this theory of divine action. In Schleiermacher's view, finite agents would not exist without continual participation in the Infinite of which they are parts. A core claim underlies the argument in the crucial second speech:

> Everything finite exists only through the determination of its limits, which must be "cut out" from the Infinite. Only in this fashion can a finite thing itself be infinite within these limits and formed on its own [or: as an individual].[23]

Schleiermacher's premise is the *sine qua non* for relating parts to the infinite whole. He writes of a chaos, "out of which nothing individual can be separated, except insofar as it is 'cut out' in time and space."[24] One can understand any individual agent only from the perspective of "infinite, undivided humanity," which religion alone is able to intuit as revealed through each individual.[25] The reason for religion's special status is that it understands the universe as active and as revealing itself to us. In seeking to comprehend this activity, religion apprehends "every individual as a part of the whole, everything limited as a representation of the Infinite."[26] One will recognize that there is only one world, one nature, only when one is ready to consider the possibility that all is the manifestation of God, "a work of this Spirit and an expression and carrying out of these laws." Only for such a person "is everything that is visible also genuinely 'world'—formed, permeated by divinity, and one."[27]

True, in 1799 Schleiermacher did not yet possess an adequate theory of divine agency. But he understood the central prerequisites for such a theory better than most contemporary theologians. He knew that the divine had to be conceived both as the all-encompassing whole (*das Ganze*) and as capable of action. He writes often of the "actions of the universe" (*die Handlungen des Universums*)[28] and notes that religious feelings are religious "only insofar as they are immediately caused by the universe."[29] He also realized that theology requires a dialectic that retains the agency of the part as well as the agency of the whole, even while the parts remain *parts of* the whole. Thus Schleiermacher speaks of the human as "a free part of the whole, who is active through his own power."[30]

Our awareness of ourselves as separate individuals is not an illusion. It's just that, in the final analysis, the priority must go to the One, the All.[31] The claim is not, *You have no individuality,* but rather, *Seek to realize your connectedness with the infinite agency, for it is the ground of your own existence as finite agent.* I suggest that Schleiermacher's stress on the feeling of utter dependence (*das schlechthinnige Abhängigkeitsgefühl*) in *The Christian Faith* implies the same dialectical position: one recognizes one's absolute dependence on God. Paradoxically, in recognizing this dependence, one also recognizes *that she is an individual who must act,* and who is capable of acting, either consonant with the whole or in opposition to it. (Is not the emphasis on kenosis or self-emptying in part III above an expression of this same principle? I will that "not my will but Thine be done.")

Just as Schleiermacher does not allow the "individual agency" pole of the dialectic to collapse, so he also fights to retain the "divine agency" pole intact—despite the strong tug of Spinoza's monism. He may insist that a religion without God *can be* better than one with God. Still, the highest notion of God is that "of a highest being, a Spirit of the universe, who rules it with freedom and understanding."[32] The goal of the process is *here and now*, "in the midst of finite, to become one with the Infinite."[33]

The author of the first-edition *Speeches* did not yet require a theistic interpretation of religious intuition—probably, I suggest, because the only theism available to him at the time was one that separated God from world. How might the conclusion have come out differently if a panentheistic theology, a theology with a stronger stress on immanence, had been available to Schleiermacher? Panentheism is present in the *Speeches* in rudimentary form, namely in the guise of Schleiermacher's notion of a world-soul (*Weltseele*). Adopting a sort of eschatological panpsychism, he suggests that the ultimate goal of the universe is that all should be pervaded by spirit. Indeed, note the remarkable parallels with Whitehead's thought in Schleiermacher's insistence, "Nothing should be 'dead mass'; everything should be . . . life."[34]

Indeed, the passages about the "world-spirit" that follow[35] offer crucial clarifications for a "dual-agency" theory of divine and human agents. In the moment of apprehension, Schleiermacher writes, my spirit *becomes* the world-spirit, and the world in this moment *is* my body, "for I permeate (*durchdringe*) its muscles and its limbs as if they were my own."[36] The Romantic exuberance of Schleiermacher's formulation makes for the more poetic position, and I in no way wish to undercut it.[37] Still, it takes only a mild reformulation of his text to make it consistent with the panentheistic-participatory theory of agency that I am advancing here. Could one not say that, in the moment of apprehension, my spirit acts in harmony with the world-spirit; the world in this moment is Spirit's body, for Spirit permeates its muscles and its limbs as if they were its own?

In the *Speeches* Schleiermacher would have us concentrate on the points "where everything that is in conflict unites itself again, where the universe manifests itself as totality, as unity in multiplicity, as system, and thus first earns its name" as uni-verse.[38] Even if the goals of this particular work led him not to use the term "God" to express this intuition of the One and All, by the 1811 *Dialectics* Schleiermacher was clear that the concept of God is required to comprehend the intuition. "Since we posit the absolute as the fundament of all thinking, we have to assume that the idea of deity is present in everything; but in this way we are in dispute with those who separate God from the world."[39] Reading the *Speeches* back through the eyes of Schleiermacher's later work, we realize that what he there attributed to human agents—

> Your personhood encompasses in a certain sense all of human nature, and this, in all its appearances, is nothing other than your own I—many times multiplied, more clearly identified, yet in all of its changes still eternal . . .[40]

—can finally be attributed to human agents only as they participate within the divine Spirit. Religion, Schleiermacher notes, perceives this process "as one of the greatest actions (*Handlungen*) of the universe."[41] For the highest calling of religion is to tie together the various appearances and actions of Spirit, "and as a consequence to recognize the Spirit by whom the whole is led."[42] Herein lies the core of a panentheistic-participatory theory of agency.

 ## Step 2: A Crucial Whiteheadian Correction

The theory is not yet complete, however. It still struggles under certain limitations that are inherent to the part-whole concept. When one *only* emphasizes that the ultimate is the whole, the universe—as Schleiermacher tended to do in the *Speeches*—then one's understanding of the agential dimension of the ultimate is truncated. The whole can have certain characteristics, including values, and perhaps it can even "broadcast" these general values, in some sense or another, to the parts (see chapter 14). But the whole as such cannot offer specific ideals to specific agents at specific times.[43]

A Whiteheadian doctrine of participation helps to overcome this limitation in Schleiermacher. For Whitehead, every entity participates in the divine experience, insofar as that experience is made available to it as a datum in its moment of becoming. But whereas the early Schleiermacher focused on agential aspects of the universe or whole, Whitehead's consequent nature of God remains agent through and through. For this reason, Whitehead can consistently maintain that God holds out to each occasion a specific valuing of its possibilities, a specific recommendation for its becoming. Schleiermacher's "universe" could broadcast out a message to all agents (perhaps, "Experience deeply! Live authentically! Rest on the bosom of the Infinite!"). By contrast, Whitehead's God, who is an agent with intentions, can intend specific goods for specific individuals at specific moments. God never simply causes (that is, coerces) another agent's response. But the divine "lure," the vision that God offers, can be as differentiated and as specific as is needed for any given occasion.

In this and the last section I have argued that thinking of these two dimensions together—God-as-whole and God-as-agent—remains one of philosophical theology's most perplexing challenges. The early Schleiermacher offers us assistance with the former concept and Whitehead contributes to our understanding of the latter. Holding the two notions in dialectical tension, I suggest, offers a richer concept of God than either one alone. Note that the two ideas stand in tension rather than contradiction, for there's no reason that the whole cannot be conceived simultaneously as having some agential characteristics. Indeed, the central insight of panentheism lies in the realization that *the whole is not just the sum of all agents but, beyond that, also agent itself.*

Step 3: The Scientific Study of Agents in the Natural World

In part I, I argued that theological theories should not trump scientific studies in scientific domains. (Incidentally, the converse also holds.) If one wants to know precisely what type of influence is exercised by various causal agents in the world, one must turn to the disciplined study of entities of that type. Only empirical studies can determine what is empirically meaningful to assert of a given entity. Thus, with a panentheistic-participatory theory of agency in place as one's overarching conceptual framework, one must join forces with physicists, biologists, primatologists, neuroscientists, social scientists—and in some cases with historians, literary theorists, and artists—to complete the account of what kinds of entities do what kinds of things in the natural world.

I list the eight major implications of this theory of divine action in outline form.[44] Because the methodological commitment to careful empirical study is a constitutive component of my theory of agency, many of these theses can (and must) be supported by more detailed scientific data and theories.

- At the lowest level, physical particles and forces exercise causal powers in a completely lawlike manner. For panentheists, such particles and forces are not external to God, hence their causal powers are still ultimately modes of divine activity. Still, since science reveals this domain to obey strict mathematical laws (for example, in mathematical physics every electron is strictly identical), one is more justified in treating physical interactions as causal than as the results of intentional actions by agents, finite or divine.
- At the biological level, variations between individual organisms influence outcomes to a greater degree. I return to the question of spontaneity in a moment.
- At the level of the higher primates, including humans, actions result from internal motivations and choices developed in a quasi-autonomous manner.
- Physical determinism would exclude free agency (*pace* compatibilism). Hence *some* degree of spontaneity in the behavior of natural entities is necessary for agency. Fortunately, quantum indeterminacy appears to leave room in principle for the required spontaneity in the physical world.
- Nonetheless, indeterminism alone is not *sufficient* for agency. Since the other conditions required for agency are lacking in the realms studied by physics and chemistry, one should not apply the category of agency to causal interactions at this level. Atoms and electrons are not themselves agents, nor are their behaviors the result of direct intentional action by God. One should thus be skeptical about direct divine influence on the outcome of such processes. Theologically, one may infer from the strict regularity of these forces and processes that God has decided to behave non-intentionally at this level, that the divine creative intent was to create a universe that is self-regulating at the physical level. God would in a sense be defeating or contradicting, or perhaps just unnecessarily complicating, God's own creative method by performing intentional actions at this level. (It's a different

matter, as we will see, when God is responding to the spontaneous agents that eventually emerge from this regularity.)

- Human thought—but presumably not *only* human thought—is not reducible to algorithms (as Donald Davidson's theory of "anomalous monism" also asserts). The regularities that are manifested in conscious agency are the result of character, language, culture, intellectual training, the attempt to be rational, the quest to be moral, and other factors. Hence no natural laws are abrogated if and when the divine agent influences the outcome of conscious processes—just as no laws would be broken if you actually come to hold some new beliefs based on reading the argument in this chapter.

- The anatomy and behaviors of at least some animals are sufficiently analogous to those of humans that one should postulate that they, too, exercise spontaneous agency. To the extent that this is true, there is no obstacle to a divine influence on their actions as well.

- More generally, wherever study of the biological world reveals sufficient spontaneity, room remains for a divine influence on behavior. (Exactly what level of spontaneity is sufficient is a matter for further reflection and study.)

 Conclusion

According to the panentheistic-participatory theory of agency defended here, the actions of all finite agents participate in the divine act, yet in such a fashion that their (partial) autonomy of action is preserved. One expects the degree of autonomy to vary widely across the levels of creation. Establishing the degree of autonomy is a matter not of philosophical stipulation but of empirical study, on which we remain permanently indebted to our scientific colleagues.

Since I've not been able to press the ethical implications of this view, it's crucial to close with a word on that topic. I have affirmed only *quasi*-autonomous action on the part of finite agents because only in the ideal case—a case that may or may not ever be actualized—is full or perfect autonomy exercised. Paradoxically, on this view *the fully autonomous action would be the one in which the agent's act is perfectly in accord with the creative intents of the divine agent in whom she participates.* Given the dual framework of participation and panentheism, to act in accord with the divine intention is to participate in the ongoing divine act. Acting in perfect harmony with the divine intent means sharing fully in the divine act, with the result that the action that ensues *is fully divine and fully human.* This perfect doubling of agency exposes the moral, and ultimately christological dimension to the theory of agency I have defended. Perfect or "pure" agency represents the ideal of one who could say, "Not my will, but Thine be done." As noted above, the theory of agency developed here links closely with, and even depends upon, a kenotic doctrine of creation (chapter 11) and a Christology based on kenosis (chapters 7 and 14). Obviously, for most, if not all, finite agents, the state of perfect accord with the divine will represents an ideal rather than a given. To understand agency as ideal rather than as given helps to explain why system and agency remain in permanent tension, but also why that tension need not be ultimate or unresolvable.

Can Contemporary Theologians Still Affirm That God (Literally) Does Anything?

T HE NOTION OF DIVINE ACTION IS CENTRAL TO THE CHRISTIAN TRADITION. The God of the Bible is continually involved in direct actions at specific times and places within the world. The Israelite prophets attest to their role by miraculous acts. Moses wins freedom for the people of Israel through the ten plagues. And Yahweh shows his superiority to the gods of the peoples by manifesting greater power than they are able to muster. In his lengthy study, *The God of the Prophets: An Analysis of Divine Action*, William Paul Griffin demonstrates the centrality of the image of God as an acting agent in the Hebrew Scriptures. In the biblical texts, God is "a thinking, valuing being who acts in ways which affect the physical and mental well-being of others," as well as being "the recipient of mental and physical activities by others."[1]

Throughout the New Testament Jesus' ministry is characterized by powerful miracles: turning water into wine, healing the sick, casting out demons, even raising the dead. And the pinnacle of the Christian *kerygma*, the decisive moment of salvation history, is the resurrection—the supernatural act by which, according to the biblical authors, God brought Jesus back to life from the dead. As Paul Gwynne writes, "The notion that God not only exists as creator and sustainer of the cosmos but is also actively involved in his creation is arguably one of the most fundamental and pervasive elements of the Christian faith."[2] It would indeed seem strange to believe that God exists but never actually does anything.

Yet the modern age has been harder on the idea of divine action than on perhaps any other religious notion. One of the foremost voices among the critics is that of David Hume. In *On Miracles* he writes:

> Though the Being to whom [an alleged] miracle is ascribed, be, in this case, Almighty, it does not, upon that account, become a whit more probable; since it is impossible

for us to know the attributes or actions of such a Being, otherwise than from the experience which we have of his productions, in the usual course of nature. This still reduces us to past observation, and obliges us to compare [on the one hand] the instances of the violation of truth in the testimony of men, with those of the violation of the laws of nature by miracles [on the other], in order to judge which of them is the most likely and probable.[3]

Hume argues that a miracle is by definition an exception to the overwhelming experience of human beings in the world. Hence, he concludes, "there is no testimony for any [miracle], even those which have not been expressly detected, that is not opposed by an infinite number of witnesses; so that not only the miracle destroys the credit of testimony, but the testimony destroys itself."[4]

The purpose of this chapter is to offer an adequate response to Hume's challenge, building further on the results of the previous two chapters. I here provide the most robust account of divine action that, in my view, can be given while still remaining consistent with the methodological parameters in part I and with the conclusions reached in the intervening chapters.[5]

➤ The Challenge to Modern Theology

What are some of the most weighty reasons for theists to be skeptical or agnostic about whether God ever actually does anything in the world? Three in particular demand the theologian's attention.

First, claims to divine action raise the problem of evil in virulent form. Imagine that God occasionally intervened in the world, setting aside the normal results of human actions or the normal consequences of natural events. What then of the cases in which God does not intervene? God did not prevent the incredible suffering of Jews and others in the Holocaust, nor did God act in 2001 to douse the fire and prevent the World Trade Center buildings from collapsing.[6] The problem of evil arises if God is *able* to prevent great suffering and evil but neglects to do so, for in this case God becomes responsible for the suffering that results. Consider the parallel: If you were able to lower a drawbridge over a river for an express train to cross, and you regularly did so, but occasionally you intentionally chose *not* to lower the bridge, so that all the passengers died in the flaming wreck, would we not hold you responsible for this conscious decision to abstain from action? Yet it seems that the defenders of occasional divine intervention face precisely this difficulty.

A second potential reason for agnosticism about divine intervention has to do with religious pluralism. We find major disagreements between the religious traditions over who God is and what God does. Divine actions have to be part of a broader set of divine intentions for human history and the history of the cosmos. But we find no unified account among the religions about the existence and nature of God, much less about the specifics of salvation history. Is God acting to reveal the law through the Jewish people, or to reveal the means of salvation through the church, or to reveal the divine will for humanity through the five pillars of Islam? Add the Eastern traditions, indigenous religions, and New Age alternatives, and the reasons for skepticism about any particular account are multiplied beyond calculation. In response, many today have grown increasingly skeptical about all claims to divine action.

Third and finally, we've seen that divine action seems to conflict with the success of scientific explanations. Thus many modern theologians have difficulties with the idea that a disembodied, supernatural God directly brings about results in the world. Let's call it *the problem of intervention*. The problem begins with the recognition that scientific research has not provided evidence that God did, or does, bring about miracles in the natural world. Indeed, such miracles don't seem to be the sort of thing for which one *could* obtain empirical evidence. Worse, the basic methodology of science seems to stand opposed to even the possibility of such events. The following four principles are often taken as basic assumptions of the scientific method.[7] Although I will later criticize some of them, these particular formulations are widely accepted by scientists and laypersons alike:

(1) If science is to be successful, it must be able in principle to explain all empirical events. Thus McLain writes, "It is the consensus of the modern effort to understand the natural and historical realms that *all* events which occur must be conceived as part of a unified and ordered world."[8]

(2) A scientific explanation of an event can be given only if the full causal history that produced that event is accessible, in principle, to scientific research and reconstruction. Imagine that you began to explore the causal history of a result in your lab, say the growth of a culture in a petri dish, or the movement of subatomic particles through a cloud chamber. Now imagine that you had to constantly consider the possibility that, a few steps back in the causal chain, God might have directly initiated part or all of the causal sequence with no physical connection to the events that preceded that intervention. The mere existence of this *possibility*, it is claimed, would conflict with the assumptions that are necessary to do empirical natural science.

(3) Science presupposes regularities in the natural world that can be formulated in terms of natural laws. The ideal toward which natural science strives is to give formal, mathematical expression to these laws. But these laws appear to leave no place for divine action (see chapter 12).

(4) In order to succeed at these first three goals, science must assume that the natural world is autonomous, closed, and physically self-explanatory. If each individual electron were a "law unto itself," or if its behaviors were a response to pushes, pulls, and tugs from outside the universe, there could be no physics. Jürgen Moltmann nicely summarizes the difficulty in his major work, *God in Creation*:

> When the machine is taken as model for the world, the underlying premise is an unbroken chain of causality which determines every event in the world. The laws of nature are eternal laws which regulate all happening. . . . [C]hance events are merely subjective impressions based on laws which are not yet comprehended.[9]

Again, these four assumptions are widely shared, even if we find ourselves forced to challenge one or another formulation (as I will do below). Note that each has its roots in one core underlying principle: the presumption of naturalism. We might formulate the presumption of naturalism as the belief that, when faced with both a naturalistic and a supernatural explanation for some event in the world, not only is one more inclined to think that the naturalistic explanation is true, *but also that one is justified in so thinking.*

➤ Liberal Responses

Of course, these challenges have not gone unanswered. A variety of conservative defenses of God's special interventions (miracles) have been offered, some of them highly intelligent.[10] And how have liberals responded to the Humean challenge?

Liberals have been particularly critical of the traditional Thomistic notion of miracles. Among his three definitions, St. Thomas suggested that a miracle can be a direct special divine act that bypasses natural causality.[11] But even Karl Rahner is reticent to accept special divine action in this sense. In his *Foundations of Christian Faith,* Rahner resists the idea of "an occasional suspension of the laws of nature." Such suspensions are always possible, as long as we believe that God is omnipotent. But we could never know for sure that a particular event in fact involved a suspension of natural law, hence "most miracles . . . can never or extremely rarely be shown certainly and positively to be a suspension of the laws of nature."[12] The theologian Walter Kasper is even less guarded in his response: "divine intervention in the sense of a directly visible action of God is theological nonsense."[13]

The most widespread response among modern theologians has been to interpret language about God's action as metaphorical, figurative, or symbolic. Schleiermacher, the father of modern theology, turned to Jesus' God-consciousness as his central attribute. Miracles, later theologians argued, were later additions, attempts to express Jesus' sense of absolute dependence on God. Bultmann continued in this tradition when he sought to give a consistently existential reading of the New Testament. Special divine action is not an essential feature of the Christian faith, he argued. Along with the three-tiered universe, heaven and hell, and the afterlife, it can be discarded. The essential, enduring message of the biblical texts is the idea of existential wholeness, of living authentically. Although Tillich's later thought moved in different directions, his most widely read book, *The Courage to Be,* likewise focuses on the existential attitude of ultimate concern as the heart of the Christian religion. Each of these authors provides a figurative reading of divine action claims as metaphors that symbolize this more fundamental existential concern.

I have no doubt that it is possible to speak of divine action in a metaphorical or figurative manner. For when one speaks that way, one makes no literal claims about the world, no claims about what has actually caused specific natural events, and no claims about what God has actually done. As critics have pointed out repeatedly, to say that all language about divine action is figurative is tacitly to grant the validity of the critics' attack.

But is metaphorical divine action enough? That brings us back to the question raised in this chapter's title. Can contemporary theologians still believe that God (literally) does anything? It seems strange to believe that God exists but never actually does anything. Some defenses of special divine action are more plausible than others. The remainder of this chapter attempts to develop a plausible constructive proposal.

➤ Special Divine Action and the Jesus Event

Recall that we are focusing on the question of special divine action. By *special divine action* I mean the claim that God (at least occasionally) carries out direct actions at specific times and places within the world. God's initial act of creating the world, or God's somehow "intending" history as a whole,[14] would thus not be sufficient for special divine action.

To address this challenge we must first agree on what is required for something to count as the result of an action. Christoph Schwöbel, drawing on the classic works by Anthony Kenny (*Will, Freedom and Power*) and G. E. M. Anscombe (*Intention*), provides an excellent brief account:

> If an event is described as the result of intentional action it is implied [1] that this event would not have occurred if it had not been brought about by an agent whose action can be named as the necessary condition for the occurrence of the event. Furthermore, it is presupposed [2] that the agent pursues a particular purpose with the action and that his or her action can be regulated to bring about the purpose. It is moreover assumed [3] that the action-directing intention is the result of a conscious choice of aims of action and that [4] the regulation of action is the result of a conscious choice of means of action. With these presuppositions we ascribe to the agent freedom of choice and freedom of action.[15]

Actions are, on this definition, intentional. They are therefore to be distinguished from behaviors such as the motion of water molecules in a cloud. Note, by the way, that Schwöbel's four criteria could be employed regardless of which position one takes in the free will debate. One may believe that free actions are compatible with determinism, or one may hold that determinism and free will are incompatible. In *either* case one could agree on something like Schwöbel's conditions for intentional action. The question is whether one can credibly ascribe any events in the world to *God's* intentional action.

Several popular responses don't actually represent answers to our question. Some affirm that they know "by faith alone" that God was acting in the life and deeds of Jesus. They maintain, for example, that supernatural power extended Jesus' own capacities to know and to do, even though they may agree that there is no way to reconcile this claim with modern science. This response, though it may be sufficient for some, bypasses rather than addresses the question that needs a response. Similarly, some affirm that both primary and secondary causes were at work in each of Jesus' actions.[16] His human insight and powers represented a string of secondary causes that can be explained in purely immanent, finite terms. The divine component represents a sort of primary supernatural cause that was also at work. Yet the two somehow coincide, even if we can't say how. But neither of these responses actually solves the problem we are wrestling with—even if they should be true.

Questions about Jesus' God-consciousness, miracles, and resurrection are among the most difficult and disputed in the Christian tradition. But the theologian has no choice. If we do not mine the resources of our tradition to see what it has to offer, we have little hope of developing a distinctively Christian response on the nature of divine action. So what are the options?[17]

Clearly one possibility for interpreting the Jesus event is that God responded individually to each of Jesus' requests—sometimes killing the virus that was harming a sick child, sometimes healing the brain lesions that were causing epileptic seizures, on one occasion introducing grape particles and alcohol molecules into water barrels, sometimes speaking audibly ("this is my son, my beloved, in whom I am well pleased"), always answering Jesus' requests and providing the power to act. Of the numerous miraculous acts of God associated with the life of Jesus, the greatest, on this account, was the resurrection, when God intervened into the natural world in order to introduce a new order of existence altogether. In this most mighty of all God's acts, God restored the body of Jesus to life (with the uncountable number of repairs that would entail), brought his spirit back from death, reunited body and spirit, provided Jesus with supernatural powers during the days after his resurrection when he was seen by numerous people, and finally raised him bodily into heaven at the ascension. Many find themselves still able to assent to these propositions, and I have no interest in proselytizing them away from their convictions. I will just say that, for many modern theologians, it has become increasingly difficult to maintain all the beliefs required by this position. Now I have no need or desire to revise the tradition any further than necessary, recognizing that the more the tradition is revised, the less justification one has in continuing to call the resulting beliefs "Christian." So what are the other alternatives?

One must first begin with the question of who Jesus was and what might have set him apart from other persons in his apprehension of God. The minimal response that the Christian theologian can make, I think, is that Jesus accessed a divine power or knowledge that is available to all humans, perhaps as someone with a good antenna can receive the radio waves that are continually streaming over the surface of the earth. Or, to use a different metaphor, perhaps Jesus tapped into a spiritual reservoir in the way that someone might dig a well and access a rich water source in an underground aquifer.[18]

Call this the *religious genius* view. Its advocates imagine God as a resource that is continually available to humanity (or, for that matter, to all living things). For example, the unchanging solace and strength of the divine presence might be available to all persons who are able to access it. Jesus knew how to mine these depths and in his teaching shared what he had learned with others. On this particular view, there is no resurrection of the individual Jesus, but one might well say that after his death the "mind of Christ"—Jesus' means of accessing the divine depths and the insights he gained—remained available to his disciples and later to their followers in the church.

The difficulty with accepting the religious genius view of the act of God in Christ is that it does not really justify one in speaking of the result of Jesus' tapping into this reservoir of spiritual truth as *God's* act. Suppose that Jesus should happen to be the greatest religious genius of all time, describing the nature of God more accurately than anyone before or since. This would be a commendable act on his part, but it would not thereby count as an act of divine revelation. Nor could God be held responsible for what Jesus (or anyone else) did or did not ascertain of the divine nature. In fact, it appears, no direct role for God in the Christ event would remain—only the indirect role of creating humans with certain generic capacities to apprehend spiritual truths.

So what *would* be necessary to constitute the life of Jesus as also involving an act of God? God would have to invite, or in some way respond to, those who seek to connect with the divine. If God makes some knowledge or experience available to those who seek it, a divine act is involved. And if a human agent such as Jesus is able to teach or act in certain ways as a result of this divine act, then the actions that he carries out can properly be spoken of as both human and divine.[19] I do not here present proofs that such special divine acts actually occurred in the case of Jesus. The first goal is to understand what it would mean for Christian theologians to affirm them and how such an affirmation can be plausible in principle.

➤ Kenotic Christology Revisited

Kenosis offers, I believe, the most attractive solution. Paul writes, "Have this mind among yourselves, which is yours in Christ Jesus, who, though he was in the form of God, did not count equality with God a thing to be grasped, but emptied himself . . ." (Phil 2:5-7, RSV). The disciples experienced Jesus as the most powerful individual they had ever met—so powerful that, they concluded, the source of his power could only be divine. And yet he did not "lord this power" over others "like the Gentiles." Instead, he "[took] on the form of a servant, being born in the likeness of man" (Phil 2:7). The sentences about Jesus' self-knowledge, his knowledge of his unique status before God, which John inserts just before Jesus begins to wash the disciples' feet (John 13:1-4),[20] continue to resonate as a moving expression of this strange juxtaposition of power and self-emptying. What was it like to be in the presence of Jesus? It was to experience a unique form of (personal, moral, intellectual, religious) power and, at the same time, to hear repeatedly "not me, but my Father who is in me. . . ."[21] How could the disciples not draw the conclusion—which Jesus may well have intended—that Jesus' incredible charisma and power were a direct result of his submitting his will to the divine will? Remember that it would have been beyond question to the disciples that God was directly responding to Jesus' prayers.

But then Jesus died. Although he somehow seemed powerful to the end, and although he continued to call out to his Father, that Father remained silent.

Scholars hold different beliefs about which events were the first catalysts for the belief in resurrection.[22] The process might have involved visions or hallucinations, or inferences drawn from celebrating the Eucharist (Luke 24), or an inner divine leading that the disciples interpreted as the direct voice of Jesus. What happened on the human side, certainly, was that the disciples began to live the life they had seen modeled in Jesus, more intensely and more confidently than they had ever done while he was with them in the flesh. In living in the way of the Christ, they seemed to experience the same divine power that Jesus had apparently drawn on. How could they *not* believe that God's Spirit, and even Jesus himself in resurrected form, was present to them and acting through them?

But what should *we* believe was happening? In chapter 7 we considered the way in which, in Pauline theology, the divine power and presence is manifested when believers share in the "mind of Christ," the kenotic mind set that affirmed, "not my will, but Thine be done." We also noted that the submission to God's will allows for the divine act to be incorporated into Jesus' experience of God and of himself. When one describes Jesus' existence in this way, one has already included the role of God in guiding, leading, and "luring" him. Recall the key passage from chapter 7, "In virtue of continually subsuming his will to the divine will, Jesus caused his actions to become *part of* the divine act. There are not two actions, but one. Jesus manifests the divine power by subsuming his will to God's. At the same time (or for the same reason, or in virtue of the same act) God acted through Jesus to manifest God's will and bring about God's intentions."[23]

This manifestation of divine power and presence *just is* (what we mean by) divine action. There is no "action" that God "performs" within the created universe other than becoming manifest. Is this view not consistent with, or even implied by, the process-theological notion of divine "luring"?[24] Just as the process theologian Lewis Ford describes divine action as "the lure of God,"[25] and just as traditional theology refuses to separate the act of God and the revelation of God, we too should understand God's intentional revealing of the divine nature through human agents who seek to submit themselves to the will of God as the essence of divine action.[26]

In the "mind" that Jesus exemplified, he set aside the natural striving that each living thing has to survive, to advance its own causes and interests, and put in its place an overriding concern with the will of God. It's my suggestion that this kenosis provides a workable model of divine action. When the principle of one's own action is that God's general nature and specific will should be manifested through what one does, and assuming the possibility of some divine leading or lure, the result can be an action that is both specifically human and specifically divine.[27]

If this "mind" was only a philosophical commitment on Jesus' part—say, something like living for the ideal of justice—one could not speak of Jesus' actions as involving any special divine action. At best they would represent another version of accessing the underground aquifer, as in the "religious genius" view discussed above. But if one accepts not only that God's nature is love, but also that God wills to manifest particular aspects of that love in particular situations through particular persons, then something interesting happens. Individual agents have the chance to become a part of the movement of divine self-manifestation, to be in their actions part of the act of God. Here we encounter again the participatory theory of divine and human agency developed in the preceding chapter.

We have already seen that modern theologians have had difficulties with a disembodied, supernatural God directly bringing about results in the world, which I labeled the problem of intervention. But it's possible that God, by an intentional act of self-limitation (kenosis), could bring about the divine purposes in the world through the actions of worldly creatures. In that case one could speak of the actions of Jesus as also acts of God. Consider the parallel: you are an extremely gifted painter, able to create beautiful works of art through subtle movements of your hand. But one day you decide to take the hand of your friend at the wrist and, using verbal cues and guiding his hand across the paper, to compose artwork. (Let's assume for the moment that he is particularly ungifted in artistic matters.) Your friend must use the muscles in his hand and be responsive to your guidance and direction. But he must also set aside (release) his desire to control his hand on his own and allow your will to act through him. The resulting painting becomes a product of his action and your action together.

Unlike the analogy, God does not physically cause Jesus to move. How, then, can one speak of divine guidance? The one whom Jesus called "the Father" could still have conveyed information, guidance, and motivation to the mind of Jesus. On this view, Jesus is open to the will of God, and the divine will fills him. It is the divine leading at the level of conscious (or at least semi-conscious) awareness that constitutes the divine act in which Jesus the person participates. How clear or explicit might we imagine this input, this conscious guiding, to be? In the case of Jesus, Christians have affirmed, it was exceptionally clear. If Jesus was indeed remarkably, even uniquely, open to the leading of the divine will, then he could have been sensitive and responsive to even subtle forms of direction from God, so that the resulting actions could indeed have represented a sort of unity of divine and human will and action. (In principle, this unity-without-dissolving-the-twoness could approach the "two-natures" doctrine of traditional Christian theology.)

Note that it's still *the man Jesus* who remains a human actor, hence whatever content is communicated in the divine act must be mediated through Jesus' own understanding and thought processes—in contrast to the conservative doctrine of plenary inspiration or dictation. One should likewise view any human apprehension of the nature or will of God as always including some human interpretation, and hence as being in part a human action. It is dangerous to claim that one's own interpretations directly and perfectly express a pre-formed propositional content in the eternal mind of God.

It may be hard to know exactly how clearly Jesus was able to hear and respond to the will of God and how precise was the content of the leading he experienced. Presumably we can barely comprehend what it would be for a human will to be perfectly in tune with the divine will in this way. But one can draw rather stronger conclusions when it comes to the case of present-day disciples. Here one rightly assumes that human wills are only imperfectly submitted to the divine will, and thus that the divine input is much less clearly received. Thus one should speak of the result-ing actions as involving a divine act only in a much more limited sense, as less of the act can be ascribed to God. Specific divine intentions may be perceived as vague lures toward goodness or "authenticity," and presumably one's conclusions about the divine component in particular actions and decisions will often involve misinterpre-tations. As religious terrorism shows, religious persons can attribute to God acts that are unspeakably evil.

The view of divine action that I am defending does entail a certain limitation regarding the rule of natural law discussed in chapter 12, however. It presupposes that human thought will not ultimately be explained in terms of physical or biological laws (nor, of course, in terms of a miraculous *breaking* of those laws).[28]

Could the divine act in Jesus' case also include physical miracles? It depends on what one means by the question. If it means, "Is it *metaphysically* possible that God could suspend natural laws and regularities?", then I suppose that one must answer in the affirmative. In the kenotic view, God *could* (metaphysically speaking) end the self-limitation if God wished—though there are strong theological reasons, having to do with the nature of God as trustworthy, to doubt that this occurs. But if the question is whether one should affirm that God worked physical miracles *through* Jesus, above and beyond the divine leading that I have emphasized to this point, then the kenotic view inclines me to answer in the negative. On this view it is the body, brain, and mind of the human being Jesus that must respond to what he apprehends to be the divine leading. The result is indeed divine action, but only as mediated through the mind and will of a human being, and only with the concurrence of his will. (Again, there are significant analogies to the classical view here.)

In the kenotic view, can Jesus still be the "firstborn of all creation"? Yes. Imagine that Jesus uniquely expressed the state of setting aside his individual will to allow God to use his thoughts and person for the divine purposes. Indeed, imagine that he did this perfectly. Then we might say that all who similarly allow God to act through them in this manner "have the mind of Christ," as Paul puts it in Philippians. "The mind of Christ" now refers to that perfect fusion of finite human will and divine will that the earthly Jesus manifested and that represents, in the Christian tradition, the highest goal for humanity. Note that this view even allows for an eschatological dimension and a resurrected state. Eschatological existence would involve finite persons retaining their personhood, character, and habits of mind. But in the heavenly state they would submit those individual distinctive abilities to God in the way in which Jesus did—in short, they would have the mind of Christ.[29]

➤ Conclusion

Could a more liberal position be developed in which the Jesus narrative is understood in *purely* immanent terms, as a series of purely human events, with no divine act involved? Yes, without question. Yet the burden of this chapter has been to show that the opposite is also possible: that the Jesus event—and by extrapolation, other events in the natural world—can also credibly be understood as representing one or more divine acts.

Of course, urgent questions remain. *Is* there a God who exercises a continual lure on humanity? *Did* the historical Jesus live in such a way that he uniquely manifested God's power? Does the future include a physical resurrection? These are equally important issues, even though I have not sought to resolve them here. This chapter's goal here was a more humble one: to develop a more-than-metaphorical account of divine action using "the mind of Christ" as a guide. If I have provided a credible description of the unique consciousness that the historical Jesus may have possessed, then one can continue to speak of special divine action, even if it is in the carefully delineated sense which I have defended here.

PART FIVE

The Theological Adventure Applied

Reflections
15 *on the* Human Quest *for* Meaning

After forays into questions of theological method and work in three major fields of contemporary theological debate, it is appropriate to turn in this final section to questions of application. Each of these final three chapters explores a topic within the theology of immanence: the quest for meaning, the renewed focus on the spiritual and ethical dimensions of religion, and the political implications of a radical theology of immanence and divine presence.

I begin in this first chapter by applying the results of an emergent theology to the question of the human person, or what was classically called theological anthropology. What can we learn theologically from the ongoing quest of individual persons to interpret their experience in a meaningful manner? And what light can theological reflection shed on the fundamental human quest for meaning?

Both emergence and panentheism lie in the background of this new inquiry, which should also extend and nuance the conclusions we've reached to this point. What criticisms do the methods and results of the social sciences raise for the present theological project? In particular, do they undercut the kinds of truth claims that theologians are wont to make? We will find that the attempt to give a rational assessment of such "meaning constructions" is rather more difficult than the theological traditions have acknowledged. The difficulties we will explore here do not in the end dismantle the question of truth or render it irrelevant. But they do add layers of complexity both to the quest of specifying what religious truth is and to the task of drawing comparative judgments between traditions.

➤ The Human Sciences and the Construction of Meaning

Some observers of the theology-science discussion sense that their interests are not fully captured by the technical concerns of the natural sciences. This lack of fit has led them to reject science (or what they call "Western science") altogether, or to turn to religion *in opposition to* science. When this occurs, something has gone deeply wrong. Many of the most important issues for theology arise within the collection of sciences known as the human or social sciences, particularly psychology, sociology, and cultural anthropology.

In contrast to the natural sciences, the human sciences are concerned in the first place with the meaning question, the task of "making sense of one's experience." This question connects inquiry in the human sciences with the religious dimension and leads to theological questions. After all, one's overall understanding of her experience will deeply affect her actions in the world. As Lindseth and Norberg write in one research article, "When our outlook on phenomena changes, our behaviour will also change."[1] If one moves from here to a metaphysics, it will invariably be a value-laden metaphysics, since in our private and social interactions we are fundamentally valuing beings. Let us therefore look closely at this set of rigorous empirical disciplines that are primarily concerned with a very different set of issues than the natural sciences: questions concerning the meaningfulness of human existence and the study of how meaning is constructed by individuals, societies, cultures, texts, and historical periods.

Consider the contrasts between the eight different levels in what we might call the hierarchy of meaning:

8. Making sense of existence as a whole
7. Integrating these worlds with the world of nature
6. Integrating multiple social/cultural worlds
5. A sense of meaningfulness derived from one's social world
4. A significant group, practice, institution, or period of life
3. A meaningful event or moment
2. The individual's project of making sense of her experience
1. Raw data from the world and other humans

Although I will treat the eight "moments" in the construction of meaning as a sort of hierarchy, one might also think of them as a heuristic path, one that can be walked in different directions depending on one's starting point. For example, in a traditional tribal culture the levels of shared social meanings (4 and 5) would probably be primary, and the sense of the self as a separate source of meaning might be secondary.

Let's take a brief look at each level. (1) One begins with the *raw data from the world and other humans*. This represents the input from the world *to an individual subject*. Imagine, for example, an infant confronted with the confusing array of experiences. (2) She must then *make sense of her experience* in order to act in the world, for agency requires an orientation in the world, an ability to act. Peter Berger writes:

> the socially constructed world is . . . an ordering of experience. A meaningful order, or nomos, is imposed upon the discreet experiences and meanings of individuals. . . . Man, biologically denied the ordering mechanisms with which other animals are endowed, is *compelled to impose his own order* on experience. Man's sociality presupposes the collective character of this ordering of reality.[2]

Developmental psychology provides a rich picture of this task. The individual must develop a sense of self. But she must also learn that her environment is predictable and safe, and that she can move from the permanence of objects and individuals to the reliability and trustworthiness of the people around her. Later she will choose role models on whom to model herself. A sense of identity emerges only as the individual solves the age-specific tasks demanded at each step. Recall the famous stages of psycho-social development proposed by Erik Ericson: trust versus mistrust (ages 0–1), autonomy versus shame and doubt (age 2), initiative versus guilt (ages 3–5), industry versus inferiority (ages 6–13), identity and repudiation versus identity diffusion (adolescence), intimacy and solidarity versus isolation (early adulthood), generativity versus self-absorption (young and middle adulthood), integrity versus despair (later adulthood).

(3) The stress on *individual meaningful events or moments* draws attention to the *particularity* of the task of assigning meaning that humans face. It is always *this* event, *this* moment that the individual must incorporate within the structure of her personality—or, at the very least, these particulars which raise for her the broader philosophical questions of her existence. Again quoting Berger:

> [Without this meaning-imposing structure] . . . the individual loses emotionally satisfying ties . . . [and] he loses his orientation in experience. In extreme cases, he loses his sense of reality and identity. He becomes anomic in the sense of becoming worldless. Just as an individual's nomos is constructed and sustained in conversation with others, so is the individual plunged toward anomy when such conversation is radically disrupted.[3]

Sociologists have labeled the failure of meaningfulness "nomic disruption," recognizing that the disruption could be individual, as in the loss of a friend or spouse, or collective, "such as the loss of status of the entire group."[4] "In both cases," Berger writes, "the fundamental order in terms of which the individual can 'make sense' of his life and recognize his own identity will be in process of disintegration. Not only will the individual then begin to lose his moral bearings, with disastrous psychological consequences, but he will become uncertain about his cognitive bearings as well."[5] The meaning project isn't marginal: it's at the center of our existence.

In the social world, events rarely occur without some significance. Everything we do either has or fails to have an underlying valence of meaning. We do not merely grow older; we pass through a series of rites of passage. In middle-class North America these might include: baptism or circumcision, confirmation, obtaining a driver's license, high school graduation, engagement and marriage, promotions, births, birthdays, retirement, and, finally, death. Humans do not merely use words and encounter objects. We fashion signs in our language and turn objects into symbols of broad affective judgments of the world. (Think of the affective weight of symbols such as the Star of David, prayer beads, the American flag, the face of Princess Diana, or the insignia of one's alma mater.)

(4) These individual events then form broader *groups, practices, institutions, and periods of life*. Think of it as a sort of "affective space" in which each person lives. Each group with which one identifies provides an important source for one's "sense of significance"—of oneself, one's relationships, and of one's life in general. These may include a church community, a fraternity or sorority, a sports team, an ethnic group, or a club.

(5) Arising out of this set of connections is *a sense of meaningfulness derived from one's social world*. This phrase for the first time captures the continuing task of the individual agent in the world, namely to create an affective or (as sociologists say) a "semantic" fit among the various components of one's subjective world. This growth task must be repeated at each phase of life, from schooling to the work place, from one's family of origin to one's adult family, from teenage crises through mid-life crises on to the crises of the loss of one's parents and (later) one's own partner or friends, and finally to the events preceding and surrounding one's final illness and death. Each loss, each ambiguity, each unanswered question again raises the urgent task of assigning meaning to a new set of events—for, again, to fail to fit the pieces of one's life together in a fashion that is meaningful for a specific individual is for her to lose the ability to act as an agent in that world.

(6) *Integrating multiple social or cultural worlds* is especially important in a pluralistic situation such as ours. Indeed, pluralism is deeply characteristic of the religious situation in which we live, since we today are more aware than ever before of the multiple religious options available to us, and hence of the many ways that our own religious traditions can be interpreted. As Berger writes, "to live in the social world is to live an ordered and meaningful life. Society is the guardian of social order and meaning, not only objectively, in its institutional structures, but subjectively as well, in its structuring of individual consciousness."[6] Society today assigns us multiple personas or roles, many stemming from deeply clashing worlds.

Some years ago I was teaching at Williams College, one of the "Little Ivies" in Massachusetts. The admissions department had the intriguing idea of offering full scholarships to Latino-American students from a high school in East Salinas, California, so that they could attend Williams. As the advisor for some of these young students, I watched the clash of worlds as they were ripped out of their mostly Spanish-speaking society and the context they knew as (mostly) second-generation immigrants in a richly Hispanic California town, and suddenly thrown into the world of a competitive, wealthy, overwhelmingly WASP liberal arts college in a small town in the heart of New England. The conflicts that were painfully evidenced in the lives of these students—many of whom survived only a semester or two before escaping back to their own home culture—were dramatic examples of the quest to integrate multiple social or cultural worlds.

(7) Alongside the integration of cultural worlds, we face the task of *integrating these subjective worlds with the objective world around us.* Society is one objective given, as Berger shows:

> The success of socialization depends upon the establishment of symmetry between the objective world of society and the subjective world of the individual. If one imagines a totally socialized individual, each meaning objectively available in the social world would have its analogous meaning given subjectively within his own consciousness. Such total socialization is empirically non-existent and theoretically impossible, if only by reason of the biological variability of individuals. However, there are degrees of success . . .[7]

One must also find one's sense of self within the natural world as well. This is no easy task. Nietzsche has most clearly expressed the tension faced by individuals in a dark universe in a passage already cited:

> Once upon a time, in a distant corner of this universe with its countless flickering solar systems, there was a planet, and on this planet some intelligent animals discovered knowledge. It was the most noble and most mendacious minute in the history of the universe—but only a minute. After Nature had breathed a few times their star burned out, and the intelligent animals had to die.[8]

(8) The Nietzsche quote shows, finally, the urgency of the highest and broadest task: to *make sense of existence as a whole.* Somehow what we know about the physical universe, with its apparently unbending laws and hostile conditions for life, must be integrated into our sense of who we are and what the world that we inhabit is. At first blush, perhaps this description does not sound radically different from the "religion and the natural sciences" discussion that is already familiar to many. But the individual and social task of constructing contexts of meaning is actually extremely significant. The impact is perhaps clearer when one adds the premise: *the construction of meaning is ubiquitous; it plays a role in all that humans do and think.*

This conclusion is, however, disturbing for most religious people. We like to think of our religious beliefs as *directly* reflecting rational reflection on the world and the self-revelation of God, rather than as the product of social construction. Many become uncomfortable to consider their religious beliefs as being the result of social factors. In order to understand the real challenge, it is not enough just to be told that sociologists can explain many of the causes of religious belief. One needs to consider the details of some of the data in order to feel their force.

➤ Religious Belief and Practice as Dependent Variables

It seems to bother theologians that religious behaviors often represent a rational choice for men and women in social contexts, quite apart from the question of whether the underlying beliefs are true.[9] "Rational choice theories" in the sociology of religion employ functionalist explanations to explore the social pressures that push individuals to, or away from, religious commitments.[10]

For example, in an important article, Richard Lee[11] reviews the findings of a number of sociologists concerning the "Success Proposition" as an explanation of religious behavior. The Success Proposition holds that religion, like many other aspects of culture, is a result of socialization, a consequence of reward and punishment. First, Lee notes that the frequency of religious behavior, such as attending church and participating in church-related activities, increases when there are opportunities for reward or praise of the individual's behavior. The reward can be as simple as the pleasure obtained by agreement with, or attention from, fellow congregation members. It can include belief in other-worldly rewards or individual recognition within the congregation. As age increases, religious participation generally does as well.

Other studies examined by Lee show how "the church lifted up the nuclear family as the norm."[12] As a result, another sociologist found that the 40 percent of congregation members who did not fit the family norm (that is, single mothers, and those divorced, older, or married to "unsaved mates") are *least* likely to conform to church norms or actively participate. Interestingly, as educational level increases, so does participation in the church. Further, when changing religious affiliations, persons are more likely to choose denominations which maintain "cultural continuity." Thus, one study found that

> Individuals reared as Episcopalians or Lutherans more often switched to Catholicism than those reared in nonliturgical Protestant traditions, and Catholics disproportionately switched to Lutheranism. Jews, having no traditions similar to their own to which to switch, were more inclined to choose nonaffiliation.[13]

Other studies demonstrate that parental choice is one of the most important, if not the singularly most important determinant in religious life choices and choice of denomination. One study of parents and high school students documented that if parents claimed no religious affiliation, neither did 85 percent of their children. Conversely, 90 percent of students who were members of evangelical congregations had parents who were members. If both parents claimed to be either Catholic or Protestant, only 4 percent of their children claimed no religious affiliation.[14]

Leiffer discovered that 40 percent of Methodists joined or continued to attend church because of friends or relatives. Schaller found that 60 to 90 percent of new church members were brought in by friends or relatives. The answer most frequently given by those surveyed as to why they attended church regularly was "to keep the family together, to strengthen the family ties."[15]

Finally, Robert Young[16] found that two factors—concern for the fate of others and rejection of the death penalty—were significantly correlated with believers' interpretations of evangelism in the communities he studied. Young hypothesized that this correlation was due to the tendency "to make situational rather than personal attributions, as well as to the relative skepticism with which [his subjects] view the American criminal justice system."[17] He found a correlation between fundamentalism and a high level of support for the death penalty, as well as between fundamentalism and higher levels of authoritarianism, particularly in white fundamentalist churches. He also noted that fundamentalist congregations that were primarily black did not share this authoritarian attitude or support for the death penalty.

Economic analyses represent an equally crucial social scientific perspective in the study of religion, although I won't be able to explore them here. The premise of economic analyses of religious behavior is that religious ideas and institutions function in an open market. Denominations do well when what they supply matches what religious consumers demand. Economists of religion explore "how people choose among religious options and what social forces govern religious taste." The resulting data, they maintain, reveal that "religious choices are akin to other cultural choices."[18]

➤ The Sacred Canopy

What is the significance of such data? Many believers find it disturbing that social factors such as these enable social scientists to reliably predict a range of religious beliefs and behaviors. Let's step back from the social sciences for a moment to attempt to understand the nature of this worry. What is the conception of religion that underlies these predictions? Does it represent a challenge to the truth of religious beliefs? If so, how might religious persons and theologians begin to answer the challenge?

Recall Nietzsche's bleak prediction about the future. In an age dominated by the new Hubble images of deep space, many feel the threat posed by Nietzsche's description of a dark, hostile universe—one that cares nothing about human existence and threatens our demise through the inexorable force of natural law at some future point in time, which we can predict only too well. As a result, many feel the urgency of the task of shielding ourselves from such a universe. One concept clearly functions to stave off the threat and resulting sense of meaninglessness: the concept of God. For if the God of the Abrahamic traditions exists, and if God is good in the way that these traditions have taught, then God will not allow the "heat death" of the universe to be the final demise of intelligent life. God will surely ensure that what is best and most valuable about our lives, both individually and as a whole, will be preserved in the end.

I do not here raise the question of *whether* God exists. We return to that question below. For the moment let's concentrate on the *function* of belief in God. A clear function of theism is to establish meaning, and thereby to make the universe meaningful for believers. The functionalist study of religious belief is most often associated with one important school in the social scientific theory, social constructivism. Only after we have examined its claims and arguments will we be in the position to ask whether theologians should endorse social constructivism, and to what extent they should (or can) resist its conclusions.

On the constructivist view, "Religion is the . . . attempt to conceive of the entire universe as being humanly significant."[19] Along with its contributions to the individual quest for meaning, religion also makes important contributions to social solidarity, at least within the in-group. Peter Berger writes that religion involves

> the establishment, through human activity, of an all-embracing sacred order, that is, of a sacred cosmos that will be capable of maintaining itself in the ever-present face of chaos. Every human society, however legitimated, must maintain its solidarity in the face of chaos. Religiously legitimated solidarity brings this fundamental sociological fact into sharper focus. The world of sacred order, by virtue of being an ongoing human production, is ongoingly confronted with the disordering forces of human existence in time. . . . Every society is, in the last resort, [persons] banded together in the face of death. The power of religion depends, in the last resort, upon the credibility of the banners it puts in the hands of [men and women] as they stand before death, or more accurately, as they walk, inevitably, toward it.[20]

The sacred is what "stands out" from the "normal" life. It is, in Rudolf Otto's famous words, a mystery that arouses both fear and fascination (*mysterium tremendum et fascinans*). The sphere of the religious is

> something extraordinary and potentially dangerous, though it can be domesticated and its potency harnessed to the needs of everyday life. . . . The cosmos posited by religion thus both transcends and includes [humanity]. The sacred cosmos is confronted by [humanity] as an immensely powerful reality other than [ourselves]. Yet this reality addresses itself to [us] and locates [our] life in an ultimately meaningful order.[21]

➤ The Fear of Functionalism

A very convincing story can be told of how religious belief functions to make sense of our total experience (level 8 in the hierarchy above). I see no point in questioning the power of the functionalist analyses of religion summarized in the last section. The explanatory power is such that the accounts speak for themselves. Clearly the sociology of religion helps to illumine the myriad ways in which religious belief functions in light of this urgent human need to make sense of our experience.

Indeed, at the functional level religious believers should be no more inclined to doubt these accounts than non-believers. Wouldn't Christians and Muslims, for example,[22] *expect* that belief in God should have the function of providing a center of meaning to one's life and a behavioral orientation that could not be matched by any nonreligious concepts or practices? Rather than being opposed to functionalist analyses of religion, perhaps the religious person should after all be their prime advocate.

Why then the widespread reticence of many believers to embrace functional analyses of religion? Presumably believers and theologians sense that these explanations are just a bit *too* powerful. Don't they account for the details of religious belief and behaviors with a bit too much detail? To put the fear bluntly: Is it possible that these explanations, given in terms of the functions of religious belief, *better* explain the existence of such beliefs than the appeal to their truth? If so, the objection continues, aren't believers better advised to suspend their belief in the actual truth of religious claims and to become, at best, agnostic? For if religious believers would continue to hold the same beliefs *even if those beliefs were false*—say, because of the benefits that are to be gained by believing them and acting in certain ways—haven't we stumbled on a reason to no longer hold them as true?

This skeptical argument involves what is generally called a *theory of error*, that is, a theory that explains why people would hold certain beliefs even if they were false. This argument is well known to students of the sociology of knowledge. If you are a passionate Republican and I show you that you hold precisely the same political beliefs as your parents do, and that the vast majority of people with an upbringing like yours mirror their parents' political beliefs to a very high degree, then I have explained why you would hold your political beliefs apart from any appeal to their actual truth. In a sense, one might fear, I've *explained them away*. Similarly, if sociological or cultural explanations are able to account for where particular religious beliefs came from, and why a person might tend to think they are true whether or not they really are, then one's reason for believing them to be true has been undercut. Herein lies the deeper worry that functionalist analyses seem to raise for religious believers: *the fact that people hold religious beliefs*—so it is claimed—*is better explained by their function than by their truth.*

Note that this worry is the analog within the social sciences to the threat of naturalism and the apparent impossibility of miracles in the natural sciences. Just as the strict regularities that physics has discovered render the idea of exceptions to physical laws increasingly unlikely, and growing neuroscientific knowledge of how brain processes produce mental phenomena makes it harder to believe that those mental phenomena are caused by a "mind" or "soul," so likewise increasing knowledge of the social and cultural functions of religious belief makes it difficult to ascribe to them a different source.

➤ Anthropology and Theology

How then are believers to answer the functionalist objection? Two forms of the functionalist critique of religion, at any rate, are easily dealt with. One is the response, "Well, that's it for religious belief! Once one accepts the human role in constructing belief, one has clearly proven that religious beliefs are false." Although one sometimes encounters bold claims of this sort, they are unjustified. Functionalist accounts do not demonstrate the falsity of (say) core Christian beliefs. Believing that God exists does not become a mistake merely because that belief functions to make one's life meaningful. Belief in God is sometimes dismissed as mere "wish fulfillment," as in Freud's famous critique. But is the fulfillment of things we wish for *always* a matter of make-believe? The functionalist critique may support agnosticism, but it provides no evidence for the falseness of religious claims.

Another criticism often raised is that there's no place for revelation after sociology, for we now know that *all* language about God is created only by human beings and only serves particular personal and social functions. But, it turns out, this objection is just as overhasty as the first. Just as religious language could be true, it also could have (at least some of) its source in a divine self-revelation.

Nevertheless, recognizing the social construction of meaning does place the believer before one sort of decision: Will she embrace or resist the analysis of the social functions of religion outlined in these pages? It seems to me that such analyses offer important insights into the nature of religious belief, and that the theologian should therefore labor to include them within his or her reflection.

On the one hand, one recognizes that the resistance of theologians and believers to functionalist analyses was unjustified. Would it not be a bit silly to try to argue that religious belief does not have psychological, social, and cultural functions? Denying the societal impact of religion, or the impact of society and culture *on* religion, leads to a truncated view of religion. Some of the major debates in science-religion discussions appear to be guilty of this error, for example, when God is introduced only in the role of initiator of the Big Bang or guarantor of the regularity of nature, in total abstraction from the meaning question. Such a God, however helpful philosophically or physically, is far from the God of actual religious belief, religious communities, and religious devotion.

On the other hand, one must be clear on the costs. Accepting the social analysis of religion means thinking harder about the status of our various statements about God. It means admitting that *some portion* of the language of worship and devotion reflects the commitments of our culture and tradition; *some kinds of God-talk tell us more about ourselves than about God.* Theology and anthropology do not exist in pristine purity, worlds apart, and none of us practices a religion that is completely culture-free. (Of course, this will also mean that theology has something to say to anthropology, as we will see.) Is this not the insight to which the sociology of religion leads us: language about God is not only inherited from above, but much of it is also constructed by humans?

What's usually not done in these discussions, however, is to embrace the social analysis, as I think we must do, *and then to give a theological account of what is occurring.* That is, critics act as if the game is over as soon as theologians grant that sociology is right about the dimension of social construction. We must thus explore what kind of a response theologians can give to the functionalist critique. For if one asserts the existence of God, one must be in the position to incorporate and explain the results of the scientific study of religion. Is it possible, then, to give a theological account of the interrelationship between religious belief and social construction? How can we integrate the two? What happens to God after Berger?

➤ Getting to the Metaphysical Questions

Social-scientific accounts of God have less tendency to usurp all place for God if they are integrated with the natural sciences and the theological questions that these sciences raise. For example, theological questions in the natural sciences concern the "before" and "after" of physics: What occurred before the Big Bang (for example, what caused it?) and what may occur after the Big Crunch, if there is one, when the universe collapses back into a singularity? Second, what is the source and significance of the regularity, the extreme lawlikeness, that characterizes the observed universe? Finally, what is the significance of the incredible "fine-tuning" that we see in the universe—a large number of variables falling within the incredibly small range that would be required for life to emerge (the so-called Anthropic Principle)?

Of course, physical notions such as the Big Bang or the emergence of complexity do not offer scientific proof for the existence of God or an "intelligent designer"— therein lies the mistake of the "intelligent design" movement. But for those who are theists, notions such as these do suggest a new task: the task of developing a theology of nature, that is, an account of the physical world around us given in theological terms. One can of course describe the world in purely physicalist terms—which is, after all, exactly what the physical sciences attempt. But in the natural sciences it is patently clear, even clearer than in the social sciences, that questions arise about the natural world which fall outside the scope of what physicists can test. (David Hume called these the questions of the "before" and "after." Today we might call them meta-physical questions).

Of course, some critics have tried to argue that metaphysical questions (including theological questions) are meaningless. Since they can't be answered in purely scientific terms, it is argued, they can't be rationally discussed at all. Would that humanity could escape its fundamental questions so easily! It has turned out to be more difficult than expected to sharply delineate between questions that can and cannot be addressed scientifically. Conceptually speaking, science shades imperceptibly from its most empirical and testable questions, through progressively more abstract ranges of theoretical reflection, and on to questions that can only be called philosophical and theological.[23] Among leading theoretical physicists one rarely finds the "science-has-all-the-answers" attitude that dominates in the popular press (and in some science classrooms). Top scientists are keenly aware of the role of *meta-empirical* questions and assumptions in theoretical physics and are often willing to explore them in great detail (as long as one does not confuse the broader discussions with what we currently know how to test).

The relation between the physical sciences and theology has direct relevance for reconsidering the relation between the social sciences and theology. I suggest that the well-known links between various physical sciences and metaphysical topics provide a corrective to a certain mistaken tendency in social scientific theory. There is nothing absurd about a dialogue between natural science and metaphysics or theology. Indeed, as I've argued, one cannot do fundamental physics without raising some of these issues. Why then should there be a resistance to recognizing the theological questions that arise out of the social sciences? The reason is surely not that sociologists and psychologists possess more powerful theories than physicists and can thus predict behaviors more precisely, rendering metaphysical questions useless. Nor is there any reason to think that the human sciences raise *fewer* broad questions than the natural sciences—to the contrary! Could it be that the relative uncertainty of social scientific explanations has caused some in this field to claim a certainty and finality for their theories that is not justified by their methods and data? If it's natural to wonder about the connections between the Big Bang and a God who might have been its cause—and I have argued that it *is* rational to reflect on this subject—then why wouldn't it be just as rational to look for connections (links, integrations) between the social sciences and metaphysics or theology?

➤ The Social Sciences and Theological Truth Claims

This topic represents, I believe, one of the most urgent questions in the entire religion-science discussion today. One must ask: What is the nature of universe, and of this particular animal *Homo sapiens* who studies it, such that humans would tend to interpret the world, and live in their respective social and cultural worlds, using religious categories in the way that we do? Why would we be the sort of animal that would be fixated on the question of meaning—the meaning of existence, of our own lives, of it all? What is the significance of our raising the question of God for the question of whether a God exists?

The transition from standard social scientific practice to a discourse in which such questions could be thematized is not difficult to sketch. One begins with humans living their lives. Social scientists use standard research methods to establish statistically significant correlations between interesting parameters that describe features of human social existence. One then formulates psychological, sociological, and anthropological theories based on those correlations. The network of these theories yields the disciplines of social psychology, sociology, and cultural anthropology as we know them today. As in the natural sciences, however, the general study of the social world gives rise to a sort of "grand theory" in the social sciences, as Quentin Skinner has argued.[24] Such broader theories shade over imperceptibly into philosophical anthropology, the philosophical reflection into the nature of humanity.[25] One area of this reflection concerns the religious dimension, the human attempt to view the universe as religiously meaningful. And one response that has been given is the theological response, the belief that human existence is meaningful because God has created the universe and wishes to be in relationship with intelligent life (or all life).

Note that what began as an empirical question in social science gradually expands to the level of philosophical worldviews. Whether one's explanations should reduce down to the biological substratum, up into theological dimensions, or remain emphatically at the level of humanity is a classic philosophical question. Such philosophical and even metaphysical questions arise naturally out of the study of human behavior, although a wealth of social scientific data bear on the debate.

➤ Conclusion

We began by examining the way in which humans make sense of their existence. We then explored the ways in which the functionalist treatment of religious belief in the social sciences appears to challenge or undercut theological truth claims. In the final section, I began to sketch a scientific, philosophical, and theological program that could respond to this challenge. In the natural sciences, it is the meta-physical questions raised by the physical theories themselves that lead to theological discussion. In the human sciences, I suggest, *the meaning question itself* can lead to theological issues. In these fields, where one speaks of metaphysics (that is, moving beyond the physical world that serves as the backdrop for human social interactions), one must include the values that pertain to agents.

It is interesting to contrast the religious and theological topics that arise out of the natural and social sciences. Typical metaphysical questions arising out of the natural sciences include:

- What occurred before the Big Bang (for example, what caused it)? What may occur after the Big Crunch, if there is one, when the universe collapses back into a singularity?
- Is Big Bang cosmology compatible with the doctrine of creation?
- What is the source and significance of the regularity, the extreme lawlikeness, that characterizes the observed universe?
- What is the significance of the amazing "fine-tuning" that we see in the universe—a large number of variables falling within the incredibly small range that would be required for life to emerge (the so-called Anthropic Principle)?

By contrast, typical metaphysical questions arising out of the social sciences include:

- What is the nature of the human animal that raises the question of the meaning of its own existence?
- Are there dimensions of human existence that require explanations at "higher" levels than the natural sciences (including sociobiology, primatology, and neuroscience)?
- Are there social scientific reasons to supplement functionalist explanations (or standard causal correlations) with other types of accounts?
- Is there a hierarchy of disciplines that points beyond the positivism typical of the most rigorous work in the social sciences today and that opens the door to philosophical and theological questions?

- Will the parallels with the other higher primates allow scientists to explain human behavior in terms of the more fundamental laws of biology (evolutionary psychology and neurophysiology)?
- Will the human being ultimately be explained using distinctively human terms and predicates?
- Or will explaining the human ultimately require that we go beyond the level of the human to include a trans-human level, for example, humans as made in the image of God and reflecting the divine nature and intentions?

The important thing about this type of explanatory project is that it does not stand in competition with the analyses of the social sciences but is a natural extension of them. We know from social scientific study that we are beings who are always *more than*, always ahead of, the particular physical environment in which we are located. The satiation of our basic physical desires and needs—food, shelter, work, reproduction—does not put an end to our striving or yearning, but rather gives rise to ever new projects of self-actualization and other-orientation. The problem of trying to make the pieces fit, of making them meaningful, continues to arise even for those whom the physical world has treated best of all.

What then of the ideas and beliefs that arise out of this process? Are *social communities*, for example, merely fictional constructions of this process, since what really exists are the individuals, the atoms of the whole process? Are the *ideals* that humans strive for—love, justice, compassion—all fictions? Or do we strive to understand some things that are actually *true of the world*? Do the sciences prove that we are alone in a hostile universe, as Nietzsche thought? Or do they provide some signs of another possibility: that humans are pervasively preoccupied with religious symbols and practices because we live in a universe that is open toward transcendence, a universe that is grounded in a reality not utterly unlike ourselves, in One who is not *less* intelligent and conscious than we are? Are there signs of One who is revealed in the physical world, in cosmic history, and somehow also in the character of human beings as it is studied by psychologists and sociologists?[26] Could not something of the divine be revealed by studying that animal that struggles with the question of God: ourselves?

Spirituality *as* Spirit *and* Spirituality *toward* Spirit

A Dialogue *with* Derrida

BOUNDARIES DRAW US. IMPORTANT THINGS HAPPEN AT THE BOUNDARIES, and most of the significant questions are decided there. The ancient Greeks saw this: *to apeiron*, the limitless or infinite, could not exist in time and space. Everything that is some-thing is what it is because of its boundaries. The Greeks knew that categories make the thing. It needs its *to ti ēn ēnai,* as Aristotle put it, its "what it is to be [this thing]." (Weren't the Rationalists saying the same things about boundaries in different words when they asserted that a thing's reason is the cause of its being?)[1] Even Quine recognized the crucial role of boundaries in his famous manifesto for mathematical logic: "To be is to be the value of a bound variable."

Boundaries are constitutive of being. Perhaps that's why there is such interest today in the boundary lands on which spirit and science meet and overlap. We sense that we would really know what science is, what theology is, if we could only know how they are different, how the one limits the other. The history of their love-hate relationship underscores this lesson. Throughout much of the modern period science derived its being, its very existence, as a field, by negating talk of Spirit. Here, truly, *omnes determinatio negatio est.* Science was the teenager whose very identity had to emerge from negating, from overcoming, the parent who had given rise to it. Think of Francis Bacon's manifesto of scientific method. Each of his famous four "idols"—the idols of the tribe, cave, theater, and marketplace—expressed a tenet he associated with the church, the negation of which alone would allow science to emerge on its own.

As the twenty-first century dawned, attention was being showered upon the boundaries between science and theology. In the centuries of the modern period, science, the former teenager, has grown into the full powers of adulthood: calm, sometimes cocky in his powers; comfortable with the riches and the powers that he now commands; sometimes lean and fit, other times a little pudgy around the middle, as he moves forward confidently to face tomorrow's challenges. Theology, by contrast many would say, has grown old, somewhat lame and hard of hearing, now weakened by the usurpation of his former powers, resting in his rocking chair at the edges of the action, no longer at the center of attention, sometimes a little melancholy, ready though to reminisce and to share his stories with anyone who will listen.

Or so it seemed a few years ago. But something happened in the last dozen or so years. There has recently been a new blaze of attention to the frontiers between science and spirituality, a series of sorties back and forth from both camps, new treaties and joint undertakings between these two great projects of the human spirit. "Frontiers" are again in the news, but now it's the frontiers of trade between two kingdoms whose interdependency is growing. Our newspapers and academic journals (and with *Contact* and its imitators, even our movies) are filled with statements by scientists and religion scholars who now stand proudly on the wall that formerly divided the kingdoms of science and Spirit, not unlike those students who stood atop the Berlin Wall on that night in November 1989, champagne bottles raised above their heads, celebrating the inconceivable: that Berlin might again be united. Of course, frontiers still confront us here, but now they are the frontiers of unexpected intercourse, cross-fertilization—the Uncrossable being crossed.

But warring nations do not become bosom buddies without transformation, even transgression. The science that consorts with theology is not the science of Bacon, Laplace, Bertrand Russell, A. J. Ayer, or even Karl Popper. And the theologian who takes the scientist in as bedfellow may find himself probed and criticized in some unexpected ways.

What this new intercourse raises is the question of sacrilege, of boundaries that one dare not cross, of liaisons that perhaps ought not to be. Indeed, does it not border on sacrilege for the theologian to enter into dangerous liaisons with scientists and deconstructionists in his or her continuing quest for Spirit? Nonetheless, I propose to turn to the French deconstructionist Jacques Derrida—and through him, to the German philosopher Martin Heidegger—during this brief exploration of the alleged demise of Spirit and the ascendance of spirituality to the throne. Like Virgil, Dante's guide in the *Inferno*, Derrida will lead us down the steps—and perhaps up again: "And dark the path we climbed, and long enough / For mortal feet to weary. Fast he led: / And I, made tireless by that hope ahead / Pursued him upward, till the rocks were rent / With first a sight of Heaven's clear firmament, / And then the earth's clean airs with learnt delight / I breathed, and round me was the beauteous night, / And overhead the stars."[2]

Our quest is clear. How is one to understand *Spirit* in these grey borderland regions in which the old boundaries are obscured—partly by their inherent ambiguity, but partly by this new trampling of boots in both directions: platoons of popular writers, armies of media coverage, the *paparazzi* of science and spirituality? A warning to the consumer: when the dust of public attention settles, the pristine purity of faith in Spirit may be harder to preserve in the regions where science and religion collide. As Heidegger once put it, "a faith that does not perpetually expose itself to the possibility of unfaith is no faith but merely a convenience."[3] In commenting on Heidegger, Arnold Come writes, this exposure of the Christian to the world of man-on-his-own is . . . a condition for the continuance of faith itself. As Kierkegaard pointed out long ago, doubt is a permanent dimension of a life of faith. . . . The Christian . . . remains a pagan in a pagan world, a pagan in the original sense of an out-lander who has not yet moved in to the City of God, who therefore is still subject to the crushing hardships and threatening dangers of life in the "far country."[4]

➤ What Then of the Future of the Spirit in an Age of Science?

Futurists speculate on the world a few decades hence. Computer science experts try to extrapolate technology trends out five or ten years. Stock market analysts can't predict a stock market collapse one week in advance. How can one possibly speculate on the future of Spirit?

The only way to look forward a century is to look back a century. By any measure, it was a staggering century. I can put the point in a single sentence. Precisely at the moment of its greatest victory, when the dominance of scientific knowledge should have been complete, the scientific endeavor slammed into insuperable limits. The irresistible force met the immovable object. The pendulum of Empedocles reached its endpoint and switched direction, one epoch began to give way to the next, or, in Californian-speak, "The age of Aquarius dawned." Of course, the conversion did not come easily. Science smashed into its limits like an out-of-control car into a brick wall (and the pieces are still flying from the impact as we speak). The collision of the individual sciences with their various concrete limits would be a book of its own. Relativity theory introduced the speed of light as the absolute limit for velocity, and thus as the temporal limit for communication and causation in the universe. Heisenberg's uncertainty principle placed mathematical limits on the knowability of both the location and momentum of a subatomic particle. The Copenhagen theorists came to the startling conclusion that quantum mechanical indeterminacy was not merely a temporary epistemic problem but reflected an *inherent* indeterminacy of the physical world itself. So-called chaos theory showed that future states of complex systems (like weather systems) quickly become uncomputable because of their sensitive dependence on initial conditions—a dependence so sensitive that a finite knower could *never* predict the evolution of the system, which is a staggering limitation when you realize what percentage of natural systems exhibit chaotic behaviors. Kurt Gödel showed in a well-known proof that mathematics cannot be complete. The list goes on and on and on.

It was truly a century of what I just called Empedocles' pendulum. (Or should it be Foucault's pendulum?) Just as the logical positivists were declaring empirical verifiability as the only criterion of meaning, Toulmin, Hanson, and Kuhn were already urging the incommensurability of competing paradigms. Just as sociology and economics were setting undreamed-of standards for quantitative precision in social science, anthropology and the interpretive sciences were already declaring "no exit" from the hermeneutical blocks to genuine knowledge of the Other. And, most recently, just as the human genome project was laying bare the very building blocks of the human machine, it turned out that there were far too few genes to code for all inherited human structures and behaviors, and top biologists such as Steven J. Gould were already describing the irreducible role of epigenetic factors and top-down causation in regulating genetic expression. To the innocent observer, it certainly appears that the project of omni-reduction to scientific explanation collapsed, perhaps permanently, at what should have been its moment of greatest victory. Could it be that we stand on the cusp of an era when science no longer represents dominance and control, sucking up and transforming everything in its path—a new era in which one speaks of science and religion using terms such as complementarity, cooperation, connection?

➤ Derrida and Heidegger on Science and Spirituality

In an era of unexpected limitations on the scope of scientific thinking, it might seem that Heidegger no longer has anything useful to say on the topics of Spirit and spirituality, science and deconstruction. After all, Heidegger's writing grew out of the *battle* between two modes of thinking, calculative and meditative thinking. Recall his analyses of technology and science. Science is not a pure pursuit of theory prior to and separate from its manifestation in technology. Rather, he held, early modern science was already an expression of technological thinking, even if it took a few centuries for the "fruits" of this mode of thinking to appear.[5] The marks of scientific technique, he thought, are calculative thinking and the will to produce. Harold Alderman puts it nicely: "The relation of science to the thought of Being is construed by Heidegger as the relation between a thought which is domineering and beings-oriented, and one which is acquiescent and Being-oriented."[6] Recall Heidegger's dichotomy: on the one side, the dominating, controlling, objectivizing actions of the Cartesian subject; on the other side, the need for passive waiting, emergence, and coming-to-be. "Beings do not become beings because they are represented to man," Alderman summarizes Heidegger, "but because they are thrust into Being by Being itself. . . . 'Man stands before Being and lets beings Be.'"[7]

Derrida uses precisely this dichotomy to set up his dilemma for theology. Calculative thinking is domineering; meditative thinking is acquiescent. Calculative thinking comprehends only efficient causes that can be quantified and reduced to underlying physical laws. Calculative thinking objectifies the world. In this manner of thinking, all of nature is "signified" by the limitless extension of the *ego cogito*.[8] Heidegger writes, "To set up an experiment means to represent or conceive the conditions under which a specific series of motions can be made susceptible of being followed in its necessary progression, i.e., by being controlled in advance by calculation" (QCT 121). But only a society that is blind to its own spiritual heritage, only a human who is blind to her own spiritual nature, could try to pretend that such calculation is ubiquitous. As Edith Wyschogrod notes, Heidegger's analysis "locates the peril of the present age in its spiritual decline, as well as in our inability to perceive this degeneration in an essential way."[9] As the epigram for her book, Wyschogrod thus uses the beautiful quotation from Ludwig Wittgenstein, "I once said, perhaps rightly: the earlier culture will become a heap of rubble and finally a heap of ashes, but spirits will hover over the ashes."

Spirits may or may not hover over the ashes of classical theology. But without a doubt spirituality does. The lordship of science, about which Heidegger was so worried, found itself under severe challenge by the end of the century, and spirituality seems to be gaining dominance instead. The widespread mutiny against science's dominion has, I suggest, three roots. First, *technē* encountered limits that appear to be inherent in nature, such as those expressed by quantum indeterminacy and in the physics of complex systems. Then many in both East and West turned aside in disgust and moral outrage in the face of Hiroshima, Chernobyl, Bopal, and the *Exxon Valdez*. Most of all, perhaps, humanity has recoiled from the emptiness and *ennui* that we feel when faced by the prospect of an allegedly spiritless, valueless, meaningless universe.

But if we turn away from calculative thinking, what is it toward which we turn?

➤ The "Spirituality" Fostered by Science and the Spirit Science Cannot Give

Heidegger's essay on Trakl advances the fundamental distinction between *geistig* and *geistlich*. (I admit that it may be discouraging for the English ear to find out that the future of the science-theology debate turns on the subtle difference between the two German suffixes *-ig* and *-lich*!) Yet Derrida's interpretation of these two terms, which I follow, underscores their centrality for theologians who struggle in this borderland region of spirituality and Spirit—this realm of permeable boundaries, of grey upon grey, where there are few guides and even the most fundamental distinctions can become obscured. Can Derrida, our mentor *par excellence* when it comes to theology's woes, also help guide us out of this morass?

Geistig represents, as Derrida puts it, "the Platonic-Christian, metaphysical or onto-theological determination of the spiritual." *Geistlich*, on the other hand, is the speaking of Spirit "now withdrawn, as Heidegger would like, from its Christian or Ecclesiastical signification."[10] We could paraphrase this latter term, *geistlich*, I suggest, as the "spirituality" that many of our popular religious leaders today fight for in the face of science, spirituality vis-à-vis science. For St. Paul the boundary was *pneuma* versus *sarx*, spirit opposed to flesh. For us it seems to be small-s spirit opposed to materialism, spirit opposed to "blind, meaningless physical law," spirit as the creative, artistic impulse that rises on outstretched wings to soar above the objectifying forces of lawlike explanation and prediction.[11]

Is this indeed the form of Spirit that will provide our liberation from the hegemony of science? I penned these words in a land called Northern California, where the term "spirituality" enjoys a renaissance of massive proportions. In the strange land from which I come—but I dare say in many other places in the United States and Europe as well—the answer is clear: the *geistig* is dead, long live the *geistlich*! *Geistig*, Platonic-Christian Spirit, now passes (ironically) as the realm of the dead letter, of organized religion, of "meaningless Scholastic distinctions," whereas *geistlich* is the realm of freedom, humanness, and authenticity. To paraphrase the Muslim call to faith, there is no God but spirituality, and Heidegger and Tillich are its prophets. In this movement—and again, I suggest, it extends across our entire culture—the question of spirit *just is* the question of human "spirituality" in an age of science.

Thus in popular culture, but no less in academics, we speak blithely of religion "versus" science, of science *or* spirit, of theology and science, and of the renewed interest in spirituality. Listening again to Derrida and Heidegger, one senses that our ears may have grown deaf to the nuances of tone, and the nuances of position, with which they are wrestling. How can we possibly speak of "the quest for spirit" when we scarcely notice the fundamental distinction between *geistig* and *geistlich*? We are even more tone-deaf to (not to say ignorant of) the wealth of resources that the Western tradition has bequeathed to us for speaking of Spirit in the metaphysical sense: the nuances of *ruach*, *pneuma*, *spiritus*, and *Geist*. Could the reason be that our age has embraced Feuerbach with a vengeance, without the sense that there even *is* an alternative? Is it "just obvious" that all talk of Spirit is merely a false projection of the human spirit—as if adding the word "human" to "spirit" were a pure tautology?

I worry that we may have become tone-deaf to Heidegger's distinction. For example, do we not immediately hear the topic of "science and spirit" as merely a question about science and the *human* spiritual quest? Note how easily the adjective "human" takes over. "Science does not exhaust the human spiritual quest," we assert confidently. But this assertion is not bold enough even to be interesting. *Obviously* there is a human spiritual quest that includes yet exceeds the quest of science! To see this, one doesn't need the complexities of contemporary Continental philosophy: watch a flower grow, play a game with a child, read Mary Midgley's book, *Poetry and Science*. Can one doubt that *Homo poeticus* is not captured by laws and equations? But these are not yet the hard questions!

I remember the response of a very famous scientist during a workshop in the "Science and Spiritual Quest" program. This agnostic was puzzled by the term "spirituality" during the entire three-day conference. At the end he noted astutely, "I am a humanist and not at all a religious person. But if you all insist on using the word 'spirituality' to mean everything that humans do, then I suppose that I too must be spiritual!" That's one way for theologians to win converts, of course. Lower the bar so far that everyone is in by definition. Indeed, how many professors begin their "Introduction to Religion" courses by trying to convince their students that they too are spiritual people and therefore should show more interest in the class they've just enrolled in? ("Don't you, too, enjoy taking a walk in an old-growth redwood forest?" the professor intones profoundly.) This strategy is reminiscent of that popular (but incorrect) reading of Tillich's theology several decades ago: "Well, if religion means whatever is 'of ultimate concern' to each of you, and since each of you must by definition be ultimately concerned about *something*, then I guess all of you are deeply religious persons!"

Such is the profanization of Heidegger's *geistlich* in contemporary culture. Set free from the metaphysical or "vertical" dimensions of *geistig*, from all Platonic or metaphysical connotations, lacking even an ear for the overtones that might turn our attention in that direction, our culture now allows "spiritual" to filter down to the lowest common denominator. If driving one's speed boat, or doing yoga, or being sexually active makes one feel fully human and fully alive, then engaging in these activities must *ipso facto* make one a spiritual being.

The theology of the future, the theology that dances with science—this new theology needs to be *geistig* as well as *geistlich*, metaphysical as well as anthropological.

When it comes to metaphysics, it is important to be minimalists,[12] to import only as much metaphysical superstructure as is necessary. But how much metaphysical superstructure is enough? Should one be satisfied with the "religiously tinged naturalism" of the philosopher Willem Drees in Holland, the "ecstatic naturalism" of the comparative religionist Wesley Wildman at Boston University, or the "religious naturalism" of the biologist Ursula Goodenough? In *The Sacred Depths of Nature,* Goodenough describes how studying the properties of the cell gives her the same sense of significance as exploring an ancient Aztec ruin; as she puts it, "same rush, same rapture." In one article,[13] Goodenough draws heavily on the work of Michael Kalton. Kalton has become a major spokesperson for a purely "horizontal" spirituality in articles such as "Green Spirituality: Horizontal Transcendence."[14] This is truly the spirituality of Heidegger's *geistlich*:

> Horizontal transcendence finds its anchor in life rather than mind, thus displacing human consciousness from its privileged place. The movement from earth to cosmos, from biosystem to life, is a form of transcendence that is characteristic of degrees of abstraction rather than a movement towards some kind of Absolute metaphysical dimension. There is no cosmos posited apart from the historically ongoing one within which we find ourselves, nor is there life apart from ongoing living, at whatever level it is considered. Instead of the typical vertical transcendence of the Greek inspired tradition, the movement of this kind of spiritual cultivation is horizontal, perfecting our relationship with the world of life about us.

> Horizontal transcendence to the vast scope of temporal process prior and consequent to human or even earth existence is a different challenge, for it does not relate to our goals and projects with either an ultimate affirmation or negation. Rather it connects with the effort itself, as our mode of manifesting and experiencing a dynamic that is coextensive with the process of life.

> In this kind of horizontally framed spirituality the question of belonging acquires a new kind of centrality. Recovering a more sacral sense of the earth and universe starts us on the way. But coming from a background of traditions premised on a discontinuity between ourselves and the rest of the natural world, inevitably many of our ordinary ways of thinking and acting carry the imprint of that discontinuity. Belonging is an achievement as well as a statement of fact, and the path to such achievement leads through a reexamination of basic habits of mind.

The Radical Immanence of God

I would argue that *geistlich*, on its own, is not enough. Human spirituality begs to be understood in the light of a "something more." Here, again, Derrida is my ally. But Derrida and I part ways—or so it will seem at first—with the statement of my next thesis. For a theologian who reads both science and Derrida, the central task becomes to think one's way from *geistlich* to *geistig*, from spirituality to Spirit. Virtually no one denies that there is a dimension of human existence in the world that is *geistlich*. Of course, one encounters those who confidently assure us that it is all "in the genes," or (for that matter) in the quarks. But for most there is little controversy in acknowledging the dimension of human spirituality—after all, religious beliefs and rituals are a firmly embedded piece of the anthropological puzzle and the archeological records.

The question, then, is one of inference to the best explanation. Is *geistlich*, the human spiritual dimension, fully explained using the vocabulary of psychology, sociology, and anthropology? Or is such a spirit "human, all too human"? For this reason I've argued in previous chapters that a metaphysics of Spirit that is tied to science must be a metaphysics of process and emergence, a panentheistic theology.

We've tarried long enough with emergent complexity. But few have thought radically enough about how to understand the process of emergence theologically. Christian thinkers have long held that God on the cross identified deeply with the world and its suffering. One thinks of Jürgen Moltmann's famous treatise on *The Crucified God*. But I would argue that we should also follow Moltmann in taking this identification of God and world even one step further. We should make it *ontological as well as soteriological*. A finite world cannot stand over against an infinite God. The world, not only at its inception, but also after its fall, was, is, and remains within the being of God. And this changes the view of God, and thus also of ourselves, far more radically than most have been willing to say.

If classical doctrines such as propitiation and the atonement for sin give rise to the picture of the "old man with the white beard," sitting outside the national order, then it's time to change the picture. On the panentheist view, the world—just as it is, as it surrounds us, without any attempt to touch up its flaws and wrinkles—is embraced by and within the divine and continues to express the divine nature. Yet panentheism maintains that God is also *more than* the world as a whole, which is why it remains a variant of theism. As long as one remains a theist, one is committed to a moment of transcendence ("vertical" transcendence) in attempting to think of Spirit.

At the same time, Jewish, Muslim, and Christian theists still have much to learn from their more *pan*theistically inclined colleagues about what belief in the *immanence of God in the world* might mean and entail. Can it really mean a God who forays occasionally into a realm separate from Godself, acting salvifically like a lightening bolt and then stepping back calmly to view the results of "his" work? Or must we not think divine Spirit as remaining intrinsically and pervasively present within this world, so that it's within the divine that "we live and move and have our being"?[15] *This*, I think, is the ultimate Christian affirmation. This is the humanism that is at the same time a transcending and overcoming of all humanism. This is what I have called the "Panentheistic Entailment" of the Christian affirmation of the world in *God and Contemporary Science*. In it, I hear the words of T. S. Eliot:

> The hint half guessed, the gift half understood, is Incarnation.
> Here the impossible union
> Of spheres of existence is actual,
> Here the past and future
> Are conquered, and reconciled . . .[16]

Panentheism and emergence—the key pieces of the puzzle are now in hand. But how are they to be fit together? Earlier I introduced the *Essay on Freedom* by Friedrich Schelling. For Schelling the stages in the emerging complexity of the universe and of life are, themselves, moments in the self-manifestation of God. Higher levels of complexity are not reducible to their physical basis—for example, biology is not merely a special case of physics—*because* the *telos* of the entire process is the manifestation of a spiritual being. Our understanding of what life is, then, must flow from the *end* of the process, not from the beginning alone. This is the future-orientation that is basic to Christian theology, as Wolfhart Pannenberg argued throughout his career. What emerges in nature *is* genuinely new, a novel expression of divine-plus-human creativity.

The Catholic philosopher Teilhard de Chardin followed the process of development through the various stages.[17] Biological organisms that develop to a sufficient degree of complexity—for instance, through the emergence of a complex central nervous system and a brain—give rise to yet another level of analysis, that of the psyche or spirit. In his hands, emergent thinking becomes a speculative hypothesis concerning the nature of Mind. Against those who claim that, someday, human thoughts and feelings will be expressible in terms of neuro-physiological states, he argued that Mind is an inherently new thing, a reality that has arisen in the course of the progressive development of life. In the end, Teilhard suggests, psychological forms develop to a sufficient degree of complexity that they give rise to a level of spiritual reality, itself not reducible to the psychological, which becomes a necessary element in any final explanation of the universe. At the end of all evolution stands God. Teilhard's narrative may be implausible as science, yet indispensable in unearthing the deeper implications of a theology of immanence.

What is it precisely that emerges in the emergence of Spirit?

➤ Toward a New Theology of Spirit

The theology of spirit is, as we've seen, a theology of emergence. Its roots lie in the one natural world that surrounds us and of which we are a part. As the "stuff" of this world becomes organized in more and more complicated ways, new properties emerge. Although their existence is dependent on the properties of the underlying particles, their behavior is irreducible to any of the underlying levels. Hence the natural world evidences the emergence of genuinely new properties. At each emerging level, new structures are established and new causal forces are at work. One extends the structure of emergence downward to address questions of fundamental physical law, but one can also extend it upwards to come to a better understanding of consciousness, mind, and spirit. The emergent causal levels thus help to elucidate the meaning and semantic range of the idea of spirit.

Though emergent thinking helps theology to reclaim the language of spirit, it also constrains that language. Herein lies the humbling of theology in an age of science. No longer can theologians build castles in the air. Henceforth, we are bound to pay attention to the actual structures of the world and to its empirical patterns. The story of spirit is not fully separate from the story of natural history, and one who would tell the former story must be prepared to tell the other latter along with it. Spirit does not reduce to matter—this is the surprising lesson of recent science. But nor does it float happily on summer breezes, cut adrift from all empirical moorings. He who would know the one must look to the other as well.

This is truly theology in a new key. We may shy away from magical interventions into the physical world, yet we still find that world "re-enchanted" as the field of action of (and in) the divine. The beauties of our planet and the richness of its life forms are not distant expressions of a far-off and distant God. They continue to manifest the divine presence. We can again look to the structures (and contents!) of individual consciousness, and to the growth and development of culture, for signs of divine creativity. Think, for example, of the means by which individuals who are agents of creativity can influence other individuals. An idea of great genius (Einstein's special relativity, Kant's critical philosophy, Gandhi's non-violent resistance) or an artistic genre (classical harmony, the sonata form in poetry) can spread like wildfire through a large number of minds or through human experience in general. Individual minds integrate into groups of minds. Individual actions influence other actions.

Of course, one cannot *demonstrate* that a given idea is Spirit-breathed or that humanity is progressing toward greater harmony with the divine will. Previous centuries offer too painful a picture of regress for such melioristic optimism to be convincing. Still, the "upwardly open" nature of human consciousness, infused as it is with intimations of immortality, offers a powerful model of the integration of mind and spirit. It allows us to speak of the mental or cultural world as upwardly open to the influence of creative Spirit.

At the end, then, we return to Derrida's distinction between *geistlich* and *geistig*, now however with a new understanding. I have shown that the contemporary focus on human spirituality hovers somewhere between the two terms, sometimes embracing and sometimes resisting the more metaphysical dimensions of Spirit. After all, isn't Derrida's primary fame as an anti-metaphysical thinker? And yet his essays are a profound grappling with metaphysical themes! Perhaps they are better interpreted not as opposed to metaphysics as such, but rather to the preliminary *closure* of metaphysics—what he calls its "foreclosure" in his book *On Spirit*.[18] For Derrida, the metaphysical question must remain radically open, since the semantic fields referred to by *ruach, pneuma, spiritus,* and *Geist* remain constantly in motion. Any new meaning can be constructed by a new semantic field, and any claims to precise meaning can be deconstructed in the same manner.

The Western discussion of God did represent a sort of foreclosure—or rather the pursuit of one line of thought until it became untenable. Specifically, it was the Aristotelian *nous noetikos* path, the conception of God as involving such perfection and purity that all real connection with the world is lost, that became untenable. Examples include St. Thomas's difficulties with a God who cannot know contingent changes in the world, Descartes's idea that God could establish even necessary truths by an act of will, and the contemporary difficulties in conceiving divine action. But Derrida, perhaps despite himself, has also signaled the direction in which to turn to address the problems. Derrida is most concerned about one particular "closure of speech" of which Heidegger is guilty: Heidegger's claim "to go beyond the European race from East to West."[19] Under the twin rubrics of emergence and panentheism, there is no longer a contentment with an East-West dichotomy or an imperialism of the West. Panentheism represents a rethinking of the divine in the direction of the East. Its openness, both ontologically and linguistically, approaches (though does not reach) the opening of which Derrida and Heidegger speak as the clearing for *geistlich.*

If one adds the metaphysics of the emergence of Spirit to the doctrine of panentheism, one obtains a framework for theology that has both systematic coherence and a sufficient fit with science to avoid contradiction with its core results. Such ideas struggle to make the trembling transition from the *geistlich*—the human spiritual quest—toward the (always preliminary) language of *Geist* or Spirit, where that quest finds its proper home.

➤ Conclusion

At the end of an exploration in theology like the present one, readers often want prophecy—not only a new vision for theology, but also clear lines of development, predictions of doctrines and structures and outcomes. What of the Trinity in the twenty-first century? Will liberals or evangelicals win the theological tug-of-war? What of the dialogue between Christians, Jews, and Muslims? What do Christ and the Buddha share in common? Which Christian doctrines will science cause the church to abandon?

Church-political debates are important. One should by no means denigrate them. And the concrete, detailed disputes between science and theology *will* have a profound impact on what theologians assert in the coming decades. But these are not the most fundamental questions. It is no coincidence that Derrida concludes his treatise *On Spirit* with an imagined debate between Heidegger and the theologians. And it is no less significant that Derrida makes himself the referee of this debate—no, much more than a referee: he *creates* both voices, contains both voices, *is* both voices. In that text, which has served as both foe and ally throughout this chapter, Derrida is both the questioning of Western metaphysics and the theologian of the future, the one who is more concerned about the origin of God-language and its ultimate *telos* than he is about systematizing inherited doctrines. A mystical tone permeates Derrida's *On Spirit*. A mist obscures the Sun, diffusing its light across the horizon, until we are no longer able to tell where the Source lies and what merely reflects the Source.

So it is today, also, in *our* quest for Spirit. The lines between Source and reflector, theology and spirituality, Holy Spirit and human spirit, *geistig* and *geistlich*, are no longer clear, though we continue to need both terms in each set. It is this diffused glow of light through mist—and in the resulting confusion of up and down, of horizontal and vertical—which our critics are labeling the demise of theology, the *Untergang* of metaphysics. It is in this diffused glow of light through mist—and in the resulting confusion of up and down, of horizontal and vertical, which our critics are labeling the demise of theology, the Untergang of metaphysics—it is here that theology must find its way."

I am no prophet. But I do know that there is value in this wandering, this seeking for a way, which is theology today and which will continue to be its fate in the coming decades. Perhaps such a theology-on-the-way is a fitting heritage of the wandering Jew from Palestine.

The Many Faces *of* Integration

Liberal Faith *between* Church, Academy, *and* World

A T THE END OF OUR JOURNEY, ONE WANTS TO KNOW: WHAT WILL THE actual mode of religious life look like when it lives out this form of theology as adventure? It takes courage to actively seek out the scientific and philosophical results that offer the greatest challenges to theism in general and to Christian belief in particular. In this new mode of religious life, doubts and uncertainties are no longer shoved away, or suppressed as sinful. Just as pursuing differences and concerns in personal relationships often leads to growth and intimacy, so wrestling with the tough challenges of our age leads to a stronger and more enduring form of faith.

The red thread that runs through these chapters is *integration*. At every point I have resisted calls to circle the wagons in order to protect inherited Christian beliefs from outside examination and criticism. Yet, like many, I find deep value in much that the Christian tradition has handed down. There is no integration if one sees contemporary culture and science as enemies from which one needs to protect her faith on every front. Nor is there integration if one retains nothing from the tradition *with which* to engage as she pursues dialogue with science, philosophy, and other religious traditions. This drive to integrate is an ethical and a deeply religious commitment that I believe lies at the very core of Christian identity in today's world.

Among all the theological traditions, there is one that has stressed the project of integration above all others. Liberal theology after Schleiermacher inherited the sixteenth-century motto, *Ecclesia reformata, semper reformanda* ("the church reformed and always reforming"), and moved this call to continually new forms of integration into its very self-definition. It may well be that, in the eyes of many, liberal theology has come to mean the gleeful overturning of the entire theological tradition. But de(con)struction of the tradition itself was not the brief of the modern theologies of integration. In this closing chapter I wish to reclaim that great integrative project—with

256 ➤

its wide-ranging conceptual, ethical, political, and personal dimensions—as the core commitment of a new liberal theology for our day.[1] The project that we have been pursuing through these pages defines a challenge, calls for a new set of methods, and, I believe, also signals a set of vibrant new answers.

The task of integration to which I am calling not only theologians but Christians in general is undertaken today in the context of what is now widely known as "the crisis of liberalism." This crisis—and the opportunities it brings—involves liberals of all stripes. A few decades ago the liberal church could give powerful and (relatively) unified expression to its identity. People knew and admired the values that the mainline churches brought to the contemporary world. Not only that, but these theologians were also able to give powerful descriptions of the *conceptual foundations* for their action. They could speak a vibrant liberal theology. Today the foundations have become obscure:

> Turning and turning in the widening gyre
> The falcon cannot hear the falconer;
> Things fall apart; the centre cannot hold;
> Mere anarchy is loosed upon the world,
> The blood-dimmed tide is loosed, and everywhere
> The ceremony of innocence is drowned;
> The best lack all conviction, while the worst
> Are full of passionate intensity.[2]

The best of us seem to lack conviction, while the worst are full of passionate intensity. Where are our "public theologians" today? Jay Adams puts the charge in harsh terms: "If I had to choose between putting a saloon or a liberal church on a corner, I'd choose the saloon every time. People who drink up the pay check in the saloon are less likely to become Pharisees, thinking that they don't need the Great Physician, than those who weekly swill the soporific doctrine of man's goodness."[3]

What has happened to liberalism? Where are the days when every intellectual American was reading that new book by Paul Tillich or one of the Niebuhr brothers? Where can one find theologians who seek a finely honed balance between inherited tradition and contemporary world in the ways that Schleiermacher, Tillich, and Rahner once did? It is a potent heritage, which in the past has had a transformative influence on society and the church as a whole: powerful convictions, powerful arguments, and powerful leaders in the church, the academy, and society. Today, one worries, the mainline churches seem to be suffering from a sort of liberal laryngitis.

➤ The Crisis of Liberalism

Recall one of those powerful liberal voices: William Sloane Coffin, chaplain at Yale from 1958 to 1975. James Carroll describes one scene from this time: Coffin approached the podium, with corduroy jacket and work boots for vestments. . . . [In his talk] there was the trademark pithiness, the rhetorical sophistication, the erudite citations, and . . . the Scriptures as a native language. [There was] the unbridled passion with which Coffin announced his gospel.

And what a gospel it was. The world he described was upside-down: the church on the side of the poor; the powerful at risk for losing everything; the disenfranchised as sole custodians of moral legitimacy. Coffin . . . was perhaps the first person from whom [I] heard that defining question: Whose side are you on? [My] answer would be the nearly ten years in coming that it took for [me] to go to jail [following a Washington protest]. . .[4]

Few liberal Christian leaders today play the role Coffin once played, and few have his impact. Clearly, the *pieces* are still there, and many—pastors, bishops, scholars, church members—still speak with resounding voices, moving and motivating those who hear them. But the liberal theology that could move mountains, that could turn a world upside down, is less obvious. Not only outsiders, but even liberal theologians themselves are struggling to say how we are different from the world. Ours is an age when the social and intellectual dividing line between church and non-church is no longer as firm and fixed as it once was. That fundamental social *and worldview* identity people once had as "church people," which was so clear to previous generations, is absent for many today.

Contrast this struggle for identity with the "loud and clear" identity enjoyed within conservative churches. One unimpeachable source describes the roots of American fundamentalism at the Niagara Bible Conference in 1878. About thirty years later, the General Assembly of the Presbyterian Church adopted a series of tenets that came to be known as the five fundamentals: "the inerrancy of the Scriptures, the virgin birth (or deity) of Jesus, the doctrine of substitutionary atonement, the bodily resurrection of Jesus, and the miracles . . . of Jesus Christ," along with his second coming.[5] In the confusing world in which we live, conservative evangelicals today have a passionate commitment to the truth of a number of propositions, and they believe that there is a clear moral imperative behind most of their actions. Evangelicals can also tell a clear narrative about modern thought and culture, using terms like "secular humanism" and "back to the Bible." In its most extreme form, as in Hal Lindsey's *The Late Great Planet Earth*, this narrative describes how the world is moving into the "last days" and how only God's direct intervention can save it now.

The contrast is at its harshest when liberals describe their religious beliefs using terms like "lifestyle choice." This language suggests that what we as liberal Christians do in the world is "what we're into," but, the world assumes, it's perfectly fine to be "into" other things as well (meditation, driving one's sports car, learning Italian). "Lifestyle choice" and "lifestyle preference," I fear, are not by themselves enough to motivate Christian identity. Talk of "my personal political convictions" is not enough. Even talk of "my spiritual journey" is not enough to ground a powerful liberal voice. Set free from our heritage, the word "spiritual" filters down to the lowest common denominator. As we saw in the previous chapter, if doing sacred dance makes me feel fully human and fully alive, then engaging in such activities must *ipso facto* make me a spiritual being. In a time when the mainline churches are seeking to rediscover their heritage and identity, when they are uncertain how to speak powerfully to the academy and the world, how can theologians provide leadership in the process?

Liberal Christians are not accustomed to speaking in ringing tones today. Why should this be? Theology since Schleiermacher has a clear and powerful heritage, albeit one that does not separate black from white as clearly as conservatives do. Our heritage, I have suggested, is the quest for a full and powerful integration. It's possible today to regain a sense of that tradition, which I call *the quest for a new integration*. I shall first try to express the core theological commitment of this integrative Christian theology, and then restate that commitment as a vision for Christians both in the academy and outside.

The Root Meaning of Integration

What is this new quest for integration? And why choose integration as *the* heritage and *the* defining characteristic of a renewed liberal Christianity? Listen for a moment to the words of a powerful Christian voice, a man whose main battle was for integration, so that (as he said) freedom might ring from every mountainside. Dr. Martin Luther King Jr. was asked, "When will you be satisfied" in your quest for integration? He answered,

> We can never be satisfied as long as the Negro is the victim of the unspeakable horrors of police brutality. We can never be satisfied as long as our bodies, heavy with the fatigue of travel, cannot gain lodging in the motels of the highways and the hotels of the cities. We cannot be satisfied as long as a Negro in Mississippi cannot vote and a Negro in New York believes he has nothing for which to vote. No, no, we are not satisfied, and we will not be satisfied until "justice rolls down like waters, and righteousness like a mighty stream." (Amos 5:24)[6]

King's was a vision of integration and of justice. Dr. King's words on the steps of the Lincoln Memorial, at the culmination of that massive march from Birmingham, remain especially prescient:

> I have a dream that one day, down in Alabama, with its vicious racists, with its governor having his lips dripping with the words of "interposition" and "nullification"— one day right there in Alabama little black boys and black girls will be able to join hands with little white boys and white girls as sisters and brothers. . . . I have a dream that one day every valley shall be exalted, and every hill and mountain shall be made low, the rough places will be made plain, and the crooked places will be made straight; "and the glory of the Lord shall be revealed and all flesh shall see it together." (Isaiah 40:4-5)[7]

That's the voice and highest calling of an integrative Christianity. These words resonate with the famous song by Holly Near, "It Could Have Been Me," written to honor the four students at Kent State who were shot to death during an anti-war rally: "It could have been me, but instead it was you; and I'll keep doing the things that you were doing until we are through. . . ."

➤ The New Integration

The priorities and tasks of classical liberal thought remain equally vital today. Its core goals have not been achieved. To achieve them, liberals need to return to and study afresh the classic texts of our heritage, those of Schleiermacher and Ritschl and Troeltsch, of Rauschenbusch and Bonhoeffer and Tillich. At the same time, there are also *new* forms of integration that demand our attention today. The need for integration at the beginning of the twenty-first century is greater than ever. Consider the fertile fields for integration in our present context:

- multiple religious traditions
- diverse cultural traditions
- science and religion
- complicated ethical questions, from bioethics to new forms of human relationship
- the continuing struggle to integrate faith and politics
- the new opportunities for constructive dialogue between liberals and evangelicals within the one church
- the "lived integration" of one's corporate beliefs with one's corporate practice

As Peter Berger writes, "The old agenda of a liberal theology was the contestation with modernity. . . . The much more pressing agenda today is the contestation with the fullness of human religious possibilities."[8] Those who practice Christianity today practice it against a rich tapestry of variegated religious options in a way that wasn't true for most Americans a few decades ago.

The task for liberals today, Peter Berger argues, is to learn to "hold convictions without either dissolving them in utter relativity or encasing them in the false absolutes of fanaticism."[9] American religion too often contents itself with one of two escape routes: the embrace of a false certainty, happily marketed by various orthodoxies, or the certainty that there *is* no access to truth, resulting in nihilism and utter relativism.[10] As we confront the pluralism of modern societies, Berger argues, we must "steer a course between a limitless tolerance which passively and yet 'progressively' reads the signs of the current age but surrenders to it with 'nothing to say,' on the one hand, and, on the other hand, a conservative fanaticism that denies the current age by writing about it 'without having ever listened' to it."[11]

➤ The Core Commitment

If one is to pursue new forms of integration, one must be able to formulate the distinctive content and the distinctive methods that once characterized liberal Christianity. A major influence on Dr. King was Reinhold Niebuhr's *Moral Man, Immoral Society*, which "tempered King's faith in humanity with an analysis of the corrupting influence of organizations over individuals."[12] Niebuhr opened King's eyes to the "big picture" approach to the gospel. He writes in *Love and Justice*:

> The gospel cannot be preached with truth and power if it does not challenge the pretensions and pride, not only of individuals, but of nations, cultures, civilizations, economic and political systems. The good fortune of America and its power place it under the most grievous temptations to self-adulation. If there is no power and grace in the Christian church "to bring down every high thing which exalteth itself against the knowledge of God," the church becomes not merely useless but dangerous.[13]

But one cannot consistently point at the influence of institutions on individual belief and action without at the same time granting their influence on *one's own belief* as well. To paraphrase the Sermon on the Mount (Matt 7:4): "How can you say to your sister, 'Let me remove the speck of institutional bias out of your eye,' when the log of cultural locatedness is in your own eye?" Integration is a radical notion, for it becomes necessary to recognize that one's own beliefs and practices, one's very definitions of "insider" and "outsider," are also products of cultural construction.

Perhaps one can conceive the new integrative theology as a form of radical Wesleyanism. Radical Wesleyans endorse a more radical sense of what has come to be known as "the Wesleyan quadrilateral." Scripture and tradition take on new meanings when integrated with present-day reason and experience. H. Richard Niebuhr beautifully formulates this vision:

> [Theology must] try to develop a method applicable not to all religions but to the particular faith to which its historical point of view is relevant. Such theology in the Christian church cannot, it is evident, be an offensive or defensive enterprise which undertakes to prove the superiority of Christian faith to all other faiths; but it can be a confessional theology which carries on the work of self-criticism and self-knowledge in the church.[14]

As Niebuhr says later, "we try to understand, not how features in our past are repeated in our present, but how our present grows out of our past into our future."[15] For "revelation is a moving thing . . . its meaning is realized only by being brought to bear upon the interpretation and reconstruction of ever new human situations in an enduring movement, a single drama of divine and human action."[16]

Three Examples of Integration in Action

Let me begin with an example from the recent discussions between science and theology. In the sciences today, most religious truth claims are seen as suspect. One encounters a fair degree of skepticism when one enters into this discussion as a Christian. The reason is that when religious conservatives have addressed science, they have repeatedly and vocally proclaimed a break with science wherever scientific results seem to conflict with traditional Christian beliefs. Some argue that science's methodological naturalism is unacceptable to Christians, who must always insist on a supernatural worldview. Others argue that explaining complex phenomena like consciousness or prayer in terms of repeatable experiments and underlying causal mechanisms is antithetical to Christianity, which must therefore oppose it. One way or another, conservatives say, walls must be built to protect Christianity from the encroachment of science.

Contrast the approach of an integrative Christian theology. It is our calling and our right to enter fully into the scientific project, either as scientists or in dialogue with scientists. As a scholar in this field, I need have no fear of any success in science. I share the excitement of each new advance in explanation. I know that it is *possible* that key beliefs I hold will in the end be accounted for by purely naturalistic mechanisms. Perhaps consciousness is not a causal force. Perhaps values are a product of the "selfish gene" in its struggle to survive the evolutionary process. Perhaps religious beliefs will ultimately be better explained by cultural and biological forces. In the end, I will accept whatever turns out to be the most successful explanation. But I *think* that purely naturalistic and value-free accounts will *not* succeed in the end, and at this point the evidence seems to support this conclusion. Across its various fields, science raises questions that cannot be answered within the natural sciences—metaphysical questions that lead right into the heart of theology. Out of physics emerge the self-replicating organisms of biology. Out of biology emerge beings with advanced cognitive capacities and cultures. Out of human existence emerge questions of the ultimate meaning of the universe and of life after death. Studying the psycho-social-physical beings that we are, one hears clear "intimations of transcendence." We need persons with the courage and the expertise to trace these lines of transcendence from their scientific origins to their ultimate theological source.

A new breed of liberal theologians, I suggest, is in an ideal position to integrate science and religion in this fashion. Because the drive toward integration is essential to our faith, because our faith is not only a given but also a quest, we do not need to build walls—indeed, we *may not* build walls—to immunize our beliefs from possible falsification. Such liberal thinkers vehemently reject a pseudo-science that is custom-designed to support supernaturalism, just as we resist a religion that is stripped of all its convictions and reduced to its purely naturalistic functions. Our quest is for nothing less than the full integration of science and religion, the full harmony between the two without the reduction of the one to the other.

Integrative theologians, students, and professors also do not need to be afraid of the social scientific study of religion (see chapter 15 above). We know that there is a psychology of religious conversion. We know that there are distinct sociological patterns within distinct denominations. We acknowledge the cultural influences on specific religious practices and beliefs. Yet we *advocate* the social scientific study of religion, for we believe it will reveal in the long run the genuinely transcendent element in religious belief. Close study will not eliminate religion, but will open insights into the God-directed aspects of human existence.

A final example: liberal American Christians generally defend a social ethics that draws from political theory and the analysis of American society today. The liberal religious voice is not defined in opposition to secular culture and all political involvement. It takes the real complexities of society as given, and *then* draws on the values of the Christian Scriptures and traditions to challenge structures of injustice, suppression, oppression, and prejudice.

➤ A Radically Incarnational Theology

This vision for a new liberal theology[17] represents a powerful calling. It takes some courage. It takes a prophetic voice. It takes a hatred of the trivial. It takes a willingness to be hard-nosed. It takes a constant refusal to become self-absorbed. At the heart of this vision lies the contention that liberal approaches to theology, by their very nature, work continually to integrate what humanity knows—our history, our science, our highest moral values, our involvement with political institutions—with the tradition handed down through the centuries.

This is a radically incarnational theology. The new integration means integrating the best of contemporary experience and contemporary reason with the inherited resources of Christian Scriptures and traditions. We each seek to wed the resources of our tradition with the unanswered problems of our own day. To be a liberal *Christian* is to return continually to the scriptures and traditions in the attempt to understand what are genuinely Christ-like responses. But to be a *liberal* Christian is not to take the inherited traditions as complete in themselves. This is the famous hermeneutical moment: only when the "horizon" of the text and tradition is fused with the horizon of our contemporary world is the Christian voice complete.

This means that scripture and tradition do not in themselves complete revelation. To claim that revelation does not end with scripture and tradition is a radical and perhaps frightening notion. It's also a powerful theological truth. Fundamentally, it's the insight of incarnation. If Jesus is fully God and fully human, that is, one who is incomplete until both dimensions are included, why would one expect that the church, the *body* of Christ, would be complete without a similar need for ongoing incarnation? If God once integrated with humanity, is it not our continual calling to integrate with ever-new contexts of knowledge, ever-new social contexts, ever-new contexts of ministry? Sadly, there is a strong inclination to overemphasize one end or the other of the "Wesleyan quadrilateral"—either scripture/tradition or experience/reason. Either one so valorizes the past that the present has no genuine input, or one so overemphasizes the present context that the past becomes mere allegory, myth, or story, contributing nothing essential. An incarnational theology means a calling to *continual integration*.

The core question behind the new integration, then, is this: What *today* are the new incarnations of scripture and tradition with reason and experience? What tomorrow will be the new fruits of their union? Integration is not the most famous feature of the conservative mind, but it has traditionally been a defining feature of liberal Christianity. The new liberal approach connotes an adventure of open inquiry, of genuine grappling with the world we live in, of honest acknowledgment of difficulties. In such grappling, integrative theologians proclaim, revelation continues to happen today. H. Richard Niebuhr gave a powerful description of this revelation:

> We climb the mountain of revelation that we may gain a view of the shadowed valley in which we dwell and from the valley we look up again to the mountain. Each arduous journey brings new understanding, but also new wonder and surprise. *This mountain is not one we climbed once upon a time; it is a well-known peak we never wholly know, which needs to be climbed again in every generation, on every new day.* There is no time or place in human history, there is no moment in the church's past, nor is there any set of doctrines, any philosophy or theology of which we might say, "Here the knowledge possible through revelation and the knowledge of revelation is fully set forth." *Revelation is not only progressive but it requires of those to whom it has come that they begin the never-ending pilgrim's progress of the reasoning Christian heart.*[18]

Consider one brief example, the integration of belief and scholarship. Widespread in the church today is the sense of a dichotomy between its mission and the striving for academic excellence. By contrast, the new liberal vision involves intellectual rigor and academic excellence as forms of service to the church, which then become part and parcel of her mission. We believe that both traditional theology and contemporary scholarship can assist in such a revisioning, both within the church and without.[19]

Some critics worry that scholarship raises too many questions and allows for too much doubt. But it is surely possible to combine critical inquiry with passionate faith. I share Peter Berger's conviction that such an approach "embodies *precisely* the balance between skepsis and affirmation that . . . defines the only acceptable way of being a Christian without emigrating from modernity."[20] This combination of openness and affirmation is, I believe, the new liberalism's greatest strength. If we were committed only to fighting for the purity of the "truth once received" or for the continuation of particular structures or a particular understanding of the church, we would have less to offer. But if liberal believers are willing to listen as well as to proclaim, to adapt what we have in order to be more effective at being who we are, we can be powerful agents of understanding and change.

A Prophetic Role for Theology

There are many ways to serve the church. The church is served by those who seek to preserve it in its current form against new challenges, and it is served by those who seek to keep its traditions fresh and alive. It is also served by those who exercise the prophetic function. Prophets are those who challenge existing structures, who call others back to what is essential. Because they ask people to look at things in a new way, to respond differently than they have responded in the past, prophets make people uncomfortable. Nevertheless, we need prophets among us. For successful communities exist not in pristine isolation but in deep integration with their surroundings. As Marjorie Suchocki writes in *God, Christ, Church*:

> On a social level, human communities are a complex bonding oriented toward the perpetuation of the community. The boundaries of the community are more or less fluid, since communities are sustained not only by their members, but by their interaction with wider societies and environment.[21]

In general, liberal education exercises three distinct functions. It teaches the great intellectual traditions. It helps students to adapt these traditions to the intellectual challenges of their day. And it offers fruitful new solutions to burning social and political problems. New forms of liberal theological education must perform three similar functions. Continue to train students in the great theological traditions of the past, though not uncritically. Help them to adapt these theologies to contemporary challenges. And exercise a prophetic function within the church and society.

Theology must retain this prophetic function as well. Recall the motto with which this chapter opened: *Ecclesia reformata, semper reformanda*; always reformed, always reforming. To grasp the core principles of the Christian proclamation, to encounter the *kerygma* associated with Jesus, is to encounter a message of resounding power, a leaven that should transform everything it comes in contact with.

What would a prophetic theology look like today? It must retain the four dimensions mentioned above. *Scripture* exercises a prophetic function, because it calls theology to look for the word of God in it. *Tradition* has a prophetic function, because it reveals the restless activity of the Holy Spirit, always bringing new insights and new ways of thinking and acting. *Experience* is prophetic, because in the heart of the individual burn experiences and insights that cannot be exactly fit into any pre-existing structure, insights with the power to transform and to create anew. And *reason*? Prophetic reason gives us words to match our convictions, clear thinking to challenge obscurities of the past, skepticism to question what may be false, a probing mind to quest for the truth wherever it lies, and arguments to persuade others of what we have found. As the famous bumper sticker reads, "If you think education is expensive, try ignorance."

Paul Tillich once wrote that prophecy "is the message of the shaking of the foundations, and not those of their enemies, but rather those of their own country. For the prophetic spirit has not disappeared from the earth."[22] Prophets, like students, are those who dream a future that may be better than the present. One reads in Joel, "Your sons and your daughters shall prophesy, your old men shall dream dreams, your young men shall see visions" (Joel 2:28), and the Proverb adds, "Where there is no vision, the people perish" (Prov 29:18). The church desperately needs institutions within it where those dreams can still be dreamed, the hard questions asked, the visions developed and nurtured for a lifetime.

The question is, will theologians foster and support the radical work of integration? Or will they follow that pattern that Max Weber called "the institutionalization of charisma"? Will they quench the spirit of experimentation and integration, of perplexity and prophecy, which I have taken as the defining feature of a truly integrative Christianity?

➤ Conclusion

Some, perhaps many, will disagree with the new liberal program I have outlined in this book. I close with a plea to those who do disagree: please don't tell us that only he or she serves the church who accepts it, relates to it, and seeks to perpetuate it in its current form. Please don't exclude from our midst those who would see differently: those who would invite into our congregations not only immigrant peoples but also their immigrant customs and ways of doing things; those who would exercise loving, long-term relationships in different forms and combinations than have traditionally been sanctioned; those who would challenge existing structures of power, whether within the church or outside it, and who would build new structures in their place; those who would use means to share their faith—rap or rock or street drama or the new liturgies of the emerging church—that make us uncomfortable because they are too loud or rude or ugly.

I think in closing of my former colleague, Mario Savio, whom history has credited with founding the free-speech movement at Berkeley in the mid-1960s. I frequently picture Mario standing on the roof of the police car to which he had been handcuffed, and saying, "Sometimes you have to throw yourself on the gears to stop the machine." Mario had prophetic courage, motivated in part (he told me at one point) by his own Catholic heritage. Listen to Mario Savio's exact words:

> There is a time when the operation of the machine becomes so odious, makes you so sick at heart, that you can't take part; you can't even passively take part, and you've got to put your bodies upon the gears and upon the wheels, upon the levers, upon all the apparatus, and you've got to make it stop. And you've got to indicate to the people who run it, to the people who own it, that unless you're free, the machine will be prevented from working at all! (http://www.savio.org/who_was_mario.html)

Integration is a messy business. If there were a formula for it, it wouldn't be integration. Peter Berger sees this clearly:

If relativity is a stormy sea of uncertainties, [our] faith does not magically make the waters recede so that we can march through them on a dry path. What it does do is give us the courage to set sail on our little boat, with the hope that, by God's grace, we will reach the other shore without drowning.[23]

A genuinely integrative theology is a high calling, and we should pursue it with pride and conviction. Let us be avant garde, think new thoughts, dream new dreams, and imagine a future that no one has imagined before. For this, I believe, is our particular vocation and our distinctive contribution.

Acknowledgments

I AM GRATEFUL TO ZACH SIMPSON, WHO HAS SERVED AS THE EDITOR for this book. The task of drawing together diverse strands from my past work and reworking them into a new systematic whole would never have been possible without his encouragement and extensive investment of support. Zach read and commented on all the material out of which this book has grown (and much more that we chose in the end not to include), making suggestions for deletions and additions. He also shared with me in the task of envisioning a new consistent whole, a coherent argument that we have sought to craft out of the various pieces.

I am grateful to Jheri Cravens for her assistance in preparing the new parts of the manuscript, and to my research assistants at the Claremont Graduate University and Claremont School of Theology, Andrea Stephenson and Ashley Riordan, for their research support. I thank Michael West at Fortress Press for his role in helping to conceive this book and to bring it to fruition, and Josh Messner and Carolyn Banks for supervising the productive process at Fortress. The book was designed by Michelle Cook, and the text was copyedited by Mark Christianson. We are also grateful for the skillful and efficient work of Richard Miller, who helped prepare the index for this volume. Inquiries regarding indexing work can be forwarded to richard.miller@earlychristianity.net.

Finally, I am deeply grateful to all the editors, journals, and presses listed below for their permission to use portions of previously published material.

Chapter 1: An earlier version of some of this material originally appeared as "Critical Faith: Theology in the Midst of the Sciences," a booklet publication in honor of Father Jan Peters, S. J., Heyendaal Institute, Nijmegen, The Netherlands, 2005. I am grateful to the Heyendaal Institute for permission to use portions of that material here.

Chapter 2: An earlier version of some of this material originally appeared as "Religious Truth and Scientific Truth: A Comparative Exploration," in *Phenomenology of the Truth Proper to Religion: An Anthology*, Daniel Guerrière, ed. (New York: SUNY Press, 1997). I am grateful to the SUNY Press for permission to use portions of that material here.

Chapter 3: An earlier version of some of this material originally appeared as "The Contemporary Science-and-Religion Discussion: A Transformation of Religious Knowledge Claims, or a Futile Quest for Legitimation?" in *Scientific Explanation and Religious Belief: Science and Religion in Philosophical and Public Discourse*, Thomas M. Schmidt and Michael G. Parker, eds. (Tübingen: Mohr Siebeck, 2005), 11–24. I am grateful to Mohr Siebeck Publishing for permission to use portions of that material here.

Chapter 4: An earlier version of some of this material originally appeared as "Process and Emergence," in *Back to Darwin,* John B. Cobb Jr., ed. (Grand Rapids: Eerdmans, 2008), 288–308. I am grateful to John B. Cobb Jr. and Bill Eerdmans Jr., of William B. Eerdmans Publishing Company for permission to use portions of that material here.

Chapter 5: An earlier version of some of this material originally appeared as "The Emergence of Spirit," *CTNS Bulletin* 20 (2000): 3–20. I am grateful to Robert J. Russell and the Center for Theology and the Natural Sciences (www.ctns.org) for permission to use portions of that material here.

Chapter 6: An earlier version of some of this material was originally delivered as "The Emergence of Spirit: From Complexity to Anthropology to Theology," The Boyle Lecture, St. Mary-le-Bow, the City of London, February 2006. That lecture was published as "The Emergence of Spirit: From Complexity to Anthropology to Theology," *Theology and Science* 4 (2006): 291–307. I am grateful to the editors of *Theology and Science*, Robert J. Russell and Ted Peters, for permission to use portions of that material here.

Chapter 7: An earlier version of some of this material originally appeared as "Toward a Constructive Christian Theology of Emergence," in *Evolution and Emergence: Systems, Organisms, Persons,* Nancey Murphy and William R. Stoeger, S. J., eds. (Oxford: Oxford University Press, 2007). I am grateful to Oxford University Press for permission to use portions of that material here.

Chapter 8: An earlier version of some of this material originally appeared as "Panentheism in Metaphysical and Scientific Perspective," in *In Whom We Live and Move and Have Our Being*, Philip Clayton and Arthur Peacocke, eds. (Grand Rapids: Eerdmans Press, 2004). I am grateful to William B. Eerdmans Publishing Company for permission to use portions of that material here.

Chapter 9: An earlier version of some of this material originally appeared as "From Substance to Subject: Panentheism and the History of Modern Philosophical Theology" in *Advents of the Spirit: An Introduction to the Current Study of Pneumatology*, Bradford Hinze and D. Lyle Dabney, eds. (Milwaukee, Wisc.: Marquette University Press, 2001). I am grateful to Marquette University Press for permission to use portions of that material here.

Chapter 10: An earlier version of some of this material originally appeared as "Pluralism, Idealism, Romanticism: Untapped Resources for a Trinity in Process," in *Trinity in Process: A Relational Theology of God*, Joseph Bracken, S. J., and Marjorie Hewitt Suchocki, eds. (New York: Continuum, 1997). I am grateful to Continuum Publishing Company for permission to use portions of that material here.

Chapter 11: An earlier version of some of this material originally appeared as "Open Panentheism and *Creatio ex Nihilo*," *Process Studies* 37 (forthcoming 2008): 166-83. I am grateful to Barry Whitney, editor of *Process Studies*, for permission to use portions of that material here.

Chapter 12: An earlier version of some of this material appeared as "Natural Law and Divine Action: The Search for an Expanded Theory of Causation," in *Zygon: Journal of Religion and Science* 39 (September 2004): 613–34. I am grateful to *Zygon* for permission to use portions of that material here.

Chapter 13: An earlier version of some of this material originally appeared as "Systematizing Agency: Toward a Panentheistic-Participatory Theory of Agency," in *Schleiermacher and Whitehead: Open Systems in Dialogue*, Christine Helmer, ed. (Berlin: Walter de Gruyter, 2004). I am grateful to Walter de Gruyter Press for permission to use portions of that material here.

Chapter 14: An earlier version of some of this material originally appeared as "Can Liberals Still Believe that God (Literally) Does Anything?" *CTNS Bulletin* 20 (2000): 3–10. I am grateful to Robert Russell and the *CTNS Bulletin* for permission to use portions of that material here.

Chapter 15: An earlier version of some of this material originally appeared as "Religion and the Social Sciences: Reflections on the Human Quest for Meaning," in *The Evolution of Rationality: Festschrift for J. Wentzel van Huyssteen*, LeRon Schultz, ed. (Grand Rapids: Eerdmans, 2006), 86–105. I am grateful to William B. Eerdmans Publishing Company for permission to use portions of that material here.

Chapter 16: An earlier version of this chapter was originally delivered as a lecture, "Spirituality as Spirit and Spirituality toward Spirit, in Dialogue with Derrida's *De l'Esprit*" at Claremont Graduate University in the fall of 2004.

Chapter 17: An earlier version of some of this material was originally delivered as my inaugural lecture at Claremont School of Theology under the title, "The Many Faces of Integration: A Vision for Liberal Theology between Church, Academy, and World" in May of 2004.

Notes

 Editor's Introduction

1. Philip Clayton, *God and Contemporary Science* (Edinburgh: Edinburgh University Press, and Grand Rapids: Eerdmans, 1997), 2.

2. See *God and Contemporary Science*, chapter 1.

3. See chapter 1 in this volume, pages 33-34, "The contemporary *religious* context for belief is a radically *inter-religious*, pluralistic context. And the *non-religious* context for belief is science, that is, the specific conclusions of the various sciences on the one hand, and the more general assumptions that underlie them, such as naturalism and empiricism, on the other."

4. See Clayton, *Explanation from Physics to Theology: An Essay in Rationality and Religion* (New Haven: Yale University Press, 1989).

5. Clayton, *The Problem of God in Modern Thought* (Grand Rapids, Mich.: Eerdmans, 2000).

6. Among many examples, see Clayton's introduction, "Conceptual Foundations of Emergence Theology," in *The Re-Emergence of Emergence,* ed. Philip Clayton and Paul Davies (Oxford: Oxford University Press, 2006), 1–31.

7. See chapter 1, page 28.

8. Clayton, "Foreword," in *Science and the Search for Meaning: Perspectives from International Scientists*, ed. Jean Staune (Philadelphia: Templeton Foundation Press, 2006), xv–xvi.

9. Wolfhart Pannenberg, *Systematic Theology,* vol. 1, trans. Geoffrey Bromiley (Grand Rapids, Mich.: Eerdmans, 1991), 56.

10. See Imre Lakatos, *Proofs and Refutations* (Cambridge: Cambridge University Press, 1976). Also see Clayton, *Explanations from Physics to Theology*, 51–58.

11. *God and Contemporary Science*, 66. This runs directly counter to a responsive reading from Andy Sanders, who asserts of Clayton's notion of panentheism that, "metaphysical panentheism strives to offer the most adequate explanation of all the available evidence, of all that is." See Sanders, "God, Contemporary Science and Metaphysics: A Response to Philip D. Clayton," *Tradition and Discovery: The Polanyi Society Periodical* 29, no. 3 (2002–2003), 28.

12. As Clayton does in his forthcoming volume with Steven Knapp, *The Challenge of Ultimacy: An Essay in Christian Minimalism* (forthcoming, 2008).

13. Clayton, "Critical Faith: Theology in the Midst of the Sciences," a booklet publication in honor of Father Jan Peters S.J., Heyendaal Institute, Nijmegen, The Netherlands, 2005, 19.

14. Chapter 1, page 32.

15. Critical Faith," 19-20. See also *Explanation from Physics to Theology*, especially chapters 3–4, and *The Problem of God in Modern Thought*, especially chapter 1.

16. Chapter 3, page 53.

17. See chapter 3, page 59, where Clayton states the following: "Why ought one to affirm 'methodological atheism' rather than methodological *agnosticism*, as discourse rationality would seem to require? Why not a methodological position that admits, as Habermas does elsewhere, that certain questions remain beyond our ability to decide them intersubjectively—so much so, indeed, that one cannot resolve them in the direction of atheism rather than theism?"

18. Clayton, "Emergence and the Epistemology of Broad Naturalism," presentation given at Ursinus University and Esalen, 2005 (paper is currently unpublished). Also see *God and Contemporary Science*, 5.

19. "Emergence and the Epistemology of Broad Naturalism."

20. See chapter 3, page 54. "There is falsification, but it is dependent on the emergence of better theories. Finally, there is a testing of theories against evidence, but this test involves a 'reflective equilibrium' (John Rawls) or broad coherence between bodies of theory, rather than an unambiguous falsification of a specific theory by a specific set of data."

21. Philip Clayton, "Von Wissenschaft zur Theologie und Zurück: Die konstruktive Metaphysik als Dialog" (English title: "Theology as Dialogue: A Dialogical Model of Religious Existence"), in *Religion im Dialog: Interdisziplinäre Perspektiven*, Tobias Mueller, ed. (Frankfurt: Probleme Lösungsansätze, 2008). Hereafter referred to as "Theology as Dialogue."

22. See *God and Contemporary Science*, 144–45.

23. John Rawls, *A Theory of Justice*, Revised Edition (Cambridge, Mass.: Harvard University Press, 1999), 113–17.

24. Ibid., 118–19.

25. Ibid., 120.

26. One could, of course, see Clayton's endorsement of "methodological agnosticism" as something akin to a "veil of ignorance." However, this only prescribes an openness to the *results* of discourse, and does not specify that one take one's beliefs out of the public sphere altogether, as Rawls might perhaps suggest. It does require, however, that one be willing to abandon one's belief if it is counter-indicated by the evidence, which similarly implies that one's belief is at least implicitly at stake in a dialogue situation.

27. Seyla Benhabib, *Situating the Self: Gender, Community and Postmodernism in Contemporary Ethics* (New York: Routledge, 1992), 167.

28. Ibid., 161.

29. Ibid., 32.

30. Clayton does give some indication in this direction in his "Theology as Dialogue," where he discusses the notion of the "Guiding Assumptions Corollary" to theological discourse.

31. Clayton, "Theology as Dialogue."

32. See "Theology as Dialogue," where Clayton notes the following: "Close dialogues of this sort are desirable because it is better to have coherence and consonance between the conclusions of the two [namely, science and theology] than to have a situation where they stand in tension. Reflective equilibrium begins with this conviction; it adds that a given individual or group should acknowledge the areas where tensions lie and work to find modifications on one or the other side that will help to minimize these tensions."

33. Benhabib, *Situating the Self*, 75.

34. Rawls, *A Theory of Justice*, 103.

35. Pannenberg, *Systematic Theology*, 24.

36. Chapter 2, 45.

37. Ibid., 44.

38. *God and Contemporary Science*, 115.

39. Pannenberg, *Systematic Theology*, 59.

40. Clayton, "Theology as Dialogue."

41. Gilles Deleuze and Felix Guattari, *What Is Philosophy?* trans. Hugh Tomlinson and Graham Burchell (New York: Columbia University Press, 1994), 197.

42. Ibid., 33–4.

43. Ibid., 111.

44. Ibid., 111.

45. *God and Contemporary Science*, 11.

46. Ibid., 175.

47. Ibid., 193ff.

48. Clayton, "Emergence and the Philosophy of Consciousness," presentation given at the University of Copenhagen, 2006.

49. *God and Contemporary Science*, 250ff.

50. Chapter 5, page 80.

51. Ibid.

52. See Chapter 6, page 91 and following. Also see Philip Clayton, *Die Frage nach der Freiheit: Biologie, Kulture, und die Emergenz des Geistes* (Frankfurt: Vandenhoeck and Ruprecht, 2007), for a somewhat different account of human agency with respect to other primates.

53. For an interesting example of global neuronal workspace theory, see Claire Sergent and Stanislaus Dehaene, "Is Consciousness a Gradual Phenomenon? Evidence for an All-or-None Bifurcation during the Attentional Blink," *Psychological Science* 15, no. 11 (2004): 720–28.

54. Chapter 12, page 197.

55. Chapter 13, page 216. Also see Clayton, "Divine Action and the 'Argument from Neglect,'" (with Steven Knapp) in Robert J. Russell et al., *Physics and Cosmology: Scientific Perspectives on the Problem of Evil* (Notre Dame, Ind.: Vatican Observatory Publications, 2007), 186, where Clayton asserts the following: "'Anomalous' signals that mental events are not nomological, not law-governed. Although one expects there to be significant patterns and detectible regularities among mental phenomena, those phenomena are not merely instances of overarching laws that govern all mental events. Intentional explanations have irreducibly holistic features; one cannot reduce them to their neurophysiological components without losing the very thing one hopes to explain: the agent's intentions. For example, there are no independent means for specifying what factors are or are not relevant to an intentional act; hence there is no way to link such acts to a specific part of the physical world in a supervenient relationship."

56. "Divine Action and the 'Argument from Neglect,'" 187.

57. Earlier, in *God and Contemporary Science*, Clayton made the critical distinction between "autonomic" divine agency, where the regularities of the laws of science are upheld through God's continuous agency, and "focal" divine agency, where God has explicit intentions for a particular event.

58. "Divine Action and the 'Argument from Neglect,'" 189.

59. Clayton, "Natural Law and Divine Action: The Search for an Expanded Theory of Causation," *Zygon* 39, no. 3 (September 2004): 630.

60. See "Divine Action and the 'Argument from Neglect,'" 192, where he states "It turns out not to matter, apparently, whether the divine influence comes in propositional or affective form. What God must refrain from doing, if the problem of evil is to be answerable, is giving us thoughts or feelings that compel an automatic or reflexive response, because otherwise God would incur an obligation to prevent or correct our mistakes whenever they might occur."

61. Chapter 12, 202.

62. "Divine Action and the 'Argument from Neglect.'"

63. Chapter 12, 202.

64. Clayton, "A Response to My Critics," *Dialog* 38, no. 4 (Fall 1999): 293.

65. *God and Contemporary Science*, 200.

66. It is interesting to contrast this view of divine influence via ontological openness to that of Pannenberg's concept of "prolepsis," where the *basileia* proclaimed by Jesus Christ becomes a condition for the openness in history.

67. Chapter 14, 224, where Clayton asserts the following: "We too should understand God's intentional revealing of God's nature through human agents who aim to submit themselves to the will of God as the essence of divine action."

68. See Clayton's unpublished presentation, "The Emergence of Spirit: From Complexity to Anthropology to Theology?" The Boyle Lecture, St Mary-le-Bow, the City of London, February 2006.

69. As quoted by Clayton, chapter 11, page 176.

70. Clayton, "Response to My Critics," 291. See, as well, *God and Contemporary Science,* 233, where Clayton asserts: "If one is to understand the agency of a personal divine being at all . . . , then surely divine agency will have to relate *in some way* to the only other type of personal agency familiar to us: our own. Divine agency will be higher, of course. . . . But if it is nothing like human

agency, we shall know nothing whatever about it." Also see Steven Crain's essay, "God Embodied in, God Bodying Forth the World: Emergence and Christian Theology," *Zygon* 41, no. 3 (Sept. 2006): 665–74, in which he remarks, "Hence, by placing the world within God, emergent panentheism provides a promising way of working out the sense in which God can act in God's own creation without intruding into it by interrupting the very natural regularities for which God is responsible in the first place" (668).

71. Clayton, "Panentheistic Internalism: Living within the Presence of the Trinitarian God," *Dialog* 40, no. 3 (2001): 212. Also see *God and Contemporary Science*, 101ff.

72. Chapter 7, page 102.

73. Chapter 12, page 198.

74. For a criticism of Clayton's notion of hierarchies, as well as its potential anthropocentrism, see Antje Jackelen's paper, "Emergence Everywhere?! Reflections on Philip Clayton's *Mind and Emergence*," *Zygon* 41, no. 3 (2006): 623–32.

75. For more on Clayton's notion of hierarchies in biology, see, in particular, his *Mind and Emergence* (Oxford: Oxford University Press, 2004), especially chapters 3 and 4.

76. Stuart Kauffman and Philip Clayton, "On Emergence, Agency, and Organization," *Biology and Philosophy* 21 (2006): 501–21. For another favorable analysis of Clayton's concept of agency, see Walter Gulick's paper, "Response to Clayton: Taxonomy of the Types and Orders of Emergence," *Tradition and Discovery: The Polanyi Society Periodical* 29, no. 3 (2002–2003): 39–40.

77. Kauffman and Clayton, "On Emergence, Agency, and Organization," 517.

78. Chapter 14, 216.

79. Ibid.

80. *God and Contemporary Science,* 210.

81. Chapter 4, 70. "Elsasser thus represents a paradigm example of scientific emergence. The leading biophysicist Harold Morowitz, heavily influenced by Elsasser, comments, 'emergence requires pruning rules to reduce the transcomputable to the computable. . . . In both Elsasser's approach and Holland's view, biology requires its own laws that are not necessarily derivable from physics, but do not contradict the physical foundations.'"

82. Also see here Stuart Kaufmann's work on complex systems dynamics in his classic, *The Origins of Order: Self-Organization and Selection in Evolution* (New York: Oxford University Press, 1993).

83. Chapter 12, 196.

84. For some additional work on causal overdetermination, see the volume, *Physicalism and Mental Causation*, ed. Sven Walter and Heinz-Dieter Heckmann (Charlottesville, Va.: Imprint Academic, 2003).

85. Chapter 1, 25.

➤ Chapter 1: Critical Faith

1. See Philip Clayton, *The Problem of God in Modern Thought* (Grand Rapids, Mich.: Eerdmans, 2000) and Philip Clayton, *God and Contemporary Science* (Edinburgh: Edinburgh University Press and Grand Rapids: Eerdmans, 1997).

2. Peter Berger, *A Far Glory: The Quest for Faith in an Age of Credulity* (New York: Free Press/ MacMillan, 1992).

3. Philip Clayton, *Explanation from Physics to Theology: An Essay in Rationality and Religion* (New Haven: Yale University Press, 1989), 167.

4. Ibid.

5. See, among many publications, Louis K. Dupré, *The Other Dimension: A Search for the Meaning of Religious Attitudes* (Garden City, N.Y.: Doubleday, 1972). I owe to Prof. Dupré my introduction to the great Dutch phenomenologist, G. van der Leeuw, and through him to the phenomenology of religion. A recent interview with Dupré, "Seeking Christian Interiority," is available at http://www.religion-online.org/showarticle.asp?title=214 (accessed July 28, 2005).

6. Clayton, *Explanation from Physics to Theology*, 138f., italics added, quoting Diderot, *Addition aux Pensées philosophiques*, par. 1, in Diderot, *Oeuvres Complètes* (1875), 1:158.

7. The classic position that doubt is a sin is defended by Gary Gutting, *Religious Belief and Religious Skepticism* (Notre Dame: University of Notre Dame Press, 1982).

8. Wolfhart Pannenberg, *Systematic Theology*, 3 vols., trans. Geoffrey Bromiley (Grand Rapids, Mich.: Eerdmans, 1991–98), 1:9f. Subsequent references to this work are prefixed by *ST.*

9. Wolfhart Pannenberg, *Jesus—God and Man* (Philadelphia: Westminster, 1963/1968), 109. Note that the Afterword to the Christology already begins to move away from the strong anti-Barthian tone. It also somewhat weakens the reliance on a "Christology from below" by adding a role for "theology from above" (*Theologie von oben*). The switch is also in evidence in Wolfhart Pannenberg, *Grundfragen systematischer Theologie. Gesammelte Aufsätze*, vol. 2 (Göttingen: Vandenhoeck & Ruprecht, 1981). See my review article, "The God of History and the Presence of the Future," *The Journal of Religion* 65 (1985): 98–108.

10. Wolfhart Pannenberg, *Theology and the Philosophy of Science*, trans. Francis McDonagh (Philadelphia: Westminster, 1976), 332. Henceforth *TPS.*

11. W. W. Bartley, *The Retreat to Commitment* (New York: Knopf, 1962).

12. Although this is the intent of all three volumes of the *Systematic Theology*, I must say that I see the footprints of this method less clearly in the second volume, and even less clearly in the third, than I see them in many of Pannenberg's earlier writings, especially in the early defense of "universal history," in the hypothetical nature of theology in his *Wissenschaftstheorie*, and in his anthropology. See Wolfhart Pannenberg, *Anthropology in Theological Perspective*, trans. Matthew J. O'Connell (Edinburgh: T & T Clark, 1985, 1999).

13. Although the position of Thomas Aquinas in *Summa Theologiae* q.2 a.3 is more profound and more complicated than this, his "five ways" do lend themselves to a reading in this fashion.

14. See the works by Edward Schillebeeckx, especially *Jesus: An Experiment in Christology*, trans. Hubert Hoskins (New York: Seabury, 1979), but also *Christ, the Sacrament of the Encounter with God*, trans. Paul Barrett (New York: Sheed and Ward, 1963), and *Christ: The Experience of Jesus as Lord*, trans. John Bowden (New York: Crossroad, 1980).

15. A phrase first coined by Steven Knapp at Johns Hopkins University and used by both of us in our work in religious epistemology. See, for example, Philip Clayton and Steven Knapp, "Belief and the Logic of Religious Commitment," in *The Rationality of Religious Belief*, ed. Godehard Bruntrup and Ronald K. Tacelli (Dordrecht: Kluwer Academic, 1999), 61-83. See also Clayton and Knapp, *The Challenge of Ultimacy* (in preparation).

16. David Wiggins, "Reflections on Inquiry and Truth Arising from Peirce's Method for the Fixation of Belief," in *The Cambridge Companion to Peirce*, ed. Cheryl Misak (Cambridge: Cambridge University Press, 2004), 114. Henceforth *CCP.*

17. Douglas Anderson, "Peirce's Common Sense Marriage of Religion and Science," in *CCP*, 181.

18. Ibid., 182. The reference is to Kelly A. Parker, "C. S. Peirce and the Philosophy of Religion," *Southern Journal of Philosophy* 28 (1990): 193–212. See also Parker, *The Continuity of Peirce's Thought* (Nashville and London: Vanderbilt University Press, 1998).

19. Although the words are Anderson's, they accurately represent Peirce's position.

20. *The Collected Papers of Charles Sanders Peirce*, 8 vols., ed. Charles Hartshorne and Paul Weiss (Cambridge, Mass.: Harvard University Press, 1931–58). Henceforth *CP.*

21. *CP*, vol. 1, 184.

22. Michael L. Raposa, *Peirce's Philosophy of Religion* (Bloomington: Indiana University Press, 1989), 13.

23. Peter Skagestad, *The Road of Inquiry: Charles Peirce's Pragmatic Realism* (New York: Columbia University Press, 1981), 18.

24. Ibid., 39.

25. Christopher Hookway, "Truth, Reality, and Convergence," in *CCP*, 127.

26. Hilary Putnam, *Realism with a Human Face* (Cambridge, Mass.: Harvard University Press, 1990), 221.

27. This notion of inquiry as self-correcting is linked to Peirce's equally important work on semiotics. Signs are never exhaustive of meaning, and meaning is always self-corrected by those constructing and receiving signs. As Skagestad notes in *The Road of Inquiry*, "The sign user's understanding, namely, is modified by further experience and is not complete until there is nothing left to experience. Hence the precise meaning of a sign is something which we can ascertain only when we have attained omniscience; indeed, only then will the sign have a precise meaning" (165).

28. See Clooney's theses in "What is Comparative Theology?" at http://www2.bc.edu/%7Eclooney/Comparative/ct.html (accessed Apr. 7, 2008).

29. Clayton, *Explanation from Physics to Theology*, 133ff.

30. See Thomas F. Torrance, *Theological Science* (Oxford: Oxford University Press, 1969, 1978).

31. See Alister E. McGrath, *A Scientific Theology*, 3 vols. (Grand Rapids, Mich.: Eerdmans, 2001–03). The three volumes are *Nature*, *Reality*, and *Theory*.

32. See my critique of Barth in *Explanation from Physics to Theology*, chapter 6, and my review of Alistair McGrath's *A Scientific Theology: Reality*, vol. 2, in *Theology Today* 61 (Apr. 2004): 121–22.

33. William Dembski, *The Design Inference: Eliminating Chance though Small Probabilities* (New York: Cambridge University Press, 1998); *Intelligent Design: The Bridge Between Science and Theology* (Downers Grove, Ill.: InterVarsity, 1999); *No Free Lunch: Why Specified Complexity Cannot Be Purchased without Intelligence* (Lanham: Rowan and Littlefield, 2002); and *The Design Revolution: Answering the Toughest Questions about Intelligent Design* (Downers Grove, Ill.: InterVarsity, 2004).

34. See Robert J. Russell, "The Relevance of Tillich for the Theology and Science Dialogue," *Zygon* 36 (2001): 269–308, especially the diagram of "creative mutual interaction" on 275.

35. *Webster's New World Dictionary*, Third College Edition.

36. There are more complex arguments that aim to show that physicalism is the only worldview that is in the end compatible with scientific inquiry. I take these arguments extremely seriously. But, whatever their strengths and weaknesses, they are certainly philosophical arguments, not statements of empirical results.

➤ Chapter 2: Religious Truth and Scientific Truth

1. I have written on this topic in Philip Clayton, *Explanation from Physics to Theology* (New Haven: Yale University Press, 1989), chapter 4, and in "Coherence and Realism: A Retrospective," in *Wahrheit—Sein—Struktur. Auseinandersetzungen mit Metaphysik*, Festschrift for L.B. Puntel, ed. Constanze Peres and Dirk Greimann (Hildesheim: Olms, 2000).

2. In the following pages "science," when used without qualifiers, will refer to the natural sciences and those social sciences that proceed according to the model of the natural sciences. That very different conclusions follow from a different model of science will be argued in due course.

3. See Martin Heidegger, *Holzwege, Gesamtausgabe*, vol. 5 (Frankfurt: Vittorio Klostermann, 1977), 71f. See also Heidegger's *Frage nach dem Ding*, translated by W. B. Barton Jr. and Vera Deutsch as *What Is a Thing?* (Chicago: H. Regnery, 1968).

4. Note that this was not Heidegger's conclusion. He always contended that science involves a concealment that undercuts the final truth of its reports.

5. See, among many others, Ian Barbour, *Myths, Models and Paradigms: A Comparative Study in Science and Religion* (New York: Harper & Row, 1974) and Paul Ricoeur, *Hermeneutics and the Human Sciences*, ed. and trans. John B. Thompson (Cambridge: Cambridge University Press, 1981).

6. See the excellent anthology edited by Maurice Natanson, *Phenomenology and the Social Sciences*, 2 vols. (Evanston, Ill.: Northwestern University Press, 1973), and Elisabeth Ströker, *Husserlian Foundations of Science*, ed. Lee Hardy (Washington, D.C.: University Press of America, 1987).

7. See Mary Hesse, *Revolutions and Reconstructions in the Philosophy of Science* (Cambridge: Cambridge University Press, 1981).

8. Namely, theoretical truth, truthfulness of expression, normative rightness. See Jürgen Habermas's *The Theory of Communicative Action*, trans. Thomas McCarthy, vol. 1, *Reason and the Rationalization of Society* (Boston: Beacon, 1984), for example, 302–309.

9. Peter McHugh, "On the Failure of Positivism," in *Understanding Everyday Life,* ed. J. D. Douglas (London: Routledge, 1971), 329.

10. Think of Mircea Eliade's claim that ontology gives place to history, in Mircea Eliade, *Myth and Reality* (New York: Harper, 1963), 108.

11. Joseph J. Kockelmans, "On the Problem of Truth in the Sciences," *Proceedings and Addresses of the American Philosophical Association* 61 (Sept. 1987): 19.

12. This is a theme that Michael Polanyi has developed as well as many recent writers. See his *Personal Knowledge* (London: Routledge and Kegan Paul, 1958).

13. See T. S. Kuhn's essay, "Logic of Discovery or Psychology of Research?" which set off the highly influential discussion contained in Imre Lakatos and Alan Musgrave, eds., *Criticism and the Growth of Knowledge* (Cambridge: Cambridge University Press, 1970).

14. Kuhn uses the term "conversion" some four times in *The Structure of Scientific Revolutions*, 2nd ed. (Chicago: University of Chicago Press, 1970). Paul Feyerabend, in *Against Method: Outline of an Anarchistic Theory of Knowledge* (London: NLB, 1975), is even less reticent to speak of the "religious" nature of these shifts: he argues, for instance, that voodoo may be as rationally justified as Western science.

15. These themes have been developed by Gerald Holton, in, for example, *The Scientific Imagination: Case Studies* (Cambridge: Cambridge University Press, 1978), and by Michel Foucault in many works, for example, and for a brief introduction, see "Truth and Power," in *Power/Knowledge*, ed. Colin Gordon (New York: Pantheon, 1980), 109–133.

16. Feyerabend develops this example in detail in *Against Method* in order to argue that there is no methodology of science, that "anything goes" even among those we hold up as our paradigms of scientific research.

17. Hans-Georg Gadamer, *Truth and Method* (New York: Crossroad, 1975), 409.

18. See Winston King, *An Introduction to Religion: A Phenomenological Approach* (New York: Harper & Row, 1968), 12f.

19. See, for example, Louis Dupré, *The Other Dimension: A Search for the Meaning of Religious Attitudes* (New York: Seabury [Crossroad], 1972).

20. This is a central thesis of Gadamer's hermeneutic theory of the human sciences in *Truth and Method*. Some of the implications of this inseparability for sociology and anthropology are explored in Bryan Wilson, ed., *Rationality* (Oxford: Basil Blackwell, 1970). Of course, the goal to objectify remains in science. We want to listen to the subject, but if we could predict her behavior with mathematical accuracy, we would be all the happier. Perhaps, though, the Other is forever unknowable, and all attempts to grasp her ultimately and necessarily fail. Given the view of science developed in this section, this would not surprise us, because the skepticism has been built into our very understanding of the *human* scientific activity. Is this not exactly the situation we deal with (with less surprise) in religion? The forever unknowable human other is just as other as the Totally Other whom we speak of as transcendent.

21. See also Philip Clayton, "Explanation from Physics to Theology" in *Philosophy of Religion*, ed. Melville Y. Stewart and Xiang Taotao, English and Chinese editions (Beijing: Peking University Press, 2005), 495–502.

22. Paul Tillich, *The Courage to Be* (New Haven: Yale University Press, 1952), 48, 175.

23. Clifford Geertz, "Religion as a Cultural System" in *The Interpretation of Cultures* (New York: Basic, 1973), 112.

24. See Wolfhart Pannenberg's still unrivalled *Theology and the Philosophy of Science*, trans. Francis McDonagh (Philadelphia: Westminster, 1977); Hans Albert, *Traktat über kritische Vernunft* (Tübingen: J. C. B. Mohr [Paul Siebeck], 1980); and Karl Popper, *Conjectures and Refutations: The Growth of Scientific Knowledge*, 4th ed. (London: Routledge and Kegan Paul, 1972). In fact, of course, few scientists will rejoice to find the hypothesis behind a major research project to be fatally flawed. Nonetheless, the professional ethic provides specific guidelines in such cases (for example, perhaps publishing a note on one's negative outcome) in a manner foreign to inter-religious discourse.

25. Gerardus van der Leeuw, *Religion in Essence and Manifestation: A Study in Phenomenology*, trans. J. E. Turner (New York: Harper & Row, 1963), 2:680.

26. See Henry Duméry, *The Problem of God in Philosophy of Religion*, trans. Charles Courtney (Evanston, Ill.: Northwestern University Press, 1969), and Louis Dupré, "Duméry's Reductions of Experience" in *A Dubious Heritage: Studies in the Philosophy of Religion after Kant* (New York: Paulist, 1977).

27. See Catherine Keller, *Face of the Deep* (New York: Routledge, 2003).

28. I am grateful to Louis Dupré and Bill Wootters for helpful criticisms of an earlier draft of this chapter.

➤ Chapter 3: The Contemporary Science and Religion Discussion

1. See Imre Lakatos, "Falsification and the Methodology of Scientific Research Programmes," in *Lakatos, Philosophical Papers*, vol. 1, ed. John Worrall and Gregory Currie (Cambridge: Cambridge University Press, 1978), 34–36, 45.

2. John Rawls, *A Theory of Justice*, 2nd ed. (Cambridge, Mass.: Harvard University Press, 1999); *Political Liberalism* (New York: Columbia University Press, 1996); *Justice as Fairness: A Restatement* (Cambridge, Mass.: Harvard University Press, 2001); "Outline of a Decision Procedure for Ethics," reprinted in *Collected Papers*, ed. Samuel Freeman (Cambridge, Mass.: Harvard University Press, 1999), 1–19; "The Independence of Moral Theory," in *Collected Papers*, 286–302; see also S. Freeman, ed., *The Cambridge Companion to Rawls* (Cambridge: Cambridge University Press, 2002), especially 139–67.

3. See Robert W. Funk, Roy W. Hoover, and the Jesus Seminar, *The Five Gospels: What Did Jesus Really Say? The Search for the Authentic Words of Jesus* (New York: Polebridge, 1993).

4. Jürgen Habermas, *Religion and Rationality: Essays on Reason, God, and Modernity* (Cambridge, Mass.: MIT Press, 2002), 108. Much could be said about the notion of truth presupposed by Habermas in this discourse theory of rationality. As is well known, his defense of a "consensus" theory of truth has come under heavy attack by German philosophers. I am convinced by the criticisms against the consensus theory raised by Lorenz Puntel in *Grundlagen einer Theorie der Wahrheit* (Berlin: Walter de Gruyter, 1990). See also the relevant articles in the Festschrift for Prof. Puntel, *Wahrheit—Sein—Struktur: Auseinandersetzungen mit Metaphysik*, ed. Constanze Peres and Dirk Greimann (Hildesheim: Olms, 2000). A discourse theory of rationality does not however commit one to such a theory of truth, as I have argued in detail elsewhere (Philip Clayton, *Explanation from Physics to Theology: An Essay in Rationality and Religion* [New Haven: Yale University Press, 1989], chapter 4). It is consistent to accept a coherence theory of truth, as I do, or even a correspondence theory of truth, and still argue that the best account of justified knowledge claims is given by discourse theory in the sense of Peirce and Habermas. The one price that must be paid, however, is that one cannot prove in advance that the "convergence of expert opinion" is sufficient for truth. The link between the ultimate consensus of experts and truth remains a wager on our part. It is, however, a justified wager, since we have no better means for ascertaining (probable) truth and eliminating errors from among our beliefs.

5. See Philip Clayton and Steven Knapp, "Ethics and Rationality," *American Philosophical Quarterly* 30 (1993): 151–61; "Is Holistic Justification Enough?" and "Rationality and Christian Self-Conceptions," in Mark Richardson and Wesley Wildman, eds., *Religion and Science: History, Method, Dialogue* (London: Routledge, 1996); and "Belief and the Logic of Religious Commitment," in *The Rationality of Religious Belief*, ed. Godehard Bruntrup and Ronald K. Tacelli (Dordrecht: Kluwer Academic, 1999), 61–83.

6. Paul Tillich, *Dynamics of Faith* (New York: HarperCollins Perennial, 1957, 2001), 25.

7. Ibid., 19, 20.

8. Ibid., 4.

9. Ibid., 23.

10. Ibid., 16.

11. Ibid., 23.

12. Tillich, *Systematic Theology*, vol. 1 (London: SCM, 1978), 10.

13. Tillich, *Dynamics of Faith*, 119.

14. Ibid., 23.

15. Ibid., 22.

16. Philip Clayton and Steven Knapp, "Belief and the Logic of Religious Commitment," in *The Rationality of Religious Belief*, ed. Godehard Bruntrup and Ronald K. Tacelli (Dordrecht: Kluwer Academic, 1999), 61–83.

17. Tillich, *Dynamics of Faith*, 26.

18. For one of many critiques of the propositional emphasis in theology, however, see George Lindbeck, *The Nature of Doctrine* (Philadelphia: Westminster, 1984). For a more radical, Derridean approach, see Mark Taylor, *Erring A Postmodern A/Theology* (Chicago: University of Chicago Press, 1984).

19. Tillich, *Dynamics of Faith*, 33.

20. Habermas, *Religion and Rationality*, 108. Compare with page 105: "unified metaphysical thought—however negatively accented—transposes solidarity, which has its proper place in linguistic intersubjectivity, communication, and individuating socialization, into the identity of an underlying essence, the undifferentiated negativity of the world-will." For further negative comments on any kind of transcendence apart from "internal transcendence," see pages 67–91. Subsequent references to this work are prefixed by *RR*.

21. Ibid., 162, translation modified.

22. See the argument to this effect in James Cushing, *Quantum Mechanics: Historical Contingency and the Copenhagen Hegemony* (Chicago: University of Chicago Press, 1994).

23. See the argument in Clayton and Knapp, "Ethics and Rationality."

➤ Chapter 4: Why Emergence Matters

1. See Karl Giberson and Mariano Artigas, *Oracles of Science: Celebrity Scientists versus God and Religion* (Oxford: Oxford University Press, 2007); Philip Clayton, *Beyond the Religion Wars: The Path from Reduction to Reenchantment* (in preparation).

2. See the introduction to the collection in Jean-Marie Lehn, "Toward Complex Matter: Supramolecular Chemistry and Self-Organization," *Proceedings of the National Academy of Sciences* 99/8 (Apr. 16, 2002): 4763–68.

3. Ibid., 4768.

4. Ibid.

5. See Giulio Tononi and Gerald M. Edelman, "Consciousness and Complexity," *Science* 282 (Dec. 4, 1998): 1846–51.

6. Wojciech Zurek, "Decoherence and the Transition from Quantum to Classical—Revisited," *Los Alamos Science* 27 (2002): 14; see also Zurek, "Decoherence and the Transition from Quantum to Classical," *Physics Today* 44 (1991).

7. See Stephen Adler, *Quantum Theory as an Emergent Phenomenon: The Statistical Dynamics of Global Unitary Invariant Matrix Models as the Precursor of Quantum Field Theory* (Cambridge: Cambridge University Press, 2004). If string theory is correct, quantum mechanics would be an emergent property of strings.

8. Numerous examples are offered by Laughlin in his recent book, Robert Laughlin, *A Different Universe: Reinventing Physics from the Bottom Down* (New York: Basic, 2005). See also the review by Philip Anderson, "Emerging Physics: A Fresh Approach to Viewing the Complexity of the Universe," *Nature* 434 (Apr. 7, 2005): 701–2.

9. See Elbio Daggoto, "Complexity in Strongly Correlated Electronic Systems," *Science* 309 (July 8, 2005): 257–62, citing 257.

10. See Pier Luigi Luisi, "Emergence in Chemistry: Chemistry as the Embodiment of Emergence," *Foundations of Chemistry* 4 (2002): 183–200. See also his book: *The Emergence of Life: From Chemical Origins to Synthetic Biology* (Cambridge: Cambridge University Press, 2006). An earlier case for the importance of emergence in chemistry was made by the process thinker Joseph Earley, for example, "Far-From-Equilibrium Thermodynamics and Process Thought," in *Physics and the Ultimate Significance of Time,* ed. David R. Griffin (Albany: State University of New York Press, 1985), 251–55; "The Nature of Chemical Existence," in *Metaphysics as Foundation,* ed. Paul Bogaard and Gordon Treash (Albany: State University of New York Press, 1992); "Self-Organization and Agency: In Chemistry and in Process Philosophy," *Process Studies* 11 (1981): 242–58; "Towards a Reapprehension of Causal Efficacy," *Process Studies* 24 (1995): 34–38; and "Collingwood's Third Transition: Replacement of Renaissance Cosmology by an Ontology of Evolutionary Self-Organization," in *With Darwin Beyond Descartes—The Historical Concept of Nature and Overcoming "The Two Cultures,"* ed. Luigi Zanzi (forthcoming).

11. Luisi, "Emergence in Chemistry," 195.

12. Ibid., 197.

13. Rui Alves, Raphael A. G. Chaleil, and Michael J. E. Sternberg, "Evolution of Enzymes in Metabolism: A Network Perspective," *Journal of Molecular Biology* 320 (2002): 751–70.

14. See Hiroaki Kitano, "Systems Biology: A Brief Overview," *Science* 295 (Mar. 1, 2002): 1662–64.

15. Ibid., 1664.

16. Ibid.

17. See Kevin Laland, "The New Interactionism," *Science* 300 (June 20, 2003): 1879–80, drawing on Matt Ridley, *Nature via Nurture: Genes, Experience, and What Makes Us Human* (New York: HarperCollins, 2003).

18. See Alvaro Moreno and Jon Umerez, "Downward Causation at the Core of Living Organization," in *Downward Causation: Minds, Bodies and Matter,* ed. Peter Bøgh Andersen, Claus Emmeche, Niels Ole Finnemann, and Peder Voetmann Christiansen (Aarhus, Denmark: Aarhus University Press, 2000), 112, 115.

19. See Harold Morowitz, "The Emergence of Intermediary Metabolism," unpublished paper, 8.

20. Barbara Smuts, "Emergence in Social Evolution: A Great Ape Example," in *The Re-Emergence of Emergence: The Emergentist Hypothesis from Science to Religion*, ed. Philip Clayton and Paul Davies (Oxford: Oxford University Press, 2006).

21. Harold Morowitz, *The Emergence of Everything: How the World Became Complex* (New York: Oxford University Press, 2002).

22. George Ellis, "Physics, Reductionism, and the Real World," *Physics Today* 59/3 (Mar. 2006): 12–14; and "Physics and the Real World," *Physics Today* 58/7 (July 2005): 49–54.

23. Philip Clayton, *Mind and Emergence: From Quantum to Consciousness* (Oxford: Oxford University Press, 2004).

24. Walter Elsasser, *Reflections on a Theory of Organisms* (Quebec: Editions Orbis, 1987).

25. Ibid., 142.

26. Ibid., 52.

27. Stuart Kauffman develops these ideas in *Investigations* (New York: Oxford University Press, 2000); and *At Home in the Universe: The Search for the Laws of Self-Organization and Complexity* (New York: Oxford University Press, 1995).

28. Elsasser, *Reflections,* 105.

29. Ibid., 142.

30. Ibid., 148.

31. Ibid.

32. Morowitz, "The Emergence of Intermediary Metabolism," 4.

33. B. C. Goodwin, "On Morphogenetic Fields," *Theoria to Theory* 13 (1979): 109–14, cited in Rupert Sheldrake, *A New Science of Life: The Hypothesis of Morphic Resonance* (Rochester, Vt.: Park Street Press, 1995).

34. Sheldrake, *A New Science of Life*, 170.

35. Ibid., 14.

36. Terrence Deacon, "The Hierarchic Logic of Emergence: Untangling the Interdependence of Evolution and Self Organization," in *Evolution and Learning: The Baldwin Effect Reconsidered,* eds. Bruce H. Weber and David J. Depew (Cambridge, Mass.: MIT Press, 2003), 273–308.

37. Ibid., 290.

38. Ibid., 288.

39. Ibid., 295.

40. Ibid., 299.

41. Deacon has developed the notion of the "autocell" in "Reciprocal Linkage Between Self-Organizing Processes is Sufficient for Self-Reproduction and Evolvability," *Biological Theory* 1 (2006): 136-149.

42. Deacon, "The Hierarchic Logic of Emergence," 299.

43. Ibid., 300.

44. Ibid., 304.

45. Ibid., 305.

46. Terrence Deacon, *The Symbolic Species: The Co-Evolution of Language and the Brain* (New York: Norton, 1997). See also Zoltán N. Oltvai and Albert-László Barabási, "Life's Complexity Pyramid," *Science* 298 (Oct. 22, 2002): 763–4. Barabási is best known for his popular presentation, *Linked: The New Science of Networks* (Cambridge, Mass.: Perseus, 2002); for a more technical presentation see Barabási and Reka Albert, "Emergence of Scaling in Random Networks," *Science* 286 (Oct. 15, 1999): 509–12. Note that embracing the core principles of network theory does not mean that it will lead to "an accurate mathematical theory of human behavior," as Barabási claims in "Network Theory—The Emergence of the Creative Enterprise," *Science* 308 (Apr. 29, 2005): 639–41.

47. Charles Darwin, *On the Origin of Species by Means of Natural Selection* (London: John Murray, 1859; reprint Holicong, PA: Wildside Press, 2003), last paragraph, pp. 489f.

Chapter 5: Emergent Realities

1. The influence of several thinkers on the following position is pervasive enough to require separate mention. Arthur Peacocke's work is so formative for this position that it rises above the level of individual footnotes. I owe my basic understanding of theological method to four years of tutelage under Wolfhart Pannenberg and to a lifetime of working through his theology. Finally, many years of conversation and correspondence with Steven Knapp have left their marks on the resulting position, and even on some of the formulations.

2. See also Philip Clayton, *Explanation from Physics to Theology: An Essay in Rationality and Religion* (New Haven: Yale University Press, 1989), especially chapter 2.

3. Terrence Deacon, "Evolution and the Emergence of Spirit," unpublished paper, 6.

4. Ibid.

5. For a version of a physicalist philosophy and theology of mind, which the author calls "non-reductive physicalism," see Nancey Murphy's contributions to Russell et al., eds., *Neuroscience and the Person* (Chicago: Notre Dame University Press, 2000); and to Warren S. Brown, Nancey Murphy, and H. Newton Malony, eds., *Whatever Happened to the Soul? Scientific and Theological Portraits of Human Nature* (Minneapolis: Fortress Press, 1998). Jaegwon Kim of Brown University was for many years the leading advocate of non-reductive physicalism, though in his more recent work he has now become one of its chief critics. See Kim, *Mind in a Physical World: An Essay on the Mind-Body Problem and Mental Causation* (Cambridge, Mass.: MIT Press, 2000).

6. Among the variety of Joseph Earley's publications on this topic, see "Far-From-Equilibrium Thermodynamics and Process Thought," in *Physics and the Ultimate Significance of Time,* ed. David R. Griffin (Albany: State University of New York Press, 1985), 251–55; "The Nature of Chemical Existence," in *Metaphysics as Foundation,* eds. Paul Bogaard and Gordon Treash (Albany: State University of New York Press, 1992); "Self-Organization and Agency: In Chemistry and in Process Philosophy," *Process Studies* 11 (1981): 242–58; "Towards a Reapprehension of Causal Efficacy," *Process Studies* 24 (1995): 34–38; "Collingwood's Third Transition: Replacement of Renaissance Cosmology by an Ontology of Evolutionary Self-Organization," in *With Darwin Beyond Descartes—The Historical Concept of Nature and Overcoming "The Two Cultures,"* ed. Luigi Zanzi (forthcoming).

7. See, for further examples, Robert Russell, Nancey Murphy and Arthur Peacocke, eds., *Chaos and Complexity: Scientific Perspectives on Divine Action* (Vatican City: Vatican Observatory, 1995).

8. Paul Cilliers, *Complexity and Postmodernism: Understanding Complex Systems* (London: Routledge, 1998), 91.

9. Niels H. Gregersen, "Levels of Complexity: From Complicatedness to Autopoiesis," unpublished paper, 7. See also Gregersen, *From Complexity to Life: On the Emergence of Life and Meaning* (Oxford: Oxford University Press, 2002).

10. Gregersen, "Levels of Complexity," 9.

11. Ibid., 10.

12. See Gregersen, "From Anthropic Design to Self-Organized Complexity," in *From Complexity to Life,* 204–34.

13. Parts of the following paragraphs were co-written with Steven Knapp, to whom I am indebted for numerous discussions and some of the formulations that follow.

14. It would be interesting to explore the origins and use of the phrase "purposiveness without purpose" in Kant's account of natural beauty in the *Critique of Judgment.* An equally important antecedent lies in Spinoza's concept of *conatus,* whereby each organism naturally strives to keep itself in existence. See Philip Clayton, *Mind and Emergence: From Quantum to Consciousness* (Oxford: Oxford University Press, 2004), chapter 3. On biosemiotics see Jesper Hoffmeyer, ed., *A Legacy for Living Systems: Gregory Bateson as Precursor to Biosemiotics* (Dordrecht: Springer, 2008).

15. For a summary see John Cartwright, *Evolution and Human Behavior* (Cambridge, Mass.: MIT Press, 2000).

16. To continue the metaphor, one might think of the environment as similar to the applause, or boos, of the audience—except that the process is not quite so gentle: in this case the acting failures are shot outright. More exactly, this "audience" rewards the hit show with babies that make babies, whereas the failures either die or are left without offspring.

17. See Philip Clayton, *In Quest of Freedom: The Emergence of Spirit in the Natural World* (Göttingen: Vandenhoeck & Ruprecht, 2008).

18. Human mental and affective experience is isolated by the conditions of natural law and biological drive, and perhaps also by human free agency.

19. See Richard Dawkins, *The Selfish Gene* (Oxford: Oxford University Press, 1976).

20. Stephen J. Gould, *The Panda's Thumb: More Reflections in Natural History* (New York: Norton, 1980), 15.

21. John Polkinghorne, *Belief in God in an Age of Science* (New Haven: Yale University Press, 1998), 63.

22. I am indebted to Steven Knapp for this formulation of the objection.

23. Wilfrid Sellars, *Science, Perception and Reality* (New York: Humanities, 1971), 40.

24. Richard J. Davidson and Anne Harrington, eds., *Visions of Compassion: Western Scientists and Tibetan Buddhists Examine Human Nature* (Oxford: Oxford University Press, 2002).

25. Francisco Varela, "Why a Proper Science of Mind Implies the Transcendence of Nature," in *Religion in Mind: Cognitive Perspectives on Religious Belief, Ritual, and Experience,* ed. Jensine Andresen (Cambridge: Cambridge University Press, 2001), 207.

26. Research reported in *New Scientist,* July 13, 1998.

27. However, since no firm conceptual or empirical distinctions can be drawn between emergent and meta-emergent properties, this locution should be used cautiously.

28. See, among other works, Bruce Weber and Terrence Deacon, "Thermodynamic Cycles, Developmental Systems, and Emergence," *Cybernetics and Human Knowing* 7/1 (2000): 21–43.

➤ Chapter 6: From World to Spirit?

1. This paper was first delivered as the Boyle Lecture for 2006. I would like to thank the organizers and sponsors of the Boyle Lecture for their generous hospitality during my stay in London, Michael Byrne for his highly professional work in administrating this complex program, and Niels Henrik Gregersen for his generous response as well as for organizing a "Boyle II" in Copenhagen a few days later.

2. See Simon Conway Morris, *Life's Solution: Inevitable Humans in a Lonely Universe* (Cambridge: Cambridge University Press, 2003) for an excellent example of the case for convergence in evolution.

3. See the introduction to the collection in Jean-Marie Lehn, "Toward Complex Matter: Supramolecular Chemistry and Self-Organization," *Proceedings of the National Academy of Sciences* 99/8 (Apr. 16, 2002): 4763–68.

4. Ibid., 4768.

5. Ibid.

6. Wojciech Zurek, "Decoherence and the Transition from Quantum to Classical—Revisited," *Los Alamos Science* 27 (2002): 14; see also Zurek, "Decoherence and the Transition from Quantum to Classical," *Physics Today* 44 (1991).

7. See Stephen Adler, *Quantum Theory as an Emergent Phenomenon: The Statistical Dynamics of Global Unitary Invariant Matrix Models as the Precursor of Quantum Field Theory* (Cambridge: Cambridge University Press, 2004). If string theory is correct, for example, quantum mechanics would be an emergent property of strings.

8. Numerous examples are offered by Laughlin in his recent book, Robert Laughlin, *A Different Universe: Reinventing Physics from the Bottom Down* (New York: Basic, 2005). Among Laughlin's examples of emergent phenomena are superconductivity, the quantum Hall effect, phase transitions, crystallization, collective instabilities, and hydrodynamics. See also the review by Philip Anderson, "Emerging Physics: A Fresh Approach to Viewing the Complexity of the Universe," *Nature* 434 (Apr. 7, 2005): 701–02.

9. See Terrence Deacon, *The Symbolic Species: The Co-Evolution of Language and the Brain* (New York: Norton, 1997); Melvin J. Konner, *The Tangled Wing: Biological Constraints on the Human Spirit* (New York: Times Books, 2002).

10. William Durham, *Coevolution: Genes, Culture, and Human Diversity* (Stanford: Stanford University Press, 1991).

11. Peter L. Berger, *The Sacred Canopy* (Garden City, N.Y.: Doubleday, 1967), 19. Emphasis added.

12. Ibid., 22.

13. Ibid., 21.

14. Friedrich Nietzsche, "Über Wahrheit und Lüge im aussermoralischen Sinne," in *Nietzsche Werke*, ed. Giorgio Colli and Mazzino Montinari (Berlin: Walter de Gruyter, 1973), pt. 3, vol. 2, 369.

15. Paraphrasing Berger, *The Sacred Canopy*, 28.

16. Ibid., 51.

17. Ibid., 26, with andocentric language removed.

18. See Peter L. Berger, "Relativising the Relativisers," in *A Rumor of Angels: Modern Society and the Rediscovery of the Supernatural* (Garden City, N.Y.: Doubleday, 1969).

19. Steven Weinberg, *The First Three Minutes: A Modern View of the Origin of the Universe* (New York: Basic, 1977), 154.

20. Jacques Monod, *Chance and Necessity: An Essay on the Natural Philosophy of Modern Being* (New York: Knopf, 1971), 167.

21. John Polkinghorne, *The God of Hope and the End of the World* (New Haven: Yale University Press, 2002), 21.

22. Michael J. Behe, "Letter to the Boston Review," http://www.arn.org/docs/behe/mb_brrespbr.htm, accessed Jan. 29, 2006. See also Behe, *Darwin's Black Box: The Biochemical Challenge to Evolution* (Boston: Free, 1996), chapter 4.

23. Quoted by Bob DeHaanin in a debate with Terry Gray; see http://www.asa3.org/archive/asa/199611/0144.html, accessed Jan. 29, 2006.

24. Each of these steps relies on a different field or type of argument. The three dimensions of the argument turn out to be complementary and mutually reinforcing in an interesting and unexpected way, despite (or perhaps precisely because of) their diversity.

25. See Philip Clayton, *Mind and Emergence: From Quantum to Consciousness* (Oxford: Oxford University Press, 2004), chapter 4.

26. Samuel Alexander, *Space, Time, and Deity*, the Gifford Lectures for 1916–18, 2 vols. (London: Macmillan, 1920), vol. 2, 361–2, 364.

27. See Ursula Goodenough, *The Sacred Depths of Nature* (New York: Oxford University Press, 1998).

28. The core concepts of and arguments for this approach are developed in the opening chapters of Wolfhart Pannenberg, *Systematic Theology*, 3 vols. (Grand Rapids, Mich.: Eerdmans, 1991).

29. 1 Cor 13:12, NRSV (adapted).

30. I am grateful to Michael Byrne and Russell Re Manning for criticisms of earlier drafts. Important segments of the argument also reflect the continuing influence of my long-time collaborator at George Washington University, Steven Knapp.

➤ Chapter 7: Theological Reflections on Emergence

1. Christoph Schwöbel, drawing on the classic works by Anthony Kenny (*Will, Freedom and Power*) and G. E. M. Anscombe (*Intention*) provides an excellent brief account: "If an event is described as the result of intentional action it is implied [1] that this event would not have occurred if it had not been brought about by an agent whose action can be named as the necessary condition for the occurrence of the event. Furthermore, it is presupposed [2] that the agent pursues a particular purpose with the action and that his or her action can be regulated to bring about the purpose. It is moreover assumed [3] that the action-directing intention is the result of a conscious choice of aims of action and that [4] the regulation of action is the result of a conscious choice of means of action. With these presuppositions we ascribe to the agent freedom of choice and freedom of action." See Christoph Schwöbel, *God: Action and Revelation* (Kampen, The Netherlands: Kok Pharos, 1992), 36.

2. Indeed, correlations between theories of self and theories of ultimate reality are ubiquitous. Vedantic philosophies of the self in the Indic traditions correlate with the philosophies of *Brahman* or ultimate reality. Buddhist and Zen Buddhist theories of the *no-self* correlate with teachings on *sunyata*, or emptiness; and physicalist or reductionist moves in the philosophy of mind correlate with agnostic or atheist metaphysics. Theists will see in mind or spirit or soul an anticipation of the nature of God—and must so anticipate, since according to all the theistic traditions humankind is made "in the image of God" (*imago Dei*). Epicurus once noted the parallels between the values of a culture and the qualities of its god or gods; here we seem to have encountered a principle no less fundamental.

3. See Arthur Peacocke, *All That Is: A Naturalistic Faith for the Twenty-First Century,* ed. Philip Clayton (Minneapolis: Fortress Press, 2007).

4. In science-based discussions one will tend to speak of mental properties, since there are no theories in the natural sciences today that offer a place for mental entities. Metaphysical and theological discussions, not working under the same strictures, tend to use the substantive "mind." What is crucial is whether distinctively and *ultimately irreducible* mental causes exist, or whether microphysical objects and forces are, in the end, the real causal agents. It seems to me that the physicalist has to wager on the latter outcome and the emergentist on the former.

5. Critics often argue that emergence theory comes closest to *property dualism*. Actually, as suggested above, it would be better to say that it is a form of *property pluralism*: many different and intriguing properties emerge in the course of natural history, and conscious experience is only one of them.

6. See Philip Clayton, *Mind and Emergence: From Quantum to Consciousness* (Oxford: Oxford University Press, 2006); and *In Quest of Freedom: The Emergence of Spirit in the Natural World* (Göttingen: Vandenhoeck & Ruprecht, 2008).

7. Samuel Alexander, *Space, Time, and Deity*, the Gifford Lectures for 1916–18, 2 vols. (London: Macmillan, 1920), 2:361–62, 364.

8. I cannot here attempt to resolve the knotty questions of the precise authority of scripture for theologians. It seems obvious that the Hebrew Bible and New Testament will remain points of reference for Christian theologians, who seek to bring those texts into dialogue with our contemporary context. But specifying exactly what balance should be found between literal and metaphorical or allegorical uses of scripture is no easy task. See Kevin J. Vanhoozer, *Is There a Meaning in This Text?: The Bible, the Reader, and the Morality of Literary Knowledge* (Grand Rapids, Mich.: Zondervan, 1998).

9. See also Philip Clayton, *The Problem of God in Modern Thought* (Grand Rapids, Mich.: Eerdmans, 2000).

10. See Philip Clayton and Steven Knapp, "Belief and the Logic of Religious Commitment," in *The Rationality of Religious Belief,* eds. Godehard Bruntrup and Ronald K. Tacelli (Dordrecht: Kluwer Academic, 1999), 61–83.

11. In contrast to much of the tradition, I do not define the incarnation first in terms of the ontological status of Jesus Christ. Most of the two-natures doctrines of the incarnation are based on the categories of a substance-based metaphysic that is foreign to how most people today think. These doctrines also require a pre-existent logos Christology that remains in tension with the fundamental humanity of Jesus, "tempted in every way, just as we are—yet . . . without sin" (Heb 4:15). This is not true of all two-natures Christologies, however, see, for example, James William McClendon Jr., *Doctrine* (Nashville: Abingdon, 1994).

12. In *The Problem of God in Modern Thought,* I tried to show why philosophical systems do matter to systematic theology and why modern thinkers were right to search for new ones.

13. Compare with Wolfhart Pannenberg, *Systematic Theology*, 3 vols., trans. Geoffrey W. Bromiley (Grand Rapids, Mich.: Eerdmans, 1991), vol. 2, chapter 7.

14. For a summary of the sciences of emergence, see Philip Clayton and Paul Davies, eds., *The Reemergence of Emergence* (Oxford: Oxford University Press, 2006). Oxford has also recently published Harold Morowitz, *The Emergence of Everything: How the World Became Complex* (New York: Oxford University Press, 2002), and Niels Gregersen, ed., *From Complexity to Life: On the Emergence of Life and Meaning* (New York: Oxford University Press, 2003). The Oxford volumes were preceded by a series of influential books on emergence and science, including John Holland, *Emergence: From Chaos to Order* (Cambridge, Mass.: Perseus, 1998); Roger Lewin, *Complexity: Life at the Edge of Chaos* (Chicago: University of Chicago Press, 1992); Albert-László Barabási, *Linked: The New Science of Networks* (Cambridge, Mass.: Perseus, 2002); Steven Johnson, *Emergence: The Connected Lives of Ants, Brains, Cities, and Software* (New York: Touchstone, 2001); Anthony Freeman, *The Emergence of Consciousness,* Philosophy Documentation Center, vol. 8, no. 9–10 (Charlottesville, Va.: Imprint Academic, 2001); Mark Taylor, *The Moment of Complexity: Emerging Network Culture* (Chicago: University of Chicago Press, 2001); and especially Terrence Deacon, *The Symbolic Species* (New York: Norton, 1997). I summarize the argument in *Mind and Emergence*, chapter 3.

15. See Philip Clayton, *God and Contemporary Science* (Edinburgh: Edinburgh University Press and Grand Rapids: Eerdmans, 1997); and *The Problem of God.* For further references, definitions, and arguments for the viability of panentheism, see Philip Clayton and Arthur Peacocke, eds., *In*

Whom We Live and Move and Have Our Being: Panentheistic Reflections on God's Presence in a Scientific World (Grand Rapids, Mich.: Eerdmans, 2004).

16. I have traced the philosophical foundations of panentheism in *The Problem of God in Modern Thought* and have applied it to the question of divine action in *God and Contemporary Science*. In three articles in *Dialog* over the last few years I have begun to work out a Christian panentheistic theology: "The Case for Christian Panentheism," *Dialog* 37 (Summer 1998): 201–8; "A Response to My Critics," Symposium on Clayton's Panentheism, *Dialog* 38 (Summer 1999): 289-93; and "Panentheist Internalism: Living within the Presence of the Trinitarian God," *Dialog* 40 (2001): 208–15. Most recently see Peacocke and Clayton, eds., *In Whom We Live.*

17. See my three-article series in *Dialog*: "The Case for Christian Panentheism," "A Response to My Critics," and "Panentheist Internalism: Living within the Presence of the Trinitarian God."

18. Philip Clayton, *God and Contemporary Science*, for example, 233–42, 257–65.

19. What analogies such as the panentheistic analogy suggest about the divine nature must be adapted, of course, to ensure that they are appropriate to the relationship between the world and its infinite Creator. Still, if one is to avoid complete skepticism about the nature of God, analogies such as this one will perforce play a rather significant role in whatever statements one makes about the nature of God, it being impossible for us to have knowledge of God that bypasses all human epistemic and cognitive abilities and limitations. It goes without saying that at least some aspects of the nature of an infinite God will remain eternally unknowable, beyond the reach of the best analogies theologians can ever conceive.

20. See the Orthodox contributions to Clayton and Peacocke, *In Whom We Live.*

21. See Peacocke, *All That Is.*

22. Individuality does not play the same role in biology as it does in, say, psychology. Where psychologists attempt to explain individual experience and behavior (what Windelband called "ideographic science"), biologists explain broad patterns and tendencies. Nonetheless, individual variance plays a far greater role here than in physics: no two phenotypes of a species are identical, and even so-called identical twins diverge from strict identity long before the moment of birth. By definition, however, laws cannot account for such variances. If biological variance indeed stands beyond the reach of law-based explanation, then it remains open to forms of individual influence, not unlike the way in which a person who knew you in infinite detail could influence your actions in ways that no laws could predict or explain. The theological significance of this fact, should biology confirm it, is obvious.

23. "If anyone is in Christ, he is a new creation; the old has gone; the new has come!" (2 Cor 5:17). The phrase "in Christ" is used some ninety times in the New Testament epistles.

24. As a woman described it to me recently at a Quaker meeting, "Perhaps God's only act is to make manifest the divine love. Is this not enough?"

25. I have told the story in Christian terms, as behooves a Christian theologian. But I presume that similar accounts could be developed within other traditions. Examples include references to the Buddha mind, the emulation of the Buddha by boddhisatvas, and the state of perfect receptiveness shown by God's prophet as he received the dictation of the Koran (as reflected, for example, in the ideals of Sufi mysticism).

26. One will note overtones of the "two horizons" hermeneutics in Hans-Georg Gadamer, *Truth and Method* (New York: Continuum, 1995).

27. I have already provided arguments against the "inside-outside dichotomy" in Philip Clayton, *Explanation from Physics to Theology: An Essay in Rationality and Religion* (New Haven: Yale University Press, 1989), 134–43.

28. See John Polkinghorne, *The God of Hope and the End of the World* (New Haven and London: Yale University Press, 2002). Paul Tillich also famously held this position (*Systematic Theology*, vol. 3), as have many mystical theologians through the ages.

29. See Polkinghorne, *The God of Hope*, 123.

30. See Marjorie Hewitt Suchocki, *The End of Evil: Process Eschatology in Historical Context* (Albany: State University of New York Press, 1988), and the volume from Eerdmans, edited by Joseph Bracken, that evaluates and extends Suchocki's process eschatology, Joseph Bracken, ed., *World Without End: Christian Eschatology from Process Perspective* (Grand Rapids: Eerdmans, 2005).

31. I am grateful to Stephen Knapp for extensive conversations on and criticisms of this topic. Many of the ideas, and some of the phrases in the text, were worked out jointly.

➤ Chapter 8: An Introduction to Panentheism

1. See Arthur Peacocke, *Theology for a Scientific Age: Being and Becoming—Natural, Divine, and Human*, enlarged ed. (Minneapolis: Fortress Press, 1993), 158f. Peacocke also makes important use of panentheism in his *Creation and the World of Science* (Oxford: Clarendon, 1979). The explanatory power of panentheism in the discussion between theology and science—for example, in the work of Peacocke and Robert J. Russell—counts, in my view, as a highly significant argument on its behalf. I have developed this argument in detail in Philip Clayton, *God and Contemporary Science* (Edinburgh: Edinburgh University Press and Grand Rapids: Eerdmans, 1997).

2. Charles Hartshorne and William L. Reese, eds. *Philosophers Speak of God* (Chicago: University of Chicago Press, 1953), 22. For an excellent (and more detailed) working-out of panentheistic metaphysics, see David Pailin, *God and the Processes of Reality* (London: Routledge, 1985), especially chapter 5.

3. See Joseph Bracken, "Panentheism from a Trinitarian Perspective," *Horizons* 22 (Spring, 1995): 7–28; see especially 12ff., where Bracken cites Thomas Aquinas, *Opera Omnia*, vol. 17 (New York: Musurgia, 1950), 342.

4. Philip Clayton, *Das Gottesproblem*, vol. 1: *Gott und Unendlichkeit in der neuzeitlichen Philosophie* (Paderborn: Ferdinand Schöningh, 1996), published in English as *The Problem of God in Modern Thought* (Grand Rapids, Mich.: Eerdmans, 2000).

5. See Baruch Spinoza, *Ethica: Ordine Geometrico Demonstrata*, E2 P21 Scholium.

6. See Friedrich Schleiermacher, *On Religion: Speeches to Its Cultured Despisers*, trans. Richard Crouter (Cambridge: Cambridge University Press, 1988), especially 103 and the surrounding argument: "All that is finite exists only through the determination of its limits, which must, as it were, be 'cut out' from the Infinite."

7. I have argued this in detail in chapter 10.

8. On "progressive" research programs, see Imre Lakatos, "The Methodology of Scientific Research Programs," in *The Methodology of Scientific Research Programs, Philosophical Papers*, vol. 1, ed. John Worrall and Gregory Currie (Cambridge: Cambridge University Press, 1978).

9. See Charles Taylor, *Sources of the Self: The Making of the Modern Identity* (Cambridge, Mass.: Harvard University Press, 1989).

10. For a book-length appeal to the biblical data, see C. John Collins, *The God of Miracles: An Exegetical Examination of God's Action in the World* (Wheaton, Ill.: Crossway, 2000).

11. Gottfried Wilhelm Leibniz, "Discourse on Metaphysics," par. 8, in *Discourse on Metaphysics and Other Essays,* ed. and trans. Daniel Garber and Roger Ariew Leibniz (Indianapolis: Hackett, 1991).

12. William James, "Does 'Consciousness' Exist?" in *Essays*, republished in *William James: Writings 1902–1910*, based on the Harvard edition of the Collected Works (New York: Penguin, 1987), 1141.

13. Augustine *Confessions* 11:28, 38.

14. *Friedrich Schleiermachers Dialektik*, ed. Rudolf Odebrecht (Darmstadt: Wissenschaftliche Buchgesellschaft, 1976); for a translation of the 1811 *Dialektik* see Terrence Tice, trans., *Dialectic, or the Art of Doing Philosophy* (Atlanta: Scholars, 1996).

15. See Philip Clayton, *The Problem of God in Modern Thought* (Grand Rapids, Mich.: Eerdmans, 2000), chapter 8.

16. Descartes *Principia* 1:51.

17. Clayton, *The Problem of God*, chapters 5, 7–9.

18. Wolfhart Pannenberg, "Fichte und die Metaphysik des Unendlichen. Dieter Henrich zum 65. Geburtstag," *Zeitschrift für philosophische Forschung* 46 (1992): 348–62.

19. I skip over a large number of subtleties and nuances that would have to be (and have been) added in a fuller treatment.

20. Many feminist theologians have argued that it has also led to a treatment of the environment as merely "instrumental," a mistake of which the consequences are palpable in the water and air and forests around us today.

21. See Joseph A. Bracken and Marjorie Hewitt Suchocki, eds., *Trinity in Process: A Relational Theology of God* (New York: Continuum, 1997).

22. See Sallie McFague, *Metaphorical Theology* (Philadelphia: Fortress Press, 1982); Janet Martin Soskice, *Metaphor and Religious Language* (Oxford: Clarendon; London: Oxford University Press, 1985).

23. I first developed the analogy in *God and Contemporary Science*, for example, 233–42, 257–62.

24. See Arthur Peacocke, *All That Is: A Naturalistic Faith for the Twenty-First Century*, ed. Philip Clayton (Minneapolis: Fortress Press, 2007); Peacocke, *Theology for a Scientific Age*.

25. See David Chalmers, "Facing Up to the Problem of Consciousness," first published in a special issue of the *Journal of Consciousness Studies* in 1995, and also available in Stuart Hameroff, Alfred Kaszniak, and Alwyn Scott, eds., *Toward a Science of Consciousness* (Cambridge, Mass.: MIT Press, 1996).

26. See Samuel Alexander, *Space, Time, and Deity*, the Gifford Lectures at Glasgow, 1916–1918, 2 vols. (London: Macmillan, 1920). Page citations are to the excellent anthology, *Philosophers Speak of God*, ed. Charles Hartshorne and William L. Reese (Amherst, N.Y.: Humanity, 2000).

27. Ibid., vol. 2, 366.

28. "A substance or piece of Space-Time which is mental is differentiated in a portion of its mental body so as to be divine, and this deity is sustained by all the Space-Time to which it belongs," ibid., 367.

29. Ibid., 367f.

30. Rabbi David Cooper, *God Is a Verb: Kabbalah and the Practice of Mystical Judaism* (New York: Riverhead, 1997).

31. I am grateful to Steven Knapp for a close reading and critique of this paper and for constructive discussions that influenced the formation and formulation of many of the ideas. Probing queries from Owen Thomas have improved the position.

➤ **Chapter 9: From Substance to Subject**

1. The strong and growing interest in "spirituality," even within the academy, should be mentioned as a third factor. But this is more a social factor than directly a philosophical one.

2. See Wentzel van Huyssteen, *Essays in Postfoundationalist Theology* (Grand Rapids, Mich.: Eerdmans, 1997).

3. And by no coincidence: Placher, like his teacher Hans Frei, remains deeply influenced by Barth in his work. See Hans W. Frei, *Theology and Narrative: Selected Essays*, eds. George Hunsinger and William C. Placher (New York: Oxford University Press, 1993).

4. According to the pre-modern notion of inertia, if motion were not added afresh at every moment all things would stop, hence God's action was *physically* necessary at every instant. We often forget that even Newton's physics in the *Principia* still required the existence of God in order to be applied to the world.

5. See Philip Clayton, *The Problem of God in Modern Thought* (Grand Rapids, Mich.: Eerdmans, 2000).

6. See Joseph F. Fletcher, *Situation Ethics: The New Morality* (Philadelphia: Westminster, 1996).

7. See Sallie McFague, *Metaphorical Theology: Models of God in Religious Language* (Philadelphia: Fortress Press, 1982).

8. William C. Placher, *The Domestication of Transcendence: How Modern Thinking about God Went Wrong* (Louisville, Ky.: Westminster John Knox, 1996).

9. Ibid., 7, my emphasis.

10. Ibid.

11. G. W. F. Hegel, *Phänomenologie des Geistes*, ed. J. Hoffmeister, PhB 114 (Hamburg: F. Meiner, 1952), 19f., my translation; compare with *The Phenomenology of Mind*, trans. J. B. Baillie (New York: Harper & Row, 1967), 80.

12. Herbert Marcuse, *Hegels Ontologie und die Grundlegung einer Theorie der Geschichtlichkeit* (Frankfurt: Klostermann, 1932), 120.

13. Clayton, *Das Gottesproblem* (Paderborn: Ferdinand Schöningh, 1996), chapter 7.

14. Gotthold Ephraim Lessing, *Die Erziehung des Menschengeschlechts* (1780) 73f.; in English see *The Education of the Human Race*, in Henry Chadwick, ed. and trans., *Lessing's Theological Writings* (London: Adam and Charles Black, 1956).

15. See K. Lachmann and Muncker, eds., *G. E. Lessings Sämtliche Schriften* (Leipzig, 1900), 15:610f.; quoted in Chadwick, *Lessing's Theological Writings*, 95; and Henry Allison, *Lessing and the Enlightenment: His Philosophy of Religion and Its Relation to Eighteenth-Century Thought* (Ann Arbor: University of Michigan Press, 1966), 158.

16. See Moritz Brasch, ed., *Moses Mendelssohns Schriften zur Metaphysik und Ethik sowie zur Religionsphilosophie*, 2 vols. (Leipzig: Leopold Voss, 1880), 1:412: "Ich Mensch, Gedanke der Gottheit, werde nie aufhören, ein Gedanke der Gottheit zu bleiben . . . so unterscheidet sich ferner diese Schule von unserm Systeme bloss in einer Subtilität, die niemals praktisch werden kann . . . ob Gott diesen Gedanken des besten Zusammenhanges zufälliger Dinge hat ausstrahlen, ausfliessen, ausströmen, oder mit welchem Bilde soll ich es vergleichen? (denn diese Subtilität lässt sich kaum anders, als durch Bilder beschreiben) ob er das Licht hat von sich wegblitzen, oder nur innerlich leuchten lassen? Ob es bloss Quelle geblieben, oder ob die Quelle sich in einen Strom ergossen habe? . . . im Grunde ist es Missdeutung derselben Metapher, die bald Gott zu bildlich in die Welt, bald die Welt zu bildlich in Gott versetzt."

17. In the interests of fairness I should admit that Spinoza sometimes came closer, for example, in the notion of an active principle or *natura naturans* (nature "naturing"), which he contrasted with *natura naturata* or nature "natured." But arguably it was not until Kant that a thinker really did full justice to the active moment in subjectivity.

18. Note, however, that this is for Kant a purely formal principle. It's not a theory of the empirical self or personhood in the sense that a social scientist might use these terms. There is an important line from Kant's theory of consciousness to the empirical social sciences (via neo-Kantianism and early German psychologists such as W. Wundt), but we will not have space to follow it here.

19. Walter Kasper, *Das Absolute in der Geschichte. Philosophie und Theologie der Geschichte in der Spätphilosophie Schellings* (Mainz: Matthias-Grünewald-Verlag, 1965), 53, quoting from *Friedrich Wilhelm Joseph von Schellings sämmtliche Werke*, 14 vols. in two divisions, ed. K. F. A. Schelling (Stuttgart and Augsburg: J. G. Cotta'scher, 1856–1861), especially 4:240, 4:325, 4:247 (emphasis added).

20. Schelling, *Sämmtliche Werke*, 8:306.

21. G. W. F. Hegel, *The Phenomenology of Mind*, trans. Baillie, 415.

22. Peter F. Strawson, *Individuals* (Garden City, N.Y.: Doubleday, 1963).

23. See Thomas Nagel, "What It's Like to Be a Bat," in *Readings in the Philosophy of Psychology,* ed. Ned Block (Cambridge, Mass.: MIT Press, 1981), vol. 1. Among the important analytic treatments of the person—to mention just a few of the major titles—see Bernard Williams, *Problems of the Self* (Cambridge: Cambridge University Press, 1973); Sidney Shoemaker, *Self-Knowledge and Self-Identity* (Ithaca, N.Y.: Cornell, 1963); Derek Parfit, *Reasons and Persons* (New York: Oxford University Press, 1984); John Perry, *The Problem of the Essential Indexical and Other Essays* (New York: Oxford University Press, 1993); Amelie Rorty, ed., *The Identities of Persons* (Berkeley: University of California Press, 1979); Harold Noonan, *Personal Identity* (New York: Routledge, 1989); Peter Unger, *Identity, Consciousness and Value* (New York: Oxford University Press, 1990); and Carol Rovane, *The Bounds of Agency: An Essay in Revisionary Metaphysics* (Princeton: Princeton University Press, 1998).

24. Including the fact that most, if not all, of these thinkers were deeply concerned about the nature of the divine subject and that their own reflections on subjectivity emerged in many cases out of reflection on the nature of God's creative activity.

25. All the references that follow are to the pagination of the 1799 edition. See Friedrich Schleiermacher, *Über die Religion. Reden an die Gegildeten unter ihren Verächtern*, ed. Otto Braun, Philosophische Bibliothek vol. 139b (Leipzig: F. Meiner, 1911); or the version edited (and copiously annotated) by Rudolf Otto, 6th. ed. (Göttingen: Vandenhoeck & Ruprecht, 1967), both of which contain page references to the first edition of the *Speeches.*

26. "Alles Endliche besteht nur durch die Bestimmung seiner Grenzen, die aus dem Unendlichen gleichsam herausgeschnitten werden müssen. Nur so kann es innerhalb dieser Grenzen selbst unendlich sein und eigen gebildet werden" (53). Wolfhart Pannenberg first drew my attention to the centrality of this passage.

27. "Nichts Einzelnes (kann) gesondert werden, als indem es willkürlich abgeschnitten wird in Zeit und Raum" (127).

28. Langdon Gilkey, *Naming the Whirlwind: The Renewal of God-Language* (Indianapolis: Bobbs-Merrill, 1969); Langdon Gilkey, *Reaping the Whirlwind: A Christian Interpretation of History* (New York: Seabury, 1976).

29. See Philip Clayton, "Neuroscience, the Person, and God," in *Neuroscience, Personhood and Divine Action,* ed. Robert Russell, Nancey Murphy, and Michael Arbib (Rome: Vatican Observatory, 1999). There is also good reason to think that psychophysical unity has strong exegetical support. The literature is immense; for one treatment that pays attention to the biblical texts as well as to scientific evidence, see Nancey Murphy et al., *Whatever Happened to the Soul?: Scientific and Theological Portraits of Human Nature* (Minneapolis: Fortress Press, 1998).

30. Ian Barbour defines an emergent level of reality as "a unit which is relatively integrated, stable, and self-regulating, even though it interacts with other units at the same level and at higher and lower levels" (draft of Vatican paper, 19).

31. See Henry P. Stapp, *Mind, Matter, and Quantum Mechanics* (Berlin: Springer, 1993).

32. I treat the voluntariness of creation in more detail in chapters 7 and 11.

33. For more detail, see Philip Clayton, *God and Contemporary Science* (Edinburgh: Edinburgh University Press; Grand Rapids, Mich.: Eerdmans, 1998).

34. This is a controversial thesis among philosophers of mind and would need extensive defense. I have argued it in more detail in *God and Contemporary Science*, chapter 8.

35. In his criticisms, John Polkinghorne has taken the analogy in a much too literalistic fashion, complaining that the universe does not reflect the sorts of physical structures that human bodies manifest.

36. Another entrée for theological reflection is belief in the givenness of direct divine revelation. Although I do not follow that path here, I do not dismiss it either.

37. Especially helpful is Wolfhart Pannenberg, *Metaphysics and the Idea of God* (Grand Rapids, Mich.: Eerdmans, 1990).

38. I am here influenced by Nicholas of Cusa's classic treatment of the not-other, *De non aliud.*

39. See Emmanuel Levinas, *The Levinas Reader,* ed. Sean Hand (Oxford: Blackwell, 1989), 128, 174. Note that "incarnated" is not a term that Levinas uses.

40. Ibid., 176.

41. See Louis Dupré, *Passage to Modernity: An Essay in the Hermeneutics of Nature and Culture* (New Haven: Yale University Press, 1993).

42. One sees this direction especially clearly in Yirmiahu Yovel's important *The Adventures of Immanence*, vol. 2 of Yovel, *Spinoza and Other Heretics*, 2 vols. (Princeton: Princeton University Press, 1989). The book chronicles the influence of Spinoza's immanence-based pantheism over the subsequent centuries. Yovel argues that, as the metaphysical side of Spinozism began to wane, the purely immanent understanding of the world came to replace any transcendence-based metaphysic. Thus in his tale the true inheritors of the Spinozistic tradition—and thus the post-philosophers who have replaced the metaphysics of old—are Marx, Nietzsche, Freud, and Richard Rorty!

43. Note that this point is not about retaining the language of transcendence but about distinguishing the transcendent and immanent dimensions of spirit in actual practice.

44. I am indebted to Van Harvey's important book on Feuerbach: Van Harvey, *Feuerbach and the Interpretation of Religion* (Cambridge: Cambridge University Press, 1995).

45. Jürgen Moltmann and Elisabeth Moltmann-Wendel, *Humanity in God* (Cleveland, Ohio: Pilgrim, 1983), 91.

46. See my notion of the "secular believer" in Clayton, *Explanation from Physics to Theology: An Essay in Rationality and Religion* (New Haven: Yale University Press, 1989), chapter 5.

47. See especially Wolfhart Pannenberg, *Anthropology in Theological Perspective*, trans. Matthew J. O'Connell (Philadelphia: Westminster, 1985).

48. These comments presuppose some reflections on "process trinitarianism" which I have pursued elsewhere; see chapters 10 and 12. I will argue that the One God is both single and undivided (monism), Ground to the world as Consequent (dualism), and active Subject who interacts with the world as Other and gives rise to a unity which relies on both (idealistic trinitarianism, or self-conscious synthesis).

49. See the previous note.

50. Similarly, Jean-Luc Marion is right to insist on a theology of ethics and of sacramental encounter in *God Without Being*, trans. Thomas A. Carlson (Chicago: University of Chicago Press, 1991).

➤ Chapter 10: The Becoming of the One Who Always Was

1. Alfred North Whitehead, *Process and Reality*, revised ed., David Ray Griffin and Donald W. Sherburne, eds. (New York: Macmillan, 1979), 15f. Subsequent references will be made to *PR*.

2. So Joseph M. Hallman, "How Is Process Theology Theological?" *Process Studies* 17/2 (1988): 112–17, following Edward Farley, *Ecclesial Man: A Social Phenomenology of Faith and Reality* (Philadelphia: Fortress Press, 1975). Hallman speaks of the "principle of positivity": "Tracy suggests . . . that we distinguish between philosophical theology, with its universal concerns, and systematics, which is hermeneutical and particular. Farley's answer is itself philosophical: one begins reflection with the particular, trying to capture the unique features of that to which one attends." More convincing is Hallman's attempt to do justice to both the provincial and the "generic" or general features of religion. In this sense he quotes Farley, "[In provincial hermeneutics,] the essential features and 'truth' of the historical faith are identified with one of its specific historical expressions" (58).

3. See Lewis Ford, "When Did Whitehead Conceive God to Be Personal?" *Anglican Theological Review* 72/3 (1990): 280–91.

4. I do not here argue for the truth of Christian revelation claims (though I do hold such arguments to be important). Our goal instead is to establish the relationship between what Christians claim and the conclusions of the best metaphysical reflection on the nature of God.

5. The debate about Whitehead's Christianity is nicely summarized in Victor Lowe, "A. N. W.: A Biographical Perspective," *Process Studies* 12/3 (1982): 137–47; and Paul G. Kuntz, "Can Whitehead Be Made a Christian Philosopher?" *Process Studies* 12/4 (1982): 232–42, especially the biographical note 6.

6. Nelson Goodman, *Ways of Worldmaking* (Indianapolis: Hackett, 1978).

7. See the works by Sallie McFague: *Metaphorical Theology: Models of God in Religious Language* (Philadelphia: Fortress Press, 1982); and *Models of God: Theology for an Ecological, Nuclear Age* (Philadelphia: Fortress Press, 1987). See also Philip Clayton, *The Problem of God in Modern Thought* (Grand Rapids, Mich.: Eerdmans, 2000), chapter 1.

8. Robert C. Neville, *Creativity and God: A Challenge to Process Theology* (New York: Seabury, 1980), 146.

9. Though the full case can't be made here, I suggest that surveying the work of contemporary thinkers who have been significantly influenced by Whitehead would show that there is scarcely a key premise of his thought that hasn't been modified or rejected. This move beyond Whiteheadian orthodoxy is what has made the project of a (neo-)process trinitarianism viable and exciting today; it will be presupposed in what follows.

10. This is one of the points of similarity with Aristotle that Rorty emphasizes in his article "Event and Form," in *Explorations in Whitehead's Philosophy*, ed. Lewis Ford and George L. Kline (New York: Fordham University Press, 1983).

11. Joseph A. Bracken, S. J., "Process Philosophy and Trinitarian Theology," *Process Studies* 8/4 (1978): 217–30, quoted from 220. Bracken adds, ". . . so that the whole exercises an agency which transcends the specific interaction of individual parts with one another."

12. David H. Jones, "Emergent Properties, Persons, and the Mind-Body Problem," *Southern Journal of Philosophy* 10 (1972): 423–433; Charles A. Krecz, "Reduction and the Part/Whole Relation," *Philosophy of Science* (1988): 71–87; Gerhard Roth, "Self-Organization, Emergent Properties and the Unity of the World," *Philosophica* (1990): 45–64; Eileen Barker, "Apes and Angels: Reductionism, Selection, and Emergence in the Study of Man (Some Recent Books)," *Inquiry* 19 (1976): 367–87; Roger Wolcott Sperry, *Science and Moral Priority: Merging Mind, Brain, and Human Values* (New York: Columbia University Press, 1983); Mario Augusto Bunge, *The Mind-Body Problem: A Psychobiological Approach* (Oxford: Pergamon, 1980); Bunge, *Scientific Materialism* (Dordrecht: D. Reidel, 1981).

13. Robert C. Neville, *A Theology Primer* (Albany: State University of New York Press, 1991), chapter 3.

14. Lewis Ford, "In What Sense Is God Infinite? A Process Perspective," *Thomist* 42 (1978): 1–13; "The Infinite God of Process Theism," *Proceedings of the American Catholic Philosophical Association* 55 (1981): 84–90. Ford himself eventually settled for the position that God could be infinite only if *fully* future.

15. Roman-numeral references are to C. Adam and P. Tannery, eds., *Oeuvres de Descartes*, 12 vols., revised edition (Paris: Vrin/CNRS, 1964-76). The English translation (*The Philosophical Writings of Descartes*, 3 vols., trans. John Cottingham, Robert Stoothoff, and Dugald Murdoch [Cambridge: Cambridge University Press, 1985ff.]) includes marginal references to the *Oeuvres*.

16. Arguably, this is the central project or goal of Wolfhart Pannenberg, *Anthropology in Theological Perspective*, trans. Matthew J. O'Connell (Philadelphia: Westminster, 1985). Such a project might appeal to our experience of (apparently) unlimited size or power or duration, such as the size of the universe or its possibly unlimited duration; to the experience of the sublime (as analyzed in Kant's *Critique of Judgment*); to the physical mathematical realms of the infinitely large and infinitely small and the infinite infinities of Cantorian set theory; and to philosophical concepts such as the infinite or Absolute.

17. Descartes also grasped this limitation: "My point is that, on the contrary, if I can grasp something, it would be a total contradiction for that which I grasp to be infinite. For the idea of the infinite, if it is to be a true idea, cannot be grasped at all, since the impossibility of being grasped is contained in the formal definition of the infinite" (5th Resp., VII, 368).

18. Here Marion is right: "Si l'infini doit se percevoir par idée, ce sera non par l'impossible représentation d'un objet, mais par la présence de l'infini même manifeste par le jeu contrasté de l'ego avec Dieu." See Jean-Luc Marion, *Sur la théologie blanche de Descartes. Analogie, création des vérités éternelles et fondement* (Paris: Presses Universitaires de France, 1981), 404. Marion adds elsewhere that "noncomprehension does not signify nonawareness": "one can (and must) know God as infinite without the clarity of a methodical object" ("The Essential Incoherence of Descartes' Definition of Divinity," in *Essays on Descartes' Meditations*, ed. Amélie Rorty [Berkeley: University of California Press, 1986], 297–338, quote 335, n. 56). On the same subject, see also his *Sur le prisme métaphysique de Descartes. Constitution et limites de l'onto-théo-logie dans la pensée cartésienne* (Paris: Presses Universitaires de France, 1986), chapter 4.

19. Descartes already realized this point with particular clarity: "I see manifestly that there is more reality in infinite substance than in finite substance, and yet that I have in some way in me a notion of the infinite that is prior to my notion of the finite—that is, the notion of God is prior to the notion of myself. For how would it be possible that I can know that I doubt and that I desire—that is, that I lack something and that I am not perfect—unless I had in me an idea of a being more perfect than me, by comparison to which I might know the defects of my own nature" (Descartes, Meditation 3, French ed., IX, 36).

20. I develop this idea in detail in *The Problem of God,* chapter 5.

21. John Cobb Jr., "Response to Neville," *Process Studies* 10/4 (1980): 98.

22. Ibid.

23. This was also the response of John Cobb Jr., *A Christian Natural Theology* (Philadelphia: Westminster, 1965).

24. Gregory Boyd, *Trinity and Process: A Critical Evaluation and Reconstruction of Hartshorne's Di-Polar Theism towards a Trinitarian Metaphysics* (New York: Peter Lang, 1992), 402.

25. On the first notion see Lewis Ford, "Temporality and Transcendence," in *Hartshorne, Process Philosophy, and Theology,* ed. Robert Kane and Stephen H. Phillips (Albany: State University of New York Press, 1989), 151–67. On the latter notion, in addition to Lewis Ford, *The Lure of God: A Biblical Background for Process Theism* (Philadelphia: Fortress Press, 1978), see especially Lewis Ford, "The Divine Activity of the Future," *Process Studies* 11 (1981): 169–79; and Lewis Ford, "Creativity in a Future Key," in *New Essays in Metaphysics,* ed. Robert C. Neville (Albany: State University of New York Press, 1987), 179–98.

26. Joseph A. Bracken, *The Triune Symbol: Persons, Process and Community* (Lanham, Md.: University Press of America, 1985). More recently, see Bracken, *The Divine Matrix: Creativity as Link between East and West* (Maryknoll, N.Y.: Orbis, 1995). See also Bracken, "Process Philosophy and Trinitarian Theology," Parts I and II, *Process Studies* 8/4 (1978): 217–30 and *Process Studies* 11/2 (1981): 83–96; and Bracken, "Energy-Events and Fields," *Process Studies* 18/3 (1989): 153–65.

27. Joseph Bracken, *Society and Spirit: A Trinitarian Cosmology* (London and Toronto: Associated University Presses, 1991), 129.

28. Ibid., 123.

29. Philip Clayton, *The Problem of God in Modern Thought* (Grand Rapids: Eerdmans, 2000), especially chapters 7–9.

30. See Antoon Braeckman, "Whitehead and German Idealism: A Poetic Heritage," *Process Studies* 14/4 (1985): 265–86. The following citations are taken from 278ff. There are certainly other important parallels, such as those between Schelling's "potencies" in *Ages of the World* and Whitehead's primordial envisagement, and the stress on the movement from potential to actual. Incidentally, I do not agree with Braeckman's reading of Schelling in exclusively Kantian (transcendental) terms. His interpretation runs into some difficulties already with objective idealism; it is untenable after the Bruno dialogue of 1803 and certainly by the time of the 1809 essay, *On Human Freedom.*

31. Braeckman, ibid., 279.

32. See, for example, chapter 4, "Subjective Spirit: The Power of Radical Self-Determination," in Bracken, *Society and Spirit.*

33. Bracken, *Society and Spirit,* 129. Bracken is perhaps the only process thinker who has been able to appropriate the insights of Schelling. See also his discussion and use of the anthropological suggestions of Wolfhart Pannenberg on 101ff. Chapter 5 attempts to mediate between Hegel and Whitehead.

34. According to Schelling, God was always the (potentially) self-manifesting God, and hence the Creator God, even though there was a phase (metaphorically, a time) when God was not manifest in anything outside of Godself. The advantage of this framework is that it allows us to say that the questions of how divinity can be (in itself) and how it can become manifest are two ways of formulating the same question (see 8:255f.). Nonetheless, there remains a real difference (probably stronger than Aristotle's metaphysics grants) between the not-yet-manifest and the now-manifest, between the "time" before and after there was a world. There may be a natural movement to the next potency, as Schelling thinks (8:275), and nature may (indeed, must) be spoken of as a potentiality vis-à-vis the godhead (8:280f.) which may (but not must!) develop eventually to something godlike; but God is only *actually* conscious, and thus actually the being whom he has become, when the actual process of creation and its subsequent development have taken place (see 8:262).

Unless otherwise indicated, citations refer to *Friedrich Wilhelm Joseph von Schellings sämmtliche Werke,* 14 vols. in two divisions, ed. K. F. A. Schelling (Stuttgart and Augsburg: Cotta'scher, 1856-1861). I indicate the four volumes of the second division as vols. 11–14, respectively. Page references to English translations are not given, since they invariably include marginal numbers keyed to the German critical edition. Major English translations of Schelling include (from vol. 7) *Schelling: Of Human Freedom,* trans. James Gutmann (Chicago: Open Court, 1936); and (from vol. 8) *The Ages of the World,* trans. Frederick de Wolfe Bolman Jr. (New York: AMS, 1942, 1967).

35. So Nathaniel Lawrence, "The Vision of Beauty and the Temporality of Deity in Whitehead's Philosophy," *Journal of Philosophy* 58 (1961): 543–53, reprinted in George L. Kline, ed., *Alfred North Whitehead: Essays on His Philosophy* (Englewood Cliffs, N.J.: Prentice-Hall, 1963), 168–78.

36. See A. N. Whitehead, *Religion in the Making* (Cambridge: Cambridge University Press, 1930), 78, 80; *Science and the Modern World* (Cambridge: Cambridge University Press, 1926), 221f.; *Process and Reality: An Essay in Cosmology,* revised edition (New York: Free Press, [1929], 1978), 345.

37. See Ivor Leclerc's excellent survey article, "The Problem of God in Whitehead's System," *Process Studies* 14/4 (1985): 301–15.

38. It might be thought that a ground is something that could not *be* creative. But the association of *esse* and creativity has been basic to process metaphysics and has been carefully defended. See Ford, "Creativity in a Future Key"; and David L. Schindler, "Whitehead's Inability to Affirm a Universe of Value," *Process Studies* 13/2 (1984): 117ff.

39. The tendency goes back, of course, to Whitehead. Lewis Ford makes the same move in his famous Trinity chapter in *The Lure of God,* for example, 106f. Among many others, see also Joseph M. Hallman, "The Mistake of Thomas Aquinas and the Trinity of A. N. Whitehead," *Journal of Religion* 70 (1990): 36–47.

40. This tension has been brilliantly worked out in the thought of Werner Beierwaltes. See, for example, Werner Beierwaltes, *Denken des Einen. Studien zur neuplatonischen Philosophie und ihrer Wirkungsgeschichte* (Frankfurt: Klostermann, 1985); and *Platonismus und Idealismus* (Frankfurt: Vittorio Klostermann, 1972).

41. See Ford in Kane and Phillips, *Hartshorne, Process Philosophy, and Theology,* 158, 162f., 171f.

42. Marjorie H. Suchocki, *The End of Evil: Process Eschatology in Historical Context* (Albany: State University of New York Press, 1988), 102. More recently, see Marjorie H. Suchocki, *The Fall to Violence: Original Sin in Relational Theology* (New York: Continuum, 1994).

43. This is also the view of Wolfhart Pannenberg, who identifies it as an orthodox Christian position; see Wolfhart Pannenberg, *Systematic Theology*, vol. 1, trans Geoffrey W. Bromiley (Grand Rapids, Mich.: Eerdmans, 1988).

44. This was also Schelling's conclusion when he shifted in his final phase to a "positive Philosophie." See his *Philosophie der Mythodologie* (vol. 12) and *Philosophie der Offenbarung* (vols. 13–14); and Edward Allen Beach, *The Potencies of God(s): Schelling's Philosophy of Mythology* (Albany: State University of New York Press, 1994).

45. It strikes me as highly unlikely that we would be able to show this. Richard Swinburne has made the attempt on various occasions; most recently, see Richard Swinburne, *The Christian God* (New York: Oxford University Press, 1994).

46. Pannenberg, *Systematic Theology*; Pannenberg, *Grundfragen systematischer Theologie. Gesammelte Aufsätze*, vol 2 (Göttingen: Vandenhoeck & Ruprecht, 1989); Jürgen Moltmann, *History and the Triune God: Contributions to Trinitarian Theology*, trans. John Bowden (New York: Crossroad, 1992); Moltmann, *The Trinity and the Kingdom of God: The Doctrine of God*, trans. Margaret Kohl (London: SCM, 1981); Eberhard Jüngel, *God as the Mystery of the World: On the Foundation of the Theology of the Crucified One in the Dispute between Theism and Atheism*, trans. Darrell L. Guder. (Grand Rapids, Mich.: Eerdmans, 1983).

47. For the details of this theory I follow Joseph Bracken; see especially Joseph Bracken, *Society and Spirit*. See also *The Triune Symbol*; *The Divine Matrix*; "Process Philosophy and Trinitarian Theology," Parts I and II; and "Energy-Events and Fields."

➤ Chapter 11: "Open Panentheism" and Creation as *Kenosis*

1. I do not here give an exposition of these schools and presuppose some familiarity with them on the part of readers. "Open theism" is often traced back to Richard Rice, *The Openness of God: The Relationship between Divine Foreknowledge and Human Free Will* (Minneapolis: Bethany, 1985). Other works to consult include Gregory Boyd, *God of the Possible* (Grand Rapids, Mich.: Baker, 2000); John Sanders, *The God Who Risks* (Downers Grove, Ill.: InterVarsity, 1998); and David Basinger, *The Case for Freewill Theism* (Downers Grove, Ill.: InterVarsity, 1996). I consider Clark Pinnock, *The Openness of God: A Biblical Challenge to the Traditional Understanding of God* (Downers Grove, Ill.: InterVarsity, 1994) to be a particularly significant statement of this view.

2. For examples of a closer dialogue between process and open theisms, see Bryan P. Stone and Thomas J. Oord, eds., *The Nature and Thy Name is Love: Wesleyan and Process Theologies in Dialogue* (Nashville: Kingswood, 2001); and John B. Cobb Jr. and Clark H. Pinnock, eds., *Searching for an Adequate God: A Dialogue between Process and Free Will Theists* (Grand Rapids, Mich.: Eerdmans, 2000).

3. Alfred North Whitehead, *Process and Reality*, corrected edition, David Ray Griffin and Donald Sherburne, eds. (New York: Macmillan, 1978), 91f., 96–98, 197–99, 205f., and so forth. Subsequent references will be made to *PR*.

4. I borrow the term from Wesley Wildman but modify its meaning. Wildman uses the term "ground-of-being cosmologies" for the view that this Ground is neither personal nor impersonal but stands above that distinction; for him the Ground is both personal or impersonal, or neither (depending on how one interprets apophatic language). A similar view is expressed in John Hick, *An Interpretation of Religion* (New Haven: Yale University Press, 1989). I use the term as neutral on the question of whether this ground of being can be both personal and impersonal at the same time.

5. Arthur Peacocke, *Paths From Science towards God: The End of All Our Exploring* (Oxford: Oneworld, 2001), 42. More recently see Arthur Peacocke, *All That Is: A Naturalistic Faith for the Twenty-First Century*, ed. Philip Clayton (Minneapolis: Fortress Press, 2007).

6. If one admits deism as a form of (extended) theism, then this requirement is not essential for theism.

7. It should be noted that St. Thomas elsewhere affirms that God knows created beings directly as individuals, whereas human agents can know others only by abstracting from the universal form (*Summa Theologiae*, I, 86, a.1). This particular claim notwithstanding, a full comparison between Thomas and Duns Scotus shows the degree to which Thomas's thought is dominated by the framework of timeless universals, for example, by the claim that all human beings *qua* human share the

same essence. Human uniqueness or "thisness"—what Scotus would later call *haecceitas*—remains underdeveloped in Thomas's thought.

8. See, for example, Alex Vilenkin, *Many Worlds in One: The Search for Other Universes* (New York: Hill and Wang, 2006).

9. See Lee Smolin, *The Life of the Cosmos* (New York: Oxford University Press, 1997). On string theory see Brian Greene, *The Elegant Universe: Superstrings, Hidden Dimensions, and the Quest for the Ultimate Theory* (New York: Norton, 1999).

10. This argument is developed in greater detail in Philip Clayton and Steven Knapp, "Divine Action and the 'Argument from Neglect,'" in *Physics and Cosmology: Scientific Perspectives on the Problem of Natural Evil*, eds. Robert J. Russell and Nancey Murphy (Notre Dame: Notre Dame University Press, 2007). Also see chapter 17 in this volume.

11. David Ray Griffin, *God, Power, and Evil: A Process Theodicy* (Lanham, Md.: University Press of America, 1991).

12. Clayton and Knapp, "Divine Action and the 'Argument from Neglect,'" 179–94.

13. See especially Joseph Bracken, *Society and Spirit: A Trinitarian Cosmology* (London and Toronto: Associated University Presses, 1991); Bracken, *The Triune Symbol: Persons, Process and Community* (Lanham Md.: University Press of America, 1985); Bracken, *The Divine Matrix: Creativity as Link between East and West* (Maryknoll, N.Y.: Orbis, 1995); Bracken, *The One in the Many: A Contemporary Reconstruction of the God-World Relationship* (Grand Rapids, Mich.: Eerdmans, 2001); and Bracken, "Process Philosophy and Trinitarian Theology," Parts I and II, *Process Studies* 8/4 (1978): 217–30 and 11/2 (1981): 83–96; and Bracken, "Energy-Events and Fields," *Process Studies* 18/3 (1989): 153–65.

14. See, for example, Alexei V. Nesteruk, *Light from the East: Theology, Science, and the Eastern Orthodox Tradition* (Minneapolis: Fortress Press, 2003); Basarab Nicolescu and Magda Stavinschi, eds., *Science and Orthodoxy: A Necessary Dialogue* (Bucharest: Curtea Veche, 2006); and "Part III, Eastern Orthodox Perspectives on the God-World Relation," in *In Whom We Live and Move and Have Our Being: Panentheistic Reflections on God's Presence in a Scientific World*, ed. Philip Clayton and Arthur Peacocke (Grand Rapids, Mich.: Eerdmans, 2004).

15. See Marjorie Hewitt Suchocki, *God, Christ, Church: A Practical Guide to Process Theology* (New York: Crossroad, 1989), chapter 3; Lewis Ford, *The Lure of God: A Biblical Background for Process Theism* (Philadelphia: Fortress Press, 1978).

16. There are a number of responses to the process objection that *don't* work. First, one might argue that the period of time before creation doesn't really count, since time becomes meaningful only when a world of creatures exists. Hence the fact that there wasn't always a world doesn't count against the nature of God as loving and as relational. This was (roughly) Augustine's response. When one reflects on it, however, one realizes that it represents a somewhat strange answer. It implicitly admits that all doctrines of creation *ex nihilo* will acknowledge two separate stages: first, a stage in the life of God before God was related to a world, and then another stage after creation. Yet, it maintains, the first does not present a problem because it really shouldn't be understood as a *time* (a temporal stage) at all. But as long as it is possible to distinguish *conceptually* between the two stages, the objection remains unanswered.

Second, one might argue that, before the creation of the world, God existed only as potentiality. God only became an actuality subsequent to the act of creation. But, I fear, this response is not adequate to answer the process criticism. For on this view God only really exists—only exists as actual—when God is related to the world, which is exactly the option that process thinkers advocate. Also, one wonders, how can God be responsible for the act of creation, and how can creation be a free and good act of God, if God does not yet exist as an agent to do the creating?

Finally, the traditional theist could maintain that it doesn't really matter at all whether a world of finite things actually exists. All that's necessary is that this drive toward love-manifested-in-relation was eternally expressed in the inner-trinitarian relations. As long as they exist, the divine love has been manifested. But I also doubt whether this answer is sufficient. There's something about *love actually expressed* that is hard to replace. Certainly this is a New Testament theme: "Greater love hath no one than this, that one lay down his life for his [or her] friends" (John 15:13), and "We know love by this, that he laid down his life for us" (1 John 3:16).

17. John D. Zizioulas, *Being as Communion: Studies in Personhood and the Church* (Crestwood, N.Y.: St. Vladimir's Seminary Press, 1985).

18. I draw here from Joseph Bracken, "*Creatio ex Nihilo*: A Field-Oriented Approach," *Dialog* 44 (2005): 246–49. Unless otherwise noted, references labeled "Bracken" are to this article.

19. Bracken, 248f.

20. I do not by contrast assert unlimited omnipotence or believe that God's omniscience extends to the future free decisions of creatures.

21. Thus Bracken writes, "So the issue for me is not so much the contrast between finite and infinite as the dynamic of independence/interdependence among the centers of activity within the field" (personal communication).

22. On creation as kenosis see, for example, John Polkinghorne, ed., *The Work of Love: Creation as Kenosis* (Grand Rapids, Mich.: Eerdmans, 2001); and D. Lyle Dabney, *Die Kenosis des Geistes: Kontinuität zwischen Schöpfung und Erlösung im Werk des Heiligen Geistes* (Neukirchen-Vluyn: Neukirchener, 1997). Jürgen Moltmann, who also advocates a kenotic understanding of creation, traces the twentieth-century roots of this concept back as far as Emil Brunner. The Jewish sources he finds in the Kabbalistic notion of *zimzum*; see Jürgen Moltmann, *God in Creation: A New Theology of Creation and the Spirit of God* (Minneapolis: Fortress Press, 1993).

23. Philip Clayton, "Kenotic Trinitarian Panentheism," *Dialog* 44 (2005): 250–55. The present argument is a revision and expansion of my earlier exploration of this topic.

24. Michael Lodahl, "From God to Creation: Pursuing the Trinitarian Reflections of Gregory of Nyssa as a Critique of *Creatio ex Nihilo*," paper presented to the American Academy of Religion, 2004 Annual Meeting, MS 4.

25. Philip Hefner, *The Human Factor: Evolution, Culture, and Religion* (Minneapolis: Fortress Press, 1993).

26. David R. Larson, "Necessarily, Essentially, Neither or Both: How Does God Love the Universe?", paper presented to the American Academy of Religion, 2004 Annual Meeting, MS 4.

27. Catherine Keller, *The Face of the Deep: A Theology of Becoming* (London: Routledge, 2003). The Hebrew term translated as "deep," *tehom*, also means "ocean" and "chaos." Keller's book offers a rich phenomenology of *tehom* and underscores the significance of this biblical term for an understanding of creation and of human freedom before God.

28. Joseph Bracken, S. J., and Marjorie Hewitt Suchocki, eds., *Trinity in Process: A Relational Theology of God* (New York: Continuum, 1997). Also see chapter 10 in this volume.

➤ Chapter 12: Natural Law and the Problem of Divine Action

1. Philip Clayton, *God and Contemporary Science* (Edinburgh: Edinburgh University Press, and Grand Rapids, Mich.: Eerdmans, 1997).

2. William James, *The Will to Believe and Other Essays in Popular Philosophy* (New York: Dover, 1956), 150.

3. Carolyn Brighouse, "Determinism and Modality," *British Journal for the Philosophy of Science* 48 (1997): 465–81.

4. Quoted in Henry Margenau, *Scientific Indeterminism and Human Freedom* (Latrobe, Pa.: Archabby, 1968), 3. In popular writings it is sometimes assumed that scientists, who are *not* omniscient, will be able to predict the future if determinism is true. But chaos theory now suggests that prediction will be impossible even in fully deterministic systems when they are "chaotic."

5. Arthur Peacocke, "Science and the Future of Theology: Critical Issues," *Zygon* 35 (2000): 35.

6. This position is developed in an important series of books under the general editorship of Robert J. Russell, stemming from a decade and a half of meetings and debates between scientists and theologians at the Vatican Observatory. See in particular *Physics, Philosophy and Theology: A Common Quest for Understanding* (Vatican City State and Notre Dame: Vatican Observatory/University of Notre Dame Press, 1988); *Quantum Cosmology and the Laws of Nature: Scientific Perspectives on Divine Action* (Berkeley and Vatican City State: CTNS & Vatican Observatory/UNP, 1993); and especially *Chaos and Complexity: Scientific Perspectives on Divine Action* (Berkeley Vatican City State: CTNS & Vatican Observatory/UNP, 1995). See the summary in Robert J. Russell, "Quantum Physics and the Theology of Non-Interventionist Objective Divine Action," in *The Oxford*

Handbook of Religion and Science, ed. Philip Clayton (Oxford: Oxford University Press, 2006), 579–95. For critical debate, see Ted Peters and Nathan Hallanger, eds., *God's Action in Nature's World: Essays in Honor of Robert John Russell* (Aldershot: Ashgate, 2006).

7. Richard Taylor, *Action and Purpose* (Atlantic Highlands, N.J.: Humanities, 1973).

8. Austin Farrer, *Finite and Infinite,* 2nd ed. (London: Dacre, 1959).

9. Aristotle, *Physica* 256a, 1984, 1:427; compare with Timothy O'Connor, *Agents, Causes, and Events: Essays on Indeterminism and Free Will* (New York: Oxford University Press, 1995).

10. I examine the literature in detail in *In Quest of Freedom: The Emergence of Spirit in the Natural World* (Göttingen: Vandenhoeck & Ruprecht, 2008). Indeterminists, of course, deny this claim, arguing instead for "genuine" or counter-factual freedom: you did this action now, but you might have done something different even in identical circumstances. As Jean-Paul Sartre (*Being and Nothingness,* trans. Hazel E. Barnes [New York: Citadel, 1956]) puts it in a classic phrase, "the indispensable and fundamental condition of all action is the freedom of the acting being."

11. Harold Morowitz, *The Emergence of Everything: How the World Became Complex* (Oxford: Oxford University Press, 2002).

12. Thomas Aquinas, *Summa Theologiae* q.44, a.1–4.

13. Wolfhart Pannenberg, *Theology and the Kingdom of God* (Philadelphia: Westminster, 1969).

14. See Philip Clayton, "The God of History and the Presence of the Future," *The Journal of Religion* 65 (1985): 98–108; Philip Clayton, "Being and One Theologian," *The Thomist* 50 (1988): 645–71.

15. Lewis Ford, *The Lure of God: A Biblical Background for Process Theism* (Philadelphia: Fortress Press, 1978).

16. Farrer, *Finite and Infinite.*

17. David Burrell, "Divine Practical Knowing: How an Eternal God Acts in Time," in *Divine Action: Studies Inspired by the Philosophical Theology of Austin Farrer,* eds. Brian Hebblethwaite and Edward Henderson (Edinburgh: T. & T. Clark, 1990); Burrell, *Knowing the Unknowable God* (Notre Dame: University of Notre Dame Press, 1986).

18. Thus my critique of Pannenberg's future ontology as "counterintuitive" (Philip Clayton, "Anticipation and Theological Method" in *The Theology of Wolfhart Pannenberg: Twelve American Critiques,* eds. Carl Braaten and Philip Clayton [Minneapolis: Augsburg, 1988]) must be taken as overly hasty.

19. Werner Heisenberg, *Physics and Philosophy: The Revolution in Modern Science* (New York: Harper & Row, 1962).

20. Quoted in P. C. W. Davies, *Other Worlds: A Portrait of Nature in Rebellion, Space, Superspace, and the Quantum Universe* (New York: Simon & Schuster, 1980), 126.

21. Quoted in ibid., 136; see also Bryce DeWitt and Neill Graham, *The Many Worlds Interpretation of Quantum Mechanics* (Princeton: Princeton University Press, 1973).

22. If the claims made on behalf of decoherence theories stand up to examination, much of the heated debate surrounding the Copenhagen interpretation will turn out to be moot; see, for example, Wojciech Zurek, "Decoherence and the Transition from Quantum to Classical," *Physics Today* 44 (1991); Zurek, "Decoherence and the Transition from Quantum to Classical—Revisited," *Los Alamos Science* 27 (2002).

23. See Henry P. Stapp, *Mindful Universe: Quantum Mechanics and the Participating Observer* (Berlin: Springer, 2007).

24. Carl Friedrich von Weizsäcker, *The World View of Physics* (Chicago: University of Chicago Press, 1952).

25. Quoted in Davies, *Other Worlds,* 132.

26. Roger Penrose, "Quantum Physics and Conscious Thought", in B. J. Hiley and F. David Peat, eds., *Quantum Implications: Essays in Honour of David Bohm* (London: Routledge and Kegan Paul, 1987), 105-120, quote 107.

27. For example, one objection imagines that a meter is set up to permanently register whether a radioactive particle has decayed at the end of a minute (assume an experimental set-up in which there is a 50 percent probability of this occurring). Two photographs are then automatically taken of the meter reading, first photo A and then photo B. The photographs are developed but no one looks at them. Imagine that ten years are allowed to pass during which no subject observes either the meter or the photos. At the end of that time a subject looks at photo B, and suppose that she observes the meter to register a radioactive decay. On Wigner's view, at that moment, but not

before, the superposition of states will be collapsed, the particle will (retroactively) have decayed, the meter will (retroactively) register its decay, and photo A (which no one has yet looked at) will suddenly show a picture of the meter in its "on" position. Before that moment photo A was still indeterminate; the observation of photo B makes A determinate—despite the fact that A was taken *before* B!

28. Alternately, they might suggest a radically different type of object: a single object with two parts that remains one even when its parts are separated by vast distances.

29. Henry Stapp, "Theory of Reality," *Foundations of Physics* 7 (1977): 313–23.

30. Ken Wilber, *The Marriage of Sense and Soul: Integrating Science and Religion* (New York: Random House, 1998), 38, 57. When concepts such as these are fleshed out into the full form of the more radical Eastern mystics, the results can be startling: "The reason is that in quantum physics the elements are not physical themselves; they do not exist as objects. Their very existence depends on the idea of their existence beforehand. They are treated as 'tendencies to exist' rather than as already existing possibilities like the sides of a flipped coin. In the quantum world the quantum coin's sides do not appear unless someone calls for them to appear" (Fred Alan Wolf, *Star Wave: Mind, Consciousness, and Quantum Physics* [New York: Macmillan, 1984], 17). And "thus we conclude that the 'new physics' introduces the element of consciousness into the material world. This consciousness will not arise from the molecule itself, as seen as a material unit, but will arise as a 'risk-taking' psyche—that is, one that chooses. These choices cannot be made willy-nilly. 'Reason' must begin to make its appearance, which surpasses the simple mechanism of cause and effect. We know that atoms do not follow the laws of cause and effect except statistically or on the average. To explain the evolution of learning, associative memory, and possibly even the more primitive forms of memory called habituation and sensitization, we must face the quantum. State of consciousness, feelings, emotional states, and psychology as a science may depend on recognition that mind, the consciousness of the universe, arises through quantum physics" (Wolf, *Star Wave*, 18–19).

31. See chapters 7 through 9.

32. Philip Clayton, "Neuroscience, the Person, and God: An Emergentist Account," *Zygon* 35 (2000): 613–52; Philip Clayton, *Mind and Emergence* (Oxford: Oxford University Press, 2004).

33. Theo Meyering, "Physicalism and Downward Causation in Psychology and the Special Sciences," *Inquiry* 43 (2000): 199.

34. See Arthur Peacocke, *Theology for a Scientific Age: Being and Becoming—Natural, Divine, and Human* (Minneapolis: Fortress Press, 1993).

35. These emerging orders of explanation may also involve an increasing role for top-down explanations. In intentional explanations it is even clearer that the goal for which the agent acts, or the broader context within which she understands her actions, influences the particular behaviors or thoughts.

36. Whether there is a God, and whether God in fact carries out these actions, is of course another question, and one that I do not seek to resolve here.

37. Farrer, *Finite and Infinite*; F. Michael McLain and W. Mark Richardson, eds., *Human and Divine Agency: Anglican, Catholic, and Lutheran Perspectives* (Lanham, Md.: University Press of America, 1999).

38. Kathryn Tanner, *God and Creation in Christian Theology: Tyranny or Empowerment?* (Oxford: Basil Blackwell, 1988), 89.

39. Thomas Tracy, *The God Who Acts: Philosophical and Theological Explorations* (University Park: Pennsylvania State University Press, 1994), 101f.

40. Wolfhart Pannenberg, "Der Gott der Geschichte," in *Grundfragen systematischer Theologie: Gesammelte Aufsätze*, vol. 2 (Göttingen: Vandenhoeck & Ruprecht, 1980), 112–28.

41. For example, David Griffin, *Reenchantment without Supernaturalism* (Ithaca, N.Y.: Cornell University Press, 2001).

42. John Puddefoot, "Information Theory, Biology, and Christology," in *Religion and Science,* eds. Mark Richardson and Wesley Wildman (New York: Routledge, 1996).

43. Stephen J. Gould, *The Panda's Thumb: More Reflections in Natural History* (New York: Norton, 1980), 15.

44. Fred Dretske, "Mental Events as Structuring Causes of Behavior," in *Mental Causation,* ed. John Heil and Alfred Mele (Oxford: Oxford University Press, 2003), 121–36.

45. Michael Behe, *Darwin's Black Box: The Biochemical Challenge to Evolution* (New York: Free, 1996).

46. The problem of evil, however, does place some further constraints on what kind and quantity of information can be imparted. See Philip Clayton and Steven Knapp, "Divine Action and the 'Argument from Neglect,'" in *Physics and Cosmology: Scientific Perspectives on the Problem of Natural Evil*, ed. Robert J. Russell and Nancey Murphy (Notre Dame: Notre Dame University Press, 2007), 179–94.

47. Carl Gillett, "Non-Reductive Realization and Non-Reductive Identity: What Physicalism Does Not Entail," in *Physicalism and Mental Causation*, eds. Sven Walter and Heinz-Deiter Heckmann (Charlottesville, Va.: Imprint Academic, 2003), 28.

48. John Holland, *Emergence: From Chaos to Order* (Cambridge, Mass.: Perseus, 1998).

49. William A. Dembski, *The Design Revolution: Answering the Toughest Questions About Intelligent Design* (Downers Grove, Ill.: InterVarsity, 2004).

50. Michael Behe, *Darwin's Black Box*.

51. See chapter 6.

➤ Chapter 13: Actions Human and Divine

1. In addition to their respective publications, see the recent highly significant volume edited by John B. Cobb Jr., *Back to Darwin: A Richer Account of Evolution* (Grand Rapids, Mich.: Eerdmans, 2008), which includes many of these authors and relates their work to the neo-Darwinian paradigm in biology.

2. See David Griffin, *Reenchantment without Supernaturalism* (Ithaca, N.Y.: Cornell University Press, 2001).

3. See Robert J. Russell, et al., *Chaos and Complexity: Scientific Perspectives on Divine Action* (Vatican City: Vatican Observatory Press; Notre Dame: University of Notre Dame Press, 1995), especially the articles by Bob Russell, Nancey Murphy, and Tom Tracy. More recently, see Robert Russell, John Polkinghorne, Philip Clayton, and Kurt Wegter-McNelly, eds., *Quantum Mechanics: Scientific Perspectives on Divine Action* (Vatican City: Vatican Observatory, 2002).

4. Alfred North Whitehead, *Process and Reality*, corrected ed. (New York: Free, 1978), 3 (henceforth *PR*).

5. See Anna Case-Winters, "System and Dynamism in Whitehead's Thought: The Category of the Ultimate and the Concept of God," in *Schleiermacher and Whitehead: Open Systems in Dialogue*, ed. Christine Helmer (Berlin: Walter de Gruyter, 2004), 135–58, quote on 146.

6. Study of Fichte's *Anweisung zum seligen Leben* and of the later editions of the *Wissenschaftslehre*, in which Fichte sought to place the self-constituting ego within the context of the whole of reality (*das Ganze*), reveals further affinities to Schleiermacher.

7. Eilert Herms, *Herkunft, Entfaltung und erste Gestalt des Systems der Wissenschaften bei Schleiermacher* (Gütersloh: Gütersloher Verlagshaus Gerd Mohn, 1974), 156.

8. In this sense, Schleiermacher was indeed the spiritual father of Wilhelm Dilthey's method of the empathetic understanding (*Verstehen*) of "the Other" and of Windeband's "idiographic" approach to social science.

9. In taking this position I break with those who would divide Schleiermacher's later work more sharply from his early, *frühromantische* phase. Although there is no doubt that Schleiermacher broke from certain tenets of the Schlegels and the Athenäum period, that his style became more academic, and that theological concerns came to weigh more heavily, this focus on individuality and experience continued to characterize all of his major writings. The growing influence of Schelling, the so-called philosopher of Romanticism, on his work after 1803 supports this interpretation; see Hermann Süskind, *Der Einfluss Schellings auf die Entwicklung von Schleiermachers System* (Aalen: Scientia, 1982). See also Manfred Frank, *"Unendliche Annäherung": Die Anfänge der philosophischen Frühromantik*, 2nd ed., STW 1328 (Frankfurt: Suhrkamp, 1998).

10. Case-Winters, "System and Dynamism," 150.

11. Giovanni Moretto, "The Problem of the Religious in Fichte and Schleiermacher," in *Schleiermacher's Philosophy and the Philosophical Tradition*, ed. Sergio Sorrentio (Lewiston, N.Y.: Edwin Mellen, 1992), 56, citing Friedrich Schleiermacher, *Über die Religion. Reden an die Gebildeten unter ihren Verächtern*, ed. Günter Meckenstock in Mechenstock, in Schleiermacher, *Kritische Gesamtausgabe* (KGA) 1/2 (Hambourg: Meiner, 1958), 221. Moretto interprets *den Augenblick* as "the generating moment of religious individuality" in his *Etica e storia in Schleiermacher* (Napoli: Bibliopolis, 1979), 205.

12. Schleiermacher, *Über die Religion. Reden*, 197.

13. So Albert Blackwell, *Schleiermacher's Early Philosophy of Life: Determinism, Freedom, and Phantasy* (Chico, Calif.: Scholars, 1982), 138.

14. Marjorie Suchocki, "System without Certainty," in *Schleiermacher and Whitehead: Open Systems in Dialgoue*, ed. Christine Helmer (New York: Walter de Gruyter, 2004).

15. Note that not all panentheistic theologies are identical. Panentheism is best understood as a family-resemblance term. A sample of the range of positions, and their common features, is provided in Philip Clayton and Arthur Peacocke, eds., *In Whom We Live and Move and Have Our Being: Panentheistic Reflections on God's Presence in a Scientific World* (Grand Rapids, Mich.: Eerdmans, 2004).

16. A quick roadmap for specialists: I have here moved from Schleiermacher's *Speeches* to *The Christian Faith* and have extrapolated in particular from his comments about the Trinity, although I do not develop that argument here. I have modified Whitehead under Hartshorne's guidance, and Hartshorne in turn has been pushed in some of the directions that Joseph Bracken has suggested in his various publications.

17. One can, for trinitarian reasons, just as easily speak of three divine agents here instead of one.

18. Donald Sherburne, *A Key to Whitehead's Process and Reality* (New York: Macmillan, 1966), 18.

19. Only the last of these types of direct influence represents a miracle in the traditional sense. See Thomas Aquinas, *Summa Contra Gentiles* III, qq. 100–103; C. S. Lewis, *Miracles: A Preliminary Study* (New York: Macmillan, 1947).

20. Philip Clayton, *The Problem of God in Modern Thought* (Grand Rapids, Mich.: Eerdmans, 2000).

21. Coleridge, *Lay Sermons*, 30, quoted in Steven Knapp, *Personification and the Sublime: Milton to Coleridge* (Cambridge, Mass.: Harvard University Press, 1985), 15.

22. Coleridge's marginalia on the seventeenth-century divine Jeremy Taylor, quoted in Knapp, *Personification and the Sublime*, 17.

23. Friedrich Schleiermacher, *Über die Religion. Reden*, 1st. edition, 53. Here and below I quote from the Philosophische Bibliothek vol. 255 (Hamburg: Felix Meiner, 1958): "Alles Endliche besteht nur durch die Bestimmung seiner Grenzen, die aus dem Unendlichen gleichsam herausgeschnitten werden müssen. Nur so kann es innerhalb dieser Grenzen selbst unendlich sein und eigen gebildet werden."

24. Scheiermacher, *Über die Religion. Reden*, 127: a "Chaos . . . , woraus nichts Einzelnes gesondert warden kann, als indem es willkürlich abgeschnitten wird in Zeit und Raum."

25. Ibid., 90f.

26. Ibid., 56: "alles Einzelne als einen Teil des Ganzen, alles Beschränkte als eine Darstellung des Unendlichen."

27. Ibid., 87: all is "ein Werk dieses Geistes und eine Darstellung und Ausführung dieser Gestze, nur [für ihn] ist alles Sichtbare auch wirklich Welt, gebildet, von der Gottheit durchdrungen und eins."

28. For example at ibid., 67.

29. Ibid., 119: "Alle religiösen Gefühle sind übernatürlich, denn sie sind nur insofern religiös, als sie durchs Universum unmittelbar gewirkt sind."

30. Ibid., 71: "ein freier, durch eigene Kraft tätiger Teil des Ganzen." Note that Schleiermacher does not place human concerns at the pinnacle of his theology. At several points he explicitly relativizes the place of humanity to a "Mittelglied" between the lowest and the whole (104f.).

31. Ibid., 132: "Strebt danach, schon hier Eure Individualität zu vernichten und im Einen und Allen zu leben."

32. Ibid., 125: the concept "von einem höchsten Wesen, von einem Geist des Universums, der es mit Freiheit und Verstand regiert."

33. Ibid., 133: the striving is, "mitten in der Endlichkeit eins [zu] werden mit dem Unendlichen."

34. Ibid., 103f.: "Nichts soll tote Masse sein.. alles soll eigenes, zusammengesetztes, vielfach verschlungenes und erhöhtes Leben sein. Blinder Instinkt, gedankenlose Gewöhnung, toter Gehorsam, alles Träge und Passive, alle diese traurigen Symptome der Asphyxie der Freiheit und Menschheit sollen vernichtet werden."

35. Such as ibid., 103, 107.

36. Ibid., 74. Compare with the famous description by Wordsworth in "Tintern Abbey" of "a sense sublime / Of something far more deeply interfused, / Whose dwelling is the light of setting suns, / And the round ocean and the living air, / And the blue sky, and in the mind of man; / A motion and a spirit, that impels / All thinking things, all objects of all thought, / And rolls through all things."

37. See David Jasper, ed., *The Interpretation of Belief: Coleridge, Schleiermacher, and Romanticism* (Houndmills, Basingstoke, Hampshire: Macmillan, 1986).

38. Schleiermacher, *Über die Religion. Reden*, 128: "wo alles streitende sich wieder veeinigt, wo das Universum sich als Totalität, als Einheit in der Vielheit, als System darstellt und so erst seinen Namen verdient."

39. Schleiermacher, *Dialectic, or the Art of Doing Philosophy*, trans. Terrence Tice (Atlanta: Scholars, 1996), 39.

40. Schleiermacher, *Über die Religion. Reden*, 99: "Eure Persönlichkeit umfaßt in einem gewissen Sinn die ganze menschliche Natur und diese ist in allen ihren Darstellungen nichts also Euer eigenes vervielfältigtes, deutlicher ausgezeichnetes, und in allen seinen Veränderungen verewigtes Ich."

41. Ibid., 99.

42. Ibid., 100.

43. Schleiermacher did make major advances beyond his position in the *Speeches* in his later theology, but that's a story for another day.

44. I gratefully acknowledge Steven Knapp's contributions to the formulation of the first and fifth points, as well as his important influence on the position developed in the latter half of this chapter.

 ## Chapter 14: Can Contemporary Theologians Still Affirm That God (Literally) Does Anything?

1. William Paul Griffin, *The God of the Prophets: An Analysis of Divine Action*, Journal for the Study of the Old Testament Supplement Series 249 (Sheffield, UK: Sheffield Academic, 1997), 11.

2. See the excellent treatment by Paul Gwynne, *Special Divine Action: Key Issues in the Contemporary Debate (1965–1995)* (Rome: Editrice Pontificia Universita Gregoriana, 1996), 7. Other central books on divine action include Thomas F. Tracy, ed., *The God Who Acts: Philosophical and Theological Explorations* (University Park: Pennsylvania State University Press, 1994); Thomas V. Morris, ed., *Divine and Human Action: Essays in the Metaphysics of Theism* (Ithaca, N.Y.: Cornell University Press, 1988); Owen Thomas, ed., *God's Activity in the World: The Contemporary Problem* (Chico, Calif.: Scholars, 1983); and, on mental causation more generally, see John Heil and Alfred Mele, eds., *Mental Causation* (Oxford: Clarendon, 1995).

3. David Hume, *Of Miracles* (La Salle, Ill.: Open Court, 1985), 53.

4. Ibid., 40.

5. I hope to extend this treatment further in a future book, coauthored with Steven Knapp, tentatively entitled *The Challenge of Ultimacy*.

6. Some Christians have argued that the collapse and the resulting deaths *were* an act of God to punish Americans for our immorality in allowing abortions and legalizing homosexual relationships. But, as Bishop Spong argued in Harvard's Memorial Church on the Sunday following September 11, if it were true that the Christian God causes terrorist attacks to punish homosexuality, I'd rather side with the atheists.

7. I am indebted here to Paul Gwynne, *Special Divine Action*, especially 122ff.

8. See F. M. McLain, "On Theological Models," *Harvard Theological Review* 62 (1969): 155–87.

9. Jürgen Moltmann, *God in Creation: A New Theology of Creation and the Spirit of God* (Minneapolis: Fortress Press, 1993), 314.

10. John Earman attacks Hume's argument against miracles in John Earman, *Hume's Abject Failure: The Argument Against Miracles* (New York: Oxford University Press, 2000). Brian Hebblethwaite defends traditional theism in answer to more liberal doctrines of God (especially Don Cupitt's) in Brian Hebblethwaite, *The Ocean of Truth: A Defense of Objective Theism* (Cambridge: Cambridge University Press, 1988). Gary Habermas defends the miracle of the bodily resurrection in Gary Habermas and Antony Flew, *Did Jesus Rise from the Dead? The Resurrection Debate*, ed. Terry Miethe (San Francisco: Harper & Row, 1987); and miracles in history in Gary Habermas and R. Douglas Geivett, eds., *In Defense of Miracles: A Comprehensive Case for God's Action in History* (Downers Grove, Ill.: InterVarsity, 1997). Luke Timothy Johnson defends the historicity of the gospels against Crossan and the Jesus Seminar in Luke Timothy Johnson, *The Real Jesus: The Misguided Quest for the*

Historical Jesus and the Truth of the Traditional Gospels (San Francisco: HarperSanFrancisco, 1996). Phillip Johnson defends God's action in evolutionary history against Darwinian accounts in Philip Johnson, *Darwin on Trial*, 2nd ed. (Downers Grove, Ill.: InterVarsity, 1993); and, for example, Philip Johnson, *Reason in the Balance: The Case Against Naturalism in Science, Law and Education* (Downers Grove, Ill.: InterVarsity, 1995). See also Geoff Price, *Miracles: True Stories of How God Acts Today* (London: Macmillan, 1995).

11. Aquinas, *Summa Contra Gentiles* III, QQ 100–103.

12. Karl Rahner, *Foundations of Christian Faith* (New York: Crossroad, 1978), 258f.

13. Walter Kasper, *Jesus the Christ* (London: Burns & Oates, 1976), 95. Quoted from Gwynne, *Special Divine Action*, 76 n. 80.

14. This is apparently the view of Maurice Wiles, *God's Action in the World* (London: SCM, 1986).

15. See Christoph Schwöbel, *God: Action and Revelation* (Kampen, The Netherlands: Kok Pharos, 1992), 36. Schwöbel continues by strengthening the status of his claims, "Only if these conditions are met does it become possible to describe an event as the result of intentional action and ascribe it to an agent who possesses knowledge of the aims and means of action and competence for the employment of these means of action. If an event can be described as the result of intentional action then the ascription of the event to the intentional agency of a free agent provides a sufficient explanation for the occurrence of the event."

16. See Brian Hebblethwaite and Edward Henderson, eds., *Divine Action: Studies Inspired by the Philosophical Theology of Austin Farrer* (Edinburgh: T & T Clark, 1990).

17. The reflections presented here stem from ongoing discussions with Steven Knapp at George Washington University. Dr. Knapp is not however responsible for any parts of the following argument that might be obscure, unclear, or obviously false.

18. See, for example, Matthew Fox, *One River, Many Wells: Wisdom Springing from Global Faiths* (New York: Tarcher/Putnam, 2000).

19. I here presuppose the complex theory of agency developed in chapter 13.

20. "Jesus knew that the time had come for him to leave this world and go to the Father. Having loved his own who were in the world, he now showed them the full extent of his love. . . . Jesus knew that the Father had put all things under his power, and that he had come from God and was returning to God; so he got up from the meal, took off his outer clothing, and wrapped a towel around his waist. After that, he poured water into a basin and began to wash his disciples' feet" (John 13:1-5).

21. "My teaching is not my own. It comes from him who sent me" (John 7:16). "The words I say to you are not just my own" (John 14:10). "These words you hear are not my own; they belong to the Father who sent me" (John 14:24). "Father, if you are willing, take this cup from me; yet not my will, but yours be done" (Luke 22:42). "Your kingdom come, your will be done, on earth as it is in heaven" (Matt 6:10). Or, most simply, "may your will be done" (Matt 26:42).

22. I would here recommend John Dominic Crossan, *The Birth of Christianity: Discovering What Happened in the Years Immediately after the Execution of Jesus* (San Francisco: HarperSanFrancisco, 1998).

23. See pages 109-110 in this volume.

24. Steven Knapp, personal communication.

25. See Lewis Ford, *The Lure of God* (Philadelphia: Fortress Press, 1978).

26. As a woman once put it at a Quaker meeting, "Perhaps God's only act is to make manifest the divine love. Is this not enough?"

27. Again, this assertion presupposes the conceptual results of chapter 13.

28. Here I follow emergentist theories of mind and the anomalous monism of Donald Davidson. See my article in Robert John Russell, Nancey Murphy, Theo C. Meyering, and Michael Arbib, eds., *Neuroscience and the Person: Scientific Perspectives on Divine Action* (Vatican City: Vatican Observatory Publications, 1999).

29. I have here developed the account in Christian terms, as one would expect from a Christian theologian. But perhaps similar accounts could be developed within other traditions. In fact, resources already exist. Examples include references to the Buddha mind, the emulation of the Buddha by *boddisatvas*, and the state of perfect receptiveness shown by God's prophet as he received the dictation of the Koran (as reflected, for example, in the ideals of Sufi mysticism). Of course, these accounts would naturally diverge in important ways from the present one.

➤ **Chapter 15: Reflections on the Human Quest for Meaning**

1. Anders Lindseth and Astrid Norberg, "A Phenomenological Hermeneutical Method for Researching Lived Experience," *Scandinavian Journal for Caring Science* 18 (2004): 145–53, quote 151.

2. Peter L. Berger, *The Sacred Canopy* (Garden City, N.Y.: Doubleday, 1967), 19.

3. Ibid., 22.

4. Ibid.

5. Ibid.

6. Ibid., 21.

7. Ibid., 15.

8. Friedrich Nietzsche, "Über Wahrheit und Lüge im aussermoralischen Sinne," in *Nietzsche Werke*, ed. Giorgio Colli and Mazzino Montinari (Berlin: Walter de Gruyter, 1973), part 3, vol. 2., 369.

9. I include here only a brief selection from the literature. Readers are encouraged to consult any of the standard textbooks in the sociology of religion (or the psychology or anthropology of religion) for further details.

10. See, for example, Christopher Ellison, "Rational Choice Explanations of Individual Religious Behavior: Notes on the Problem of Social Embeddedness," *Journal for the Scientific Study of Religion* 34 (1995): 89–97.

11. Richard R. Lee, "Religious Practice as Social Exchange: An Explanation of the Empirical Findings," *Sociological Analysis* 53 (1992): 1–35.

12. Ibid., 10.

13. Ibid., 15.

14. Murray H. Leiffer, "Why do we choose the churches we attend?" *Christian Advocate* (Feb. 2, 1956): 29ff.

15. Lyle E. Schaller, "Evaluating the potential for growth," *Christian Ministry* 10 (1979): 55–8.

16. Robert L. Young, "Religious Orientation, Race, and Support for the Death Penalty," *Journal for the Scientific Study of Religion* 31 (1992): 76–87.

17. Ibid., 85.

18. See Darren E. Sherkat and John Wilson, "Preferences, Constraints, and Choices in Religious Markets: An Examination of Religious Switching and Apostasy," *Social Forces* 73 (1995): 993–1026, quotes 994.

19. Berger, *The Sacred Canopy*, 28.

20. Ibid., 51.

21. Ibid., 26.

22. Particular issues are raised by the centrality of observance rather than belief in Judaism that distinguish it from the other two major Abrahamic traditions.

23. See Philip Clayton, "Tracing the Lines: Constraint and Freedom in the Movement from Quantum Physics to Theology," in *Quantum Mechanics: Scientific Perspectives on Divine Action,* ed. Robert Russell, Philip Clayton, John Polkinghorne, and Kirk Wegter-McNelly (Vatican City: Vatican Observatory Press, 2002). Also see chapter 4 of this volume.

24. Quentin Skinner, *The Return of Grand Theory in the Human Sciences* (Cambridge and New York: Cambridge University Press, 1985).

25. One thinks of the "philosophische Anthropologie" of the early twentieth century (Arnold Gehlen, Helmuth Plessner, Max Scheler, et al.); see Louis P. Pojman, *Who Are We? Theories of Human Nature* (New York: Oxford University Press, 2006); and Wolfhart Pannenberg, *Anthropology in Theological Perspective*, trans. Matthew J. O'Connell (Philadelphia: Westminster, 1985).

26. See Peter L. Berger, "Relativising the Relativisers," in *A Rumor of Angels: Modern Society and the Rediscovery of the Supernatural* (Garden City, N.Y.: Doubleday, 1969).

➤ **Chapter 16: Spirituality as Spirit and Spirituality toward Spirit**

1. Isn't this why Hegel's dictum, "the real is the rational; the rational is the real," works as the *Grundmotiv* for so many of the moderns?

2. *The Inferno*, Canto XXXIV, from Dante, *The Divine Comedy*, available online in S. Fowler Wright's translation at http://history.hanover.edu/courses/excerpts/344dan.html, accessed Apr. 7, 2008.

3. Martin Heidegger, *An Introduction to Metaphysics*, trans. Ralph Manheim (New Haven: Yale University Press, 1959), 7.

4. Arnold Come, "Advocatus Dei-Advocatus Hominis et Mundi," in James M. Robinson and John B. Cobb Jr., *The Later Heidegger and Theology* (New York: Harper and Row, 1963), 119.

5. See Heidegger, *The Question Concerning Technology*, trans. William Lovitt (New York: Harper and Row, 1977). Henceforth QCT.

6. Harold Alderman, "Heidegger's Critique of Science and Technology," in *Heidegger and Modern Philosophy: Critical Essays,* ed. Michael Murray (New Haven: Yale University Press, 1978), 35–50, quote 35.

7. Ibid., 37.

8. See the classic treatment by Joseph Kockelmans, *Heidegger and Science* (Washington, D.C.: University Press of America, 1985).

9. Edith Wyschogrod, *Spirit in Ashes: Hegel, Heidegger, and Man-Made Mass Death* (New Haven: Yale University Press, 1985), 177.

10. Jacques Derrida, *Of Spirit: Heidegger and the Question* (Chicago: University of Chicago Press, 1987), 12.

11. This "spirit" is beautifully described by Mary Midgley, *Science and Poetry* (London: Routledge, 2001).

12. See "minimal personalist theism" in Philip Clayton, *God and Contemporary Science* (Grand Rapids, Mich.: Eerdmans, 1997), chapter 8.

13. Ursula Goodenough, "Vertical and Horizontal Transcendence," *Zygon* 36 (Mar. 2001): 21–31.

14. See especially Michael Kalton, "Green Spirituality: Horizontal Transcendence," in *Paths of Integrity, Wisdom and Transcendence: Spiritual Development in the Mature Self,* ed. M. E. Miller and P. Young-Eisendrath (New York: Routledge, 2000). The following quotations are taken from this piece.

15. Acts 17:38. See Philip Clayton and Arthur Peacocke, eds., *In Whom We Live and Move and Have Our Being: Panentheistic Reflections on God's Presence in a Scientific World* (Grand Rapids, Mich.: Eerdmans, 2004).

16. T. S. Eliot, "The Dry Salvages," No. 3 in *Four Quartets* (London: Faber and Faber, 1944).

17. Pierre Teilhard de Chardin, *The Appearance of Man*, trans. J. M. Cohen (New York: Harper & Row, 1965); *Building the Earth*, trans. Noel Lindsay (Wilkes-Barre, Pa.: Dimension, 1965); *Christianity and Evolution*, trans. Rene Hague (New York: Harcourt Brace Jovanovich, 1971); *The Future of Man*, trans. Norman Denny (New York: Harper, 1964); *The Phenomenon of Man*, trans. Bernard Wall (New York: Harper, 1959); *Science and Christ*, trans. Rene Hague (New York: Harper, 1968).

18. Derrida, *Of Spirit,* 100.

19. Ibid., 101.

➤ Chapter 17: The Many Faces of Integration

1. Note that in speaking of a new liberal theology, I do not identify with neo-liberalism in economic theory, a policy advocated by Milton Friedman with disastrous consequences for international economics and United States foreign policy.

2. W. B. Yeats, "The Second Coming," in W. B. Yeats, *The Poems* (New York: Macmillan, 1983).

3. See http://www.monergism.com/thethreshold/articles/topic/liberaltheology.html, accessed Feb. 2005.

4. Foreword to William Sloane Coffin, *Credo* (Louisville, Ky.: Westminster John Knox, 2004), xi.

5. Cited from *Wikipedia*, an online encyclopedia; see http://en.wikipedia.org/wiki/Fundamentalist_Christianity, accessed Mar. 28, 2005.

6. Anders Breidlid et al., eds., *American Culture: An Anthology of Civilization Texts* (New York: Routledge, 1996), 86. The speech is also widely available online. I quote it from http://www.americanrhetoric.com/speeches/mlkihaveadream.htm, accessed Apr. 7, 2008.

7. Breidlid et al., eds., *American Culture*, and the same online sources.

8. Peter Berger, *The Heretical Imperative: Contemporary Possibilities of Religious Affirmation* (Garden City, N.Y.: Anchor/Doubleday, 1979), 183.

9. Peter Berger, *A Far Glory: The Quest for Faith in an Age of Credulity* (New York: Free/MacMillan, 1992), 46.

10. See ibid., 18–19. I here modify a formulation from Tino Garcia.

11. Tino Garcia, personal communication, modified, quoting Peter Berger, *A Far Glory*, 15–16.

12. See http://www.sparknotes.com/biography/mlk/terms.html, accessed Mar. 2005.

13. Reinhold Niebuhr, *Love and Justice: Selections from the Shorter Writings of Reinhold Niebuhr*, ed. D. B. Robertson (Louisville, Ky.: Westminster/John Knox, 1957), 97.

14. H. Richard Niebuhr, *The Meaning of Revelation* (New York: MacMillan, 1960), 18. I am grateful to Zach Simpson for assistance on the Niebuhr research.

15. Ibid., 128.

16. Ibid., 136.

17. Again, reference to a new liberal theology does not associate this position with neo-liberalism in economic theory (Milton Friedman); see note 1 above.

18. H. Richard Niebuhr, *The Meaning of Revelation*, 137 (italics added).

19. My thesis is simple, though the details aren't: it has always been the fundamental nature of liberal Christianity to speak a voice that is both revisionary and yet in continuity with the Christian tradition. Put differently, the prophetic voice of liberal Christians has been to bring the resources of the Christian faith to bear on contemporary society in a way that transforms *both* the society *and* the Christian faith itself.

20. Peter Berger, *Questions of Faith: A Skeptical Affirmation of Christianity* (Malden, Mass.: Blackwell, 2004), viii, emphasis added.

21. Marjorie Suchocki, *God, Christ, Church: A Practical Guide to Process Theology* (New York: Crossroad, 1989), 118.

22. Paul Tillich, *The Shaking of the Foundations* (New York: Scribner, 1948), 7–8.

23. Berger, *A Far Glory*, 211.

Index